T5-CPY-346

Current Security Management & Ethical Issues of Information Technology

edited by

Rasool Azari
University of Redlands, USA

IRM Press
Publisher of innovative scholarly and professional
information technology titles in the cyberage

Hershey • London • Melbourne • Singapore • Beijing

Acquisitions Editor:	Mehdi Khosrow-Pour
Senior Managing Editor:	Jan Travers
Managing Editor:	Amanda Appicello
Copy Editor:	Alana Bubnis
Typesetter:	Jennifer Wetzel
Cover Design:	Michelle Waters
Printed at:	Integrated Book Technology

Published in the United States of America by
    IRM Press (an imprint of Idea Group Inc)
    701 E. Chocolate Avenue, Suite 200
    Hershey PA 17033-1240
    Tel: 717-533-8845
    Fax: 717-533-8661
    E-mail: cust@idea-group.com
    Web site: http://www.irm-press.com

and in the United Kingdom by
    IRM Press (an imprint of Idea Group Inc)
    3 Henrietta Street
    Covent Garden
    London WC2E 8LU
    Tel: 44 20 7240 0856
    Fax: 44 20 7379 3313
    Web site: http://www.eurospan.co.uk

Copyright © 2003 by IRM Press. All rights reserved. No part of this book may be reproduced in any form or by any means, electronic or mechanical, including photocopying, without written permission from the publisher.

Library of Congress Cataloging-in-Publication Data

Azari, Rasool.
  Current security management & ethical issues of information
technology / Rasool Azari.
     p. cm.
  ISBN 1-931777-43-8 (soft cover) -- ISBN 1-931777-59-4 (ebook)
  1. Computer security. 2. Computer networks--Security measures. I.
Title.
    QA76.9.A25A93 2003
    005.8--dc21

                        2002156229

British Cataloguing in Publication Data
A Cataloguing in Publication record for this book is available from the British Library.

New Releases from IRM Press

- **Multimedia and Interactive Digital TV: Managing the Opportunities Created by Digital Convergence**/Margherita Pagani
  ISBN: 1-931777-38-1; eISBN: 1-931777-54-3 / US$59.95 / © 2003
- **Virtual Education: Cases in Learning & Teaching Technologies**/ Fawzi Albalooshi (Ed.),
  ISBN: 1-931777-39-X; eISBN: 1-931777-55-1 / US$59.95 / © 2003
- **Managing IT in Government, Business & Communities**/Gerry Gingrich (Ed.)
  ISBN: 1-931777-40-3; eISBN: 1-931777-56-X / US$59.95 / © 2003
- **Information Management: Support Systems & Multimedia Technology**/ George Ditsa
  (Ed.), ISBN: 1-931777-41-1; eISBN: 1-931777-57-8 / US$59.95 / © 2003
- **Managing Globally with Information Technology**/Sherif Kamel (Ed.)
  ISBN: 42-X; eISBN: 1-931777-58-6 / US$59.95 / © 2003
- **Current Security Management & Ethical Issues of Information Technology**/Rasool Azari
  (Ed.), ISBN: 1-931777-43-8; eISBN: 1-931777-59-4 / US$59.95 / © 2003
- **UML and the Unified Process**/Liliana Favre (Ed.)
  ISBN: 1-931777-44-6; eISBN: 1-931777-60-8 / US$59.95 / © 2003
- **Business Strategies for Information Technology Management**/Kalle Kangas (Ed.)
  ISBN: 1-931777-45-4; eISBN: 1-931777-61-6 / US$59.95 / © 2003
- **Managing E-Commerce and Mobile Computing Technologies**/Julie Mariga (Ed.)
  ISBN: 1-931777-46-2; eISBN: 1-931777-62-4 / US$59.95 / © 2003
- **Effective Databases for Text & Document Management**/Shirley A. Becker (Ed.)
  ISBN: 1-931777-47-0; eISBN: 1-931777-63-2 / US$59.95 / © 2003
- **Technologies & Methodologies for Evaluating Information Technology in Business**/Charles
  K. Davis (Ed.), ISBN: 1-931777-48-9; eISBN: 1-931777-64-0 / US$59.95 / © 2003
- **ERP & Data Warehousing in Organizations: Issues and Challenges**/Gerald Grant (Ed.),
  ISBN: 1-931777-49-7; eISBN: 1-931777-65-9 / US$59.95 / © 2003
- **Practicing Software Engineering in the 21st Century**/Joan Peckham (Ed.)
  ISBN: 1-931777-50-0; eISBN: 1-931777-66-7 / US$59.95 / © 2003
- **Knowledge Management: Current Issues and Challenges**/Elayne Coakes (Ed.)
  ISBN: 1-931777-51-9; eISBN: 1-931777-67-5 / US$59.95 / © 2003
- **Computing Information Technology: The Human Side**/Steven Gordon (Ed.)
  ISBN: 1-931777-52-7; eISBN: 1-931777-68-3 / US$59.95 / © 2003
- **Current Issues in IT Education**/Tanya McGill (Ed.)
  ISBN: 1-931777-53-5; eISBN: 1-931777-69-1 / US$59.95 / © 2003

Excellent additions to your institution's library!
Recommend these titles to your Librarian!

To receive a copy of the IRM Press catalog, please contact
(toll free) 1/800-345-4332, fax 1/717-533-8661,
or visit the IRM Press Online Bookstore at: [http://www.irm-press.com]!

Note: All IRM Press books are also available as ebooks on netlibrary.com as well as
other ebook sources. Contact Ms. Carrie Skovrinskie at [cskovrinskie@idea-group.com] to receive
a complete list of sources where you can obtain ebook information or
IRM Press titles.

Current Security Management
&
Ethical Issues of
Information Technology

Table of Contents

Preface

As *Time* magazine proclaimed 20 years ago, "The 'information revolution' that futurists have long predicted has arrived...America will never be the same. In a larger perspective, the entire world will never be the same" (January 3, 1983, p. 14). Since the dawn of civilization our lives have been improved and sometimes also uprooted by evolving technologies, but there is no precedent to the explosive pace of innovations experienced in this time and age, and we are told by experts that this is just the beginning.

The information technology is a major force of this ongoing revolution. What started with the cumbersome, oversized dinosaurs of the first generation computers has mushroomed into the age of mobile computing, the Internet, and the open access worldwide networks. Information technology has increased productivity, shortened the product life cycle, diminished the importance of distance, and globalized markets and economies. New communication technologies centered around information technologies are linking markets, institutions, and populations all over the globe and are radically altering our lives and work. Increased use of technology and the development of e-business are transforming established organizational patterns and are profoundly changing current business structures. Products and services are becoming more and more knowledge and information dependent. The labor force composition has reversed from being seventy percent blue-collar and farm workers into seventy percent white-collar and service providers within the last century. Nearly sixty percent of the American gross national product comes from information and knowledge sectors; some experts even argue that these knowledge assets are at least as important as physical and financial assets in ensuring the survival of organizations (Laudon, 2002).

Because of the need for new and different organizational infrastructures, management is pressured to reconsider its purpose and its methods of operation. Information technology not only challenges and alters the way we produce new goods and services, but it also triggers far-reaching change in institutional arrangements, social norms, and cultural values. It is playing a crucial role in economic well being and introducing a form of relationship among societies and nations never experienced before. Even educational institutions are being revolutionized through distance learning by the new computer-mediated communication technology and Internet-based support.

In addition to adjusting to these changes, societies will also have to come to terms with the unprecedented speed with which change occurs. And this pace is accelerating because the increasingly powerful technologies facilitate the exponentially multiplying pool of knowledge and vice versa. 'Faster, cheaper, smaller' are more than slogans for the information technology. The speed and reach of electronic transmission and distribution and the increasing computing power of microprocessors allow new technologies to reach a quarter of all households in less than a decade, compared to the span of two generations half a century ago. As Alfred Chandler, a Harvard Business historian argues, the driving force in the market is now the economics of speed, not the economies of scale (Grupp, 2001). Speed has become a source of competitive advantage.

These dizzying developments bring an array of unknowns. In uncharted territories, people are faced with questions of law, ethics, and security, brought on by the unfamiliar circumstances created by the new technologies. The astonishing possibilities promised tend to obscure the sobering fact that technology is, and always has been, like a two-sided sword — it may cut both ways. Its destructive potential can outdo its beneficial powers, because it is exactly those marvelous benefits which make possible the potential risks. On the one hand, people are getting closer to each other but on the other hand they are becoming more virtual, anonymous, and impersonal. While extensive use of networks and the Internet, easy access to technology, and advances of wireless telecommunication all raise the likelihood of progress and growth and can benefit both organizations and individuals, they simultaneously raise risks of computer hacking and criminality. The concurrent growth in interdependence, anonymity, and location independence all add to this vulnerability.

As populations become more and more comfortable with the extensive use of networks and the Internet, as our reliance on the knowledge-intensive technology grows, and as progress in the computer software and wireless telecommunication increases accessibility, "there will be a higher risk of unmanageable failure in either physical or social systems that underpin survival...the spread of information technology makes it easier to violate basic privacy or civil rights and to engage in criminal practices ranging from fraud and theft to illegal collusion" (OECD, 2001, p.15). The increasing importance of information technology for production, storage, and distribution of our scarce resources demands that we ensure the reliability, accuracy, and security of our systems and pay special attention to the ethical issues involved.

The ethical issues raised by information technology relate, among others, to privacy, the ownership of information, and intellectual property rights. What is meant by property rights? How can we protect privacy? What are common security weaknesses? How is network security defined? What is the social contract? What is responsibility? What does corporate and social responsibility mean? How does information technology create ethical problems? How does information technology cause change in society and vice versa? Can we reduce the digital divide? There are no easy answers to these or other related questions. The chapters in this book try to address some of the challenges. Most of these topics relate directly or indirectly to questions of risk. To decrease the systems' vulnerability and to minimize risks of breaches of security and computer crimes, we need to develop policies and procedures and design control structures that incorporate the vigilance necessary to stay abreast of the changing technology and its demands for security. Embracing security management programs and including them in the decision making process of policy makers helps to detect and surmount the risks with the use of new and evolving technologies. Raising awareness about the technical problems and educating and guiding policy makers, educators, managers, and strategists is the responsibility of computer professionals and professional organizations.

However, no matter how secure systems may be, insecurities will remain. People are constantly concerned with the search for more security in their lives, homes, jobs, and relationships. How secure is secure? Technology alone is not the solution. As Schneier (2000) put it: "If you think technology can solve your security problems, then you don't understand the problems and you don't understand the technology." Security is not only about software packages, good encryption, and symptomatic remedies.

In an increasingly interdependent world in which our decisions have greater significance to others, moral standards must be critically re-examined. It is more essential to include everyone affected in the decision making process. It is important to move away from compartmentalized thinking that fails to recognize all perspectives involved and thereby does not consider the consequences of our actions. Adhering to a holistic approach not only fosters an agile and alert mind necessary to constructively deal with the many upheavals, disruptions, and changes stemming from the new technologies, it also facilitates the responsible thinking needed in a globalized world. If ethical consideration and social responsibility do not drive technological advance, human misery may be increased. Since technology is used in all of our institutions, "in a social context rich with moral, cultural, and political ideas," (Johnson, 2001) and thus directly and substantially affects all of our lives, it is the responsibility of all businesses, governments, educational institutions, and citizens to exert our social responsibility in steering its moral course.

Securing and harnessing the powers of present and especially future technologies is and will stay a formidable task that requires concerted efforts. Information and education will be a major asset to the achievement of this goal.

This book contributes by encouraging and furthering the dialogue. It brings together ideas and expertise from different fields. It is a response to the many questions raised by the rapid development of information technology that concern security management and ethical issues. It seeks to shed some light on the problems society is facing because of these technological changes and it suggests some solutions.

STRUCTURE OF THE BOOK

The chapters in this book are self-standing. The content of this book is organized into two sections. The first section (Chapters I-VII) focuses on the technical aspects of dealing with the heightened need for security brought on by increasingly powerful information technologies. It discusses and presents models designed to address these pressing issues.

Section two (Chapters VIII-XV) attempts to define and describe ethics and social responsibility in the new age of information systems and takes the reader through some of the impacts these transforming technologies have on the characteristics and quality of institutions, on individuals, and society in general. Both sections contribute to the ongoing discussion so urgently needed for dealing with these complex phenomena.

A brief description of each chapter follows:

Section I: Information System Security

Chapter I titled, "Network Security Software," by Göran Pulkkis, Kaj J. Grahn, and Peik Åström of Arcada Polytechnic (Finland), provides a brief topical overview of state-of-the-art network security software and related skills and education needed by network users, IT professionals, and network security specialists. It presents a broad area of topics, such as protection against malicious programs, firewall software, cryptographic software, security administration software, security software development, network security software skill levels, and network security software skills in higher education.

Chapter II titled, "A Forensic Computing Perspective on the Need for Improved User Education for Information Systems Security Management" by Vlasti Broucek and Paul Turner of the University of Tasmania (Australia), identifies common security and privacy weaknesses that exist in e-mail and Web browsers, underlines some of the implications for organizational security, and tries to raise awareness amongst users. It recommends improved user training and education and concludes that IS security management can be achieved through a balanced and cooperative approach.

Chapter III titled, "Integrating Cooperative Engagement Capability into Network-Centric Information System Security" by Alexander D. Korzyk, Sr., of the University of Idaho (USA), suggests a departure from the traditional decentralized approach to security systems by adapting a system for industrial commercial organizations similar to the new concept of a Cooperative Engagement Capability used by the military to centralize the command over the entire suite of defensive assets.

Chapter IV titled, "A Methodology for Developing Trusted Information Systems: The Security Requirements Analysis Phase" by Maria Grazia Fugini and

Pierluigi Plebani of Politecnico di Milano (Italy), presents a methodology for designing security in advanced distributed Information Systems. It provides architecture for secure transmission of data among e-services and identifies the need for a plan of action in case of intrusion.

Chapter V titled, "A National Information Infrastructure Model for Information Warfare Defence" by Vernon Stagg and Matthew Warren of Deakin University (Australia), introduces an enhanced National Information Infrastructure model that provides greater defense against threats to information systems. The authors describe many threats that are not dealt with adequately in the current infrastructure and offer an enhanced model within the ICT sector.

Chapter VI titled, "Biometrics: Past, Present and Future" by Stewart T. Fleming of the University of Otago (New Zealand), aims to review the current state of the art of biometric systems. It conducts a detailed study of the available technology, examines end-user perceptions of such systems, and discusses a framework which is intended as a step towards providing more detailed guidelines to designers of interactive systems that incorporate biometric data. The importance of ethical and societal implications is mentioned.

Chapter VII titled, "User Types and Filter Effectiveness: A University Case Study" by Geoffrey Sandy and Paul Darbyshire of Victoria University (Australia), reports on Web-filtering software, in particular the filter squidGuard, used in a number of Australian universities. It describes three trials utilized to test its effectiveness and concludes that the ease by which the filter is bypassed points to the filter as superficial at best in trying to block against offensive material.

Section II: Ethics and Social Responsibility in the Information Age

Chapter VIII titled, "What is the Social Responsibility in the Information Age? Maximising Profits?" by Bernd Carsten Stahl of the University College Dublin (Ireland), argues that the idea of social responsibility is not a clearly defined concept and that it is essential to come to a concise definition to avoid confusion. The author then analyzes it and discusses its meaning in the information age. He hopes thereby to start a discussion with the purpose of rendering the term social responsibility useful.

Chapter IX titled, "The Social Contract Revised: Obligation and Responsibility in the Information Society" by Robert Joseph Skovira of Robert Morris University (USA), introduces the social contract as a basis for responsibility and obligation. It discusses the changes in this contract brought about through the Internet. It depicts three traditional social contracts — the Hobbesean, Lockean, and Rousseauean — and raises the question of what it means to take responsibility for one's behavior as an individual or corporation in the information society.

Chapter X titled, "The Influence of Socioeconomic Factors on Technological Change: The Case of High-Tech States in the U.S." by Rasool Azari and James Pick of the University of Redlands (USA), investigates the association of technological development with socioeconomic factors for 74 counties in 12 high-tech states in the United States. The findings are addressed relative to the research literature. Unequal access to technology, ethics, and social responsibility are discussed. Policy implications are examined.

Chapter XI titled, "Social Responsibility and the Transition Toward a Knowledge-Based Society in Latin America" by Heberto J. Ochoa-Morales of the University of New Mexico (USA), talks about the digital gap in the countries of South America and discusses the role of private and public institutions in closing the digital gap.

Chapter XII titled, "Information Systems Ethics in the USA and in the Arab World" by Husain Al-Lawatia and Thomas Hilton of Utah State University (USA), explores the similarities and differences between Arab and American students in information systems ethics through a survey on the use of personal computers at work. The findings point to interesting statistical differences in the average strength of several responses, but there is no disagreement as to the ethicality or non-ethicality of any survey item.

Chapter XIII titled, "Lemon Problems in the Internet Transactions and Relative Strategies" by Li Qi and Zhang Xianfeng of Xi'an Jiaotong University (China) discusses the information asymmetry which exists, not only in traditional business environments, but also in the Internet. This asymmetry encourages the sale of inferior products and services through Internet transactions. Some strategies are offered for avoiding or lessening the likelihood of these "lemon problems" to occur.

Chapter XIV titled, "Reputation, Reputation System and Reputation Distribution — An Exploratory Study in Online Consumer-to-Consumer Auctions" by Zhangxi Lin of Texas Tech University (USA), Dahui Li of the University of Minnesota Duluth (USA), and Wayne Huang of Ohio University (USA), explores the value of reputation in the area of e-commerce by evaluating data directly collected from eBay.com. Inherent problems of the existing reputation systems are pointed out. A stochastic process model is used to analyze the formation of the distribution.

Chapter XV titled, "Privacy Perspective from Utilitarianism and Metaphysical Theories" by Hasan A. Abbas and Salah M. Al-Fadhly of Kuwait University (Kuwait) talks about the concept of privacy in the information age and tries to present the topic from philosophical perspective.

REFERENCES

Chandler, A. (1991). *Scale and Scope*. Cambridge, MA: Harvard University Press.

Grupp, H. & Maital, S. (2001). *Managing New Product Development and Innovation: A Microeconomic Toolbox*. Cheltenham, UK: Edward Elger.

Johnson, D. (2001). *Computer Ethics (3rd Ed.)*. Upper Saddle River, NJ: Prentice Hall.

Laudon C. K. & Laudon, J. P. (2002). *Management Information Systems: Managing the Digital Firm (7th Ed.)*. Upper Saddle River, NJ: Prentice Hall.

OECD. (1998). *21st Century Technologies: Promises and Perils of a Dynamic Future*. City, County: OECD.

Schneier, B. (2000). *Secret and Lies: Digital Security in a Network World*. New York: Wiley Computer Publishing.

Rasool Azari
School of Business
University of Redlands, USA
February 2003

Acknowledgments

This book is the work of many people whose expertise and diligence contributed in numerous ways. I thank them all. I am deeply indebted to Mehdi Khosrow-Pour, a friend and the senior editor of Idea Group Publishing Inc. for introducing me to this timely and interesting project. My special thanks also go to other members at Idea Group Inc., especially Jan Travers and Amanda Appicello who organized and coordinated the process from its inception through its completion.

Furthermore, credit certainly is due to all the authors of the chapters for taking the time and energy to contribute to this book. In addition, my gratitude is extended to the blind reviewers who worked on the early drafts of these chapters and whose contribution cannot be measured easily. And I gladly credit my colleague, Professor James Pick, whose helpful insights and advice I have gratefully accepted many times. Finally I want to acknowledge my wife, Gabriele Azari, who keeps position with me on the home front throughout whatever weather is blowing our way. I thank her for her patience and encouragement.

Rasool Azari
School of Business
University of Redlands, USA
February 2003

Section I:

Information System Security

Chapter I

Network Security Software

Göran Pulkkis
Arcada Polytechnic, Finland

Kaj J. Grahn
Arcada Polytechnic, Finland

Peik Åström
Arcada Polytechnic, Finland

ABSTRACT

This chapter is a topical overview of network security software and related skills needed by network users, IT professionals, and network security specialists. Covered topics are protection against viruses and other malicious programs, firewall software, cryptographic software standards like IPSec and TLS/SSL, cryptographic network applications like Virtual Private Networks, secure Web, secure email, Secure Electronic Transaction, Secure Shell, secure network management, secure DNS and smartcard applications, as well as security administration software like intrusion detectors, port scanners, password crackers and management of network security software management. Tools and API's for security software development are presented. A four-level network security software skill taxonomy is proposed and implications of this taxonomy on network security education is outlined. University and polytechnic level network security education is surveyed and the need for inclusion of network security software development skills in such education is pointed out.

Copyright © 2003, Idea Group Inc. Copying or distributing in print or electronic forms without written permission of Idea Group Inc. is prohibited.

INTRODUCTION AND BACKGROUND

The steadily growing international computer network user community needs an expanding staff of well educated network security professionals to guarantee the reliability of the global IT infrastructure of computer nodes in wired and wireless networks. Network security tools are usually software tools. Network security professionals should know these tools, how to use and develop them, and know what kind of network security they can provide.

In accordance with Oppliger (1999, preface) we define network security as "a set of procedures, practices and technologies for protecting network servers, network users and their surrounding organizations." Network security software (computer programs) covers the area defined above. In order to give a more structured picture of network security software, the material has been organized into the following topics:

- Protection against malicious programs
- Firewall software
- Cryptographic software
- Security administration software
- Security software development
- Network security software skill levels
- Network security software skills in higher education

The text gives a topical overview of network security software: the topics are not covered in detail, and most topics are briefly introduced and left for further study. The main objective is to present "State-of-the-Art" of network security software and to discuss related skills and education needed by network users, IT professionals, and network security specialists.

PROTECTION AGAINST MALICIOUS PROGRAMS

Malicious software exploits vulnerabilities in computing systems. In Bowles and Pelaez (1992) is presented a taxonomy, in which malicious programs are divided into two categories:

1. *Host program needed*
   - **Trap door**
   A trap door is a secret entry point bypassing normal authentication procedures to a program. Trap doors have for many years been used legitimately in program development for debugging and testing purposes. Malicious use of trap doors is a serious security threat.

Copyright © 2003, Idea Group Inc. Copying or distributing in print or electronic forms without written permission of Idea Group Inc. is prohibited.

- **Logic bomb**

A logic bomb is one of the oldest malicious program types. A logic bomb embedded in some legitimate program can be triggered by some condition — for example a particular time on a particular date — to "explode," which means some damage in the host computer, like an unexpectedly formatted hard disk, deleted files, etc.

- **Trojan horse**

A Trojan horse is a program fragment hidden in some useful program performing unwanted or harmful operations.

- **Virus**

A virus is a program that can infect other programs by modifying them. The modification includes a copy of the virus program that can go on to infect other programs.

2. *Self-contained malicious program*
   - **Bacteria**

A bacteria is a self-replicating but otherwise harmless program, which eventually may take up all capacity in the target computer.

   - **Worm**

A worm is a program spreading from computer to computer through network connection. An activated worm may behave like a virus or bacteria, or it could implant Trojan horses.

Antivirus Protection Software

A virus is the most common malicious program. Virus types are defined in Stallings (2000, Chap. 9) and Stephenson (1993). As can be seen from Table 1, viruses use different ways to hide their presence or otherwise complicate antivirus operations. Some viruses even use self-encryption to hide themselves or are embedded in encrypted data communication, like file attachments in secure email or script viruses on protected web pages or in secure HTTP mail messages. Retroviruses attack antivirus programs trying to destroy or neutralize these programs. Multi-partition viruses use multiple infection techniques in order to survive disinfection operations.

The ideal antivirus approach is prevention, which means that a virus is not allowed to enter a computer system. In practice, 100% virus prevention is difficult to achieve, that is why prevention must be combined with detection, identification and removal of such viruses for which prevention fails (Stallings, 2000).

Four generations of antivirus software are described in Stephenson (1993):

1. *First Generation:* Simple scanners that search files for any known virus "signatures" and check executable files for length changes.

Copyright © 2003, Idea Group Inc. Copying or distributing in print or electronic forms without written permission of Idea Group Inc. is prohibited.

Table 1. Different types of viruses

Type of virus	Description
Parasitic	Attaches itself to executable files and replicates when the infected program is executed.
Memory-resident	Lodges in main memory as part of a resident program and infects every program executed.
Boot Sector	Infects a (master) boot record and spreads when a system boots up from the infected disk (original DOD viruses).
Macro	Takes advantage of the macro script features of some types of documents (e.g., MS Word and MS Excel documents).
Script	The virus is similar to macro viruses and uses scripting languages of the operating system or applications like the web. It is application and platform independent.
Stealth	Explicitly designed to hide itself from detection by antivirus software (e.g., using compression).
Polymorphic	Mutates with every infection, making detection by "signature" impossible.

2. *Second Generation:* Scanners that use heuristic rules and integrity checking to search for probable virus infection. Look for more general signs than specific signatures (code fragments common to many viruses); check files for checksum or hash changes.

3. *Third Generation:* Programs called "activity traps" that are memory resident and identify virus actions (e.g., opening executable files in write mode, scanning many files).

4. *Fourth Generation:* Antivirus software packages that use a variety of the best of antivirus techniques in conjunction.

Examples of recent advanced antivirus techniques are *Generic Decryption (GD)* and *Digital Immune System (DIS)* technology. GD is used for efficient detection of complex polymorphic viruses (Nachenberg, 1997). GD works by running executable files through a GD scanner. The GD scanner consists of three

Copyright © 2003, Idea Group Inc. Copying or distributing in print or electronic forms without written permission of Idea Group Inc. is prohibited.

components, the CPU emulator, the virus signature scanner and the emulation control module. The comprehensive approach *DIS*, proposed by IBM in 1997, was developed in response to the weaknesses in integrated mail systems and mobile program technology. DIS consists of three components, a monitoring program, the administrative machine and the virus analyst machine. Both *Generic Decryption* and *Digital Immune System* antivirus approaches are described in Stallings (2000, Chap. 9).

Modern antivirus programs can also be divided into classes based on the level of antivirus protection it provides:

- Gateway level protection
- File server level protection
- End user level protection

Gateway level antivirus protection consists of mail server and firewall protection. Mail server protection is implemented by monitoring incoming and outgoing SMTP traffic. Malicious code in scripts in HTTP email messages and in file attachments is automatically detected, identified and removed. Firewall protection is implemented by detection, identification and removal of viruses passing through firewalls. HTTP, FTP and SMTP traffic is automatically scanned for malicious code as data comes through the firewall from the Internet. Examples of gateway level antivirus software are F-Secure Anti-Virus for Firewalls, F-Secure Anti-Virus for Internet Mail, McAfee WebShield and Symantec Anti Virus Gateway Solution.

File server level antivirus protection consists of software that resides on the server. User profiles of the file system are updated periodically and whenever data is downloaded and uploaded.

End user level antivirus protection is achieved by programs and modules attached to communication applications. The basic antivirus software consists of scanners that scan local files and monitor memory for viruses. As an addition to these, antivirus modules are needed. These modules are add-ons that implement antivirus protection to other programs. Examples of such programs are web browsers, email software and other cryptographic applications. For example, web browsers need antivirus protection integrated into decryption of HTTPS communication, and email clients need antivirus protection to scan encrypted HTTP email messages and encrypted file attachments during decryption. Embedded end user level antivirus modules are needed whenever data communication is encrypted, because encryption disables gateway level antivirus security.

There are commercial end user level antivirus programs for detection of, and protection from viruses (McAfee, 2002; Symantec, 2002; F-Secure Download Center, 2002):

- VirusScan Online
- Norton AntiVirus™
- F-Secure Anti-Virus™

Copyright © 2003, Idea Group Inc. Copying or distributing in print or electronic forms without written permission of Idea Group Inc. is prohibited.

Many of these commercial end user level antivirus programs can be down-loaded from the Internet as free TRIAL versions that only work for a specific period of time.

There are also freeware or shareware antivirus programs such as:

- AntiVir® Personal Edition (H+BEDV, 2002)
- AVG Free Edition (Free Site, 2002)
- AVG 6.0 Free Edition (AVG AntiVirus, 2002)
- F-Secure Antivirus™ (F-Secure Download Center, 2002)

Different levels of antivirus protection should be combined to achieve depth in antivirus defense. The first defense line is gateway level antivirus protection, where viruses are detected and removed before files and scripts reach a local network. The next defense line is file server antivirus protection, where viruses are detected and removed from network user files and script, even before the users try to use these files and scripts from network connected workstations. The ultimate defense line is end user antivirus protection, where viruses undetected in outer defense line are detected and removed.

The defense lines in antivirus protection are illustrated in Figure 1. Viruses can enter a system through a network connection and through infected files and scripts on external media (CD, floppy) inserted into the system. In both cases viruses can be hidden in encrypted information

When using a network connection, viruses may try to enter the network through a gateway, where the gateway level antivirus protection software is installed. But when viruses are hidden in encrypted information the gateway level antivirus protection is always penetrated and the server level antivirus protection is usually penetrated.

Viruses hidden in encrypted information may try to enter also the server level from infected installation files, which have been encrypted.

When antivirus protection is installed, virus definition databases should be kept updated. New viruses and modifications of earlier viruses are constantly introduced. Providers of commercial antivirus protection software usually develop protection against newly detected viruses and virus modifications within hours, and include this new protection in their virus definitions databases, which are available to their customers. Commercial antivirus protection software can usually be configured to update virus definition databases automatically or on request from:

- a management server updated by the antivirus protection provider,
- a network server directory updated by local network administrator, or
- the web page of the antivirus protection software provider.

Virus definition databases can, of course, also be updated manually.

Copyright © 2003, Idea Group Inc. Copying or distributing in print or electronic forms without written permission of Idea Group Inc. is prohibited.

Figure 1. Defense lines in antivirus protection

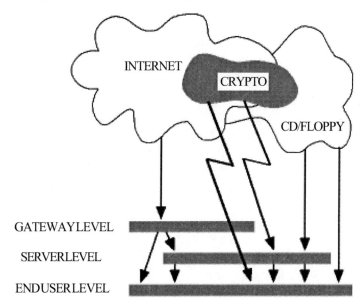

Trojan Horse Defense Software

One defense option against Trojan horse attacks is the use of a secure, **trusted operating system**, in which attempts to implant Trojan Horses are disallowed by a reference monitor using a *security kernel access database* (Stallings, 2000, p. 334). The concept of a trusted system is also explained. Example illustrations of Trojan Horse defense in a secure, trusted operating system are published in Boebert Kain, and Young (1985).

FIREWALL SOFTWARE

Firewalls are used to protect a local computer or network of computers from external network-based security threats. There are three common types of firewalls:

1. *Packet-filtering router:* The router applies a set of rules to each incoming IP packet and then forwards or discards the packet. IP packet filtering occurs in both directions.
2. *Application-level gateway:* The gateway is also called proxy server. It acts as a relay of application level traffic.
3. *Circuit-level gateway:* The gateway is a stand-alone system or performs specialized functions through an application level gateway. Typically it relays TCP segments from one connection to another without examining the contents.

Copyright © 2003, Idea Group Inc. Copying or distributing in print or electronic forms without written permission of Idea Group Inc. is prohibited.

The platform for a packet-filtering router is, of course, the router itself, in which the filtering rules are hardware and/or software implemented. Most TPC/IP routers support basic user defined IP packet filtering rules.

A packet-filtering firewall can also be a stand-alone device on a network link. For example, a PC/Linux computer with two network connections can be used as a platform for an IP packet filtering router for the IP traffic between the two network connections (Conry-Murray, 2001, Chap. 9). Such Linux firewall platforms usually use IPTables screening firewall software (Web Portal of the Netfilter/IPTables Project, 2002), which is integrated into the Linux kernel. For example, the following lines in the firewall initialization script, which is executed at boot time in the Linux firewall platform, allow data communication to and from the SSH port (port number 22) of the same Linux computer:

```
# SSH TCP 22 OUT
iptables -A INPUT -i eth0 -p tcp —sport 22 -m state —state ESTABLISHED
    -j ACCEPT
iptables -A OUTPUT -o eth0 -p tcp —dport 22 -m state —state
    NEW,ESTABLISHED -j ACCEPT

# SSH TCP 22 IN
iptables -A INPUT -i eth0 -p tcp —dport 22 -m state —state
    NEW,ESTABLISHED -j ACCEPT
iptables -A OUTPUT -o eth0 -p tcp —sport 22 -m state —state ESTAB
    LISHED -j ACCEPT
```

Another example of a stand-alone firewall device is Cisco Secure PIX 500 Firewall with IP packet traffic, controlled by a stateful connection oriented algorithm (Adaptive Security Algorithm, ASA) and user authentication/authorization based on an efficient Cut-Through Proxy functionality (Cisco Firewalls, 2002).

For some routers advanced firewall functionality is available as add-on software. An example is Cisco IOS Firewall add-on module to Cisco Internetwork Operating System, which is the control software of many Cisco routers and routing switches (Cisco IOS Firewall Feature Set, 2002). Cisco IOS Firewall can be configured to filter network layer, transport layer, and application layer traffic. Cisco IOS Firewall can be configured to permit specific TCP and UDP traffic when the connection is initiated from the protected network. Cisco Firewall add-on software thus implements packet filtering features and application level gateway features, as well as circuit level gateway features on routed TCP/IP connections.

A typical application level gateway is a protocol oriented proxy server — for example a PC/Linux computer with two network connections executing proxy software — on a network link, for example a HTTP proxy, a SMTP proxy, a FTP proxy, etc. An HTTP proxy can also be used as a web page cache for web users in the proxy protected network.

Copyright © 2003, Idea Group Inc. Copying or distributing in print or electronic forms without written permission of Idea Group Inc. is prohibited.

The platform for an application-level gateway firewall or for a circuit-level gateway firewall is called a **bastion host**. A single-homed bastion host forwards incoming data traffic and filters outgoing data traffic. A dual-homed bastion host filters data traffic in both directions. Usual configurations for firewall-protected networks consist of a one or two packet filtering routers and a bastion host (Stallings, 2000, p. 329).

Firewall software can also protect individual computers connected to a public TCP/IP network. Examples of firewall software for individual workstations in a TCP/IP network are ZoneAlarm® (Zone Labs, 2002), Sygate Personal Firewall (Sygate Technologies, 2002) and Norton Personal™Firewall (Symantec Corporation, 2002).

CRYPTOGRAPHIC SOFTWARE

Classification

Cryptographic software for network security consists of secure network applications and implementations of

- secure network level data communication (IPSec) and
- secure transport level data communication (TLS/SSL).

TCP/IP network standards proposed by IETF are available for secure data communication on these two levels of the protocol stack, as well as for many secure network applications (Active IETF Working Groups, 2001). Many cryptographic software applications use standardized X.509 certificates of the Public Key Infrastructure (PKI) on the Internet (IETF Public-Key Infrastructure Working Group, 2002). PKI client software like ID2 Personal (2001) is a necessary component of such applications. Protection of sensitive cryptographic data and operations is usually implemented as smartcard applications (Rankl, 2000).

Software for Secure Network Level Data Communication

Most software implementations of secure network level data communication in TCP/IP networks are based on the Internet Protocol Security (IPSec) protocol suite developed by IETF IP Security Protocol Working Group (2002). A detailed tutorial on IPSec is found in Doraswamy and Harkin (1999).

The IPSec protocol suite adds security to TCP/IP communication by introducing a new layer in the TCP/IP protocol stack below the IP layer. IPSec adds authentication and optionally encryption to all transmitted data packets. Authentication ensures that packets are from the right sender and have not been altered. Encryption prevents unauthorized reading of packet contents. Two computers connected to the same TCP/IP network can implement end-to-end security through the network if IPSec software with encryption is installed and properly configured

Copyright © 2003, Idea Group Inc. Copying or distributing in print or electronic forms without written permission of Idea Group Inc. is prohibited.

in both computers. When normal IP packets reach the IPSec node they are no longer routed through the network. They are instead used as optionally encrypted payloads of new IP packets (IPSec packets). The IPSec packets are then routed through the IP network, such as the Internet, until they reach an IPSec node, where the packet payloads are — for encrypted payloads first decrypted and then — unpacked to traditional IP packets.

Key management and security associations, the IPSec parameters between two IPSec nodes, are negotiated with the Internet Key Exchange (IKE). IKE is based on the Diffie-Hellman key exchange protocol. IKE creates an authenticated, secure tunnel between two IPSec nodes and then negotiates the security association for IPSec. This process requires that the two entities authenticate themselves to each other and establish shared keys.

IPSec defines a new set of headers to be added to usual IP packets in order to create IPSec packets. These new headers are placed after the IP header and before the Layer 4 protocol (typically Transmission Control Protocol [TCP] or User Datagram Protocol [UDP]) header. These new headers provide information for securing the payload of the IP packet as follows:

Authentication Header (AH)

This header, when added to an IP datagram, ensures the integrity and authenticity of the data, including the invariant fields in the outer IP header. It does not provide confidentiality protection. AH uses a keyed hash function rather than digital signatures, because digital signature technology is too slow and would greatly reduce network throughput.

Encapsulating Security Payload (ESP)

This header, when added to an IP packet, protects the confidentiality, integrity, and authenticity of the data. If ESP is used to validate data integrity, it does not include the invariant fields in the IP header.

IPSec provides two modes of operation — transport and tunnel modes. In transport mode original IP headers are used, but in tunnel mode new IP headers are created and used to represent the IP tunnel endpoint addresses. IPSec tunnel mode is thus an example of IP tunneling in TCP/IP networks.

The core elements of IPSec are shown in Figure 2. ISAKMP is the name of the standardized negotiation protocol used by Internet Key Exchange (IKE). Security Association Databases (SAD) and Security Policy Database (SPD) are databases needed by IPSec and IKE.

IPSec is also integrated with Windows 2000 and Windows XP Professional to provide a platform for safeguarding TCP/IP data communication (see Microsoft TechNet, 2002).

Copyright © 2003, Idea Group Inc. Copying or distributing in print or electronic forms without written permission of Idea Group Inc. is prohibited.

Figure 2.   Elements of IPSec

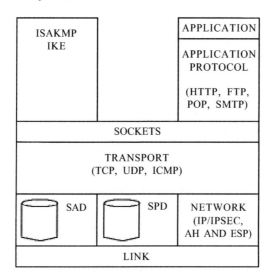

The introduction of DNSSEC may however change the status of IPSec in the future.

A widely used IPSec application is Virtual Private Network (VPN) software for providing secure LAN functionality for geographically distributed LAN segments and computers interconnected by a public TCP/IP network, like Internet. VPN software thus implements IPSec tunnel mode. VPN software developers have founded an international trade consortium, VPNC. The primary purposes of VPNC are (VPN Consortium, 2002):

- Promote the products of its members to the press and to potential customers
- Increase interoperability between members by showing where the products interoperate
- Serve as a forum for the VPN manufacturers and service providers throughout the world
- Help the press and potential customers to understand VPN technologies and standards
- Provide publicity and support for interoperability testing events

The two fundamental VPN types are:
1. *Access VPN:* A secure connection to a LAN through a public TCP/IP Network
2. *Connection VPN:* A secure remote connection between two segments of the same logical LAN through a public TCP/IP network

An Access VPN example is a notebook PC with installed VPN Client software securely connected to a Home LAN over Internet (see Figure 3). The router

Copyright © 2003, Idea Group Inc. Copying or distributing in print or electronic forms without written permission of Idea Group Inc. is prohibited.

Figure 3. Access VPN example

(Notebook PC|VPN Client)↔Internet↔(VPN Server|Router)↔Home LAN

Figure 4. Connection VPN example

Segment A↔(Router|VPN)↔Internet↔(VPN|Router)↔Segment B

connecting the Home LAN to Internet implements the transformation between incoming/outgoing IPSec packets on the Internet connection and traditional IP packets in the Home LAN with installed and properly configured VPN server software.

A connection VPN is, for example, when two segments A and B of the same logical LAN are connected with routers to the Internet (see Figure 4). Both routers implement the transformation between incoming/outgoing IPSec packets on the Internet connection and traditional IP packets in the LAN segment with installed and properly configured VPN software.

There are some free VPN programs available (see Linux FreeS/WAN, 2002). VPNlabs is an open community for researching, reviewing, and discussing Virtual Private Networks (see VPNlabs, 2001). There are also many commercial VPN applications available. Information about commercial VPN solutions can be found on the web portal of VPNC (see VPN Consortium, 2002).

Software for Secure Transport Level Data Communication

Many applications in TCP/IP networks are based on the Transport Layer Security (TLS) standard proposed by (IETF Transport Layer Security [TLS] Working Group, 2002). TLS is based on version 3.0 of the Secure Socket Layer (SSL) protocol. Version 1.0 of SSL was introduced in 1994 by Netscape Communications for secure data communication based on the HTTP protocol.

The TLS/SSL protocol is based on an established client-server TCP connection between two communicating computers and uses the socket interface for data communication. After the establishment of a TCP connection both computers execute the SSL Handshake Protocol in order to agree on the cryptographic algorithms and keys to be used in the actual data communication (Stallings, 2000, p. 214). In this context, X.509 certificates may be used for server and/or client authentication. For the actual data communication the SSL Record Protocol is used. Sending side protocol steps are shown in Figure 5.

Application data is divided in data fragments, which are first optionally compressed. A **message authentication code** (MAC) is computed for each

Copyright © 2003, Idea Group Inc. Copying or distributing in print or electronic forms without written permission of Idea Group Inc. is prohibited.

Figure 5. Sending side SSL record protocol steps

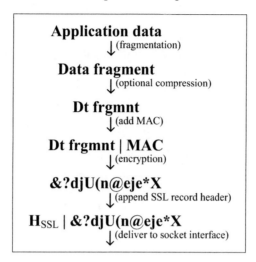

compressed data fragment. The compressed fragment | MAC-packet is encrypted and appended with a SSL record header. Finally the SSL record header and the encrypted packet are delivered to the socket interface of the established TCP connection. On the receiving side, SSL record headers are stripped of the data received from the socket interface. Received data packets are decrypted, the integrity of decrypted data is MAC-checked, checked data is decompressed if necessary, and finally data fragments are re-assembled to application data.

Secure TLS/SSL versions of HTTP and also of other application level TCP/IP protocols have been implemented and made available to the Internet community (see Table 2).

Reading mail from a remote mailbox using POP3S or IMAPS protects mailbox passwords and the contents of fetched email messages against attacks based on eavesdropping on network traffic.

Table 2. Secure application level protocols running on the top of TLS/SSL (Oppiger, 2000, p. 135)

Secure protocol	Port	Description
HTTPS	443	TLS/SSL protected HTTP
POP3S	995	TLS/SSL protected POP3
IMAPS	993	TLS/SSL protected IMAP4
SMTPS	465	TLS/SSL protected SMTP
NNTPS	563	TLS/SSL protected NNTP
LDAPS	636	TLS/SSL protected LDAP

Copyright © 2003, Idea Group Inc. Copying or distributing in print or electronic forms without written permission of Idea Group Inc. is prohibited.

Web Security

There are two basic web security services that need to be considered, access level security and transaction level security (Zouridaki, Abdullah, & Qureshi, 2000). Access security is provided with solutions using firewalls that guard the network against intrusion and unauthorized use. Transaction security requires protocols that secure sensitive, private information between a client and a server using a TCP/IP connection. To ensure that sensitive information is safe while passing between a Web browser and a Web server through an Internet link, there are three Internet protocols (Karve, 1997):

1.   HTTPS, the SSL Secured HTTP Protocol
2.   S-HTTP, Secure Hypertext Transfer Protocol
3.   PCT, Private Communication Technology

S-HTTP is an extension to the HTTP protocol to support sending data securely over the World Wide Web. S-HTTP was developed in 1994 by Enterprise Integration Technologies as an implementation of the RSA encryption standard (see Webopedia, 2002). The protocol implements a flexible choice of key management mechanisms, security policies and cryptographic algorithms by supporting option negotiation between parties for each transaction (Graham, 1995). S-HTTP allows the client and server to negotiate the strength and type of cryptographic option, supports PKI, Kerberos and pre-arranged keys. S-HTTP does not require that the client possesses a public key certificate, which means that secure transactions can take place at any time without individuals needing to provide a key as in session encryption with SSL (Karve, 1997). S-HTTP supports secure end-to-end transactions by adding cryptography to messages at the application layer. S-HTTP is thus tied to the HTTP protocol. S-HTTP encrypts each message on an individual basis.

Microsoft introduced the Private Communication Technology (PCT) protocol in its first release of Internet Explorer in 1996.

HTTPS is a protocol using HTTP on top of SSL. Although HTTPS was originally introduced by Netscape for secure HTTP communication to and from the Netscape Navigator browser, it is now a globally accepted de-facto standard for secure Web communication and supported by practically all web browsers. The use of the protocols S-HTTP and PCT is today insignificant.

When using the Netscape Navigator browser, a user can tell that the session is encrypted by the key icon in the lower-left corner of the screen. When a session is encrypted, the key, which is usually broken, becomes whole, and the key's background becomes dark blue. In Internet Explorer there appears a lock in the lower-right corner of the screen signaling that the connection is encrypted. When browsing to a secure web page, the identities of the server and of the organization that issued the server certificate can be inspected:

•   In Netscape Navigator, click **once** on the locked lock icon
•   In Microsoft Internet Explorer, **double-click** on the locked lock icon

Copyright © 2003, Idea Group Inc. Copying or distributing in print or electronic forms without written permission of Idea Group Inc. is prohibited.

Then, by inspecting the shown certificate, the trustworthiness of the server can be determined. Browser information can be found in Netscape (2002), Microsoft (2002) and Opera (2002).

The URL in the browser also shows if a web page is secured. When a secure link has been opened, the first part of the URL at the top of the browser will change from http:// to https://.

HTTPS communication must, of course, be supported by the web server. HTTPS communication normally uses port 80, but HTTPS communication uses port number 443 by default. Server level support for SSL and HTTPS is included in most web servers (see Apache Software Foundation, 2002; Microsoft Internet Information Services, 2002).

Email Security

Email traffic to and from email servers can be secured by the SMTPS protocol, the SSL protected version of the SMTP protocol. Sessions with email client programs can be secured:

* by using the SSL protected versions POP3S and IMAPS of the email mailbox access protocols POP3 and IMAP4 or
* if the email client program uses a HTTPS web page as user interface.

However, full email security requires email client program extensions for signing and/or encrypting outgoing email messages as well as for decrypting and/or signature checking incoming email messages.

The most widely used email client program security extensions are Pretty Good Privacy (PGP) and Secure/Multipurpose Internet Mail Extension (S/MIME) (see Stallings, 2000, Chap. 5). Neither PGP nor S/MIME are based on the TLS/SSL protocol, but S/MIME uses – like TLS – X.509 certificates and the PKI on the Internet for authentication purposes.

Internet Mail Consortium (IMC) is an international organization focused on cooperatively managing and promoting the rapidly expanding world of electronic mail on the Internet. The goals of the IMC include greatly expanding the role of mail on the Internet into areas such as commerce and entertainment, advancing new Internet mail technologies, and making it easier for all Internet users, particularly novices, to get the most out of this growing communications medium (see Internet Mail Consortium, 2002).

PGP is a public key encryption program originally written by Phil Zimmermann in 1991. PGP is actually a hybrid cryptosystem, combining some of the best features of both conventional and public key cryptography. PGP uses compression of data, conventional encryption/decryption with temporary session key, public key encryption/decryption and digital signing. The combination of the two cryptographic methods combines the convenience of public key cryptography with the speed of conventional cryptography. The keys, measured in bits, in public cryptography are stored in encrypted form in two key ring files. The public keys (and PGP certificates)

Copyright © 2003, Idea Group Inc. Copying or distributing in print or electronic forms without written permission of Idea Group Inc. is prohibited.

of your recipients are added to your public key ring and your own private keys are stored, encrypted using a pass phrase, on your private key ring.

Public key digital signatures enable checking of information authenticity and integrity. They also provide non-repudiation, proof of sender. These features are fundamental features in secure communication. To keep data volumes in reasonable size, i.e., keeping the system fast, PGP uses one-way hash functions in the creation of digital signatures. The hash function produces a fixed-length output and ensures that, if the information is changed in any way — even by just one bit — an entirely different output value is produced.

An important issue within public cryptographic systems is ensuring that the correct person's keys are used. It is possible to post a key with false name and user ID. It is important that the public key to which you are encrypting data is in fact the public key of the intended recipient and not a fake. In practice you can only trust those keys which physically have been handed to you. Digital PGP certificates are used to establish trust public keys. A digital PGP certificate consists of:

- a public key,
- information about the owner, such as name, user ID, and
- one or more digital signatures.

PGP Certificates are utilized when it's necessary to exchange public keys with someone else. For small groups of people who wish to communicate securely, it is easy to manually exchange diskettes or emails containing each owner's public key. This is *manual public key distribution,* and it is practical only to a certain point. Beyond that, it is necessary to put systems into place that can provide the necessary security, storage, and exchange mechanisms so coworkers, business partners, or strangers could communicate if needed. These can come in the form of storage-only repositories called *Certificate Servers,* or in more structured systems that provide additional key management features. These are called *Public Key Infrastructures (PKIs)* (see Network Associates, Inc., 1999).

The digital signatures on a PGP certificate are to state that the PGP certificate information has been attested to the authenticity of the certificate as a whole; it vouches only that the signed identity information is bound to the public key. The digital signature proves that the certificate information is valid. The public key of the sender is needed to check the signature.

Validity of a signature in a signed email can also be proved if sufficient trust can be derived from the signatures in the PGP certificate of the sender. There must be at least one completely trusted signature or at least two partly trusted signatures. Every PGP user collects PGP certificates in their own public key ring.

A PGP user can add own signature to any PGP certificate in own public key ring.

A PGP user can also attach a trust level to any PGP certificate in own public key ring:

Copyright © 2003, Idea Group Inc. Copying or distributing in print or electronic forms without written permission of Idea Group Inc. is prohibited.

- Unknown trust in the signature of the certificate owner,
- No trust in the signature of the certificate owner,
- Marginal trust in the signature of the certificate owner (partly trusted signature), and
- Complete trust in the signature of the certificate owner.

PGP stores the attached trust value in the signature made by the PGP user on the trusted PGP certificate. A PGP user always has complete trust in own signature.

Trust propagation means that a PGP user will accept the trust levels which by him/her completely trusted certificate owners attach to other PGP certificates.

The **PGP trust network** in the public key ring of every PGP user (Stallings, 2000, Figure 5.7, p. 134) remains updated only if:

- An updated PGP certificate (a new signature has been added or the trust level value in a signature has been changed) is always immediately sent to the certificate owner, who then also immediately updates own PGP certificate, not only in own public key ring, but also where it is published — on own web homepage, on key servers, etc.
- Own PGP certificate is attached by the sender to a signed email message or the email contains information about how to obtain the updated PGP certificate of the sender

A **trust propagation example** for PGP v6.5 in Linux is described. The following symbols are used in Figure 6 a-f:

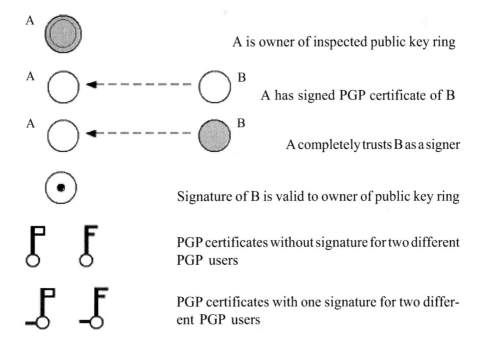

A is owner of inspected public key ring

A has signed PGP certificate of B

A completely trusts B as a signer

Signature of B is valid to owner of public key ring

PGP certificates without signature for two different PGP users

PGP certificates with one signature for two different PGP users

Copyright © 2003, Idea Group Inc. Copying or distributing in print or electronic forms without written permission of Idea Group Inc. is prohibited.

Figure 6a.

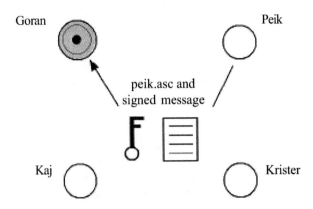

Peik, **Goran**, **Krister** and **Kaj** are PGP users.

1.   **Peik** sends a signed message with own PGP certificate peik.asc as a file attachment to **Goran**
2.   **Goran** adds PGP certificate of **Peik** to own public key ring. → pgp –ka peik.asc
3.   **Goran** checks signature of signed message from **Peik**: *invalid signature from peik*
4.   **Goran** adds own signature to PGP certificate of **Peik**. → pgp –ks peik
5.   **Goran** checks again signature of signed message from **Peik**: *good signature from peik*
6.   **Goran** extracts PGP certificate of **Peik** to the file peik_updated.asc.
     → pgp –kxa peik peik_updated.asc
7.   **Goran** emails the file peik_updated.asc to **Peik**
8.   **Peik** updates own PGP certificate in own public key ring. → pgp –ka peik_updated.asc
9.   **Goran** attaches complete trust in **Peik** as a signer. → pgp –ke peik
     "Would you trust 'Peik Åström' <peik.astrom@arcada.fi>" to act as an introducer and certify other people's public keys to you?
     (1 = I don't know (default); 2 = No; 3 = Usually; 4 = Yes, always) ? 4
10. **Kaj** has earlier attached complete trust in **Goran** as a signer.
11. **Peik** signs the PGP certificate of **Krister**, sends it to **Krister**, who updates his own PGP certificate in his public key ring
12. **Krister** extracts his PGP certificate from his public key ring into the file krister.asc, and sends the file as an attachment to a signed message to **Kaj**
13. **Kaj** first updates his public key ring with the file krister.asc
14. **Kaj** checks how PGP certificate of **Krister** is signed. → pgp –kc krister
15. **Kaj** notices that the PGP certificate of **Krister** is signed by a, for him, unknown "number ID" user (= **Peik**)

Copyright © 2003, Idea Group Inc. Copying or distributing in print or electronic forms without written permission of Idea Group Inc. is prohibited.

Figure 6b.

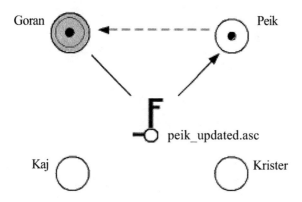

Figure 6c.

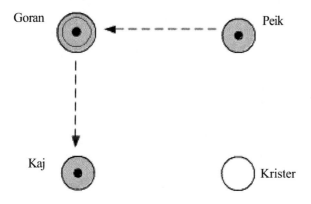

Figure 6d.

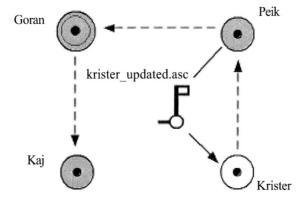

Copyright © 2003, Idea Group Inc. Copying or distributing in print or electronic forms without written permission of Idea Group Inc. is prohibited.

Figure 6e.

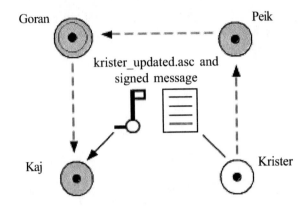

16. **Kaj** asks **Krister** to send the PGP certificate of the "number ID" PGP user
17. **Kaj** gets the missing PGP certificate of **Peik** and updates his public key ring
18. **Kaj** checks the signature of the message from **Krister**: *good signature from krister,* because PGP certificate of **Krister** is signed by **Peik**, and PGP certificate of **Peik** is signed and completely trusted by **Goran**, who is completely trusted by **Kaj**

PGP has some legal issues that users should be aware of, but those have not stopped PGP from becoming a de-facto standard for secure email on the Internet. These problems have caused PGP to be divided into four distinct versions (see University of London, 2002):

• The original, monolithic work, not explicitly integrated into Internet mail (**PGP 2**)

• A standard, which integrates PGP Classic into Internet mail, using MIME (**PGP/MIME**)

Figure 6f.

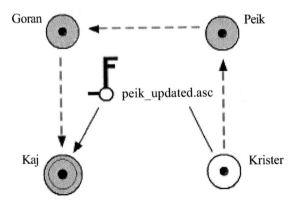

Copyright © 2003, Idea Group Inc. Copying or distributing in print or electronic forms without written permission of Idea Group Inc. is prohibited.

- Versions using non-RSA algorithms (**PGP 5.0/6.0/7.0**)
- IETF standards for an open PGP specification, fully integrated with MIME (**OpenPGP**)

There is an active IETF OpenPGP Working Group (openpgp) that provides IETF algorithm standards and formats of PGP processed objects (see IETF OpenPGP Working Group, 2002). The current work on PGP/MIME is being done in the IMC (see Internet Mail Consortium, 2002).

PGP Freeware for non-commercial use is available for many different platforms, including Windows, UNIX, MS-DOS, OS/2, Macintosh, Amiga and Atari (see The International PGP Home Page, 2002). PGP for commercial use can be found at OpenPGP Alliance (2002).

PGP, version 7.0, works with a number of different email applications using specific email plug-ins. Plug-ins are available for a number of supported email applications in Windows:

- Qualcomm Eudora
- Microsoft Exchange
- Microsoft Outlook
- Microsoft Outlook Express
- Lotus Notes

S/MIME is a secure email standard based on the unsecured email standard MIME, which is based on technology from RSA Data Security (RSA Security Inc.). S/MIME accomplishes privacy and authentication by using encryption and digital signatures. S/MIME combines traditional symmetric ciphers, public key cryptography, hashing, and public key certificates. The reason why these various methods are combined within S/MIME is efficiency. By using the strength of each method in the appropriate place, the result is a reasonably secure scheme that still runs quickly in practical use (Connell, 2001).

S/MIME is designed to work within a Public Key Infrastructure (PKI), which secures communication between two or more parties. The S/MIME standard has been developed by the Internet Engineering Task Force (IETF) and is based on the PKCS #7 (Public Key Cryptography System #7) standard for messages, and the X.509v3 standard for certificates (see Secure Solution Experts, 2002). Corresponding work is done in IETF S/MIME Working Group (2002).

S/MIME provides the following functions, described in Stalling (1998, Chap. 5):

Enveloped Data

Such data consists of encrypted content of any type and encrypted content encryption keys for one or more recipients.

Copyright © 2003, Idea Group Inc. Copying or distributing in print or electronic forms without written permission of Idea Group Inc. is prohibited.

Signed Data

A digital signature is formed by taking the message digest (hash) of the content to be signed and then encrypting that with the private key of the signer. The content plus signature are then encoded using base64 encoding. A signed data message can only be viewed by a recipient with S/MIME capability.

Clear-Signed Data

As with signed data, a digital signature of the content is formed. However, in this case, only the digital signature is encoded using base64. As a result, recipients without S/MIME capability can view the message content, although they cannot verify the signature.

Signed and Enveloped Data

Signed-only and encrypted-only entities may be nested. Encrypted data may be signed, and signed data or clear-signed data may be encrypted.

In S/MIME v3 — presently the latest version of S/MIME — it is still a recommendation, but no longer a precondition, for an email user to own a X.509 security certificate, in which his/her email address is included, in order to obtain all security services from a S/MIME email client extension (IETF S/MIME Working Group, 2002).

Many of the latest commercial email programs have built in S/MIME support that allows users to use the security features of S/MIME (IETF S/MIME Working Group, 2002). Microsoft Outlook and Netscape Messenger are examples of email client programs with S/MIME support. To add S/MIME support to early versions of these email client programs third-party utilities are used (see Slipstick Systems, 2002).

Microsoft Outlook 2000 Service Release 1 (SR-1) and Outlook 2002 support S/MIME v3. TrustedMIME is an email client program plug-in with S/MIME v3 support. TrustedMIME provides support for both Microsoft (Outlook, Exchange, and Messaging) and Lotus Notes platforms. TrustedMIME is compatible with smartcards and tokens from Setec, Rainbow, Aladdin, Gemplus, Siemens, De La Rue, Oberthur, Schlumberger, and Bull, and it has support for PKCS #15, the Swedish SEIS standard, and FINEID smartcard profiles. For further information, see Secure Solutions Experts (2002).

Although PGP and S/MIME offer similar services to users, the two secure email client program extensions have very different certificate formats and can therefore not interoperate. There are many differences between X.509 certificates in S/MIME and PGP certificates. Users can create own PGP certificates, but in S/MIME users must request and be issued X.509 certificates from a Certification Authority. X.509 certificates natively support only a single name for the key's owner, PGP certificates supports multiple names. X.509 certificates support only a single digital signature for

Copyright © 2003, Idea Group Inc. Copying or distributing in print or electronic forms without written permission of Idea Group Inc. is prohibited.

creating trust in a public key. PGP supports multiple signature validation (see Network Associates, 1999).

Secure E-commerce (SET, SEMPER, etc.)

Secure Electronic Transaction (SET), originally introduced by MasterCard and Visa, is an open encryption and security specification designed to protect credit card transactions on the Internet (Nachenberg, 1997). SET provides three services:
1. a secure communication channel among all parties involved in a transaction,
2. trust by the use of X.509v3 digital certificates, and
3. ensures privacy because the information is only available to parties in a transaction when and where necessary.

A core transaction in SET is a **purchase transaction**, which consists of **order information (OI)** encrypted by the public key of the merchant (KPubM), and **payment information (PI)** encrypted by the public key of the credit card issuer (KPubB). A credit card issuer will shortly be called a bank. All encrypted information is signed (a dual signature) with the private key of the cardholder (KPrivC). The purpose of the dual signature is to create a unique, unambiguous, and irreproducible association between specific order information and specific payment information. All encrypted information with the dual signature and a certificate for the public key of the cardholder (X.509$_C$) is sent to the merchant, who can verify the dual signature, check the cardholder certificate, and decrypt the order information. The merchant, who can't decrypt the payment information, passes the encrypted PI, a hash of OI, the dual signature, and the cardholder certificate to the bank through a payment gateway. Also, the bank can verify the dual signature, check the cardholder certificate and further decrypt the payment information. However, the bank can't find out OI from the received hash, which is needed for verifying the dual signature. After verification of the payment information the bank informs the merchant about the payment authorization.

The "cryptographic logic" of a purchase transaction is shown in Figure 7. Some transaction details have been streamlined on purpose in order to show more clearly how security and privacy are ensured in one and the same transaction. An exact but still compact description of SET is found in Stallings (2000, Chap. 7.3). A detailed description is found in Macgreogor, Ezwan, Ligouri, and Han (1997). The official web site of SET is http://www.setco.org (2001).

Figure 7. "Cryptographic logic" of a purchase transaction in SET

cardholder -----> $Sig_{KPrivC}(E_{KPubM}(OI) \mid E_{KPubB}(PI) \mid X.509_C$ -----> merchant
gw(bank) <------ $Sig_{KPrivC}(E_{KPubM}(OI) \mid E_{KPubB}(PI) \mid X.509_C$ <------ merchant
gw(bank) -----------> info about payment authorization -----------> merchant

Copyright © 2003, Idea Group Inc. Copying or distributing in print or electronic forms without written permission of Idea Group Inc. is prohibited.

The SET protocol can only be used to secure payment transactions with credit cards in TCP/IP networks. Other steps in electronic commerce (orders, confirmations, deliveries, etc.) are not supported. A project for standardization of the security architecture of value chains in electronic commerce is the SEMPER (Secure Electronic Marketplace for Europe) project of the European Union (Lacoste, Pfitzmann, Steiner, & Waidner, 1999; SEMPER Secure Electronic Marketplace for Europe, 2001). An overview of electronic payment systems is published in Oppliger (2001).

Secure Shell (SSH)

The Secure Shell (SSH) protocol is an application level protocol introduced for secure remote login in TCP/IP networks (Ylönen, 1996). Presently SSH is an established de-facto Internet security standard, which is being further developed by a dedicated Internet Engineering Task Force Security Area Working Group (IETF Secure Shell Working Group, 2002). The Working Group attempts to assure that the SSH protocol:

- provides strong security against cryptanalysis and protocol attacks
- can work reasonably well without a global key management or certificate infrastructure
- can utilize existing certificate infrastructures (e.g., DNSSEC, X.509) when available
- can be easy to deploy and take into use
- requires minimum or no manual interaction from users
- is reasonably clean and simple to implement
- will operate over TCP/IP or other reliable but insecure transport

Features of SSH include (SSH Communications Security, 2002):
- protects all passwords and data
- full replacement for TELNET, RLOGIN, RSH, RCP, and FTP
- fully integrated secure file transfer and file copying
- graphical user interface on Windows
- automatic authentication of users
- multiple strong authentication methods to prevent spoofing of user identity
- authentication of both ends of a connection
- agents enabling strong authentication to multiple systems with single sign-on
- transparent and automatic secure tunneling of X11 sessions
- secure tunneling of arbitrary TCP/IP-based applications
- encryption and compression of data for security and speed
- multiple built-in methods for password, public key, and host-based authentication

Copyright © 2003, Idea Group Inc. Copying or distributing in print or electronic forms without written permission of Idea Group Inc. is prohibited.

- multiple ciphers for encryption, 3DES, Blowfish, and the AES candidate TWOFISH

The SSH protocol is available in two incompatible varieties: SSH1 and SSH2 (OpenSSH, 2002). The new SSH2 protocol provides several improvements over SSH1 (Ylönen, 1996):
- much better understood and more secure protocol
- new design, which requires much less code to be run with root privileges
- totally rewritten code that improves security
- new routines for cryptography and mathematics, resulting in considerable improvements in speed
- easy to use file transfers using the integrated file transfer agent in SSH for Windows, and the SCP (Secure file copy) and SFTP (Secure File Transfer Protocol) applications on UNIX
- support for multiple public key algorithms, including DSA and Diffie-Hellman key exchange

A free version of the SSH protocol suite of network connectivity tools called OpenSSH can be found in OpenSSH (2002). OpenSSH has been primarily developed by the OpenBSD Project (see OpenBSD, 2002). The goal for the OpenSSH project is simple: all operating systems should ship with support for the SSH protocol included. The current OpenSSH release is OpenSSH 3.4, released in June 2002. It contains support for both SSH1 and SSH2 protocols. The Linux clients in the newest releases of OpenSSH support smartcard login.

The current commercial release from SSH Communications Security of SSH is release 3.2. It is based on the SSH2 protocol with enhanced performance and smartcard support, as well as with major new server features. It includes a Windows client that supports smartcard login (SSH Communications Security, 2002).

Secure Network Management

Network management and monitoring software for TCP/IP networks is usually based on the Simple Network Management Protocol (SNMP), an application level protocol. The first versions of SNMP have practically no security features. SNMP managers could neither securely authenticate themselves to managed SNMP agents nor protect the message transfer between themselves and the managed SNMP agents. The access control of managed SNMP agents was also insecure. In Version 3, secure authentication and encryption features were incorporated in the specifications for SNMP managers and secure access control features were incorporated in the specifications for SNMP agents (see IETF SNMP Version 3 Working Group, 1998). A detailed description of the security features in SNMPv3 is published in Stallings (2000, Chap. 8)

Copyright © 2003, Idea Group Inc. Copying or distributing in print or electronic forms without written permission of Idea Group Inc. is prohibited.

Secure DNS (DNSSEC)

The Domain Name System (DNS) is vital to the Internet, providing a distributed mechanism for resolving host names into Internet Protocol (IP) addresses and IP addresses back into host names. The DNS also supports other Internet directory-like lookup capabilities to retrieve information belonging to DNS Name Servers. Unfortunately there are many security problems surrounding IP and the protocols carried by it. The DNS is not immune to these security problems.

The accuracy of the information contained within the DNS is vital in many aspects of IP-based communications. DNS is missing services that provide data integrity and authentication for data within the DNS. This also causes security threats to other protocols that rely on DNS data for access control.

DNS Name Servers are subjected to many types of attacks (Liu, 1998):

- Denial of service
- Buffer overruns
- Discovered attacks are patched

Name servers are relatively easily spoofed. Security measures, like access lists, and mechanisms, like credibility, can make spoofing more difficult, but not impossible.

A better, more secure version of the DNS protocol is therefore needed. To address this problem IETF formed DNSSEC Working Group to develop the DNSSEC standard. The development work has been overtaken by IETF DNS Extensions Working Group, which addresses these security issues in cooperation with IETF DNS Operations Working Group, (see IETF Working Group DNS Extensions (dnsext), 2002; IETF DNS Operations Working Group (dnsop), 2002). The objective is a standard for secure DNS that provides both authentication and integrity to the information contained within the DNS. DNSSEC can accomplish both of these goals through cryptography. DNSSEC primarily relies on public key technology to create cryptographic digital signatures on information contained within the DNS (Davidowicz & Vixie, 2000).

As defined in Davidowicz (1999), the security extensions to the DNS can be summarized into three services:

Key Distribution

Allows for the retrieval of the public key of a DNS name, to verify the authenticity of the DNS zone data, and provides a mechanism through which any key associated with a DNS name can be used for purposes other than DNS.

Data Origin Authentication

Relieves such threats as cache poisoning and zone data compromise on a DNS server.

Copyright © 2003, Idea Group Inc. Copying or distributing in print or electronic forms without written permission of Idea Group Inc. is prohibited.

DNS Transaction and Request Authentication

Provides the ability to authenticate DNS requests and DNS message headers, guaranteeing that the answer is in response to the original query and that the response came from the server for which the query was intended.

To support the new security capabilities of DNSSEC several new types of DNS Resource Records (RRs) were created. These records allow mapping of uniquely identified host names into IP addresses, i.e., identify an IP address for a given DNS name (a record).

The most important new types of RRs are (Davidowicz, 1999):
1. *KEY RR:* Used for verification of a DNS RRSet's signature.
2. *SIG RR:* Used for storing the RRSet.
3. *NXT RR:* Used to cryptographically assert the nonexistence of an RRSet.
4. *CERT RR:* Used to provide public key certificate within the DNS to other applications outside the DNS.

DNSSEC is still a work in progress. However, any organization that relies on the Internet should consider DNSSEC a critical component of its security infrastructure because the DNS protocol is still vulnerable to malicious misuse. Only DNSSEC, through its strong cryptographic techniques, will provide authentication and integrity to all aspects of DNS in one package (Davidowicz & Vixie, 2000).

BIND (Berkeley Internet Name Domain) was originally written at University of California at Berkeley as a graduate student project. BIND is an implementation of the Domain Name System (DNS) protocols and provides an openly redistributable reference implementation of the major components of the Domain Name System (Internet Software Consortium, 2002). The BIND DNS Server is used on most name serving machines on the Internet. Cryptographic authentication of DNS information is possible through the DNS Security (*DNSSEC*) extensions, defined in RFC 2535 (Nominum, 2001). (For more information concerning BIND compatibility with DNSSEC, see Internet Software Consortium (2002).

The tool package Net::DNS::SEC has DNSSEC functionality (see RIPE NCC, 2001). The DNSSEC functionality is written in PEARL and it works as an extension to the Net::DNS package (Fuhr, 2002).

Smartcard Applications

The computationally secure randomness applied to key creation in public key cryptography may cause security problems, if encryption and decryption operations use the main memory of network-connected computers. Intruders may identify keys as random areas in the main memory, since code and data are usually structured. An identified area of 1024 bits may be a private RSA key being used in an encryption or decryption operation. This is a possible security problem. That is why a private key

Copyright © 2003, Idea Group Inc. Copying or distributing in print or electronic forms without written permission of Idea Group Inc. is prohibited.

should be stored on a smartcard together with the code of the cryptographic operations using it. Then all cryptographic operations using the key can be executed on board the smartcard and the key, after installation, will never leave the smartcard. Once installed, a private key should never leave a smartcard. The use of keys on a smartcard is protected by pin codes or biometrically by digital fingerprint comparison and/or by digital voice recognition. A numerical keypad dedicated to the smartcard is necessary for pin code security.

The characteristics of present smartcards are defined by several ISO 7816 standards (see Portal of International Organization for Standardization ISO, 2002). Smartcards exchange byte sequences — called APDU's in ISO 7816 — with smartcard readers. The file structure of many current smartcard operating systems is based on the pkcs#15 standard (RSA Security, 2002).

Smartcard applications call functions of some Application Programming Interface, when information and operations coded on smartcards are needed. Examples of such API's are implementations of the pkcs#11 standard (RSA Security, 2002) and Microsoft CryptoAPI (MSDN, 2002). Moreover, API's for smartcard applications need interface software to smartcard reader drivers. Usually such interface software is an implementation of the PC/SC Specifications, see (PC/SC Workgroup, 2002). The software architecture of smartcard applications in a PC/Windows computer is shown in Figure 8.

An example of a smartcard-based digital personal identity is the Finnish Electronic Identity Card (FINEID card) introduced in December 1999 and managed by the Finnish Population Register Centre. The implementation details of FINEID are published in Finnish Population register Centre (2002).

SECURITY ADMINISTRATION SOFTWARE

Security administration software includes **intrusion detection**, **management software** for security software and **vulnerability checking**.

An Intrusion Detection System (IDS) monitors traffic in a network and/or user behavior in a host computer to identify possible intruders and/or anomalous behavior and/or misuse (Stallings, 2000, Chap. 9).

Network security software in host computers and in other network nodes, like routers, configurable switches, is often controlled by management software. An example is the distributed IDS described in Heberlein, Mukherjee, and Levitt (1992). Management software is also available for multiple installations of Cisco Secure PIX Firewalls (Cisco PIX 500 Firewalls, 2002). The Digital Immune System described in Stallings (2000, Chap. 9) as well as security software developed and delivered by F-Secure (F-Secure Enterprise Solutions, 2002) are also centrally managed and updated.

A major vulnerability of password protection is insufficient password quality. Passwords can be too short or easily guessed or cracked. A potential intruder could

Copyright © 2003, Idea Group Inc. Copying or distributing in print or electronic forms without written permission of Idea Group Inc. is prohibited.

Figure 8. Software architecture for smartcard applications in a PC/Windows computer

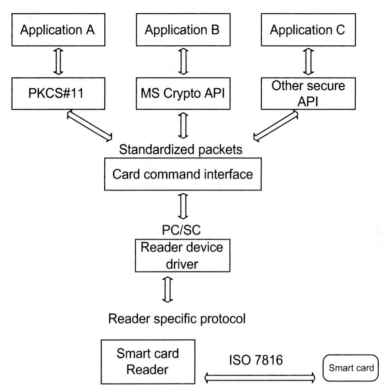

run a password cracker on the encrypted passwords stored in a computer. A system administrator should often do the same, disable user accounts with bad passwords, and urge users to use only good passwords. A freeware password cracker, L0phtCrack, can be downloaded from @stake Research Labs (2002)

Intrusion into a computer in a TCP/IP network occurs through open ports. Intrusion prevention thus requires administration based on regular vulnerability scans for open ports. The vulnerability scan procedure is described in Conry-Murray (2001). How the three-step "handshake" to establish a TCP connection can be manipulated in intrusion attempts is described in Scambray, McClure and Kurtz (2001). A freeware port scanner, Nmap, can be downloaded from Insecure.Org (2002). Information on available commercial port scanners is available at Atomic Tangerine (2002).

SECURITY SOFTWARE DEVELOPMENT

Antivirus protection programming skills require studies of self-modifying code programmed in assembler, in high level programming languages, and in scripting

Copyright © 2003, Idea Group Inc. Copying or distributing in print or electronic forms without written permission of Idea Group Inc. is prohibited.

languages, as well as of virus sensitive vulnerabilities in common operating system environments.

Firewall software programming skills are based on knowledge of software implementations of the TCP/IP protocol stack. Programming exercises and projects to design software of the IP, TCP, UDP and application level protocols should therefore be included in advanced network security education.

For development of network applications with built-in application level security the open source toolkit OpenSSL is available (The OpenSSL Project, 2001). OpenSSL can be installed on UNIX, Windows, and Macintosh computers as a library of C functions available to a C compiler. Also, commercial development tools for SSL-protected network applications are available. RSA Security and Certicom offer software developer kits based on C and Java (see RSA BSAFE, 2001; Certicom, 2001).

There are a number of IPSec implementations and patches available for Linux, such as portable, open source, tunnel and reference implementation. (References can be found in R4knet, 2002; Ringström, 2002; Linux FreeS/WAN, 2002; and NIST/ITL, 2002). The KAME project aims to provide free reference implementations of IPv6 and IPSec (see KAME Project, 2002).

There are also available commercial IPSec developer products such as SSH QuickSec ™ Toolkit. This toolkit includes full IPSec based VPN functionality, an integrated stateful inspection firewall with support for multiple Application Level Gateways, dynamic addressing and configuration, and integration to existing infrastructures (authorization, authentication and accounting). It provides the industry's latest Internet standards, including IPv6, NAT Traversal, and robust PKI support (press release, 2002).

VPN software is implemented as add-on or integrated software controlled by operating systems of workstations, servers, and routers (F-Secure Security Solutions, 2002; Cisco Systems, 2002; Linux FreeS/WAN, 2002). Development skills for VPN software and other IPSec applications require a deep knowledge, especially in IKE — the encryption key management protocol in IPSec. Education of IPSec specialists should include installation, configuration, and test use of VPN software, as well as source code studies of VPN implementations combined with programming exercises in which new features and/or modifications are introduced into the examined VPN software.

There are a number of S/MIME toolkits and packages available from different commercial companies or non-commercial organizations. With these toolkits S/MIME features can be implemented to existing software that do not support S/MIME and to applications under development that need S/MIME support.

A freeware S/MIME v3 toolkit is available in the S/MIME Freeware Library (SFL). SFL works under the MS Windows NT/98/2000/XP, Linux and Solaris 2.8 operating systems (see Getronics, 2002).

Copyright © 2003, Idea Group Inc. Copying or distributing in print or electronic forms without written permission of Idea Group Inc. is prohibited.

There is an S/MIME Toolkit for cross-platform development of S/MIME applications available from The Mozilla Organisation. The Mozilla S/MIME Toolkit provides S/MIME functionality via an API that can be integrated with a variety of MIME parsers and generators (see Mozilla Organization, 2002).

Phaos S/MIME is a package in pure Java. With the Phaos S/MIME Toolkit secure S/MIME messaging applications and applets can quickly be built. The Phaos S/MIME Toolkit is platform-independent, and executes on newer versions of the Java platform. With the Phaos S/MIME Toolkit you can incorporate the S/MIME secure messaging protocol into Java applications (Phaos, 2000).

RSAEuro is an open source cryptographic toolkit providing various preprogrammed functions in C. RSAEuro can be downloaded; for example, from ftp.funet.fi (FUNET ftp server, 2001).

In smartcard application development usually some development kit for smartcard programming is used. Microsoft offers a Smart Card Toolkit based on the use of visual programming tools (Windows for Smart Cards Toolkit for Visual Basic 6.0, 2001).

NETWORK SECURITY SOFTWARE SKILL LEVELS

Every computer and computer network user needs skills:

* to understand the significance of antivirus protection and to perform virus scans with installed antivirus protection software;
* to understand the basic principles of firewalls; to install and use firewall software for protection of a workstation connected to a public TCP/IP network;
* to manage settings of network security software embedded for example in web browsers and remote access software like SSH; and
* to understand the basic principles of PKI and digital signatures.

This skill level could be called **user level,** including basic understanding of PKI and digital signatures. User level skill examples are management of security settings of a web browser (see Figure 9) and inspection of the signature of a signed email message (see Figure 10).

User level skills in network security software should be acquired in all medium- and higher-level education

The next level of network security software skills is the **network administrator level**, which should include skills to install, configure and update network security software (see Figure 11). Education of IT engineers and other IT professionals should provide network administrator skills in network security software.

Copyright © 2003, Idea Group Inc. Copying or distributing in print or electronic forms without written permission of Idea Group Inc. is prohibited.

Figure 9. Security settings in Netscape Communicator v4.79

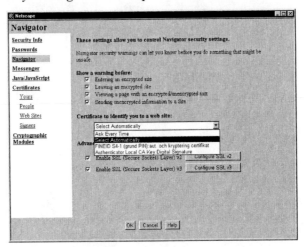

The highest level of network security software skills is the **software development level**, in which a profound and detailed knowledge of:

- behavior of viruses and other malicious programs
- TCP/IP and other network protocols
- cryptographic algorithms, protocols and standards

is combined with advanced programming skills. Figures 12-14 illustrates the knowledge and skills needed for development of PKI client software based on the PKCS#11 standard. Education of software and programming professionals should provide software development skills in network security software.

Figure 10. Inspection of the signature of a signed email message in Netscape Messenger v4.79

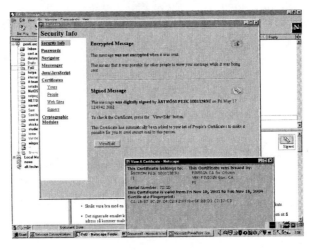

Copyright © 2003, Idea Group Inc. Copying or distributing in print or electronic forms without written permission of Idea Group Inc. is prohibited.

Figure 11. SSL variables in the configuration file of a web server configured for HTTPS — the secure HTTP protocol

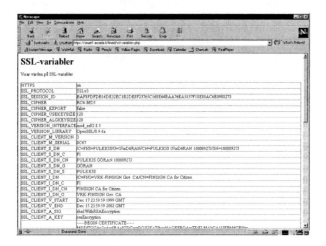

An even higher skill level could be introduced, the **network security scientist level**, which covers knowledge and skills:

- to propose new protection methods against viruses and other malicious programs,
- to propose new firewall types and configurations,
- to further develop the mathematics of cryptography, and
- to propose new cryptographic algorithms, protocols and standards.

Figure 12. Presentation of the PKCS #11 standard on a Web page of RSA Laboratories

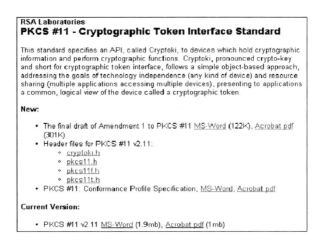

Copyright © 2003, Idea Group Inc. Copying or distributing in print or electronic forms without written permission of Idea Group Inc. is prohibited.

Figure 13. PKCS #11 function declarations published by RSA Laboratories

It should be possible to acquire this skill level in postgraduate IT education in universities.

NETWORK SECURITY SOFTWARE SKILLS IN HIGHER EDUCATION

Education of computer scientists and IT professionals in universities and polytechnics includes, as a rule, courses in computer and network security (Rubin, 2002). Several universities also offer MSc programs in information security (see Eastern Michigan University, 2002; James Madison University, 2002; Queensland University of Technology, 2002; University of Glamorgan, 2002; University of London, 2002; University of Westminster, 2002). Usually these courses and programs cover information security administration, antivirus protection, firewall techniques, intrusion prevention and detection, theory and applications of cryptography, and information security standards. Computer scientists and IT professionals

Copyright © 2003, Idea Group Inc. Copying or distributing in print or electronic forms without written permission of Idea Group Inc. is prohibited.

Figure 14. PKCS #11 function declaration in include file pkcs11f.h published by RSA Laboratories

```
/* pkcs11f.h include file for PKCS #11.  2001 June 25 */
/* This function contains pretty much everything about all the */
/* Cryptoki function prototypes.  Because this information is */
. . . . . . . . . . . . . . . . . . . . . . . .
/* Signing and MACing */

/* C_SignInit initializes a signature (private key encryption)
 * operation, where the signature is (will be) an appendix to
 * the data, and plaintext cannot be recovered from the
 *signature. */
CK_PKCS11_FUNCTION_INFO(C_SignInit)
#ifdef CK_NEED_ARG_LIST
(
CK_SESSION_HANDLE hSession,    /* the session's handle */
CK_MECHANISM_PTR pMechanism,  /* the signature mechanism */
CK_OBJECT_HANDLE hKey        /* handle of signature key */
);
#endif
```

educated by these courses and programs should have knowledge as well as skills about installation, configuration, use, and user support of present network security software. However, university and polytechnic level network security education seldom covers network security software development skills like programming TLS/SSL applications, IPSec applications, SET applications, PKI applications, authentication solutions, applications with digital signatures, antivirus protection software, firewall software, and smartcard programming.

Education of IT professionals in Arcada Polytechnic includes an undergraduate course on Computer and Network Security and specialization courses on IPSec Applications and TLS/SSL Programming. Arcada Polytechnic has, in cooperation with the LM Ericsson IPSec Competence Center, implemented a multimedia IPSec tutorial, in which the characteristics of IPSec and especially IKE are illustrated with audio-supported text presentations, pictures and animations.

CONCLUSIONS

The rapidly spreading use of computers and computer networks and the many advantages of open global network interconnections also have created increasing needs of improved information security. Software solutions and tools are irreplace-

Copyright © 2003, Idea Group Inc. Copying or distributing in print or electronic forms without written permission of Idea Group Inc. is prohibited.

able cornerstones in network security. As can be seen from this chapter, network security software is today a large and complex topic area in a rapidly expanding state. Network security software skills are a necessity, not only for IT and security specialists, but for every computer and computer network user. All this has profound implications on IT education, but also on all education in which use of computers and computer networks is inevitable.

The highest level of IT education, the university and polytechnic level, education for network security software skills should include:

- installation, configuration, and test use of all categories of available network security software solutions and products,
- source code inspection exercises of open source network security software solutions, and
- programming exercises and projects with TLS/SSL application development environments, cryptographic toolkits like RSAEuro, IPSec applications, SSH applications, PKI applications, and smartcard applications.

More emphasis should be put on network security software development skills in present upper level network security education, especially in postgraduate educational programs focusing on information security. Also, student participation in related research should be supported.

REFERENCES

@stake Research Labs. Retrieved June 2, 2002, from http://www.atstake.com/research/lc3/download.html.

Active IETF Working Groups. (2002). Retrieved January 7, 2002, from http://www.ietf.org/html.charters/wg-dir.html.

Apache Software Foundation. (2002). *Apache Projects*. Retrieved June 18, 2002, from http://www.apache.org.

Atomic Tangerine. (2002). *Security portal*. Retrieved April 20, 2002, from http://www.securityportal.com.

AVG Antivirus. (2002). *AVG 6.0 Free Edition*. Retrieved June 26, 2002, from http://www.grisoft.com.

Boebert, W., Kain, R., & Young, W. (1985, July). Secure computing: the secure Ada target approach. *Scientific Honeyweller*..

Bowles, J., & Pelaez, C. (1992, August). Bad code. *IEEE Spectrum*.

Certicom. (2002). *SSL Plus Products*. Retrieved September 25, 2001, from http://www.certicom.com/products/ssl_plus_prod.html.

Cisco Firewalls. (2002). *Cisco Secure PIX 500 Firewalls*. Retrieved March 6, 2002, from http://www.cisco.com/warp/public/cc/pd/fw.

Cisco IOS Firewall Feature Set. (2002). *Cisco IOS Firewall*. Retrieved March 6, 2002, from http://www.cisco.com/warp/public/cc/pd/iosw/ioft/iofwft.

Copyright © 2003, Idea Group Inc. Copying or distributing in print or electronic forms without written permission of Idea Group Inc. is prohibited.

Cisco Systems. (2002). *VPN Solutions*. Retrieved June 16, 2002, from http://www.cisco.com/warp/public/44/solutions/network/vpn.shtml.

Connell, C. (2001). *Enhancing email security with S/MIME.* Retrieved June 20, 2002, from: http://www-10.lotus.com/ldd/today.nsf/0/d2b3eda4956e165a85256b1700175f47/$FILE/SMIME.pdf.

Conry-Murray, A. (2001, April). Vulnerability assessment tools. *Network Magazine.*

Davidowicz, D. (1999). *My DNSSEC paper*. Retrieved June 29, 2002, from http://compsec101.antibozo.net/papers/dnssec/dnssec.html.

Davidowicz, D. & Vixie, P. (2000). *Securing the domain name system*. Retrieved June 20, 2002, from http://www.networkmagazine.com/article/NMG20000509S0039/2.

Doraswamy, N. & Harkin, D. (1999). *IPSec The New Security Standard for the Internet, Intranets, and Virtual Private Networks.* New Jersey: Prentice-Hall.

Eastern Michigan University. (2002). *EMU Information Security Program.* Retrieved January 5, 2002, from http://www.emich.edu/public/bted/default.htm.

Finnish Population Register Centre. (2002). *The Electronic ID Card.* Retrieved May 25, 2002, from http://www.fineid.fi.

Free Site. (2002). *AVG Free Edition.* Retrieved June 26, 2002, from http://www.thefreesite.com/Free_Software/Anti_virus_freeware.

Fuhr, M. (2002). *Net::DNS*. Retrieved May 15, 2002, from http://www.net-dns.org.

FUNET ftp server. (2001). Retrieved June 12, 2001, from ftp://ftp.funet.fi/pub/crypt/cryptography/libs.

F-Secure Download Center. (2002). *F-Secure Antivirus™* Retrieved June 26, 2002, from http://www.f-prot.com.

F-Secure Enterprise Solutions. (2002). *Network security solutions.* Retrieved June 12, 2002, from http://www.f-secure.com/products.

F-Secure Security Solutions. (2002). *F-Secure VPN+.* Retrieved June 16, 2002, from http://www.f-secure.fi/products/vpnplus.

Getronics. (2002). *S/Mime Freeware Library*. Retrieved June 28, 2002, from http://www.getronicsgov.com.

Graham, I. (1995). *HTTP Documents*. Retrieved June 18, 2002, from http://www.utoronto.ca/webdocs/WG/drafts.html.

H+BEDV. (2002). AntiVir® Personal Edition. Retrieved June 26, 2002, from http://www.free-av.com.

Heberlein, L., Mukherjee, B., & Levitt, K. (1992, October). Internetwork security monitor: An intrusion-detection system for large-scale networks. In *Proceedings of the 15th National Computer Security Conference.*

ID2 Personal. (2001). *Bringing end-user security for the Internet economy.* Retrieved September 25, 2001, from http://www.id2tech.com/products/2d.html.

IETF DNS Extensions Working Group, (dnsext). Retrieved June 20, 2002, from http://www.ietf.org/html.charters/dnsext-charter.html.

Copyright © 2003, Idea Group Inc. Copying or distributing in print or electronic forms without written permission of Idea Group Inc. is prohibited.

IETF DNS Operations Working Group (dnsop). Retrieved June 20, 2002, from http://www.ietf.org/html.charters/dnsop-charter.html.

IETF IP Security Protocol Working Group. Retrieved July 6, 2002, from http://www.ietf.org/html.charters/ipsec-charter.html

IETF OpenPGP Working Group. Retrieved June 26, 2002, from http://www.ietf.org.

IETF Public-Key Infrastructure Working Group. Retrieved July 6, 2002, from http://www.ietf.org/html.charters/pkix-charter.html.

IETF S/MIME Working Group. Retrieved June 20, 2002, from http://www.ietf.org.

IETF Secure Shell Working Group. Retrieved June 20, 2002, from http://www.ietf.org/html.charters/secsh-charter.html.

IETF SNMP Version 3 Working Group. Retrieved June 20, 2002, from http://www.ietf.org.

IETF Transport Layer Security (TLS) Working Group. Retrieved June 20, 2002, from http://www.ietf.org.

Insecure.Org. (2002). *Nmap Free Security Scanner*. Retrieved June 28, 2002, from http://www.insecure.org.

The International PGP Home Page. Retrieved June 20, 2002, from http://www.pgpi.org.

Internet Mail Consortium. (2002). *About Internet Mail Consortium*. Retrieved May 18, 2002, from http://www.imc.org/.

Internet Mail Consortium. (2002). *S/MIME and OpenPGP*. Retrieved June 20, 2002, from http://www.imc.org/smime-pgpmime.html.

Internet Security Solution Optimized for Network Edge and Network Access Devices (Press release). (2002). Retrieved July 5, 2002, from http://www.ssh.com/about/press/detail.cfm?id=1265.

Internet Software Consortium. (2002, May 1) *ISC BIND*. Retrieved June 10, 2002, from http://www.isc.org/products/BIND.

James Madison University. (2002*). InfoSec Masters program with a Concentration in Information Security*. Retrieved January 5, 2002, from http://www.infosec.jmu.edu.

KAME Project. (2002). *Overview of KAME Project*. Retrieved July 1, 2002, from http://www.kame.net/project-overview.html#overview.

Karve, A. (1997). *SSL and S-HTTP*. Retrieved June 18, 2002, from http://www.networkmagazine.com/article/NMG20000727S0002/2.

Lacoste, G., Pfitzmann, B., Steiner, M., & Waidner, M. (Eds). (1999). SEMPER – Secure Electronic Marketplace for Europe. *Lecture Notes in Computer Science, 1854*.

Linux FreeS/WAN. (2002). *IPSec Community*. Retrieved July 1, 2002, from http://www.freeswan.org.

Liu, C. (1998). *The DNS Security Extensions*. Retrieved June 20, 2001, from http://www.acmebw.com/resources/papers/dnssec.pdf.

Macgreogor, R., Ezwan, C, Ligouri, L., & Han, S. (1997). *Secure electronic*

Copyright © 2003, Idea Group Inc. Copying or distributing in print or electronic forms without written permission of Idea Group Inc. is prohibited.

transactions: Credit card payment on the web in theory and practice. IBM RedBook.

McAfee. (2002). *McAfee VirusScan*. Retrieved June 26, 2002, from http://www.mcafee.com.

Microsoft. (2002). *Internet Explorer 6*. Retrieved June 18, 2002, from http://www.microsoft.com/windows/ie/default.asp.

Microsoft Internet Information Services. (2002). *Web and Application Services*. Retrieved June 18, 2002, from http://www.microsoft.com/windows2000/technologies/web/default.asp.

Microsoft TechNet. (2002). *IP Security and Filtering*. Retrieved May 27, 2002, from http://www.microsoft.com/technet/treeview/default.asp?url=/technet/prodtechnol/winxppro/reskit/prcc_tcp_erqb.asp?frame=true.

Mozilla Organization. (2002). *S/MIME Toolkit*. Retrieved June 28, 2002, from http://www.mozilla.org.

MSDN. (2002). *The Crypto API and Cryptographic Service Providers*. Retrieved January 6, 2002, from http://msdn.microsoft.com/library/en-us/dnw98bk/html/thecryptoapicryptographicserviceproviders.asp.

Nachenberg, C. (1997, January). Computer virus-antivirus coevolution. *Communications of the ACM* .

Netscape. (2002). *Browser Central*. Retrieved June 18, 2002, from http://browsers.netscape.com/browsers/main.tmpl.

Network Associates, Inc. (1999). *An Introduction to Cryptography*. Retrieved June 26, 2002 from ftp://ftp.pgpi.org/pub/pgp/6.5/docs/english/IntroToCrypto.pdf.

NIST/ITL. (2002). *NIST Cerberus, an IPSec Reference Implementation for Linux*. Retrieved July 1, 2002, from http://www.antd.nist.gov/cerberus.

Nominum. (2001). *BIND 9 Administrator Reference Manual*. Retrieved June 10, 2002, from http://www.nominum.com/resources/documentation/Bv9ARM.pdf.

The Official Web Site of SET. Retrieved June 3, 2001, from http://www.setco.org.

OpenBSD. (2002). *Project Goals*. Retrieved June 20, 2002, from http://www.openbsd.org.

OpenPGP Alliance. (2002). *Working together to protect your privacy*. Retrieved June 26, 2002, from http://openpgp.org.

OpenSSH. (2002). *Project Goals*. Retrieved June 20, 2002, from http://www.openssh.com/goals.html.

The OpenSSL Project. Retrieved September 15, 2001, from http://www.openssl.org.

Opera. (2002). *Opera 6.04*. Retrieved June 18, 2002, from http://www.opera.com/index.html.

Oppliger, R. (2000). *Security technologies for the World Wide Web*. USA: Artech House.

PC/SC Workgroup. (1996). *Specifications Overview*. Retrieved January 6, 2002, from http://www.pcscworkgroup.com.

Copyright © 2003, Idea Group Inc. Copying or distributing in print or electronic forms without written permission of Idea Group Inc. is prohibited.

Phaos. (2000). *Secure Messaging*. Retrieved June 28, 2002, from http://www.phaos.com/e_security/prod_smime.html.

Portal of International Organization for Standardization ISO. Retrieved January 6, 2001, from http://www.iso.org.

Queenslands University of Technology. (2002*). Faculty of Information Technology – Courses, Master of Information Technology*. Retrieved January 5, 2002, from http://www.qut.edu.au/pubs/hbk_current/courses/IT50.html.

R4knet. (2002). *IPSec for FreeBSD*. Retrieved June 20, 2002, from http://www.r4k.net/ipsec.

Rankl, W. & Effing, W. (2000). *Smart Card Handbook e2*. UK: Wiley.

Ringström. (2002). *An IPSec tunnel implementation for Linux*. Retrieved July 1, 2002 from http://ringstrom.mine.nu/ipsec_tunnel.

RIPE NCC. (2001, April 24). *DISI and DNSSEC on the reverse tree*. Retrieved May 15, 2002, from http://www.ripe.net/disi.

Royal Holloway College, University of London. (2002). *The MSc programmes*. Retrieved January 7, 2002, from http://www.isg.rhul.ac.uk/msc/msc_home.shtml.

RSA BSAFE. (2002). *Security protocols*. Retrieved June 13, 2001, from http://www.rsasecurity.com/products/bsafe.

RSA Security. (2002). *Public-Key Cryptography Standards*. Retrieved January 7, 2002, from http://www.rsasecurity.com/rsalabs/pkcs.

Rubin, A. (2002). *List of crypto and security courses*. Retrieved January 5, 2002, from http://avirubin.com/courses.html.

Scambray, J., McClure, S., & Kurtz, G. (2001). *Hacking Exposed e2*. USA: Osborne/McGraw-Hill.

Secure Solution Experts. (2002). *TrustedMIME*. Retrieved June 26, 2002, from http://www.sse.ie/tm_emailsec.html.

SEMPER. (2001). *Secure Electronic Marketplace for Europe*. Retrieved May 27, 2001, from http://www.semper.org.

Slipstick Systems. (2002). *Security Tools*. Retrieved June 28, 2002, from http://www.slipstick.com/addins/security.htm#smime.

SSH Communication Security. (2002). *SSH Secure Shell*. Retrieved May 27, 2001, from http://www.ssh.com/products/ssh/features.html.

SSH Secure Shell Support Page. Retrieved September 25, 2001, from http://www.ssh.com/support/ssh/index.cfm.

Stallings, W. (2000). *Network security essentials: Applications and standards*. New Jersey: Prentice-Hall.

Stephenson, P. (1993, November). Preventive Medicine. *LAN Magazine*.

Sygate Technologies. (2002). *Sygate Personal Firewall*. Retrieved March 6, 2002, from http://www.sygate.com.

Symantec. (2002). *Symantec AntiVirus™*. Retrieved June 26, 2002, from http://www.norton.com.

Copyright © 2003, Idea Group Inc. Copying or distributing in print or electronic forms without written permission of Idea Group Inc. is prohibited.

Symantec Corporation. (2002). *Norton Personal Firewall*. Retrieved March 10, 2002, from http://www.symantec.com.

University of Glamorgan, Courses of School of Computing. (2002*). MSc Information Security and Computer Crime*. Retrieved January 5, 2002, from http://babylon1.isd.glam.ac.uk/Prospectus/view.php3?ID=849&sfrom=easy&dosommat=school.

University of London. (2002). *Secure Web Servers*. Retrieved June 17, 2002, from (http://www.isg.rhul.ac.uk/msc/teaching/sec3/sec3slides/Sec3week2.pdf.

University of Westminster. (2002). *MSc Information Technology Security*. Retrieved January 5, 2002, from http://www.wmin.ac.uk/item_new.asp?ID=3888&wp=pg.

VPN Consortium. Retrieved June 20, 2002, from http://www.vpnc.org.

VPNlabs. (2001). *VPN links*. Retrieved May 17, 2002, from http://www.vpnlabs.org.

Web Page of the Finnish Electronic ID Card. Retrieved May 27, 2001, from http://www.fineid.fi.

Web Portal of the Netfilter/IPTables Project. Retrieved June 26, 2002, from http://www.iptables.se/doc/nag2.

Webopedia. (2002). *S-HTTP*. Retrieved June 18, 2002, from http://www.webopedia.com/TERM/S/S_HTTP.html

Windows for Smart Cards Toolkit for Visual Basic 6.0. Retrieved February 6, 2001, from http://www.microsoft.com/windowsce/smartcard/start/datasheet.asp

Ylönen, T. (1996, July). SSH - Secure Login Connections over the Internet. In *Proceedings of the Sixth USENIX Security Symposium,* San Jose, CA, USA.

Zone Labs, Inc. (2002). *ZoneAlarm*. Retrieved March 6, 2002, from http://www.zonelabs.com.

Zouridaki, H., Abdullah, M. & Qureshi, W. (2000). *Comparing Secure Hypertext Protocol (S-HTTP) to Secure Socket Layer (SSL)*. Retrieved June 18, 2002, from http://ece.gmu.edu/crypto/zouridaki/presentations/secure_www_seminar.pdf.

Copyright © 2003, Idea Group Inc. Copying or distributing in print or electronic forms without written permission of Idea Group Inc. is prohibited.

Chapter II

A Forensic Computing Perspective on the Need for Improved User Education for Information Systems Security Management

Vlasti Broucek
University of Tasmania, Australia

Paul Turner
University of Tasmania, Australia

ABSTRACT

This chapter is divided to two parts. Part one identifies common security and privacy weaknesses that exist in e-mail and WWW browsers and highlights some of the major implications for organisational security that result from employees' online behaviours. This section aims to raise awareness of these weaknesses amongst users and to encourage administrators to mitigate their consequences through enhanced security and privacy-focused user education and training. Part two makes recommendations for improved user education as a component of information systems security management practices. These recommendations have been generated from a forensic computing perspective

Copyright © 2003, Idea Group Inc. Copying or distributing in print or electronic forms without written permission of Idea Group Inc. is prohibited.

that aims to balance the complex set of issues involved in developing effective IS security management policies and practices. From this perspective these policies and practices should improve security of organisation and the privacy of employees without compromising the potential need for future forensic investigation of inappropriate, criminal, or other illegal online behaviours.

INTRODUCTION

In the age of hacktivism, malware and cyber-warfare, increasing numbers of publications are being produced by computer security specialists and systems administrators on technical issues arising from illegal or inappropriate on-line behaviours. Technical advances — in the ability of information systems to detect intrusions, denial of services attacks and also to enhance network monitoring and maintenance — are well documented and subject to constant research and development.

To date, however, there has been limited research into a range of other issues impacting on information systems (IS) security and its management. From a forensic computing (FC) perspective IS security management emerges as part of a much broader debate on the risks and challenges posed by digitalisation for legal, technical and social structures (Broucek & Turner, 2001a, 2001b). This perspective highlights that IS security management cannot be addressed by technical means alone. Indeed the development of effective security management relies on recognition of the need to balance a complex set of technical, legal and organisational issues (Lichtenstein & Swatman, 2000).

This chapter explores one of these issues, "user education" and identifies its relevance for, and interrelationships with, other IS security management issues. This exploration is conducted through an examination of the two most common Internet applications used in organisations: electronic mail (e-mail) and World Wide Web (WWW) browsers. By identifying common security weaknesses in both types of applications, the chapter examines how the security management problems are compounded by common online user behaviours. Retaining a FC perspective, the chapter makes recommendations for improving IS security management.

PART ONE

At a technical level, systems administrators are very aware of the security risks and security weaknesses prevalent in Internet applications and, in particular, in e-mail and WWW browsers. Significantly, while technical solutions are available (at a cost) to alleviate most of the major security challenges, the manner in which most users continue to utilise these applications compounds organisational IS security problems. While technical responses may be able to treat some of the symptoms of inappro-

Copyright © 2003, Idea Group Inc. Copying or distributing in print or electronic forms without written permission of Idea Group Inc. is prohibited.

priate and/or illegal user behaviours, they do little to treat the causes of these or future problematic behaviours (Broucek & Turner, 2002b). The focus here is on "user education", however, it is important to note that most technical solutions employed to detect intrusions, denial of services attacks and/or to engage in network monitoring/maintenance are not currently designed to collect forensic data (Broucek & Turner, 2002a).

As a result, user education of security risks and weaknesses must be treated as an important element in developing effective IS security management practices. For the purposes of user education of security management issues in an organisational context, users can be categorised in three major groups:

1.   Employees lacking awareness of the implications of their online behaviours for organisational security;
2.   Employees who are security conscious but who, in taking steps to protect their on-line privacy, remain unaware of the implications of these behaviours for organisational security; and
3.   Employees who may deliberately exploit technical and managerial weaknesses to engage in inappropriate and often illegal online behaviours.

For all three types of users, targeted education, training and raising awareness emerge as critical to minimising these risks and improving IS security management practices and policies.

The following section examines some of the major security weaknesses of e-mail, their relationships with employees online behaviours and their implications for IS security and employees privacy.

E-Mail

Electronic mail (e-mail) has emerged as a major communication tool in academic, business and social environments. However, e-mail — or more techni-cally Simple Mail Transfer Protocol (SMTP) as defined by RFC821 (Postel, 1982) and the proposed new standard RFC2821 (Klensin, 2001) — remains inherently insecure as a communications medium. As a result e-mail per se is not suitable for the transfer of any information that has to be kept secret. Significantly, most employees and many corporate managers remain unaware that e-mail, unless encrypted, is transferred in plain text, and that during its transfer from sender to receiver journeys through numerous computer systems that could provide points of access to the content of the e-mail. More worryingly, most e-mail systems in use still deploy the very efficient, but simple Post Office Protocol version 3 (POP3) (Myers & Rose, 1996). In most instances POP3 based e-mail clients send passwords in clear unencrypted text across computer networks, thereby enabling sniffing/spoofing type security breaches. Although partial solutions for both these weaknesses are available in the form of TLS/SSL capabilities of e-mail clients (Hoffman, 1999; Newman,

Copyright © 2003, Idea Group Inc. Copying or distributing in print or electronic forms without written permission of Idea Group Inc. is prohibited.

1999), their acceptance is very slow and often hindered by the lack of support for such capabilities in common e-mail software. For example, the version of SMTP daemon *sendmail* distributed by SUN Microsystems with their operating system Solaris 8 does not support TLS/SSL.

These security weaknesses are further compounded by the fact that, as has often been observed, many employees do not bother to have separate passwords for e-mail and other systems that they use in the course of their work. This "one password for everything" approach means that POP3 e-mail client sniffing/spoofing type security breaches may become access points for all organisational information systems.

Awareness of these security weaknesses in e-mail has led many systems administrators to enhance security and restrict access to organisational e-mail systems. From the user's perspective this has led to the perception of organisational e-mail systems as being "unfriendly." This is mainly because these systems tend not to be accessible outside the organisational "firewall" and/or because organisational policy prohibits their utilisation for private communications. As a result of the increasingly important social dimension to e-mail usage most employees solve this "problem" of lack of anytime/anywhere access to e-mail by subscribing to one of the numerous free Web-mail services, e.g., hotmail.com, yahoo.com, excite.com, etc. This user response to the need for e-mail access introduces further risks for organisational IS security management.

As was mentioned above, the tendency of employees to adopt the "one password for everything" approach means that the same password is used on organisational e-mail systems as well as on private Web-mail accounts. This dramatically increases the possibility of password sniffing/spoofing type security breaches. Web-mail services also appear susceptible to a higher incidence of direct or double-click attachment-based viruses that can easily migrate to the organisational information systems as a result of employee online behaviours. More significantly, most of these free Web-mail systems also allow the checking of POP3 e-mail accounts. Employees using these services are rarely aware that in doing so they may be allowing unauthorised access to organisational information.

From the authors' own experiences in network administration within a university environment, it is evident that more than 70% of current students opt for a free Web-mail account in addition to their university e-mail accounts. From class discussions the main reason given by students was the concern that university administrators could gain access to their university e-mail accounts, making them feel concern that their personal e-mail would be read. Following open discussions of the security weaknesses and risks of Web-mail accounts with a class of 30 postgraduate students, all but one opted to stop utilising Web-mail and to use the University e-mail system providing POP3 access internally and SSL protected Web based access from outside of university firewall.

Copyright © 2003, Idea Group Inc. Copying or distributing in print or electronic forms without written permission of Idea Group Inc. is prohibited.

Finally, it is also worth noting how, at a time when legal principles providing for privacy and data protection in the on-line environment have become increasingly common and users privacy expectations have continued to grow, there has been an exponential growth in inherently insecure digital communications that provide individuals with little or no privacy (Broucek & Turner, 2002b).

WWW Browsers

Web browsers, like e-mail, have become central to the development of the information age. But they also exhibit many security weaknesses that combine with users' online behaviours to compound IS security management problems. These include:

- Web browser history and cache files being kept on local drives:
  Generally users are unaware of this and its implications for their privacy, including the ease with which the sites they have visited can be viewed. This problem becomes even more significant for privacy in environments where computers are shared;
- Extensive use of cookies:
  This is problematic because many sites now do not work if cookies are disabled in browsers. This raises issues not just because of the privacy of the user, but also because organisational information is disclosed through the TCP/IP address and through other details available from browsers;
- Possible disclosure of information about computers running the browsers:
  The majority of browsers, if not "hardened," enable the collection of information about themselves and the underlying software and hardware they run on. This can be used by hackers for collecting information about computers and software. This "fingerprinting" generates information that can subsequently be used to find systems vulnerabilities that hackers can exploit to hack into these systems;
- Corporate users assuming that being behind corporate firewall/cache/proxy means that their true identity is not exposed to browsed Internet sites:
  This is often not the case because many corporate installations pass through the HTTP_X_FORWARDED_FOR environment variable;
- Active pages — using Java applets, Java scripts, ActiveX technologies:
  Introducing executable elements into Web pages creates potential risks for the spread of malware, viruses, etc.;
- Data collected from browsers can be used for Internet user profiling and consequently for targeted advertising and context:
  For example, a person that once visits "porn site" will later on be targeted by receiving "e-mails" advertising "porn sites," they may be subject to pop-up screens redirecting them from browsing legitimate site to sites considered to be inappropriate and often illegal.

Copyright © 2003, Idea Group Inc. Copying or distributing in print or electronic forms without written permission of Idea Group Inc. is prohibited.

Having highlighted the major weaknesses of browsers, it is perhaps worth mentioning that from a forensic computing perspective, it is these very weaknesses that are often exploited to create the invaluable resources that form the basis for forensic investigations.

Access to Internet through Web browsers creates further privacy issues for both users and IS management. Many organisations use proxy/cache for speeding up, controlling and monitoring access to Internet by using proxy authentication. Proxy authentication and monitoring can create amongst users the perception of a modern form of "Panopticon" (Dishaw, 2002). In particular, this perception can be created if such monitoring and/or authentication are introduced without proper policies, and if the purpose of their introduction is not explained to users. Proxy authentication is often used only for statistical purposes, however it often can create a "big brother" type of surveillance fear amongst the users. Unfortunately, current available proxy authentication tools and proxy authentication implementations in major Web browsers do not support any sophisticated forms. As a result, passwords used for proxy authentication travel across the wire in "BASE64 uuencoded" format that is close to plain text. These issues have been further compounded by some implementations of proxy authentication requiring users to use the same password as for their e-mail.

PART TWO

In the context of the above discussion, this part of the chapter aims to generate recommendations for improving user education as a component of IS security management practices. From a forensic computing perspective these recommendations remain conscious of the need to balance improved security for the organisation and the privacy of employees, without compromising the potential for future forensic investigation of inappropriate, criminal, or other illegal online behaviours.

Clearly a major element in any organisational IS security management approach must be to provide detailed explanations and demonstrations to users of how their online behaviours with these two applications could potentially damage the organisation. As part of this education, it will be important to address head-on employees' privacy concerns and to introduce transparent and documented procedures for any investigations over particular behaviours. Users must also be made aware that using anonymous e-mails, proxies and anonymizers will not prevent future forensic investigations from being able to track and trace their online activities. It is also imperative that the risks associated with computer viruses are explained, along with the potential fallibility of current antivirus software. In particular, the importance of not running or opening files (usually referred to as "double clicking") received via e-mail from unknown or unreliable sources should be explained.

In addition to explanations and demonstrations it is important that organisations put in place IS security management policies that balance employee privacy concerns with the need for improved security. These policies must be transparent

Copyright © 2003, Idea Group Inc. Copying or distributing in print or electronic forms without written permission of Idea Group Inc. is prohibited.

and developed in cooperation with employees. Where deterrents to inappropriate online behaviours are introduced, they should be explained and discussed. If organisations feel the need to have the option of monitoring online behaviours or conducting forensic investigations, then staff should be informed of the procedures and the results of any investigations or monitoring. Creating a "big brother surveillance" perception amongst employees may well be counter-productive in terms of IS security and/or wider organisational goals (Dishaw, 2002). Effective IS security management will increasingly rely on informing users of the risks and allaying privacy concerns they may have as the need for monitoring and forensic investigation become increasingly common.

CONCLUSION

This chapter has highlighted a series of security and privacy problems with e-mail and Web browsers, and suggested how improved and targeted user education can significantly improve IS security management within organisations. With the dramatic growth in malware and cyber-attacks that looks set to continue, it has become increasingly important that organisations improve their IS security management policies and practices through a balanced and cooperative approach.

REFERENCES

Broucek, V. and Turner, P. (2001a). *Forensic computing: Developing a conceptual approach for an emerging academic discipline.* Paper presented at the 5th Australian Security Research Symposium, (July 11) Perth, Australia.

Broucek, V. and Turner, P. (2001b). Forensic computing: Developing a conceptual approach in the era of information warfare. *Journal of Information Warfare, 1*(2), 95-108.

Broucek, V. and Turner, P. (2002a). *Bridging the divide: Rising awareness of forensic issues amongst systems administrators.* Paper presented at the 3rd International System Administration and Networking Conference, (May 27-31) Maastricht, The Netherlands.

Broucek, V. and Turner, P. (2002b). Risks and solutions to problems arising from illegal or inappropriate on-line behaviours: Two core debates within forensic computing. Paper presented at the *EICAR2002 Conference*, (June 8-11) Berlin, Germany.

Dishaw, M. T. (2002). *Monitoring Internet use in the workplace: Caution is advised.* Paper presented at the 2002 Information Resources Management Association International Conference, Seattle, WA, USA.

Hoffman, P. (1999). *RFC2487 — SMTP service extension for secure SMTP over TLS.* Retrieved July 14, 2002, from the Internet Society's Internet Engineering Task Force Web site: http://www.ietf.org/rfc/rfc2487.txt?number=2487.

Copyright © 2003, Idea Group Inc. Copying or distributing in print or electronic forms without written permission of Idea Group Inc. is prohibited.

Klensin, J. (2001). *RFC2821 — Simple Mail Transfer Protocol*. Retrieved December 12, 2001, from the Internet Society's Internet Engineering Task Force Web site: http://www.ietf.org/rfc/rfc2821.txt?number=2821.

Lichtenstein, S. and Swatman, P. M. C. (2000). *Issues in e-Business security management and policy*. Paper presented at the 1st Australian Information Security Management Workshop, University of Deakin, Australia.

Myers, J. and Rose, M. (1996). *RFC1939 — Post Office Protocol — Version 3*. Retrieved July 14, 2002, from the Internet Society's Internet Engineering Task Force Web site: http://www.ietf.org/rfc/rfc1939.txt?number=1939.

Newman, C. (1999). *RFC2595 — Using TLS with IMAP, POP3 and ACAP*. Retrieved July 14, 2002, from the Internet Society's Internet Engineering Task Force Web site: http://www.ietf.org/rfc/rfc2595.txt?number=2595.

Postel, J. B. (1982). *RFC821 — Simple Mail Transfer Protocol*. Retrieved December 12, 2001, from the Internet Society's Internet Engineering Task Force Web site: http://www.ietf.org/rfc/rfc0821.txt?number=821.

Copyright © 2003, Idea Group Inc. Copying or distributing in print or electronic forms without written permission of Idea Group Inc. is prohibited.

Chapter III

Integrating Cooperative Engagement Capability into Network-Centric Information System Security

Alexander D. Korzyk, Sr.
University of Idaho, USA

ABSTRACT

The U.S. military's concept of a Cooperative Engagement Capability should serve as a useful referent for those attempting to design/develop large scale, organization-wide information security systems. This concept involves centralizing command over the entire suite of defensive assets (naval, air, ground) available in some region or locale; whenever a threat is directed against any US force element (a ship, an infantry unit, etc.), this central authority would then be expected to direct the deployment of whatever appears to be the most efficient countermeasure...in light of prospective as well as actual threats. This is a dramatic departure from the traditional decentralized approach, whereby each force element was expected to draw on its own defensive measures to counter any threat directed at it from any source.

Copyright © 2003, Idea Group Inc. Copying or distributing in print or electronic forms without written permission of Idea Group Inc. is prohibited.

Industrial/commercial organizations might draw on the logic of the Cooperative Engagement Capability *logic in devising a system to secure its informational assets.*

INTRODUCTION TO NETWORK-CENTRIC INFORMATION SYSTEM SECURITY

Network-Centric Security

The end of the "Forty Years War," as historians of the 23rd century may note, marked the end of the 20th century Cold War. For 40 years the world lived in the specter of nuclear holocaust or an apocalyptic catastrophe of the magnitude of the Great Flood. The two superpowers waged a nuclear arms race for nearly a quarter-century based on a doctrine of deterrence. Industrial nations silently conducted espionage of governments and corporations with thousands of intelligence and counter-intelligence agents. President Nixon even claimed that World War III had begun with the ratification of the first Strategic Arms Limitation Treaty. However this war would be a global economic war based on information assets. The foundation of today's society has moved to the accessibility and availability of valuable information. It is important to note the great economic differences in the value of information. Much information is literally worthless and is called garbage information. Many citizens of today's society have not been able to sift through the garbage information because of the glut of worthless information. Those individuals who have found the crown jewels of information (i.e., Bill Gates, Larry Ellison, Paul Allen, etc.) have accumulated great wealth at an astonishing rate (almost beyond comprehension). They have replaced the Sheiks of Arabia and the Sultan of Brunei, once the wealthiest individuals in the world because of a physical asset called oil. Thus, in the shift from an industrial to an information-centered economy, information and economic value are nearly synonymous. The way in which a nation-state wages war is similar to how it accumulates wealth (Toffler, 1980). Information warfare is fought on digital battlespace in which information assets are considered the strategic assets worthy of conquest or destruction. Information systems and critical infrastructure assets supporting those information systems become the new first-strike strategic targets of the post-Cold War era (Jones, 2000, p. 39). The new strategic defense weapons can be based on the Cooperative Engagement Capability Doctrine.

Evolution of Network-Centric Information Systems

Before discussing how Cooperative Engagement Capability may become an information security strategic defense weapon, let me first recall the concept of network-centric warfare from an information warfare perspective and how Cooperative Engagement Capability is part of network-centric warfare. Early computing

Copyright © 2003, Idea Group Inc. Copying or distributing in print or electronic forms without written permission of Idea Group Inc. is prohibited.

solutions required specialized hardware and software custom-made from scratch, much as the craftsmen of the pre-industrial revolution. Early computer manufacturers developed large human labor-intensive computers performing a single function/ mission. Mass production took two centuries to be developed for the industrial age, but only two decades to be developed for the information age. However, from the beginning, hardware technology outstripped software technology and continues to do so today. Early information systems slowly integrated into the business world, with some of the first being developed to perform accounting tasks (IBM) (Laudon & Laudon, 1997, p. 4). These systems simply documented existing procedures and automated the accounting tasks, which could be repeated. Actual business processes finally changed in the early 1990s during the business process reengineering fad to take advantage of data integration. During this reengineering process, information systems made a radical shift from stovepipes to enterprise network-centric information systems. The focus shifted from hardware to information and from stovepipe function to network integration. Considering the overall forms of Information warfare [command and control, information-based, electronic, psychological, hacker, economic information, and cyber (Libicki, 1995)], the Cooperative Engagement Capability would be considered under command and control warfare. I will attempt to indicate how Cooperative Engagement Capability may also be considered for information-based and economic information warfare.

BACKGROUND OF ADVANCED INFORMATION WARFARE

Network-Centric Warfare

Network-centric warfare to date has three levels of command and control fusing more information at each level (Joint Vision, 1995). The highest level is the domain of Cooperative Engagement Capability. The Cooperative Engagement Capability could control economic information as an information weapon. The Global Information Grid contains a middle command and control layer below Cooperative Engagement Capability called Link 16, which integrates data network weapons and forces with radar supporting Cooperative Engagement Capability. The bottom Cooperative Engagement Capability Layer is the Global Command and Control System (GCCS), which coordinates joint forces and joint planning networks. Each service then has its own Command and Control System connected to the Global Command and Control System via the secret Internet, which is largely unknown and inaccessible to the general public. The Global Information Grid is only one part of a triumvirate network-centric warfare structure. The Information Grid part provides information transmission, protection, and assurance. The Sensor Grid part provides both persistent and transient signals from various sources and allows certain sensor data to be amplified and fused across the electromagnetic spectrum in near real-time.

Copyright © 2003, Idea Group Inc. Copying or distributing in print or electronic forms without written permission of Idea Group Inc. is prohibited.

The Engagement Grid also provides a new capability called distributed precision strike using integrated forces management as the new potential weapon delivery formation against mobile targets and their center of gravity. The architecture of Cooperative Engagement Capability provides security and reliability (Birman, 2000, p. 54).

Currently, Cooperative Engagement Capability responds to new threat scenarios that are sudden and unexpected against U.S. Forces only. Cooperative Engagement Capability is now based on Naval Battle Groups. Future versions of Cooperative Engagement Capability enabled systems may support coalition battlespace by extending CEC to NATO forces. This could provide a common fire control picture to all involved nation-states, so forces receive a common command and decision to fire immediately. Data from anti-submarine sensor grids may also be fused into Cooperative Engagement Capability, to add yet another dimension. One must consider all of the discussed features of CEC to devise a system to secure informational assets for a corporation, which could be a lucrative economic information warfare target.

Economic Information Warfare

Similar to the Armed Forces organizational environment consisting of the Army, Navy, Marines, and Air Force departments, a corporation could consist of major divisions, each with their own companies. Division A controls all of its intra-organizational informational assets separate from Division B and Division C. Yet, there is a higher command and control system at the corporate level integrating (but mostly aggregating) inter-organizational information to report to stakeholders/stockholders. The operational picture at each level is very different from the other levels. The Chief Executive Officer sees and wants to see similar information in a higher Command and Control level format much like Cooperative Engagement Capability. If Cooperative Engagement Capability Logic is implemented at the Fleet level, then radar and other sensor grid data should be available for the Fleet Commander. This starts to form a common picture of the naval battlespace and the threat. Similarly, short-term projections, forecasts, and other industry information can be fused to populate the business battlespace. The Engagement grid data also must be available in order to give a common command for executing a decision. If Division A is considered a Fleet Level organization, then the information a business analyst produces for short-term planning after analyzing a particular market may indicate a threat or action being taken by a competitor. This action could be as a result of information from an act of economic information warfare, information-based warfare, or even hacker warfare, or all of the above. In the case of economic-information warfare, Division A would likely send an early warning notification to the affected company in Division A. Should the Division A Director determine that the entire Division could be affected economically, then the Division A Director would likely send a similar early warning notification to the Corporate Headquarters

Copyright © 2003, Idea Group Inc. Copying or distributing in print or electronic forms without written permission of Idea Group Inc. is prohibited.

indicating the potential damage estimates based on different scenarios. The three levels of organization in the corporation could see a common picture and make a common decision to execute an action. This action may even be a preemptive precision strike designed to prevent the competitor from taking the predicted action. A routine secret messaging system may be sufficient to handle this situation because of having sufficient time for a decision window; however, this is not the case in the hacker information warfare scenario.

MAIN THRUST OF THE CHAPTER
Issues, Controversies, Problems of Corporate Information Warfare

At 2:30 a.m., the network administrator on duty at Corporate Headquarters notices slightly increased network activity appearing to come from Division A. Unknown to the network administrator, Division A ceases normal information operations between 12:00 midnight and 5:00 a.m. to run daily backup procedures. The network administrator assumes that Division A is running routine queries against the corporate database without checking any details of the increased activity. At 2:32 a.m., the network administrator notices a large increase in the corporate system network traffic and becomes suspicious. The network administrator tries to execute a "view rlogin" command that fails. By 2:33 a.m. the network administrator tries to execute a root command and discovers that the network administrator's session has been "killed." The attempts to log-in are unsuccessful. The network administrator now suspects foul play, but is powerless because a hacker has taken control of the corporate network. At 2:35 a.m., the network administrator vainly looks for the Standard Operating Procedures book once kept in hardcopy form, but cannot find it. Luckily, he has his boss' phone number and calls him. The Chief Network Officer answers his cell phone and gets a status report from the network administrator. The Chief Network Officer knows that the CEO has an important meeting later that day about a possible acquisition. At 2:37 a.m., the Chief Network Officer calls the Chief Information Officer at home with a recommendation to shut down the network because they have no means or system to engage the attacker and track his movements, let alone take back control of the system. The CIO immediately concurs with the Chief Network Officer's recommendation and decides to call the CEO. The Network Administrator receives the order to shut down the system at 2:40 a.m. However, the attacker had already downloaded two gigabytes of corporate data. The Chief Network Officer knows that it will take days, even using sophisticated tools, to determine which files have been compromised. Unfortunately, the corporation has not encrypted any stored files. Files have only been encrypted when transmitted outside the corporation, but not automatically. Another alternative and cheaper technique than encryption could have been digital watermarking, which

Copyright © 2003, Idea Group Inc. Copying or distributing in print or electronic forms without written permission of Idea Group Inc. is prohibited.

provides value-added protection on top of encryption (Yeung, 1998, p. 32). Digital watermarking is the embedding of unobtrusive marks or labels that can be represented in bits in digital content. Marking valuable data with a digital watermark clearly identifies the data if it is ever copied illegally or stolen. The velocity of information warfare is so fast that a human cannot possibly absorb and comprehend all the data from their systems in a fast enough manner to detect, defeat, or counter such an attack. In the example sited, the corporation had a pull-the-plug policy for such attacks because they had no other defense. A corporate network with Cooperative Engagement Capability-like enabled features may have allowed early warning, immediate detection and possible preemption of this attack. However, to prosecute the attacker, not only would the corporation need the CEC-like enabled system, the FBI and local legal authorities would most likely also need to have the CEC-like enabled system in order to have the common picture. In a larger view of cybercrime, the FBI instituted a program called INFRAGARD Partnerships for Protection to coordinate the resources of the FBI, local authorities, and companies to fight attacks from various threats. Some of these threats include: (1) internal threats such as disgruntled employees, industrial espionage spies, vendors, and contractors; and (2) external threats such as crackers, virus writers, criminal groups, foreign and domestic terrorist organizations, activists, extremists, and vandals (Yurcik et al., 2000, p. 2). If security data from the hacker scenario discussed above involved the FBI or local authorities, then the security data would be shared among any other corporations similarly attacked or attacked near the same time. If this were a widespread attack, the shared data would aid in the possible apprehension of the attacker. A recent sting of two hackers blackmailing a British company involved the FBI, London MetroPol, and Kazakhstan authorities (Armstrong, 2000, p. 24). One of many tools that they used was an intrusion detection system, which is simply analogous to a burglar alarm system or perimeter defense with an unarmed sentry (Stillerman et al., 1999, p. 65). One of the problems still unresolved, unfortunately, is that burglar alarms often go off when there is no burglar. Researchers have developed a prototype intrusion detection system that cooperates with other host computers across decentralized but connected computer networks (Frincke, 2000, p. 2). If host-based Intrusion Detection Systems are analogous to a guard dog for each computer, then network-centric Intrusion Detection Systems are the neighborhood police patrols riding in cars with no weapons (Durst et al., 1999, p. 55).

Solutions and Recommendations

Macrocybernetic Security

The use of macrocybernetic theory for corporate network-centric information system security may allow the use of CEC-like logic for securing enterprise-wide informational assets of industrial/commercial organizations. A set of sensor/engagement function specific security subsystems with the macrocybernetic (supra system) (Sutherland, 1997, p. 218) would handle the fusing of integrated multimedia

Copyright © 2003, Idea Group Inc. Copying or distributing in print or electronic forms without written permission of Idea Group Inc. is prohibited.

data sources and invoking real-time multi-countermeasure subsystem responses without human intervention. The architecture offered by the use of the JAVA programming language that provides network-centric computing is called JINI. JINI consists of federations where most of the power belongs to local authorities with the federal authorities having only the authority to ensure local entities work together (Waldo, 1999, p. 80). The enterprise system protected information system boundary includes all the subsystems such as network subsystem, database subsystem, application subsystem, and security subsystems. The network boundary includes both intra- and inter-organizational networks up to, and even through, the Internet/ Information networks. The database boundary includes client/server and Internet databases. The application boundary similarly includes client/server and Internet applications. Within each of these subsystem boundaries a microcybernetic structure handles sensor data. Interfacing subsystem's security data received from a database sensor and a network sensor requires a macrocybernetic to handle integrated sensor data. Integrating **information systems security** subsystems from multiple information systems within an organization necessitates a supra macrocybernetic to handle engagement data. At the inter-organizational level required for FBI and local authority coordination, humans from the corporation, FBI, and local authorities must become involved because of socio-political ramifications (Armstrong, 2000, p. 24). This involvement may simply be the corroboration of a recommended countermeasure to be executed by the supra macrocybernetic. The result is an ensemble of interconnected sets at the supra macrocybernetic level representing cellular structures (Sutherland, 1998, p. 166), which are the information system security subsystems.

Engagement Macrocybernetic

The corporate enterprise system would contain the engagement cybernetic, which would be based on the threat and synthesized countermeasures primarily for active and restorative countermeasures. The macrocybernetic would determine the sequence, length, and intensity of the engagement. Some rules of engagement could be mode-based. A decision to engage covertly to gain counter-intelligence (industrial espionage) information prior to choosing the best course of action may only be acceptable for unknown or not recognized threats. A decision to engage by pursuit may involve calling in for reinforcements (FBI and local authorities). The CEC-like common security picture may involve other organizations such as the FBI and local law enforcement officials coordinating information security subsystem sensor data to obtain total awareness of the intruder and his intentions. The decision then could be to set an ambush with the cooperation of the FBI and local authorities (Korzyk, 2000, p. 74). The engagement macrocybernetic could also choose a restorative countermeasure. Either the macrocybernetic predicted that the damage from the threat would be such that the best course of action is to allow the attack to proceed and use the containment rule of engagement. If the macrocybernetic uses the

Copyright © 2003, Idea Group Inc. Copying or distributing in print or electronic forms without written permission of Idea Group Inc. is prohibited.

containment rule of engagement then the system must try to limit damage, maintain system availability, and allow recovery of full operating capabilities as soon as possible (Jajodia, 1999, p. 73). Extreme examples include quarantining or shutting down services provided by the system in order to prevent the spread of malicious code. A vaccine, security patch for updating system files or anti-virus definition file updates allow quick reconstitution of the system and continued corporate information operations.

Efficient Allocation of Countermeasures

A countermeasure is a safeguard achieved through adding a step or an improvement in system design that mitigates or eliminates the vulnerability making the threat irrelevant or reducing the damage from the threat to acceptable levels (National Research Council, 1991, p. 13). Countermeasures are the union of passive, active, and restorative countermeasures $C \in C_A \cup C_P \cup C_R$ as shown in the Enterprise System Security Planning Model (Korzyk, 2000, p. 75). The use of countermeasures involves a cost for each countermeasure. The maximum utility function, noted as $\text{Utility}_{max} [C_1, C_2, ...C_n[T]]$, determines which countermeasure provides the maximum utility to counter the threat at an acceptable risk and cost. Thus, the resource or asset chosen to counter a threat would be made on efficiency criteria rather than a response from the attacked system. Each major type of countermeasure involves more than just risk and cost. The maximum utility function, $\text{Utility}_{max} [C_1, C_2, ...C_n[T]$, uses the multi-criteria function, $f_{mc} = \alpha + \beta + \phi + \lambda + \sigma$, where $\alpha = \{$cost of implementing $C_n[T]\}$, $\beta = \{$future likelihood of recurrence$\}$, $\phi = \{$known second order effects$\}$, $\lambda = \{$the likelihood of concurrent SI in the enterprise$\}$, $\sigma = \{$minimum exposure time$\}$. The synthesized **enterprise system security** array uses the results of the multi-criteria function with the minimum expected value $E(V)_{min}$. The multi-criteria function includes the decision to use one or more of the following countermeasures.

Passive Countermeasures

A passive countermeasure, C_P, is defined as a safeguard achieved through safeguards taken to prevent the threat from exploiting the vulnerability, safeguards taken to prepare for the threat, safeguards taken to detect the threat, or safeguards taken to protect the system during the security incident. Passive countermeasures have been by far the mode of choice for various reasons. The passive mode is similar to the martial arts' philosophy to defend against an attack, rather than to be the aggressor, unless counter-attacking becomes necessary to defeat the attacker. Defending is almost always less expensive than counter-attacking. Current techniques and tools require human corroboration to counter-attack. The security practitioners and researchers are spending considerable resources in the area of intrusion detection. As techniques and tools for intrusion detection become adequate enough, a macrocybernetic structure could determine if there was enough intelligence to switch from passive to active mode.

Copyright © 2003, Idea Group Inc. Copying or distributing in print or electronic forms without written permission of Idea Group Inc. is prohibited.

Active Countermeasures

An active countermeasure, C_A, is a safeguard achieved through safeguards taken immediately to respond to the threat upon exploitation of the vulnerability (reactive), safeguards taken to remediate or stabilize the system enough to continue information operations, safeguards taken to isolate the point of penetration and then track the attacker as long as the attacker is in the system, safeguards taken to counter-attack and, if successful, pursue the attacker to expose the attacker's identity to law enforcement officials. Active countermeasures also include covert security safeguards taken to confuse and expose the attacker, which enables the attacked organization to gather counter-intelligence about the attacks unknown to the attacker (proactive). Gaining valuable counter-intelligence about the attack gives the attacked organization time to observe the attacker in order to choose the best course of action, including pursuit and calling reinforcements. This employs the military strategy of cooperative engagement capability because, while the attacked company lures the attacker to a fake site or an ambush site, a cooperating agency from the National Infrastructure Protection Center, such as the FBI could be gathering real-time intelligence on the origin of the attacks. This places the cooperating agency in an advantageous position over the attacker. Taking immediate countermeasures, determined by the countermeasure array could minimize damage and financial losses by most efficiently allocating the countermeasures.

Restorative Countermeasures

A restorative countermeasure, C_R, is a safeguard achieved through containing or limiting the extent of damage caused by the security incident and a safeguard achieved through quarantining or shutting down services provided by the system in order to prevent catastrophic failure (failsafe). If an enterprise system has deliberate redundancy designed into it, then the damage to the operational system can be minimized by the immediate shut down of the attacked system and instantaneous cut-over to the backup or redundant system. For example, shutting down the email server to prevent the further spread of a virus, which attaches itself to email messages, a safeguard achieved through reconstituting the system with resources remaining that are still able to function or operate adequately and a safeguard achieved through recovering from the security incident as quickly as possible, e.g., installing security patches for the operating system or updating anti-virus files.

Enterprise System Security Arrays

The synthesized enterprise system security array consists of the threat array and the countermeasure array. There are multitudes of threats that form the basis of the threat array. Threats become dangerous when the threat exploits a corresponding vulnerability of the information system. Most, but not all threats and vulnerabilities are known. The threat is assigned a probability of occurring given vulnerability. A Markov-based approach will model the threat sequence over time.

Copyright © 2003, Idea Group Inc. Copying or distributing in print or electronic forms without written permission of Idea Group Inc. is prohibited.

Figure 1.   Enterprise system security planning model

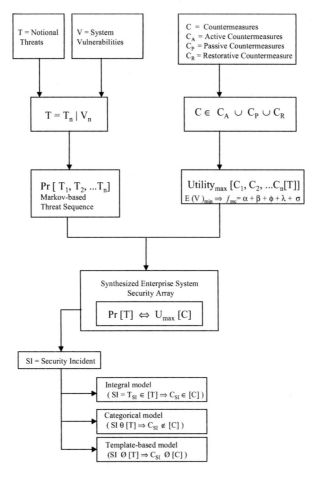

Countermeasure interdiction too late in the threat cycle could lead to a serious degradation of available countermeasure at a much higher cost, possibly catastrophic. Countermeasures interdicted too early may change the attacker's strategy for the worse. Since the Markov-based approach models state-level transformations, it can be used to decide which countermeasure method to use against the threat. Using high cost countermeasures against a low-level threat, which could just be a decoy, could leave the enterprise system in the horrible position of just having used all available high cost countermeasures against lower level threats when a larger threat follows with just low cost countermeasures left. Those remaining countermeasures are known to be ineffective against the larger threat, thus leaving the enterprise completely exposed to the primary attack. The cooperative engagement capability may have allowed the enterprise system to more efficiently allocate the countermeasures to produce the best performance with minimum damage and at minimum cost.

Copyright © 2003, Idea Group Inc. Copying or distributing in print or electronic forms without written permission of Idea Group Inc. is prohibited.

Various vulnerabilities form the basis of the countermeasure array. The countermeasure array corresponds to a maximum utility function of the exploited threat. IS managers typically practice trading off security for performance or trading off security for funding as a matter of course (Korzyk, 1997). Upper management accepts this motis operandi until the first security catastrophe, after which the typical reaction is to throw money at the problem to prevent a reoccurrence of the catastrophe (Korzyk, 1998).

The $[T] \times [C]$ Array is the cross product of the threat array and the countermeasure array producing several combinations to be used by the cybernetic mechanisms. The countermeasures used by the macrocybernetic entity model depend upon the probability of whether the particular threat and countermeasure combination exist in the synthesized enterprise system array noted as $\Pr [T] \Leftrightarrow U_{max}$ $[C]$.

Future Trends

Model-Base Versus Database Structures

Traditional database structures are generally insufficient to store and process real-time systems. Network-centric information systems rely upon real-time processing and storage. Even object-oriented databases have not been able to support real-time processing and storage. The concept of a model base structure is not new. It has not been commercially developed by some of the database software manufacturers. Recent model-base structures constructed by researchers have been able to support real-time processing and storage.

Model-Base Security Structures

Three basic classes of model-base structures serve as the basis for enterprise system security planning. The type of model-base structure used by the enterprise system security-planning model depends upon whether the threat is known, given known vulnerabilities and a corresponding countermeasure.

The integral model provides countermeasures for a fully predicted security incident. When the threat is known, given a certain vulnerability, and the countermeasure for that threat is known, given maximum utility, constitutes a fully predicted security incident noted as $(SI = T_{SI} \in [T] \Rightarrow C_{SI} \in [C])$.

The categorical model provides countermeasures for a partially predicted security incident. When the threat is within a certain range or category of threats (given a certain vulnerability) but the countermeasure for that particular threat is not known for a certain threat, but are known for a range or category of threat; this constitutes a partially predicted security incident noted as $(SI \theta [T] \Rightarrow C_{SI} \notin [C])$.

The template-based model provides countermeasures for an unpredicted security incident. When the threat is not known within a certain range or category of threats, or vulnerabilities for the unknown threat are not known and the countermeasure for the unknown threat is not known; this constitutes an unpredicted security incident noted as $(SI \varnothing [T] \Rightarrow C_{SI} \varnothing [C])$.

Copyright © 2003, Idea Group Inc. Copying or distributing in print or electronic forms without written permission of Idea Group Inc. is prohibited.

CONCLUSION

The use of a Cooperative Engagement Capability logic clearly shows great potential for preventing the competition (enemy) from capturing the ability to control supply chain or value chain (friendly) information assets and insuring survivability of those resources (assets). CEC-like logic may increase the ability of enterprise network-centric information systems to handle increasingly complex security technology.

REFERENCES

Armstrong, I. (2000). Security Fights for Internet Foothold. *SC INFO Security*, *11*(10), 23-30.

Birman, K. (2000). The Next-Generation Internet: Unsafe at any speed? *IEEE Computer*, *33*(8), 54-60.

Durst, R., Champion, T., Witten, B., Miller, E., & Spagnuolo, L. (1999). Testing and Evaluating Computer Intrusion Detection Systems. *Communications of the ACM*, *42*(7) 53-61.

Frincke D. (2000). Balancing Cooperation and Risk in Intrusion Detection. *ACM Transactions on Information and System Security*, *3*(1), 1-29.

Jajodia, S., McCollum, C. D., & Ammann, P. (1999). Trusted Recovery. *Communications of the ACM*, *42*(7), 71-75.

Joint Vision. (1995). *Joint Vision 2010*. Washington, D.C.: U.S. Department of Defense.

Jones, A. (2000). The Challenge of Building Survivable Information-Intensive Systems. *IEEE Computer*, *33*(8), 39-43.

Korzyk, A. (2000). Towards a cybernetic perspective for enterprise system security. In *Proceedings of the 4th World Multiconference on Systemics, Cybernetics, Informatics* (pp. 72-77).

Korzyk, A. (1998). A forecasting model for internet security attacks. In *Proceedings of the 21st National Information Systems Security Conference* (pp. 99-110).

Korzyk, A. (1997). Who should be in charge of information systems security in the federal government? In *Proceedings of the 20th National Information Systems Security Conference* (pp. 295-304).

Laudon, K., & Laudon, J. (1997). *Essentials of management information systems organization and technology* (2nd ed.). Upper Saddle River, NJ: Prentice Hall.

Libicki, M. (1995). *What is information warfare?* Washington, D.C.: National Defense University Press.

National Research Council (1991). *Computers At risk*. Washington, D.C.: National Academy Press.

Copyright © 2003, Idea Group Inc. Copying or distributing in print or electronic forms without written permission of Idea Group Inc. is prohibited.

Stillerman, M., Marceau, C., & Stillman, M. (1999). Intrusion detection for distributed applications. *Communications of the ACM, 42*(7), 62-69.

Sutherland, J. (1998). Integrative systems: Assessing requirements and capabilities for intra- and inter-organizational context. *IEEE Transactions on Systems, Man, and Cybernetics—Part A: Systems and Humans, 28*(2), 159-182.

Sutherland, J. (1997). A Prospective on Macrocybernetic Process Management System. *Journal of Technological Forecasting and Social Change, 55*, 215-248.

Toffler, A. (1980). *The Third Wave.* New York: William Morrow & Company.

Waldo, J. (1999). The JINI Architecture for Network-Centric Computing. *Communications of the ACM, 42*(7), 76-82.

Yeung, M. (1998). Digital Watermarking. *Communications of the ACM, 41*(7), 30-33.

Yurcik, W., Loomis, D., & Korzyk, A. (2000, September). Predicting internet attacks: On developing an effective measurement methodology. In *Proceedings of the 18th International Communications Forecasting Conference* (pp. 1-9).

Copyright © 2003, Idea Group Inc. Copying or distributing in print or electronic forms without written permission of Idea Group Inc. is prohibited.

Chapter IV

A Methodology for Developing Trusted Information Systems: The Security Requirements Analysis Phase

Maria Grazia Fugini
Politecnico di Milano, Italy

Pierluigi Plebani
Politecnico di Milano, Italy

ABSTRACT

In building cooperative distributed information systems, a methodology for analysis, design and implementation of security requirements of involved data and processes is essential for obtaining mutual trust between cooperating organizations. Moreover, when the information system is built as a cooperative set of e-services, security is related to the type of data, to the sensitivity context of the cooperative processes and to the security characteristics of the communication paradigms. This paper presents a methodology to build a trusted cooperative environment, where data sensitivity parameters and security requirements of processes are taken into account. The phases are illustrated

Copyright © 2003, Idea Group Inc. Copying or distributing in print or electronic forms without written permission of Idea Group Inc. is prohibited.

and a reference example is presented in a cooperative information system and e-applications. An architecture for trusted exchange of data in cooperative information system is proposed. The requirements analysis phase is presented in detail.

INTRODUCTION

Recently, the widespread use of information technology and the availability of networking services have enabled new types of applications in the field of Information Systems, characterized by several geographically distributed interacting organizations exchanging data through the network and the Web. For example, *Cooperative Information Systems* (*CoopIS*) are distributed information systems that are employed by users of different organizations under a common goal (Mylopoulos et al., 1997). Another extension consists of *e-applications* (Mecella et al., 2001), namely, *e-services* provided by different organizations on the net. The data exchange and the interleaved execution of processes in such systems bring about security issues bound to inter- and intra-organizational structures, to a plurality of actors in the distributed system, and in the heterogeneity of policies existing at the various sites where a distributed process is executed.

In advanced information systems, new security issues, besides traditional ones, arise, such as (1) cooperating organizations may not know each other in advance; (2) data exchanged in a cooperative environment can be either internally generated or acquired from other sources. Newly created data can have different security levels according to their acquisition mode (e.g., manual data entry vs. automatic capture) and their information acquisition process; (3) e-applications can be invoked in a distributed way at design and at run-time and, whereas in traditional "closed" CoopIS mutual knowledge and agreements upon design of applications are the basis for the cooperation, the availability of a complex platform for CoopIS (Mecella et al., 2001) allows for "open" cooperation among different organizations that may not know and/ or trust each other.

A major obstacle in securing new information systems lies in the lack of concepts and methods that, differently from traditional systems where security problems are well known [see for instance (Icove et al., 1995) for an overview], allow security developers to identify, design, and implement security requirements and policies that integrate different security needs in a heterogeneous system (Chung et al., 2000; Schneider, 2000).

For example, for CoopIS few requirements and policies are known at design time: at run time, policies need to be negotiated among the cooperating processes or new policies must be added. In these cases, determining the suitable requirements and policies is based on the identification of the "normal" behaviour of the system users (Mukkamala et al., 1999), known as user profiling methods. The need arises

Copyright © 2003, Idea Group Inc. Copying or distributing in print or electronic forms without written permission of Idea Group Inc. is prohibited.

to identify, verify, and strengthen the security policies in order to allow the e-applications to securely authenticate each other and to exchange data in a trusted way.

This paper proposes a policy- and mechanism-based security methodology called TRUMET (TRUsted METodology), where we organize application data and control data of e-applications of a CoopIS in a sequence of development steps. Moreover, an architecture for secure exchange of information in the CoopIS based on the security level is proposed. This architecture is a development of a proposal contained in (Dall'Agnola et al., 1999) where the results of a project (Demostene Project) sponsored by the Italian National Research Council 1998-2000 for security in federated information systems are presented. There, the basic architecture for secure cooperation of Organization Units in the Public Administration domain have been studied, leading to a federation of sites with their own database and Web protection policies to be mediated by a federated security engine that automatically builds and maintains the federated security rules.

Then, the requirements analysis phase is illustrated in more detail, where data and process analysis is interleaved with security analysis. The methodology premises start from our work described in (Fugini et al., 2002).

Some proposals for architectures for new information systems, e.g., e-service and workflow-based, have been presented in the literature (Casati et al., 2001; Mecella et al., 2001). The concept of cooperative process (Schuster et al., 2000) defines as a complex business process involving different organizations. An e-service represents a contract on which an organization involved in the cooperative process agrees.

In order to integrate features of *data security* in a CoopIS/e-application, we have to handle (Bertolazzi et al., 2001):

- security of data handled *within* one e-service/process; and
- security of data exchanged *among* cooperating e-services/processes and therefore of the *cooperation* among individually trusted e-services.

The methodology presented in this paper extends the traditional waterfall method by providing a set of steps that, starting from the user security requirements and policies, brings to the development of a *secure*, or *trusted*, distributed system.

Basic Assumptions

In the remainder of the chapter, we make a set of assumptions.

1. First, we assume that each e-services has been designed (e.g., as a workflow) according to internal security requirement and policies and is therefore a *trusted* or secure (set of) *process(es)*. The focus of the methodology is on data and process security during the *cooperation* among processes [VLDB-TES 2000] (Casati et al., 2002).

Copyright © 2003, Idea Group Inc. Copying or distributing in print or electronic forms without written permission of Idea Group Inc. is prohibited.

2.   Secondly, we consider that organizations cooperating in CoopIS/e-applications
     can be of two types:
     • *trusted organizations*: data transmission occurs among organizations which
     trust each other in a network due to organizational reasons (e.g., homogeneous
     work groups in a departmental structure, or supply-chain relationships among
     organizations in a virtual enterprise);
     • *untrusted/external organizations*: data are transmitted among cooperating
     entities in general, possibly accessing external data sources. Every time mutual
     knowledge among organizations participating in CoopIS/e-applications is not
     given in advance, mechanisms are needed to ensure that mutual trust be
     established dynamically, during cooperative process executions.
3.   Trust regards mainly two aspects:
     • the sensitivity of data being managed within a process; and
     • a secure *information exchange* to guarantee sensitive information.

Sensitivity concerns both correct authentication of cooperating organizations
and the process of guaranteeing that only authorized organizations can read, use, and
generate data in the cooperative process. To guarantee sensitivity of information,
security technologies and mechanisms must be used, e.g., based on the use of digital
certificates and signatures, to allow the cooperating organizations to establish a
secure communication environment.

The paper is organized as follows. We present the methodology schema through
its steps. We then detail the phases of the methodology and then illustrate the phase
of requirements analysis. Finally, we draw the remarks and discuss the envisioned
use of the framework in order to cope with development issues aspects that can
regard other types of distributed Information Systems, such as Multi-Channel
Information Systems.

METHODOLOGY SCHEMA

Security requirements and policies are the knowledge of a specific domain
about features of interest for the identification and verification of security issues and
mechanisms in the CoopIS. Starting from captured requirements and policies, the
sequence of phases is identified as follows:

•   A *requirements analysis* phase, where the sensitivity of *user data* is stated
     for those data (mainly databases and business data, such as customer
     directories or collections of documents) pointed out as core-business data for
     the CoopIS.
•   A *design phase*, where *system security* data (such as password, security files,
     log files, authentication data and so on) are designed and ways for exchanging
     data in a secure way are identified.

Copyright © 2003, Idea Group Inc. Copying or distributing in print or electronic forms without written
permission of Idea Group Inc. is prohibited.

Figure 1. Sequence of steps of the TRUMET the methodology

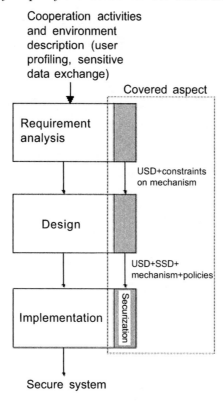

A *securization phase*, where user data and system security data are implemented on a security platform made of selected products and solutions for authentication, access control, audit, communication, and so on.

All these steps consider in parallel the development of e-applications and of their security, referring, for example, to a workflow development methodology described in (Baresi et al., 1999), where the cooperative system is modeled as a workflow. The close relationship between the development method and the security development steps are a key issue in the success of the development of a truly secure system. In this paper we will limit the connection between applications and security to the overall TRUMET structure, while we go into details of the requirements analysis phase in order to concentrate on novelties of security aspects in cooperation.

To illustrate the development methodology, in this chapter we refer to a "***Goods purchase and payment***" case study, whose UML activity diagram (Booch et al., 1998) is shown in Figure 2 and is also described in its security aspects in (Fugini et al., 2001). This e-application is composed of two e-services: a good ordering e-service and a payment e-service, which can possibly interact by exchanging the customer card data.

Copyright © 2003, Idea Group Inc. Copying or distributing in print or electronic forms without written permission of Idea Group Inc. is prohibited.

Figure 2. UML activity diagram of the "goods purchase and payment" application

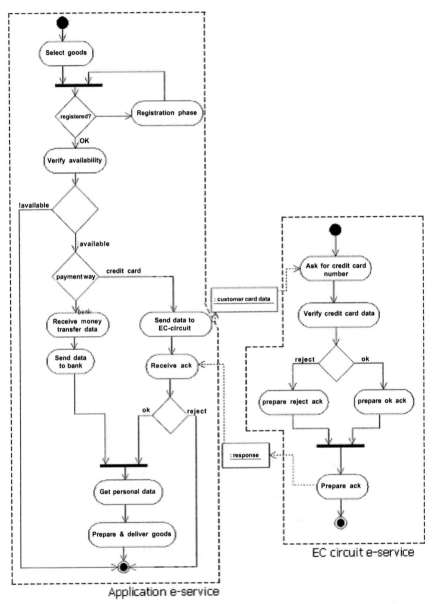

This is a typical e-commerce application whose flow goes as follows. First, the customer browses the product catalogue published on the company's Web site. In order to buy the chosen goods, the customer has to register into the application providing his/her personal data. In this way, the system can identify each customer by using a unique identifier (called username), and authenticate him/her using a password.

Copyright © 2003, Idea Group Inc. Copying or distributing in print or electronic forms without written permission of Idea Group Inc. is prohibited.

Upon request of goods by a customer, the system verifies the availability of the needed quantity of that good; the customer can then pay in two different ways: (1) by credit card or (2) using his/her own bank's payment circuit.

In the first case, the e-services cooperate as follows. Application control passes from the ***goods selection*** e-service to the e-service of the credit card electronic circuit (EC-Circuit). The EC circuit's Web site manages information about the credit cards and has the responsibility for checking the customer data and the card validity. As illustrated in the figure, the EC circuit's Web site is activated by the dispatch of the customer data sent by the Goods e-service (this is usually modeled and implemented as a trigger in workflows). In this case, security of exchanged data is an issue handled by our methodology.

If the second payment mode (bank circuit) applies, the payment validity is checked within the same system process and no communication exists among e-services, hence no security issues that are treated by our methodology occur.

Once the payment task has been completed, the system prepares and sends to the customer the invoice and the goods.

A set of security information regarding users that access the application are stored in the system in order to (1) authenticate the customers during the registration phase; and (2) to monitor the user actions on the system for log purposes.

However, privacy about the customer must be preserved when storing all this information in a *profiling database*; therefore, the choice of what data have to be stored, under which format, and with which access rules is a critical aspect to be designed in the development. Good purchasing tracking should be forbidden according to national and international security and privacy rules.

THE METHODOLOGY PHASES

The TRUMET phases for secure information systems development is based in the following assumption:

If the completion of the steps of the methodology eventually leads to trusted agents/roles who handle sensitive data in a correct way (that is, according to the security requirements and policies and according to the implemented security mechanism), then data are handled, processed and exchanged in a secure way and therefore the Information System is secure.

This methodology can be applied when:

- a new Information System is built;
- the CoopIS is built out of existing systems that are aggregated to compose a *federated system* and this is the most frequent case; and
- part of an existing system (e.g., a new e-services or a new version thereof) is developed.

Copyright © 2003, Idea Group Inc. Copying or distributing in print or electronic forms without written permission of Idea Group Inc. is prohibited.

Figure 3.   Methodology data, policies, and mechanisms

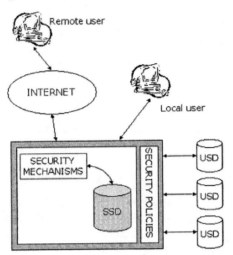

In the two latter cases, the methodology must take into account the different policies of the existing systems and mediate them into a *common federated security policy* for data protection (Castano et al., 1997).

In TRUMET, we classify sensitive data in two classes:

1. *User Sensitive Data (USD)* — Data that are sensitive for the user (databases, data files, documents, and so on)
2. *System Sensitive Data (SSD)* — Data that constitute the security mechanisms and hence are sensitive for the system (e.g., password files, crypto keys, protected databases, log files, audit traces) and arise from the choice of the mechanisms that will ensure the protection of the USD.

This classification leads to a *recursive* definition of sensitive data. This recursion consists in the fact that some sensitive data (USD) are protected through other sensitive data (SSD), which are in turn to be protected. To stop the recursion, the methodology has to be based on a set of *security policies* able to protect the sensitive data independently of technological (hardware or software) issues or devices. This is shown in Figure 3, where the methodology block (denoted by a gray background) represents the target of the methodology, which is composed of two sub components: the security mechanisms that use the SSD, and the policies. In this way, access to the sensible data of USD type occurs only through the gray-background module that will be implemented through the methodology.

We assume that, in a preliminary requirement collection phase, interviews and checklists have been submitted to the users in order to capture the core business of the CoopIS and list the basic categories of data that need to be protected.

For our example, a requirement list is shown in Table 1. External payment means payment via EC credit card. Agent means the operator of the e-service. The

Copyright © 2003, Idea Group Inc. Copying or distributing in print or electronic forms without written permission of Idea Group Inc. is prohibited.

Table 1: Sample checklist with requirements and policies used as input to TRUMET

	Core Business Description	Funct.l req.s	Non Funct.l req.s	Security Policies
Target	A.Goods selling via e-commerce	A.1.Separate order from payment phase	A.1. Efficiency: goods delivered within 5 days	A.1.1Customer must be registered in customer db
		A.2.Allow for external and internal payment modes	A.2.Provide fast Web access	A.2.1.Keep audit data regarding both orders and browsing session
				A.2.2.Authentication required between e-services in case of external payment
				A.2.3 Same agent can not handle order and payment
		A.3. Filter accesses	A.3 Keep filtering transparent	A.3.1 Use firewall with web bastion host
	B. Fidelization of customers	B.1.Manage credit line data	B.1 Provide fast access to credit data by agents	B.1.1 Keep secrecy and integrity of credit line data
	C. Expand business	C.1.Examine audit data about browsing	C.1 Limit amount of stored analysis data	C1.1 Keep secrecy of data about customers
				C1.2 Treat data statistically only
USD	Customer database, Order database, OrderHistory database, CreditCard Database, AgentIds			
SSD	Passwords, Clients(browser) authentication data, Agent authentication data			

numeration assigns a letter to the business targets, a number to functional and non-functional requirements and gives a "dot" level to the security policies regarding the sub-target and the requirements. A hierarchy in a tree can be constructed from this table to study derived policies. Finally, we have listed some USD and SSD data for this application.

Requirements Analysis Phase

This phase will be detailed later in the chapter. The goals of the phase are the following:

1. The identification of the *USD*. The emphasis is on data that need to be protected: indirectly, security information is derived on who (agents or roles or Organization Units) is authorized to operate on these data, from which sites/ workplaces, under which policies (e.g., separation of duties, need-to-know, binding of duties [Castano et al., 1995]).

Copyright © 2003, Idea Group Inc. Copying or distributing in print or electronic forms without written permission of Idea Group Inc. is prohibited.

3.   The identification of *constraints on security mechanism (and therefore on SSD)*: these data will be derived precisely in the design phase. Here, only constraints on what security mechanisms the user wants or does not want (e.g., password only instead of digital certificates) are considered. Thanks to the identification of constraints, we can apply the methodology presented in this paper not only to a new system, but also to an existing system, which is represented basically in terms of constraints.

Once the USD have been identified, we classify them according to the four "traditional" *sensitivity properties*:
- Integrity;
- Confidentiality;
- Non-repudiation; and
- Authenticity

with respect to a set of studied attacks and threats, e.g., those described in Aleph (1996) or Garfinkel (1997).

In fact, the need to preserve these properties leads to different levels of security in data protection and the four properties constitute the *Security Level* of both the USD and the SSD data. They are used for secure storage and secure transmission of data.

Referring to the **Goods Purchase** example, let us consider the case where we are building a new system which has to communicate with the e-service provided by the EC credit card circuit system. There exists a set of sensible data which are transmitted over the communication channel, say via Internet, and, in order to protect these data, we have to create a secure channel to ensure both the integrity and the confidentiality of the data. The USD of the application could be the *personal data* used by the system to deliver the acquired goods. The Security Level SL of these data is represented by the values of the four items — SL = <integrity, confidentiality, authenticity, non-repudiation> — where each can assume the Top, High, Confidential, or Unrelevant value. In fact, the privacy law requires the use of a set of mechanisms to guarantee the confidentiality and the integrity of the personal data.

Hence, in order to satisfy a given order request forwarded to the application, the step of authentication to the application can rely on the use of the login-password method. This is a typical *application constraint* belonging to those that we have called SSD constraints.

Design Phase

The input of this phase is the set of USD produced in the requirement analysis phase and the security constraints regarding the SSD.

In this phase we have to identify the suitable mechanisms that permit not only to protect the USD, but also to meet the constraints. On the basis of the adopted

Copyright © 2003, Idea Group Inc. Copying or distributing in print or electronic forms without written permission of Idea Group Inc. is prohibited.

mechanisms, a particular set of *security (or control) data* will be used to enforce it: these are the data that we have called SSD.

For example, if we chose to protect stored data using the Access Control Lists (ACL) mechanism, there will be a list of users for whom access is denied. Only the system administrator can manage those data.

Finally, as done with USD, we have to define a Security Level SL for the SSD too. In particular, for data exchange the design phase specifies an architecture that ensures security when data are transmitted between e-services. The architecture is composed of two standard virtual devices:

- a SecureSender and
- a SecureReceiver

that, on the basis of the mutual trust between the communicating e-services and of the Security Level of the exchanged data, wrap the data in a *secure package*.

The presence of this abstract device allows us to face the security design problems with no need to specify the characteristic of a particular data transmission channel.

Referring to the "***Goods purchase and payment***" example, in order to protect the USD (the personal data), the mechanism should allow access to these data only from the data owner and from the authorized system personnel.

First of all, we have to create a mechanism that authenticates the user who wants to operate with the USD. In order to satisfy the existing SSD constraints, we create this secure mechanism on the basis of the login-password method, so that every login-password pair identifies a *subject*.

After identifying all the *objects* composing the system, we have to define the Access Control Lists for them so that we can create a rule set able to permit or deny the access to an object by a subject.

In this context, information like login and password are the SSD. In order to explain the role of the policies in our methodology, let us consider the typical situation where the identified SSD are to be stored into a dedicated protected database which is accessible only by a restricted set of operators, such as the system administrator or the account managers. These users are also *subjects* of the system, that can be authenticated in two different modes:

- Using the same login-password used for the normal system users. In this way, the authentication data related to these operators are located at same Security Level of the other users.
- Using different and stronger authentication methods, like smart-card-based or digital certificates-based. In this case, we create another set of SSD.

The design phase is completed when the protection of all of the identified USD has been covered by a mechanism and when all the SSD are protected by security mechanisms or by a set of security policies.

Copyright © 2003, Idea Group Inc. Copying or distributing in print or electronic forms without written permission of Idea Group Inc. is prohibited.

Let us assume that the authentication phase for the account manager implies the use of a smart-card; in this context a security policy could define the behavior of both the account manager and the system administrator. For example:

- "the operator must securely store his/her smart card every time he/she leaves the work place";
- "in case of theft/lost, the operator must inform immediately the system administrator to disable the smart-card."

Summarizing, the USD are protected by realizing an ACL that implies the definition of the **login password pair** (SSD). The SSD are protected using the same method that, now, adopts the smart-card approach; therefore another SSD is introduced.

Eventually, all these SSD are protected by a correct behavior of the user, who has to follow the security policies.

Securization

In recent years, quite a number of system and application software have suffered from several vulnerabilities, such as the buffer overflow vulnerability (Aleph, 1996), which have been exploited by the attackers to obtain system access privileges. In the securization phase, designed protection issues have to be implemented into a set of security mechanisms that allow one to flexibly meet the security policies.

Under the term "securization" we consider:

- The realization of the mechanisms selected in the design phase. It is important to note that the realization of the security mechanisms is a typical task of the implementation phase specified in the software waterfall model.
- The implementation of the whole software code using the secure programming technique (Wheeler 1999) in order to avoid the buffer overflow vulnerabilities, as well as all other vulnerabilities deriving from wrong code.

Considering this definition of the securization phase, it is difficult to locate this phase with a specific role into the whole system implementation phase. A continuous cycle of hardware/software implementations and verifications has to be performed in order to meet the non-functional requirements of the e-applications.

Moreover, during the implementation other kinds of issues have to be taken into account, such as the characteristics of the transmission channel, or the authentication method adopted by existing e-services (in case a new service has to be integrated) or the costs and technique needed to securize the transmission channel.

Central to this phase is the implementation of the standard virtual devices *SecureSender* and *SecureReceiver* specified in the design phase. They can be viewed as a sort of wrapper that mediates the various security level of the transmitted data among the e-services.

Copyright © 2003, Idea Group Inc. Copying or distributing in print or electronic forms without written permission of Idea Group Inc. is prohibited.

THE REQUIREMENTS ANALYSIS PHASE

The requirements analysis phase collects all the information emerged through the meetings with the customers to generate a set of requirement documents. These documents must describe as accurately as possible the operational context of the system, the resources to be protected, and the constraints. Eventually, the analysis must clarify *what* needs to be protected with no details on *how*.

The five issues on which the requirements analysis is based are:

1.   Domain knowledge about the business, through which the analysis perimeter is defined.
2.   Requirements collection, through meeting with the customers.
3.   Classification and grouping of the requirements.
4.   Resolution of conflicts within the analysis (such as contradictory policies or constraints).
5.   Ordering of requirements, according to the risk level, to define the priorities in the security implementation.

First of all, it is needed to identify the system requirements, to analyze the threats and the vulnerabilities related to users, machines, and data, and finally to perform a risk analysis to correctly identify the basic elements of defense for the system.

The requirements analysis phase can be partitioned into the five following sub-phases, shown in Figure 4.

1.   Information collection: all the information useful to structure effective security solutions are collected. Issues must be clarified regarding the system where the security measures will be inserted, the users, and the integration with existing systems. Such information is composed in an overall document, describing:
     - the problem;
     - the environment; and
     - the existing constraints.
2.   Identification of system constraints: the constraints that must guide the development cycle for the system are listed. Examples are the functional and non-functional properties related to security, such as the quality of service, the availability of the security measures, and the scalability.
     If the system has to be integrated with other existing systems, the structure of existing systems in the federation must be analyzed, and possibly identify the security issues that have already been identified.
3.   Analysis and classification: the key elements of security are grouped into categories such as: users, data, threats. Internal and external types are defined, vulnerabilities that can be used by intruders to perform and attack are considered.
4.   Risk analysis: costs due to a possible attack are studied and decisions are made regarding the identification of primary threats from which the system must be

Copyright © 2003, Idea Group Inc. Copying or distributing in print or electronic forms without written permission of Idea Group Inc. is prohibited.

Figure 4.   Sub-phases in the requirements analysis phase

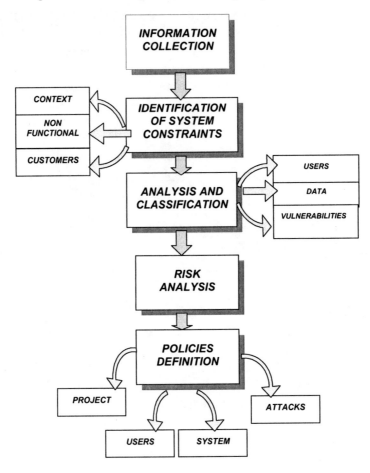

protected. This sub-phase defines what has to be protected and under which financial effort.

5.   Policies definition: the system rules and the user security policies and roles are defined, trying to standardize all the possible operations, hence lowering the probability that subjective behaviors and decisions may be a threat for the security of both the single workstations and the whole system.

The above listed sub-phases can be performed according to three basic moments:

1.   set-up of the development team with the users and customers;
2.   definition of the work plan for the team on the collected data;
3.   involvement of the business management in the team to fix the investment cost for the security measures and to state the policies that grant the respect of the security regulations.

Copyright © 2003, Idea Group Inc. Copying or distributing in print or electronic forms without written permission of Idea Group Inc. is prohibited.

Information Collection

This sub-phase is performed through interviews with the system customers. The team must be made knowledgeable of the business core elements. This can be obtained through two combined ways: using the analysis documents produced during the software and system development cycle (assuming the applications have been implemented with no security aspects) and by interviewing the users.

The interviews must be targeted to get knowledge about all the system issues that might be related with security and with the security development process (context, system perimeter, composed of both trusted system and simple clients, the project time-lining, the constraints on non-functional system properties). All of this information is necessary for those who must then find solutions, and it is therefore useful to adopt clear and simple questionnaires. In this way, the information will be already structured and the meetings will be short and productive.

We consider the adoption of two different questionnaires:

General Information: people will be interviewed about the business purpose of the system, about the systems to be connected to the organization system and, in particular, what kind of *trust* exists in the relationships among internal parts and with external parts. Other elements are the user typologies, and the users' roles and responsibilities. This allows the team to identify, among other aspects, the legal responsibility bound to the compromising of personal user data.

Constraints: a set of questions must be related to constraints related to non-functional system properties and particularly to security properties: from one side, this regards constraints on the communication types with external systems, on the other side constraints on protection methods of data within the system.

This initial information is reported in a first specification document whose structure is denoted in Table 2. To this table, the set of compiled questionnaires are annexed.

The final document does not describe *how* the security properties are to be obtained but only *which* properties have to be implemented.

Identification of System Constraints

It is necessary to identify the constraints to be met by the system. The types of *constraints* to be identified belong to three categories:
1. Related to the context;
2. Related to non functional properties; and
3. Needed by the users/customers.

Constraints **related to the context** are made by the decisions that are made implicitly when the problem is first analyzed, although they should be made along all the phases of the development.

Depending on the customer, for example, choices related to the type of operating system to be employed are evident: consider a system that must be

Copyright © 2003, Idea Group Inc. Copying or distributing in print or electronic forms without written permission of Idea Group Inc. is prohibited.

Table 2.   Structure of the specification document

INTRODUCTION	Description of the system and of the interfaces to the users and to other cooperating systems, business scopes of the system, forecast about system installation times, estimates of system workload at full operation time
GLOSSARY	Definition of technical terms
FUNCTIONAL PROPERTIES	Services offered by the system, ordered according to the business priorities
NON FUNCTIONAL PROPERTIES	Constraints on the system that are in relation with security and that might condition the system design
SYSTEM EVOLUTION	Assumptions on which the system is based and on possible changes that the system will undergo due to evolutions of hw/sw and of user requirements
CONSTRAINTS	List of constraints imposed by the customer

developed in a highly secure environment (e.g., in a military environment): commercial solutions can not be taken into consideration, but rather proprietary, or *trusted,* operating systems must be assumed.

In a normal development cycle, these choices are typical of the last phases (implementation): however, we underline that these needs/constraints, inserted from the initial moments, can influence the design phase and guide in the implementation choices.

Moreover, if the system has to be integrated with other existing applications, constraints can exist on the type of security policies and on the minimum-security level to be granted for all communications among systems belonging to the federation.

Concerning constraints imposed by *non-functional properties*, it must be considered that there are some non-functional properties strictly bound to security: constraints on these properties can consequently influence architectural and securization/implementation choices. The schema of Figure 5 shows the dependencies of non-functional properties.

Non-functional properties describe the system behavior with reference to quality properties regarding the business services. The final system performance will deeply depend on the security properties. Consider, for example, an environment where it is necessary to have asymmetric key cryptographic systems that encipher

Copyright © 2003, Idea Group Inc. Copying or distributing in print or electronic forms without written permission of Idea Group Inc. is prohibited.

Figure 5. Dependencies of non-functional properties

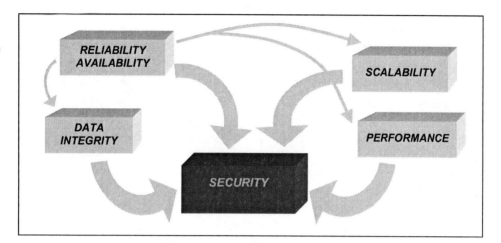

large quantities of data before the emissions into insecure channels or before the data storage phase. The system performance will surely be lower than those offered by symmetric cryptography. The service availability is directly bound to the system ability to resist attacks aimed at consuming the machine resources, thus reducing the system availability until its complete block.

In systems that can undergo denial of service attacks, it is necessary to consider the reliability level that one wants to grant for offered service. Some systems must be available for the whole daytime, and hence the security levels must be adequate to face DoS attacks. Moreover, it could be needed to use redundant systems to grant a given service when the security measures have been broken. Also, the secondary system has to implement security measures able to guarantee the inviolability.

Other systems have to guarantee a continuous service. They can therefore afford some inactivity periods with no damage for the business or for users or applications. In these cases, it will not be a primary requirement to ensure *"always available"* services; hence, the security choices will be taken under these constraints.

Finally, various constraints exist that are given by the ***customer*** during the information collection step. These constraints can regard the system security policy, the ease of use of the mechanisms, the grant/revocation of privileges to ***users***, the privacy rules applying to their company, the fidelization policies of their business with respect to their customers, and so on. These constraints can imply relevant choices to be taken about the system architecture or simply are in relation with implementation choices such as authentication through passwords rather than through smart-cards.

All of the constraints that emerge from this phase can be characterized in a two-fold manner: first, by grouping them on the basis of the development phase which they

Copyright © 2003, Idea Group Inc. Copying or distributing in print or electronic forms without written permission of Idea Group Inc. is prohibited.

refer to; and then by classifying them according to a priority ordering, with the aim of solving possible conflicts due to constraints or implementation choices that can not co-exist during the implementation phase.

The results obtained in this step of TRUMET will be used not only during the design and implementation phases, but also (as we will see in the risk analysis) to guide the decisions on which costs/protection balance levels will be obtained.

Analysis and Classification

This sub-phase has the aim to produce a set of documents containing structured information on users, protected data, cooperation modes, and system vulnerabilities.

In some cases, this information will remain unchanged, such as the typology of dangerous users that will hardly vary unless the business organization is changed. As far as information regarding vulnerabilities, these considerations unfortunately do not apply because vulnerabilities change day-by-day and new patches emerge frequently. Therefore it is necessary to update these data constantly through periodical and scheduled controls to minimize intrusion risks due to unexecuted updates.

Figure 6 reports a graph describing the course of the system risk, where it clearly appears that, after a system update, the danger lowers to zero. The curve family reported in the figure is parametric with the single vulnerability.

Now, let us discuss the three elements of analysis and classification also using some examples described in UML. Aspects related to protection from vulnerabilities will be described in the design and in the implementation phases: at the analysis level, it is important to understand the threats and how to describe them.

Users

User analysis considers all the actors interacting with the system: the *internal* ones, represented by employees, and the *external* ones, that is, the users that get

Figure 6. Temporal distribution of risk

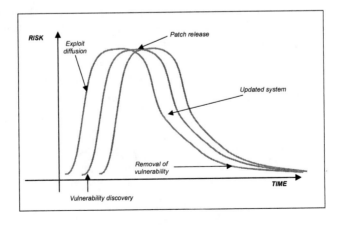

Copyright © 2003, Idea Group Inc. Copying or distributing in print or electronic forms without written permission of Idea Group Inc. is prohibited.

connected to the system for business reasons and, from the security viewpoint, also to execute illegal actions.

Internal users may become a threat voluntarily or involuntarily. In fact, due to a low sensibility to security problems, users can behave so as to vanish the implemented security systems.

An example is a system using SSL as secure communication protocol: an intruder willing to perform a *man in the middle* attack can acquire a digital certificate from a *Certification Authority* and exhibit it together with the public key used instead of the server's key at the moment of *handshaking* with the client. However, the user can become aware of the tricky action since the *domain name* at the basis of his/her contract does not correspond to the one reported on the certificate. The same system would report a *warning* to the user to signal the difference. The users, both because scarcely export or scarcely interested in the system protection, seldom read in-depth and understand the meaning of these messages, and can therefore create communication channels to be possibly used by attackers.

Therefore, internal users who behave both maliciously or accidentally can provoke damages that can be higher than damages caused by external and strongly motivated attackers.

External users act maliciously in order to get access to the system with various scopes, ranging from the simple personal challenge to penetrate or breach the system to industrial espionage, just to mention a few (not to mention terrorist attacks aimed at breaking infrastructures of vital importance for a country). In order to achieve an effective protection it is necessary to identify the users' typologies, studying them in their organizational and operational aspects.

Table 3.   Organizational features

Typology	Organization	Motivation	International Links
HACKER			
Isolated individual	None	Attraction from intellectual challenge	Possible interactions via computer network
Groups	Low structured	Competition among groups	Possible interactions with other groups
CRIMINALS			
Espionage	Supported by hostile agents or competitors	Money – Ideology Political matters	Yes
Fraud	Small groups of criminals	Money	Limited
VANDALS			
External	Individuals or small groups	Revenge Challenge Money	
Internal	Employees	Revenge Challenge Power	

Copyright © 2003, Idea Group Inc. Copying or distributing in print or electronic forms without written permission of Idea Group Inc. is prohibited.

Table 4.   Operational features

Typology	Planning	Experience level	Used techniques
HACKER			
Isolated individual	System study	Medium - High	Script
Groups	Detailed	High	Proprietary tools
CRIMINALS			
Espionage	Very detailed due to money availability	High	Any
Fraud	Accurate	Medium	
VANDALS			
External	Usually high	Various	Usually Script Kiddies
Internal	Sometimes detailed	Various	Trojan – Data Modification

Tables 3, 4 and 5 report a general classification of possible intruders and of their organizational and operational features. These lists are not exhaustive, but are to be considered as a basis for the development team in the identification of possible *opponents*, and to then be completed and personalized according to the usage context.

User classifications that need to emerge from the requirements analysis must be complete and accurate, also considering the typologies of intruders that are not dangerous in principle, or whose threat is scarcely probable.

The UML tools allowing us to classify system users are Use Case Diagrams. They help to describe the intruder type and, through textual notations, to list notes about motivations and tools possibly available to intruders.

Here are the basic elements of a use case diagram and their meaning:

Actor
- External users such as single crackers, vandals
- Internal users already identified in the requirements analysis phase as possible threats
- External user groups acting under the same purpose

Use Case
- Abuses that ill-intentioned actors want to perform on the system
- Actions executed autonomously by the system that influence external cooperating system or actors

Copyright © 2003, Idea Group Inc. Copying or distributing in print or electronic forms without written permission of Idea Group Inc. is prohibited.

Table 5.   Available resources

Typology	Training	Minimal tools	Support structures
HACKER			
Isolated individual	Experience via trials	Computer - modem	Web
Groups	High level	Computer - modem	Other groups
CRIMINALS			
Espionage	Various levels	Sophisticated devices	Intelligence agencies
Fraud	Various levels		Affinity groups
VANDALS			
External	Low– High		Groups
Internal	Medium-Good Knowledge of ICT techniques	Direct access to the system	None

Description

- The description that usually is given here can be structured schematically by specifying:
  - causes/targets
  - resources
  - consequences
  - interested use cases
- The motivations and ultimate scope of the attack can be clarified; the temporal, personnel, and technical resources available to the attacker are illustrated; the state of the system after the attack and the relationships between the current diagram and other use cases are listed.
- The description of consequences can serve two purposes:
  1. to check whether the intruder or the attack can be easily detected by an *Intrusion Detection* system or by security responsibles,
  2. to permit the identification of compromised resources and to make decisions on patches and solutions.
- By listing other use cases involved in the present one, it is possible to implicitly identify the actions that intruders will perform on the system before and after.

UML diagrams do not allow the creation of relationships among actors. Therefore, it is impossible to describe the interactions within groups that are planning attacks or to represent *zombie* systems able to generate a *Distributed DoD*. We use a *stereotype* for actors constituting a set of users. Different, special purpose links express the relationships of these intruders with the system. Moreover, we need to

Copyright © 2003, Idea Group Inc. Copying or distributing in print or electronic forms without written permission of Idea Group Inc. is prohibited.

Figure 7. Stereotype icons

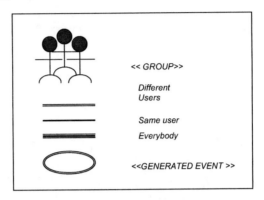

express interaction generated directly by the system. This is not allowed in standard OMG UML 1.3 where the use cases are defined as interactions of the system following external stimuli (Booch, 1997). We introduce a stereotype to denote messages sent by the system to external and internal actors. As an example, consider a *DoS* attack where the system under development is a zombie and starts to flood an external machine with TCP SYN messages to perpetrate a *Syn Flood* attack.

The graphical notation for these extensions is shown in Figure 7.

The Use Case of Figure 8 describes a scenario with stereotypes describing some possible system states. We report only some interactions showing how single intruders or groups of opponents can threaten the system by collecting information, installing code to execute distributed attacks or modifying or substituting one or more we pages.

The diagram shows the use of the proposed stereotypes: the opponent group; the relationship linking the group to the use case, Information Collection showing the

Figure 8. Use Case diagram

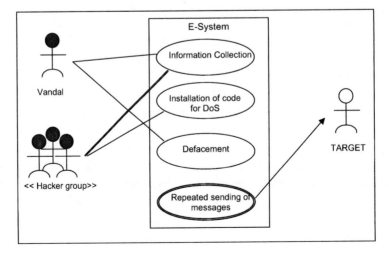

Copyright © 2003, Idea Group Inc. Copying or distributing in print or electronic forms without written permission of Idea Group Inc. is prohibited.

Table 6: Description of the "installation of code for DoS" Use Case

Name:	Installation of code for DoS
Date:	08-08-2002
Causes:	the group of hackers, after acquiring sufficient data about the system, tries to install code on the system to execute a DoS attack to block an external cooperating system. The installation might occur on a single machine or on more machines within a local network.
Resources:	the group has normal-power computing resources and large band connections. They will use both automated tools and proprietary programs. The group has a high expertise in both ICT in general and in programming languages and can cooperate with other groups to get a deeper knowledge about the system.
Consequences:	after installing their software, the intruders will try to modify the log file of the operating system to remove tracks of their access. The file system will be modified, but the presence of new code will be hardly identifiable. There will be no relevant proofs on the fact that the system has been compromised: only a targeted analysis will enable to detect the installed code.
Use Case:	Info Collection Sending of SYN messages

possibility that the interactions with the system are executed by different users within the group, and the use case Repeated sending of messages describing the spontaneous interaction of the system with the external system.

Table 6 shows an example of textual notations attached to the Use Case taken from the diagram of Figure 8 related to attacks to an e-service.

In particular, in this case it is difficult to detect the intrusion *a posteriori*: the related use cases have to be analyzed to identify which actions executed during other interactions are traceable, thus helping to forecast and prevent the attack. In this specific example, it is useful to analyze the system accesses identifying anomalous behaviors, thus obtaining the definition of new filtering rules in the *firewall* system.

Note how the proposed stereotypes have been used in the diagram. The actor representing the opponent group is graphically represented by the icon defined in the figure. The relationship links the group with the use case of info collection, by which it is outlined the possibility that the interactions with the systems in the analysis phase are executed by different users within the group. Note also the Repeated Sending of Messages use case, describing the spontaneous interaction of the system with the external world.

The user typologies can be characterized in various ways: the Use Case Diagrams are a good starting point to gain a clear vision of the whole set of attackers,

Copyright © 2003, Idea Group Inc. Copying or distributing in print or electronic forms without written permission of Idea Group Inc. is prohibited.

but to better classify the intruder categories we can also employ the Class Diagrams. The different types of opponents are represented by classes and structured as packages to categorize them on the basis of their danger level.

Data

The requirements analysis phase has to identify sensitive data that are stored, exchanged or used in the system. These elements are the *Business Sensitive Data BSD* that must necessarily be protected, since they are a basic part of the business and a primary asset of the system/company.

Sensitive data represented by BSD are, as described in Fugini and Plebani (2002), classified in two categories:

User Sensitive Data (USD)

Refers to information of users and composed of:

- *Internal User Sensitive Data (IUSD)* — All sensitive data for internal users such as files, documents, databases, financial, marketing and strategic information. We consider also a *Knowledge Base* represented by all the knowledge acquired by the security system during the applications lifetime.
- *External User Sensitive Data (EUSD)* —The data that are sensitive for external users interacting with the system, such as personal data. The treatment of these data has to guarantee privacy and integrity.

System Sensitive Data (SSD)

Data that constitute the security mechanisms and are therefore sensitive for the system, such as crypto keys, passwords, and log files. These data derive from the choice of the mechanisms that will be used to protect the USD.

Since the system will cooperate to implement distributed services, the information to be protected could be not stored on physical devices in static memories, but rather be present only on volatile devices such as RAM memories on communication links. These data need to be granted the same integrity and privacy of other information according to internal or external constraints.

All the identified data have to be classified according to the four properties:

1. Integrity
2. Confidentiality
3. Authenticity
4. Non-repudiation

Vulnerability

Vulnerabilities of a system can be physical and/or software. Physical ones refer to threats to which the system installations are exposed (natural catastrophes,

Copyright © 2003, Idea Group Inc. Copying or distributing in print or electronic forms without written permission of Idea Group Inc. is prohibited.

persons, terrorism actions). Physical security regards the protection of machines from faults due to environmental conditions where the system operates. TRUMET takes these issues into considerations during the risk analysis phase.

Software threats are problems deriving from a bad system design or configuration, from wrong protocols and from wrong design and operation of the applications.

To correctly list these threats, we consider three information sources:

1.   the list of the most widespread vulnerabilities published by the *SANS Institute* in collaboration with *FBI* (SANS, 2002);
2.   information contained in the documents where system actors have been classified; and
3.   the attack trees.

Table 7 gives the list of vulnerabilities of the information system and the method to identify them.

Table 7. List of vulnerabilities

Vulnerability	Description	Identification
Redefined installations of the OS and of applications	By default, some functions are enabled that are not strictly necessary and that can be used as ports to the system	
Account with weak authentication		Use of password crackers
Poorly protected backup		
High number of active services	Only the right number of ports necessary to the correct operation of the system can be opened to the external environment	Netstat Portscanner
Packets not correctly filtered	The source and destination addresses are not checked to avoid DoS attacks	Sending of spoofed packets and control of firewall and log behavior
Nonexistent or incomplete logs	In case of intrusion, the log files should be as complete as possible	
Vulnerable CGI	Programs available with the Web Servers used to provide interactivity to pages. Many are vulnerable and allow one to get privileges on the server	Scanner for CGI testing
Buffer Overflow	Bad written code in the servers leads to execute wrong checks in the detection of errors. In particular, too long input strings are not blocked.	Use of scanners (SAINT, SARA)
R commands	Used in Unix systems, these allow trust relations to administer the system. R allows access one to a remote system with no passwords; authentication occurs via IP checking.	Control of configuration of the etc/host.equiv /.rhosts files

Copyright © 2003, Idea Group Inc. Copying or distributing in print or electronic forms without written permission of Idea Group Inc. is prohibited.

Interactions of actors with the system described in the diagrams written in the initial phases of the analysis help to identify the system weaknesses. For example, the information in the use case diagrams can be reused and extended by analyzing the methods for attackers to exploit the vulnerabilities.

We use Class Diagrams by structuring vulnerabilities into packages each representing a particular vulnerability and each single class is a possible exploit to obtain system access. The classes are in turn grouped in packages according to their danger level.

Consider the use case diagram of Figure 8 where we analyze only the interaction Information Collection. We obtain the class diagram shown in Figure 9.

The example considers, for simplicity, two vulnerabilities only related to info collection: in fact, to obtain information, an intruder could exploit other vulnerabilities such as the employee behavior, *network enumeration,* and so on.

If we consider as an example a Use Case Diagram where an interaction is called System Block, we can deduce that the cause of this vulnerability is represented by a possible DoS attack and that hence the vulnerability can be due to a bad configuration of the values of *Committed Access Rate* (CAR) in the routers, or to the lack of tools aimed at filtering the input traffic.

High vulnerabilities can emerge not from the Use Case diagrams, but be obtained from the *Context Diagram* or from the documents related to constraints imposed by the customers on the system: an example is given by the vulnerabilities due to the geographical location of the system installations (e.g., seismic areas) or to the interaction with pre-existing systems with which access to resources must be shared, and if not correctly managed, can turn out to be a vulnerability.

This new data also can be described using a *Class Diagram* to structure the vulnerabilities and the scenarios of abuse according to the danger level and the

Figure 9.   Class diagram referred to information collection

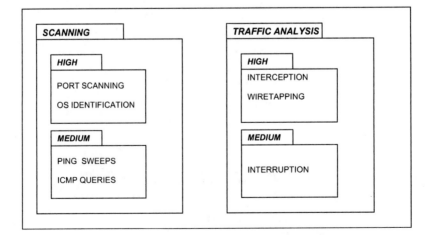

Copyright © 2003, Idea Group Inc. Copying or distributing in print or electronic forms without written permission of Idea Group Inc. is prohibited.

Figure 10. Sequence Diagram

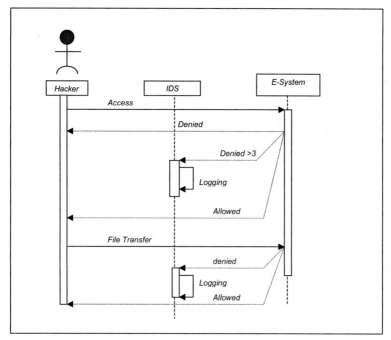

Sequence Diagram, through which the interactions can be represented between the attackers and the system.

In the sequence diagrams we can model the interactions among various entities with special attention to the temporal sequence. In order to express, in a more representative way, the constraints and the security characteristics, the *link*s connecting the various objects/entities can be enriched with a set of *constraints* or *tagged value*.

Figure 10 represents a Sequence Diagram describing the threat related to an unauthorized installation of executable code, evidencing the interactions with the system, and the log in actions that this executes at the moment where the user seems to be unauthorized.

In the design phase, these Sequence Diagrams will be extended by introducing a set of stereotypes and creating the *Intrusion /Recovery Diagram* where, in the normal flow of messages or in general application, some elements are inserted representing intrusions or dangerous or exceptional situations that can modify the execution flow. To these, an execution flow will follow that will try to roll the system back to a secure state.

Moreover, as reported in Schneider (2000), an attack can be decomposed by using the *attack trees:* this tree decomposition provides a methodology to describe the threats against a system from which it is possible to identify a set of counter figures.

Copyright © 2003, Idea Group Inc. Copying or distributing in print or electronic forms without written permission of Idea Group Inc. is prohibited.

The root of this tree represents the intruder's target, the trees are different modes according to which one can gain the result.

It is possible to assign values to the various nodes that can be used to analyze the more viable attack ways. One can so show how it is possible to attack a system using cryptographic systems with no need to use *brute force* attacks and tremendous computing power, but simply analyzing all the possible ways and choosing the simplest one.

Risk Analysis

The high costs derived from a total protection of the system against the risks make security a *trade off* between costs and advantages. Therefore it is necessary to perform a risk analysis to set up an acceptable security level for a company.

Risk analysis is a method for quantifying the impact of a potential attack due to a system vulnerability. The result of this phase helps to list a set of risks, both software vulnerabilities or threats to physical security of site, that need to be prevented, moved, or accepted while balancing risks and costs.

In terms of *risk management*, a company must evaluate risks and linked opportunities.

Decisions are based on financial factors, on strategic motivations, or on the need to follow a given regulation. Examples of the last type are: the company needs to obtain a certification of adherence to a given standard (e.g., the international ITSEC standard required by the legislation for some security devices) or to the low (minimal security measures established by the privacy low) (Allen, 2001). These motivations can also be found among the constraints identified in the phase of identification of system constraints.

Risk analysis is a dynamic process: every day new vulnerabilities are discovered and *patches are released*. Moreover, the context where the system operates changes frequently, thus imposing that the *risk analysis* process is repeated periodically.

We remind the reader of only some basic concepts of risk analysis:

- *Proactive Assessment:* before an accident
- *Reactive Assessment:* after an attack

The analysis can be qualitative or quantitative:

- *Qualitative:* based on an intuitive evaluation with no numerical data
- *Quantitative:* based on statistical data and on probabilities

Asses, or company resources to be secured have been identified previously: data, machines, installations and people.

In order to obtain correct decisions, it is necessary to gain the best knowledge about the specific risks, in particular those bound to the ICT environment, to which the system is exposed.

Copyright © 2003, Idea Group Inc. Copying or distributing in print or electronic forms without written permission of Idea Group Inc. is prohibited.

To compute a value of estimate of annual risk, we mention the following formula:

Annual Risk = Value of Asset **x** *Exposure Factor* **x** *Occurrence Frequency*

Policies Definition

Here, the security analysis defines the system security policies. The *security policies* are a set of principles, rules and procedures through which information is protected, contained in the information system, and to which the system users must conform in order not to vanish all the development efforts.

The policies that must be defined to guarantee system security must take into account the constraints expressed in the constraints identification phase.

In fact, when developing a cooperative distributed system, it is quite possible that some policies are already present in the component systems related to the behavior of the local users. In this case, after defining the new policies for the global CoopIS, the team must evaluate the possible differences and decide whether different policies for the various subsystems can be maintained or if they have to be unified. Some local policies can be so strict as to influence all the other ones and eventually the whole process of definition of the new system.

In order to define effective policies, the policies must be regularly reviewed and corrected.

Since the policies regard different system aspects and involve various people and roles, it can be a good rule to have these policies developed totally or partially (with the help of the team) by the security responsible of the target Information Systems, together with the most involved users.

First of all, the information set produced in the analysis and implementation of the system applications must be protected; then, the policies that rule out the system usage must be defined; then, a training plan oriented to education to system security must be settled; finally, the policies that are needed to make the system secure must be defined by specifying the constraints of administrative type.

In the following, we list the *Policies Guidelines* regarding their definition:

Project

Information written in the analysis and design documents is very important: a malicious user could get these data in order to gain information about the system architecture, about the enciphering techniques, on the policies and on other security decisions and parameters.

Hence, the *Information Collection* phase, that takes about 80% to 90% of the time that a potential intruder spends to get access to the system, would be reduced dramatically allowing one to obtain a sufficient set of data needed to plan an attack in the short run.

It must be defined the set of people who can access these data and guarantee to each person and to each developer access only to the needed data on a need-to-

Copyright © 2003, Idea Group Inc. Copying or distributing in print or electronic forms without written permission of Idea Group Inc. is prohibited.

know basis. This avoids the complete knowledge of the system also from within the company. Usually, attacks coming from the inside are executed by personnel with a high skill in ICT.

The policies should set up the following guidelines:
- Persons in the development team who can access all the information.
- On a role basis, authorizations allowed to access the various information types.
- Location for design documents maintenance.
- Data, and related constraints, that can be exchanged among the development team members.
- Documents that can be shared with external personnel.
- Upon completion of system development, where and how development information are stored.

Users

Users are the weak point of each system even though a good security level has been defined; their behavior can make efforts and expensive security techniques vanish. Rules must be established to minimize the risk. Since these policies basically map into rules that restrict the user actions and choices, it is useful to involve them in the policies definition and to plan an education intervention.

Policies related to users' behavior depend on the user role:
- Define the type of removable supports that can be introduced at the sites.
- Access to these supports.
- Responsibility of each individual and obligations to guarantee security.
- Allowed modifications to the system hardware.
- Use of the applications, of the software and of the administration tools and of the Web browser.
- Allowed download/installation of software.
- Accessible information.
- Allowed circulation of information via network.
- Allowed operations on the system data (e.g., log file).
- As far as users' training, the policies must define:
    - Who will organize and teach security seminars (external personnel or internal specialists).
    - Training frequency.
    - Structure of meetings based on the roles.
    - System administrators, network administrators and members of a *Response Team* must be trained to the use of tools reacting to intrusions via practical simulations.
    - Expected user response after the meetings.
    - If and how to evaluate the usefulness of training actions.

Copyright © 2003, Idea Group Inc. Copying or distributing in print or electronic forms without written permission of Idea Group Inc. is prohibited.

System

Here we report the set of policies referred to the system itself: they rule out the system usage and administration.

These policies will be considered not only during the normal use of the system but must be consulted during the design phase to guide architectural choices.

Security policies must:

- Guarantee that the use of resources is performed only by authorized personnel and in a correct way.
- Classify the system resources, both hardware and software, on the basis of the typology of authorized users.
- Decide who and how accesses are granted and if there exists a central authorization entity of the CoopIS.
- Define the needed services that must be offered on a need to know basis and, if possible, each service must run on a dedicated host.
- Decide the authentication modes of local and remote users.
- Establish which information will be gathered about users' activities (*logging* of sessions).
- Decide how, where and for how long log and security data must be kept.
- Define which information to keep recorded during the accesses by external users, where and how to keep them.

Attack

To avoid panic upon an intrusion, an action line must be pursued to limit the damage. Policies must be identified to help the personnel (both security responsible and common users) in the phase of response to the intrusion.

The policies must:

- Define roles and responsibilities to security personnel.
- Establish which measures are to be undertaken (e.g., legal) on the basis of the severity of the attack.
- Identify the system information and the users' data that can be examined during the inquiry phases.
- Define the conditions to isolate from the net the compromised machine(s).
- Describe the inspection procedures.
- List the investigation team's permissions and rights during the inquiry phase.
- Establish a list with the ordering of reactivation of the services depending on the type of attack and considering the priorities bound to the collection of data related to the intrusion.
- Indicate the persons to which the inquiry results must be shown.
- Explain how the final documents of the inquiry must be signed, stored and maintained.

Copyright © 2003, Idea Group Inc. Copying or distributing in print or electronic forms without written permission of Idea Group Inc. is prohibited.

- Establish if and how to publish the intrusion news and the causes (both internally and externally to the company).
- Describe how to identify and delimit the perimeter of the attack.

CONCLUDING REMARKS

In this paper, we have outlined the steps of a methodology for designing security in advanced distributed Information Systems. Central to the methodology is the identification of User Security Data, that is, of information (records, databases, messages, etc.) that is perceived as sensible by the users. A second featuring element is the identification of System Security Data, which follow from User Security Data. These are expressed as constraints (e.g., a password scheme and a public-key encryption mechanism must be used to protect the data) and rule out the choice of security mechanisms that are both application compliant and cost/budget compliant.

An architecture for secure transmission of data between e-services has been sketched in the paper. More details on these wrapper-based architecture can be found in Bertolazzi et al. (2001), where we have identified the wrapping techniques for data exchanges among e-services.

Then, we have detailed the phase of requirements collection about security of data and about users' interaction with the cooperative system within and outside a "circle of trust." This work will proceed by detailing the design phase and the securization phase, instantiated on examples of e-services, and drawing the specifications of the SecureSender and SecureReceiver tools.

A further step consists obviously in extending TRUMET to virtual information systems, and to multichannel systems, such as Mobile Information Systems. These are distributed information systems that forward a user request on different communication channels, depending on the availability of the multichannel communication infrastructure. The security of these systems is multi-aspect and has to consider how a variety of metaphors and protocols of security can be integrated; for example, in the multichannel access to specialized portals offering services to citizens and enterprises in the Public Administration field. We are experimenting in technique of user profiling and security based on single sign on in Web services.

ACKNOWLEDGMENTS

This work has been partially supported by the Italian MIUR Project "Data Quality" COFIN 2002 and by the VISPO project about virtual enterprises. We thank the Master student Emanuele Bianchi for work on this paper ideas.

Copyright © 2003, Idea Group Inc. Copying or distributing in print or electronic forms without written permission of Idea Group Inc. is prohibited.

REFERENCES

Aleph One. (1996). Smashing the stack for fun and profit. *Phrack Magazine,* 7 (49).

Allen, J. (2001). *The CERT Guide to System and Network Security Practices.*Addison-Wesley.

Baresi, S. Casati, S. Castano, M.G. Fugini, Mirbel, I., & Pernici, B. (1999). Workflow development methodology. In *Proceedings of the Intl. Joint Conference on Work Activities Coordination and Collaboration.* San Francisco, CA: WACC'99.

Bertolazzi, P., Fugini, M. G., Mecella, M., Pernici, B., Plebani, P., & Scannapieco, M. (2001). *Supporting trusted data exchanges in cooperative information systems.* Submitted for publication.

Booch, G., Rumbaugh, G., & Jacbson, I. (1998). *The UML User Guide.* Addison Wesley.

Casati, F., Castano S., & Fugini M.G. (2002) Managing workflow authorization constraints through active database technology. *Journal of Information Systems Frontiers, Special Issue on Workflow Automation And Business Process Integration.*

Casati, F., Sayal, M., & Shan, M.C. (2001). Developing E-Services for composing E-Services. In *Proceedings of the 13th International Conference on Advanced Information Systems Engineering.* Interlaken, Switzerland: CAiSE.

Castano, S., Fugini, M.G., Martella, G., & Samarati, P. (1995). *Database security.* Addison-Wesley.

Chung, C., Gertz, M., & Levitt, K. (2000). Discovery of multi-level security policies. In *Proceedings of the 14th IFIP 11.3 Working Conference on Database Security.*

Dall'Agnola, G., Fugini, M.G., Lioy, A., Maino, F., Maio, F., & Mazzocchi, D. (1999). Securing applications in the Demostene project. In *Proceedings of Information Security Solutions Europe.* Berlin: ISSE'99.

Fugini, M.G., & Plebani, P. (2001). Security aspects in B2M2C applications. In *Proceedings of Information Security Conference IS2.* Prague.

Fugini, M.G., & Plebani, P. (2002). A methodology for development of trusted cooperative information systems. *In Proceedings of IRMA Conference 2002.* Seattle, WA.

Garfinkel S., & Spafford, G. (1997). *Web security & E-Commerce.* O'Reilly & Associates, Inc.

Icove, D., & VonStorch, W. (1995). *Computer crime: A crimefighter's handbook.* O'Reilly Associates, Inc.

Mecella, M., & Pernici, B. (2001). Designing wrapper components for e-Services in integrating heterogeneous systems. *VLDB Journal, Special Issue on e-Services.*

Copyright © 2003, Idea Group Inc. Copying or distributing in print or electronic forms without written permission of Idea Group Inc. is prohibited.

Mukkamala, R., Gagnon, J., & Jajodia, S. (1999). Integrating data mining techniques with intrusion detection methods. In *Proceedings of the 12ᵗʰ IFIP 11.3 Working Conference on Database Security*.

Mylopoulos J., & Papazoglou, M. (Eds.). (1997). Cooperative Information Systems. *IEEE Expert Intelligent Systems and their Applications*, *12*(5).

SANS (2002). SANS Institute - FBI 2002. The twenty most critical Internet security vulnerabilities. Retrieved from http://www.mediacity.com/~norm/CapTheory/ProtInf.

Schneider, B. (2000). *Secret and lies: Digital security in a networked world.* Wiley Computer Publishing.

VLDB-TES. (2000). *Proceedings of the 1st VLDB Workshop on Technologies for E-Services.* Cairo, Egypt: VLDB-TES.

Wheeler, D.A. (1999). *Secure Programming for Linux and Unix HOWTO.* Available online: http://www.dwheeler.com/secure-programs/.

Copyright © 2003, Idea Group Inc. Copying or distributing in print or electronic forms without written permission of Idea Group Inc. is prohibited.

Chapter V

A National Information Infrastructure Model for Information Warfare Defence

Vernon Stagg
Deakin University, Australia

Matthew Warren
Deakin University, Australia

ABSTRACT

Information infrastructures are an eclectic mix of open and closed networks, private and public systems, the Internet, and government, military, and civilian organisations. Significant efforts are required to provide infrastructure protection, increase cooperation between sectors, and identify points of responsibility. The threats to infrastructures are many and various, and are increasing daily: information warfare, hackers, terrorists, criminals, activists, and even competing organisations all pose significant threats that cannot be sufficiently dealt with using the current infrastructure model. We present a National Information Infrastructure model that is based on defence against threats such as information warfare.

Copyright © 2003, Idea Group Inc. Copying or distributing in print or electronic forms without written permission of Idea Group Inc. is prohibited.

INTRODUCTION

Information technology has removed many of the traditional barriers that exist between organisations, both nationally and internationally. As links are formed within and between organisations, resources, services, and information are integrated into infrastructures of interrelated, interoperable, and interconnected elements. These infrastructures have rapidly grown to incorporate not only equipment and services, but elements deemed critical for survival or necessary for national capability.

Information infrastructures have become necessary and vital elements for nations worldwide, and are an eclectic mix of open and closed networks, private and public systems, the Internet, and government, military, and civilian organisations. They are important vehicles for the generation of wealth, and can influence the power and capability not only of organisations, but also nations (Westwood, 1996). However a problem with many infrastructures is that they are excessive, continually growing, regularly reconfigured and reengineered, and lack suitable staff and resources to oversee them (Brock, Jr., 2000). With the growing trend for private ownership of critical infrastructure elements, responsibility shifts from government to private organisations and raises issues of who is involved, what their responsibilities and requirements are, and determining a focal point of authority for infrastructure control (Cordesman, 2000; PCCIP, 1997b; Waltz, 1998).

Numerous countries have developed national information infrastructures to reap the benefits they offer. However, with the growing demand on these infrastructures, along with the reliance and dependability on their operation, the threats and vulnerabilities they face have also increased (Stagg & Warren, 2001). This requires new methods of protection and security, especially when dealing with new and emerging threats such as information warfare.

NATIONAL INFORMATION INFRASTRUCTURE

A National Information Infrastructure (NII) has been defined as *a system of high-speed telecommunications networks, databases, and advanced computer systems that make electronic information widely available and accessible* (OMB, 1995). It has also been described as *an inchoate, multidimensional phenomenon, a turbulent and controversial mix of public policy, corporate strategies, hardware and software that shapes the way consumers and citizens use information and communications* (Wilson, 1997).

Defining and describing an NII is no easy process. Wladkowski (1996) describes an NII as a hierarchal structure with a base consisting of networks belonging to the power industry, a middle level of networks belonging to the telecommunications industry, and a high level of multiple networks involving government, business, finance, transportation, emergency functions, and the military. Garigue (1995) points out that with the introduction of such infrastructures, the strict

Copyright © 2003, Idea Group Inc. Copying or distributing in print or electronic forms without written permission of Idea Group Inc. is prohibited.

organisational hierarchies, structures, and boundaries of time, space, and physical barriers are broken down or removed.

Another important consideration is that many elements within the NII, as well as those used to protect and defend it, come from the public and private sectors, particularly Commercial off the Shelf (COTS) software and hardware. With the growing trend of government and military organisations to procure commercial products, along with the need for system interoperability, there will be a greater amalgamation of government, military, and civilian infrastructures (Campen et al., 1996; Garigue, 1995).

The responsibility of the defence of an NII has primarily been the domain of government and military departments. However, with the increasing use of commercial hardware and software elements within an NII, the issue of who is responsible for defence has broadened considerably. The level of security and defensive measures has primarily focused on those elements deemed critical for the nation's survival, creating the concept of critical information infrastructure.

A critical information infrastructure considers the essential elements of a nation and implements special hardening, redundancy, recovery, and other protection mechanisms (Anderson et al., 1999; Nash & Piggott, 1999). The United States Presidential Critical Infrastructure Protection Commission (PCCIP, 1997a) identified five critical sectors:

- Information and communications
- Banking and finance
- Energy, including power, oil, and gas
- Physical distribution
- Vital human services

Much of the focus on NII protection has focused on the critical aspects, especially due to many of these elements being privately owned and operated. This has led to numerous debates on who is responsible for providing protection, who should be in control, who should be involved in recovery procedures, and to what extent. Figure 1 outlines the current situation regarding the NII and highlights the emphasis on the critical aspects.

As described, an NII is a diverse and eclectic mix of systems, networks, people, and processes, and with the growing trend for private ownership and control of many infrastructural elements, the whole notion of the NII needs to be reconsidered. Figure 2 revises the current model of the NII, identifying the separate yet intertwined nature of critical elements and the need to address key issues across the whole infrastructure (Stagg & Warren, 2002). Certainly, many critical elements exist within the NII, but there are also elements that reside outside of the NII model. We can consider these elements to be key critical aspects, and primarily the attention of government and military concerns. The sectors derived from the PCCIP apply equally to Critical

Copyright © 2003, Idea Group Inc. Copying or distributing in print or electronic forms without written permission of Idea Group Inc. is prohibited.

Figure 1. Critical elements clearly defined

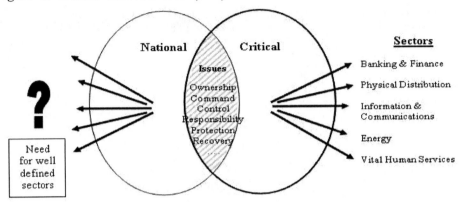

as well as National Information Infrastructure, along with additional sectors for inclusion within the NII. The issues of protection are applied to the whole model and can be divided into Critical and Non-Critical Levels (Stagg & Warren, 2002). Before we examine this new model we need to consider the factors involved in infrastructure protection, and the emerging threat known as information warfare.

INFRASTRUCTURE PROTECTION

Numerous problems exist in the protection of infrastructures. Aside from the obvious technical, legal, and financial aspects involved, there are also numerous misunderstandings between business and government over what protecting the infrastructure entails. An interesting dichotomy arises with businesses wishing to

Figure 2. Re-examining the NII

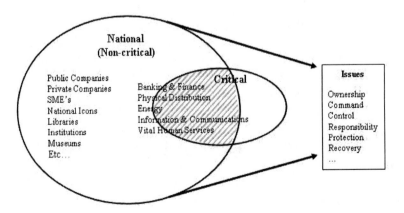

Copyright © 2003, Idea Group Inc. Copying or distributing in print or electronic forms without written permission of Idea Group Inc. is prohibited.

Figure 3. Comparison of computer-related attacks (source: www.cert.com)

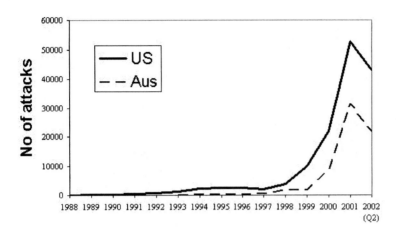

avoid and prevent attacks while governments want to detect, trail, and then prosecute the attackers. This raises numerous concerns over liability, information sharing, and vulnerability issues that have been plaguing infrastructure protection since day one. Another problem arises as governments become increasingly removed from owner-ship of critical infrastructure elements, limiting their ability to protect them, requiring sector-by-sector solutions instead (Willemssen, 2000).

Countries such as Australia, Canada, and the United Kingdom recognise they pose a lesser threat toward such attacks as those faced by super-power nations, along with their inability to commit the substantial resources needed to follow the United States (U.S.) model of Information Infrastructure and Information Warfare protection (Dudgeon, 1997; Westwood, 1996). Figure 3 shows that while a country such as Australia has less reported computer attacks the scale is proportionate to the U.S. With most of the effort and research on Information Infrastructure and Information Warfare protection emanating from the U.S. however, the U.S. model provides a suitable framework with which to base strategies upon.

The finance sector has long understood the necessity of preserving customer confidence and the integrity of business information. The awareness of information security, implementation of policy, and protective measures is especially strong within this sector (Mitchell et al., 1999). The concern within other sectors is that many organisations do not yet realise the sheer scale of the steadily growing threats they face. The approaches they take to protective measures are often closed, secretive, and compartmentalised in nature, and do not take into consideration the impact their systems have on other elements of infrastructure (Cordesman, 2000). By identifying these interdependencies within the NII a greater level of security can be provided for defending against such infrastructure attacks.

Copyright © 2003, Idea Group Inc. Copying or distributing in print or electronic forms without written permission of Idea Group Inc. is prohibited.

INFRASTRUCTURE ATTACKS

The last few years have seen a steady rise in the number and type of attacks against infrastructures, which have had significant impacts upon organisations and nations (Power, 2002). The nature of these attacks has also changed, from harmless and annoying pranks, to menacing and malicious concerted efforts. The attackers themselves have also become more sophisticated and coordinated, often with clear political, social, environmental, religious or financial objectives in mind. The availability and accessibility of tools and techniques to use in carrying out their attacks have also grown rapidly since the introduction of the Internet (Stagg & Warren, 2000). The resultant cost, time, and effort required in recovering after an attack can be enormous and, without suitable recovery methods in place, many organisations may not be able to face the challenge.

One of the significant challenges that emerged from the PCCIP was the concept of the cyber threat. While many of the physical threats identified could be addressed, the new security challenges presented by the cyber threat of networked information systems were fundamentally different to existing methods (PCCIP, 1997b). Indeed, many organisations are still struggling with the concept of what constitutes a cyber attack (Willemssen, 2000).

Attacks against infrastructures are relatively new, shifting the threat focus from low-level attacks on individual, system-level elements to high-level, system-wide attacks. These types of network-centric attacks are considered to be a version of an emerging issue known as information warfare (Alberts et al., 1999).

INFORMATION WARFARE

Information Warfare is still a relatively new issue, not clearly understood in the commercial sector, yet more than just hype or a buzzword (Gershanoff, 2000). Originating from the military sector, a certain amount of disparity exists between the various definitions and concepts of Information Warfare developed among various military and defence departments (Gray et al., 1997). Derived from various sources, Information Warfare can be considered as *actions taken to affect a competitor's information, information systems, and information-based processes whilst protecting one's own information, information systems, and information-based processes. These actions may be directed at an individual, a corporation or multinational body, and may occur during peacetime or conflict between nations or societies* (Arquilla & Ronfeldt, 1993; JCS, 1998; Schwartau, 1994).

When considering the Information Warfare threat to an infrastructure, we need to determine the potential adversaries, their motives, and their objectives. Such adversaries could include nation states, criminals, terrorists, hackers, hacktivists, spies, ideological and cultural adversaries, insiders, and competing organisations (Brand, 2000; Luiijf, 2000). By identifying the objectives and motives of attackers,

Copyright © 2003, Idea Group Inc. Copying or distributing in print or electronic forms without written permission of Idea Group Inc. is prohibited.

it is possible to qualify the potential effort, skill, and expense the attacker is willing to invest in exploiting vulnerabilities.

Information Warfare presents significant challenges to those responsible for developing policy regarding the protection of the NII (Ryan & Ryan, 1996). In 2000, a Forrester report found that 89% of companies surveyed saw information warfare as a possible risk, with 6% saying they had first-hand experience of such an attack (Prince et al., 2000). Whilst organisations may not be able to defend against large-scale attacks against the NII, they are more likely to successfully defend against attacks on smaller, more constrained infrastructures. A report by the Defense Science Board (1996) stressed that to understand the information warfare process, and identify information warfare attacks, will require a determined effort to collect, consolidate, and synthesize information from various infrastructure elements.

Examples

One of the problems faced with infrastructure protection, and the possibility of information warfare attack, is there is a distinct lack of precedents to compare against, or capabilities to simulate such events (Rattray, 1999). There is also a substantive lack of information available regarding potential attackers, their capabilities and strengths, the targets they may attack, attacks already carried out, and the success of such attacks (Dudgeon, 1997). A number of infrastructure incidents highlight the fragility of many of their elements, with the resultant chaos and losses from such attacks or disruptions making it clear that the risks are not merely speculative. Examples of such attacks include:

- The resultant chaos from the 1992 London Square Mile bomb explosion provided the Provisional IRA with a strategy to disrupt infrastructure services, in particular the Underground and London financial district services (Luiijf, 2000).
- In 1997, malicious calls from a Swedish hacker jammed the 911 emergency telephone lines in Miami, disrupted service, harassed the operators, and diverted 911 calls. He also accessed a telephone system and generated 60,000 unauthorized calls. He was tried as a juvenile in Sweden and fined the equivalent of $US345 (Correll, 1998).
- Australia faced a number of infrastructure breakdowns with power outages in Queensland, Sydney's water crisis, and the Victorian gas stoppage, all in 1998. Although relatively short in downtime, these disruptions caused widespread domestic inconvenience and financial losses for many businesses (ABC, 1998). More recently there was an intentional infrastructure attack in November 2001 against a Queensland sewage facility that has become a reference case for U.S. investigations into cyber attack (Barker, 2002).
- In 2000, a spate of distributed denial-of-service attacks caused massive disruptions for a number of prominent online companies including Amazon,

Copyright © 2003, Idea Group Inc. Copying or distributing in print or electronic forms without written permission of Idea Group Inc. is prohibited.

eBay, and Yahoo. The loss of business has been estimated at over $US1 billion (McCombie & Warren, 2000). Although not fundamentally new in approach, these attacks achieved an effect where hundreds, even thousands, of systems would attack a particular system.

- The Love Bug virus swept the world in 2000, affecting over 55 million computers. Numerous companies, government organisations, and educational institutions were forced to shut down their mail servers, many for up to one week. The resultant financial loss of this attack has been mooted at over $US8 billion (Erbschloe & Vacca, 2001). More recently, viruses such as Code Red, Nimda, SirCam, BadTrans, and Slapper have had similar devastating effects.
- Wik (2000) pondered the enormous financial cost that would have occurred had the telecommunications hub and conduits been damaged during the 1993 attack on the World Trade Center (WTC). Theory became reality in September 2001 when the WTC was destroyed by terrorist attacks. A cost close to $US5 billion has been estimated just for the financial services infrastructure (Williams & Kennedy, 2001). This figure could have been much higher, had it not been for the efforts of organisations in securing their infrastructures during recent years (Rountree, 2001).
- Computer hackers, routing through networks operated by China Telecom and servers in the U.S., gained access to a California power system. Although there was no threat to the power grid, the hackers came close to accessing critical parts of the system and could have disrupted the movement of power (Vatis, 2001).

NII MODEL

As seen, the issues of infrastructure protection, infrastructure responsibility, and Information Warfare threats and attacks are becoming harder to deal with for organisations that are part of, or connected to, the current infrastructure model. Infrastructure protection cannot simply be addressed by compartmentalised solutions that have derived from methods and practices out-of-touch, and out-of-date, with today's sophisticated and complex technologies.

In developing our model of the NII (see Figure 4), we have applied three main criteria for selection:

1. Focus on the non-critical elements
2. Determine their position (national, state, local) and function (strategic, operational, tactical) within the NII
3. Their category according to information warfare

There are a growing number of non-critical elements that are becoming part of an NII (Stagg & Warren, 2002). These elements include public and private corporations, small-to-medium enterprises, institutions, museums, national icons, and

Copyright © 2003, Idea Group Inc. Copying or distributing in print or electronic forms without written permission of Idea Group Inc. is prohibited.

other entities that may be directly or indirectly related to critical elements of infrastructure, or be adversely affected by infrastructure attack.

We initially consider that elements have a *primary* position within an NII and exist at either a national, state, or local level (of course, many of these will cross over a mixture of these levels, even internationally). These levels will then be equated with the strategic, operational, or tactical function that they provide to the NII.

As defined, the three main categories of information warfare are information, information systems, and information-based processes. This will help categorise infrastructure elements and enable clear and decisive methods of protection based against potential information warfare threats.

Applying this model from our criteria, we can then begin to determine the necessary steps required at each level for developing suitable security measures. Some of these issues will include:

- National/Strategic/Information
  - Critical infrastructure protection
  - Government and military measures
  - Information sharing and analysis centres
  - Apply standards, criteria, policies, etc.
  - Determine interdependencies between sectors (see Figure 5)
- State/Operational/Information Systems
  - Coordinate between strategic and tactical levels
  - Non-critical elements
  - Determine relationships between elements of each sector
  - Sector-specific measures
  - Sharing of information within sectors
  - Identify threats and vulnerabilities to each sector
  - Determine relationships within sectors (see Figure 5)

Figure 4. NII model

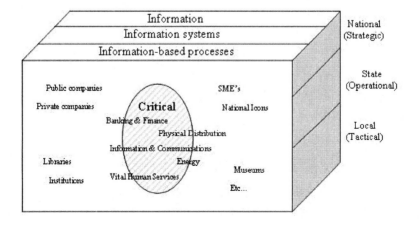

Copyright © 2003, Idea Group Inc. Copying or distributing in print or electronic forms without written permission of Idea Group Inc. is prohibited.

Figure 5. Identify dependencies and relationships

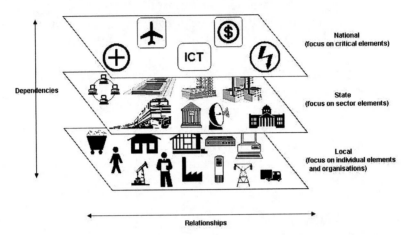

- Local/Tactical/Information-based processes
  - Individual elements per sector: hardware, software, people, etc.
  - Apply the relevant security measures
  - Implement relevant tools and techniques

By determining the non-critical elements, we can identify crucial support functions that flow vertically (control and cooperation), horizontally (strategy, structure and rivalry), or both ways. The efforts in protecting the horizontal elements can consist of methods, policies, and procedures relevant to that sector; many of these will already be in place. The vertical levels can be strengthened with applicable security measures, e.g., the use of strong encryption, secure channels, redundancy, and recovery systems for the information and communications sector.

Many of the entities involved will have strict rules and procedures in place for information collection, management, distribution, retention, and deletion. These procedures can provide a viable framework for Information Sharing and Analysis Centers (ISAC) to work within. A common hurdle to ISAC's is the unwillingness of organisations to share sensitive information with others (Brock, Jr., 2000), especially on a large scale. The proposed model would enable information to be filtered from the horizontal elements to develop statistics and analysis that could then be shared among the vertical levels. This information could also be combined with other infrastructure sectors, along with federal resources, to better protect the NII (Willemssen, 2000).

CONCLUSION

One of the significant differences between offence and defence is that defence is required to ensure against all threats and vulnerabilities, while a successful offence

Copyright © 2003, Idea Group Inc. Copying or distributing in print or electronic forms without written permission of Idea Group Inc. is prohibited.

need only exploit one of these (Anderson et al., 1999). This situation is further exacerbated by the continual growth in performance and power of information and communications technologies, the availability and accessibility of information and tools (Stagg & Warren, 2000), and the relative low costs that enable almost anyone to launch an attack against an infrastructure. On the other hand, the cost to detect, repair, recover, respond, research, and retaliate against such attacks is significantly higher (West-Brown & Kossakowski, 1999).

It is important to realise the growth of infrastructures presents shared risks, which in turn creates shared responsibilities for protection (West-Brown & Kossakowski, 1999). Organisations must work together to safeguard their infrastructure networks, which will further help strengthen the NII. Of course, mass attack on the NII resulting in the total shutdown of systems is not likely without a high level of planning, coordination, skilled personnel, and funds (Cobb, 1997). The possibility of attack on elements of the NII is much more feasible with minimal outlay of technology, funds, and personnel required.

The prospect of an Information Warfare attack against an NII is becoming more realistic as we add to, and depend upon, these infrastructures. Most efforts to date have focused on Critical Information Infrastructure protection and have not incorporated the diversity and inherent dependencies that an NII creates. The model presented here applies the characteristics of Information Warfare to an NII model that recognises both Critical and Non-Critical elements, and the roles they have within the overall infrastructure. Further work is planned on refining this model, along with an accompanying Information Warfare framework.

RECOMMENDED SITES

Australian Institute of Network and Information Warfare, http://www.infowarzone.com

Business Government Task Force on Critical Infrastructure (Australia), http://www.cript.gov.au/cript/

Carnegie Mellon University's Computer Emergency Response Team, http://www.cert.org/

Critical Infrastructure Assurance Office (U.S.), http://www.ciao.gov

Financial Services Information Sharing and Analysis Center, http://www.fsisac.com/

Forum of Incident Response and Security Teams, http://www.first.org/

Information Technology Information sharing and Analysis Center, https://www.it-isac.org/

Infowar Australia, http://www.infowar.com.au

National Infrastructure Protection Center (U.S.), http://www.nipc.gov/

National Infrastructure Security Coordination Centre (UK), http://www.niscc.gov.uk/

National Office for the Information Economy (Australia), http://www.noie.gov.au/

Copyright © 2003, Idea Group Inc. Copying or distributing in print or electronic forms without written permission of Idea Group Inc. is prohibited.

Office of Critical Infrastructure Protection and Emergency Preparedness (Canada), http://www.ocipep.gc.ca/
Partnership for Critical Infrastructure Security (U.S.), http://www.pcis.org/
World Wide Information sharing and Analysis Center, http://www.wwisac.com/

REFERENCES

ABC. (1998). Class Actions. *The Law Report,* Australian Broadcast Corporation.

Alberts, D. S., Garstka, J. J., & Stein, F. P. (1999). *Network centric warfare: Developing and leveraging information superiority* (2nd ed.), CCRP Publication Series.

Anderson, R. H., Feldman, P. M., Gerwehr, S., Houghton, B. K., Mesic, R., Pinder, J., Rothenberg, J., & Chiesa, J. R. (1999). *Securing the U.S. Defense Information Infrastructure: A Proposed Approach* (Report MR993). CA: RAND Corporation.

Arquilla, J. J. & Ronfeldt, D. F. (1993). Cyberwar is coming! *Comparative Strategy, 12*(2), 141-165.

Barker, G. (2002, July). Cyber Terrorism a Mouse-click Away, *The Age.*

Brand, G. (2000). *Protecting the United States Against Information Warfare* (Strategy Research Project), Carlisle, PA: U.S. Army War College.

Brock, Jr., J. L. (2000). *Critical Infrastructure Protection: Challenges to Building a Comprehensive Strategy for Information Sharing and Coordination* (Testimony). Washington, D.C.: United States General Accounting Office.

Campen, A. D., Dearth, D. H., & Goodden, R. T. (1996). *Cyberwar: Security, Strategy and Conflict in the Information Age.* AFCEA International Press.

Cobb, A. (1997). *Australia's Vulnerability to Information Attack: Towards a National Information Policy* (Working Paper). Canberra: Strategic and Defence Studies Centre, Australian National University.

Cordesman, A. H. (2000). *Defending America: Redefining the Conceptual Borders of Homeland Defense* (Final Draft). Washington, D.C.: Center for Strategic and International Studies.

Correll, J. T. (1998). War in Cyberspace. *Airforce Magazine, 81*(1), 32-36.

DSB. (1996). *Report of the Defense Science Board Task Force on Information Warfare — Defense* (Report). Washington D.C.: Office of the Under Secretary of Defense for Acquisition and Technology.

Dudgeon, I. (1997). *Australia's National Information Infrastructure: Threats and Vulnerabilities* (Report). Canberra, Australia: Defence Signals Directorate.

Erbschloe, M. & Vacca, J. R. (2001). *Information Warfare.* McGraw-Hill.

Garigue, R. J. (1995). *Information Warfare: Developing a Conceptual Framework* (Draft Version 2.1). Decision Analysis Laboratory, Carleton University.

Copyright © 2003, Idea Group Inc. Copying or distributing in print or electronic forms without written permission of Idea Group Inc. is prohibited.

Gershanoff, H. (2000). Information What? *Journal of Electronic Defense, 23*(12), 10.

Gray, J. V., Barlow, W. J., Barnett, J. W., Gerrity, J. L., & Turner, R. D. (1997). *Information Operations: A Research Aid* (D-2082). VA: Institute for Defense Analyses.

JCS. (1998). *Joint Doctrine for Information Operations* (Joint Pub 3-13). Washington D.C.: Office of the Joint Chiefs of Staff.

Luiijf, E. A. M. (2000, February). *Information assurance under fire.* Paper presented at the SMI Conference on Information Assurance and Data Security, London.

McCombie, S. & Warren, M. J. (2000). *A profile of an Information Warfare attack* (Technical Report TRC 00/09). Victoria: Deakin University.

Mitchell, R. C., Marcella, R., & Baxter, G. (1999). Corporate Information Security Management. *New Library World, 100*(5), 213-227.

Nash, C. L. & Piggott, C. K. (1999, June). *'Help! I've Been Attacked!' Researching ways to recover a command and control system following an Information Warfare attack.* Paper presented at the 1999 Command and Control Research and Technology Symposium, USA.

OMB. (1995). *NII Security: The Federal Role* (Report). National Information Infrastructure Security Issues Forum, Office of Management and Budget.

PCCIP. (1997a). *Critical Foundations: Protecting America's Infrastructures.* President's Commission on Critical Infrastructure Protection.

PCCIP. (1997b). *Critical foundations: Thinking differently* (Report Summary): President's Commission on Critical Infrastructure Protection.

Power, R. (2002). CSI/FBI computer crime and security survey. *Computer Security Issues & Trends, 8*(1), 1-22.

Prince, F., Howe, C. D., & Voce, C. (2000). *B2B Information Warfare* (Report). Forrester Research.

Rattray, G. J. (1999). *Defensive Strategic Information Warfare: Challenges for the United States.* Paper presented at the Seminar on Intelligence, Command and Control, Harvard University.

Rountree, D. (2001). Disaster's effect on financial systems measured. *Bank Technology News, 14*(10), 7.

Ryan, D. J. & Ryan, J. C. H. (1996). Protecting the National Information Infrastructure against Infowar. *Colloquy, 17*(1), 21-25.

Schwartau, W. (1994). *Information Warfare: Chaos on the electronic superhighway.* NY: Thunder's Mouth Press.

Stagg, V., & Warren, M. J. (2000, November). *Computer hacker information still available on the Internet!* Paper presented at the 1st Australian Information Security Management Workshop, Geelong, Australia.

Stagg, V. & Warren, M. J. (2001, November). *A business information infrastructure.* Paper presented at the Second Australian Information Security Management Workshop, Perth, Australia.

Copyright © 2003, Idea Group Inc. Copying or distributing in print or electronic forms without written permission of Idea Group Inc. is prohibited.

Stagg, V. & Warren, M. J. (2002, May). *Defending infrastructures against Information Warfare.* Paper presented at the Information Resources Management Association International Conference, Seattle, WA, USA.

Vatis, M. A. (2001). *Cyber Attacks during the War on Terrorism: A predictive analysis* (Report): Institute for Security Technology Studies, Dartmouth College.

Waltz, E. (1998). *Information Warfare: Principles and operations.* Boston, MA: Artech House.

West-Brown, M., & Kossakowski, K. P. (1999). *International Infrastructure for Global Security Incident Response* (Draft Report): CERT Coordination Center, Carnegie Mellon University.

Westwood, C. J. (1996). *Military Information Operations in a conventional warfare environment* (Paper Number 47). Canberra: Air Power Studies Centre.

Wik, M. W. (2000, May). *Revolution in information affairs: Tactical and strategic implications of Information Warfare and Information Operations.* Paper presented at the Third Association of Old Crows International Electronic Warfare Conference, Switzerland.

Willemssen, J. C. (2000). *Critical Infrastructure Protection: Comments on the proposed Cyber Security Information Act of 2000* (Testimony). United States General Accounting Office.

Williams, F. & Kennedy, M. (2001). Technology, Planning Came Through After the Attack. *Pensions and Investments, 29*(20), 4.

Wilson, E. J. (1997). The what, why, where and how of National Information Initiatives. In B. Kahin & E. J. Wilson (Eds.), *National Information Infrastructure Initiatives: Vision and Policy Design,* (p. 22) Cambridge, MA: MIT Press.

Wladkowski, F. (1996). The Threat to National and Corporate Information Networks. In S. J. League (Ed.), *A View to the Future* (pp. 145-150).

Copyright © 2003, Idea Group Inc. Copying or distributing in print or electronic forms without written permission of Idea Group Inc. is prohibited.

Chapter VI

Biometrics: Past, Present and Future

Stewart T. Fleming
University of Otago, New Zealand

ABSTRACT

This chapter discusses the current state of the art of biometric systems. The use of biometrics is an important new part of the design of secure computer systems. However, many users view such systems with deep suspicion and many designers do not carefully consider the characteristics of biometrics in their system designs. This chapter aims to review the current state of the art in biometrics, to conduct detailed study of the available technologies and systems and to examine end-user perceptions of such systems. A framework is discussed that aims to establish guidelines for the design of interactive systems that include biometrics.

INTRODUCTION

In the recent movie adaptation of Philip K. Dick's short story "Minority Report," a man walks through a crowded shopping mall. As he passes by, electronic billboards scan his irises. Their presentations instantly change, with electronic actors calling the man's name aloud to attract his attention, immediately tailoring their presentations to suit his pre-recorded profile of preferences.

Copyright © 2003, Idea Group Inc. Copying or distributing in print or electronic forms without written permission of Idea Group Inc. is prohibited.

As with any movie presentation, this vision of a dystopia of corporate advertising linked to biometrics outwith the control of the individual contains just enough grains of truth to make us wonder. We can trace through many of the technologies that would be necessary for this vision to become reality and ask, "Is this possible?" We can trace through many of the societal realities of today and ask, "Is this already happening?"

In fact, we can readily identify many complex issues relating to biometrics in our current societies and there is a need to consider their implications from social and ethical perspectives. The technical aspects of acquiring and comparing biometrics have matured in much the same way that multimedia technologies matured in the 1990s. That is, we know how to do things with these new technologies; we must now figure out how they should be applied and the potential effect they will have on our societies.

It is important to consider these issues at this juncture because if we do not define and choose which reality we prefer one will be imposed on us. Such an imposition would not necessarily be from government, but merely as a result of technical development, where one alternative finds widespread support and eventually squeezes out all others. Indeed, at this time, the rate of development of biometric devices and their uptake in public society far exceeds the rate of development of ethics or policy regarding their use.

This chapter will review some of the complex issues relating to the use of biometrics in our current societies. The nature of biometrics and some of the characteristics and limitations of contemporary devices will be discussed. A framework based on privacy, consent and awareness will be presented and it will be shown how cryptographic techniques can be employed to provide the important properties of privacy and non-repudiation in a biometric system.

Definitions of Biometrics

A biometric is some measurement of the biological characteristics of an (human) individual. There are many forms of biometric data for which capture and verification is possible via some device. Fingerprints, voice recognition, and retinal, face or hand scanning are all feasible with current technology. However, the nature of biometric data is such that there are significant risks associated with its capture and use in a secure environment (Schneier, 1999).

We can define two broad classifications for the method of acquiring biometric data: direct and indirect. A direct biometric is data that represent a measurement that is made of some physical characteristic of an individual, for example a fingerprint or a retinal scan. An indirect biometric is data that represent a measurement that is made of an individual's actions, such as the rhythm of typing on a keyboard.

Direct biometrics generally have a higher probability than indirect biometrics of establishing a 1:1 correspondence between the identity of an individual and the biometric. The method of acquisition is generally more invasive than indirect

Copyright © 2003, Idea Group Inc. Copying or distributing in print or electronic forms without written permission of Idea Group Inc. is prohibited.

biometrics, normally involving measurement by scanning the physical characteristic and the digitization of the measurement.

Indirect biometrics tends to be less invasive in a direct physical sense than direct biometrics. For example, a sensor attached to a keyboard could monitor typing patterns without interacting with the user at all during operation.

Biometric data can be acquired from an individual either in their presence or remotely. Measurements can be obtained from an individual with or without their consent and, in some cases, with or without their knowledge. Issues regarding the nature of the biometric — direct or indirect — are technical ones; issues regarding consent and awareness lead us to the need to consider the social and ethical perspectives of how the data are acquired and used.

Note here that consent and awareness are not equivalent. An individual could know that biometric data was being acquired, but not consent to it. Or the individual could simply be unaware that a biometric was being captured.

For identification purposes, a desirable characteristic of a biometric is that it should be unique to an individual. The acquisition of the biometric in the presence of the individual provides a confirmation of the identity of the individual — at that moment. In order to maintain this 1:1 correspondence, the integrity of the entire biometric system must be maintained.

The uniqueness of a biometric to an individual can be guaranteed only to a certain degree. For some well-established biometrics, such as fingerprinting or DNA signatures, the probabilities of the same biometric being obtained from two different individuals are quite low (of the order 10^{-8} or less). However, even here, the biometrics are not infallible and can lead to false associations. Fingerprint data can be misread or "planted"; DNA samples can be cross-contaminated. For individuals with very similar genetic makeup, such as identical twins, unique identification may be more difficult (Jain, Prabhakar & Pankanti, 2002).

As soon as the measurement is transformed into some digital representation, there is a risk that this direct correspondence with identity will be lost. A collection of bits can be copied perfectly and communicated from place to place very easily. The biometric data once acquired directly from the individual can now be reproduced by means of transformation of digital information. A collection of bits representing a biometric could be associated with a different individual. Essentially, a directly-acquired biometric becomes equivalent to an indirectly-acquired one and loses the ability to identify an individual uniquely.

There is a temporal aspect to biometric data. A measurement of a physical characteristic taken at a particular time provides a correspondence between that data and an individual. However, the physical characteristic may quite naturally develop or change over time and future comparisons with that measurement may not match — even though it was valid at the time of acquisition. Indeed, the physical characteristic may even be lost, or damaged so severely that it can no longer be used as the basis for measurement. Many contemporary systems do not address the temporal aspects of biometric data.

Copyright © 2003, Idea Group Inc. Copying or distributing in print or electronic forms without written permission of Idea Group Inc. is prohibited.

Uncertainty in the biometric device leads to the notions of false acceptance and false rejection. In false acceptance, we incorrectly authenticate the biometric for an individual. In false rejection, we incorrectly reject the biometric for an individual. The uncertainty in the biometric often leads to a trade-off between the false acceptance and false rejection rates of a device. Such trade-offs will impact on the usability and the security of the biometric system. The level of the uncertainty depends on both the degree of uniqueness of the particular measurement being used and the precision of the device used to take the measurement.

Common Perceptions

There is a common perception that biometrics can uniquely identify an individual. This is true to the extent that a biometric can be used to confirm the identity of a person *in their presence*. There is a common perception that if a biometric matches that acquired from an individual, that it somehow confirms their identity. This is also true, depending on the level of integrity that exists within the system that administers the biometric comparison. There is a perception, often held by organizations marketing security solutions, that biometrics on their own can eliminate the problems of collusion, copying and theft that plague conventional security systems based on keys, passwords and so on.

On the other hand, there is a view in the security community that there are major concerns with the use of biometric data in secure systems. As Bruce Schneier points out: *"Biometrics are not secrets"* (Schneier, 1999). If biometric data is compromised, it is impossible to return to a totally secure situation. Many researchers have pointed out vulnerabilities with biometric devices: voiceprint recorders have been fooled by tape-recorders, fingerprint scanners by fake fingers made of gelatin.

As biometric devices find wider application, the general population may encounter them more frequently. Retinal scanners are commonplace in the military; fingerprint or iris scanners are common in secure commercial facilities; a Seattle grocery chain launched a fingerprint-based system for purchasing; face scanners linked to closed-circuit television cameras, particularly in airports and at border crossings, are becoming more common. There is a growing undercurrent of distrust about the use and potential abuse of such devices. Many drivers in the state of Connecticut in the United States voiced opposition to a scheme that would embed digital images and other biometric data in their driver's licenses. In another study (Fleming, 1998), users who were not familiar with technology showed reluctance to use a system that captured biometric data. It is expected that many users will have suspicions about the use of biometric devices.

Objectives

First of all, the capabilities of some contemporary biometric devices are discussed and some technical and societal issues noted. Different devices have different capabilities and limitations and their implications of use affect privacy,

Copyright © 2003, Idea Group Inc. Copying or distributing in print or electronic forms without written permission of Idea Group Inc. is prohibited.

awareness and consent in different ways. We then examine the vulnerabilities of some of these devices. From this discussion, the important principles of irrevocability and non-repudiation emerge and we consider how cryptographic techniques can be employed to solve various technical problems associated with biometric devices.

The latter part of the chapter describes scenarios in which biometrics and cryptography techniques are combined to guarantee confidentiality, integrity, authentication and non-repudiation — the classic characteristics of a secure system (Clarke, 1998).

This consideration of the capabilities and context of use of biometric devices leads to the development of a framework based on principles of privacy, awareness and consent. This framework has been developed and used as a guideline for the design of systems that incorporate biometrics.

Finally, some future trends in the use of biometrics are noted. These technologies represent a growing area and one that should concern us as we look at the implications for both our individual privacy and the security of our societies.

BIOMETRICS – TECHNOLOGIES AND ISSUES
Characteristics of Contemporary Devices

Many types of biometric devices exist for measuring, either directly or indirectly, some physical characteristic to create biometric data. These devices can be used for many different purposes: to identify or confirm the identity of an individual, to authorize access, to eliminate fraud, to confirm the presence of an individual at a certain location and time. Some of these types of devices are briefly discussed below, along with some notes regarding advantages, disadvantages or limitations with respect to the framework of privacy, awareness and consent that is described later in this chapter. Davies (1994) provides an interesting set of case studies regarding the use of biometrics, and it is interesting to see how the societal implications — the need for security versus the need for individual privacy — have remained the same, while the technology has developed.

Fingerprint Scanning

Fingerprint scanners work by taking a high-resolution image of a fingertip and extracting features (known as minutiae) that can be compared. Fingerprint devices normally reduce the image data to a more compact template that stores information about these distinct elements of the fingerprint scan. The accuracy of such scanners can often be adjusted by controlling the number of key features that are compared between fingerprints. These techniques for extraction are similar to the simple graphics algorithms used in automated fingerprint matching systems operated by law enforcement. However, most of the common fingerprint scanners in use adopt proprietary algorithms for reducing the image scans and matching the resulting

Copyright © 2003, Idea Group Inc. Copying or distributing in print or electronic forms without written permission of Idea Group Inc. is prohibited.

templates. Some researchers have indicated that identifying fingerprints based only on matching minutiae may not be sufficient to confirm identity (Pankanti, Prabhakar & Jain, 2001).

Fingerprint scanners often provide sensors for "liveness," that is they attempt to ensure that the finger that is presented for scanning belongs to a live human. Some of these sensors can be fooled easily — Professor Matsumoto famously demonstrated that many contemporary devices could be fooled by presenting a fake finger with a mould of the original fingertip embedded in gelatin (Matsumoto, 2002). Rumours abound of a South African incident where the finger of a dead person was used to gain authorization.

Fingerprint scanners are a reasonably good technology solution where a biometric identifier is needed. Typical accuracy rates are of the order of 1×10^{-6} false acceptance and 3×10^{-6} false rejection. Acquisition of fingerprint samples must be conducted with the knowledge of the individual concerned. The templates generated by most contemporary devices are normally of the order of a few hundred bytes and are suitable for storage in databases or on smart cards.

Eye Scanning

Retinal scanning is commonplace in military organizations. It provides the greatest stability of recognition over time. Templates are formed by scanning the pattern of capillary blood vessels at the back of the eye (retinal scanning) or on the iris. Retinal scans are claimed to be extremely reliable, with a zero probability of false acceptance and very small probability of false rejection.

Retinal scanning is more invasive than iris scanning. For a retinal scan, the individual must look into the scanner, which often incorporates a light source. The scanner can determine liveness via measurement of pupil dilation when looking into the light.

Iris scanning can be performed remotely. A high-resolution camera can be used to acquire an image from an individual's iris and used to form a compact template in a similar manner to a retinal scan. Iris scans are less reliable than retinal scans, but the ability to perform them remotely can be an advantage in some situations, such as the identification of dangerous prisoners without direct physical contact.

The templates formed from eye scans are extremely compact, often less than a hundred bytes. Comparisons against a database of samples can be done extremely quickly, often hundreds of samples per second.

Facial Scanning

Facial scanning works by extracting a key set of facial features (such as the relative position and dimensions of the eyes, ears and mouth) from an image of an individual's head or face. Proprietary algorithms reduce the image data to a template that identifies these features and is used to compare data between individuals. The reliability of the method depends on the quality of the images obtained. In many deployments of facial scanning technology, there is a significant difference in the

Copyright © 2003, Idea Group Inc. Copying or distributing in print or electronic forms without written permission of Idea Group Inc. is prohibited.

environment — camera angle, lighting, etc. — of the enrollment and acquisition/comparison stages.

In one of the more high-profile uses of biometrics in recent years, the Tampa Bay Police Department deployed facial scanning equipment at the 2001 Superbowl. Closed-circuit television cameras (CCTV) were linked to facial scanning systems in an attempt to identify individuals from a database of images of known criminals. According to reports, the system not only did not lead to any arrests, it failed to identify a single criminal and even made basic mistakes such as confusing race and gender of individuals. It did, however, lead to some intense and undeserved discomfort for one individual (Meeks, 2001).

Facial scanners find application in situations where a large number of candidate individuals must be processed. A feed from a camera overlooking a controlled entry point can scan and compare the images of many individuals. Since this is a non-invasive process, the individuals may not even be aware that their image has been captured and/or processed. There are major ethical concerns regarding the reliability and use of facial scanners, particularly in public areas.

Hand Geometry

Hand geometry adopts measurements based on various features of the hands (including finger length). An individual places their hand on a scanner, which makes the measurements, reducing them to a very compact template. These systems seem to find a higher level of acceptance among end-users since they are less invasive than other forms of scan. There may also be a perception that they do not have the same potential for abuse as fingerprints (which might be used to match with criminal records held by law-enforcement).

Voiceprint Identification

In voiceprint recognition, an individual speaks a certain phrase into a micro-phone and the system compares with prerecorded data. The level of complexity can range from speaking a simple sequence of numbers to a pass-phrase or to selection of one from several prerecorded phrases. Voiceprint recognition has developed along with more general speech recognition systems to improve reliability and increase the flexibility of the system.

Voiceprint recognition systems may be prone to being fooled by recordings of an individual's voice, although many recent systems claim immunity to such techniques. A voiceprint system provides the ability to include challenge-response protocols in the authentication procedure. An individual could be asked to repeat on of a set of prerecorded phrases, or they could be asked to answer a question to which they could not have known the answer in advance. Such developments have greatly improved the reliability of voiceprint technology as a technique for biometric identification.

Copyright © 2003, Idea Group Inc. Copying or distributing in print or electronic forms without written permission of Idea Group Inc. is prohibited.

DNA Fingerprinting

DNA fingerprinting works by taking a sample of genetic material from an individual and comparing short segments that are known to vary significantly between individuals. DNA profiling provides a reliable way to exclude an individual (i.e., to reject a match between an unknown sample and that provided by an individual). However, it only provides a probability measure that two samples match. Hence there is an extremely low false acceptance rate, but an uncertain false rejection rate.

The disadvantages of using DNA fingerprinting as a biometric are the speed of processing and the need for a controlled environment for the acquisition and comparison of the sample. Contamination of the sample with foreign DNA will increase the likelihood of a false acceptance.

Very large databases of DNA samples do exist. In the United States, large-scale programs are in place to obtain DNA samples from convicted criminals and these are added to databases. Refinements in the accuracy of DNA testing permit law-enforcement officers to revisit existing cases and compare samples against these larger databases.

Despite the appearance of infallibility, DNA evidence and biometrics must be considered most carefully. Recently, Alec Jeffreys, commonly regarded as the "father" of DNA profiling, hinted that there were flaws at the heart of current profiling techniques. Indeed, the reliability of DNA profiling is in its ability to exclude an individual — in other words to guarantee a rejection — that make it inappropriate for the wide-scale identification of individuals. There is considerable reluctance to adopt DNA fingerprinting as a general method for identification and most countries restrict its use to controlled organizations, such as law-enforcement or immigration, or those that are directed by the courts, such as paternity agencies.

Keystroke Patterns

Keystroke patterns are a form of indirectly-acquired biometric that are obtained by monitoring the pace of typing of an individual user on a keyboard. Individual users have distinct patterns of typing and the monitoring of typing pace of key phrases may provide some indication of user identity.

Keystroke patterns have been used to "harden" password entry. When the user is prompted to enter their password, the system not only checks the password matches the one stored on file, it checks the pace at which it was entered with a profile of pre-recorded typing patterns for that user. This effectively forms a challenge-response protocol using a biometric.

Keystroke patterns are notoriously variable and changes over time can be significant. A dramatic variation in a short time period may be an indicator of a change of user at a terminal and may provide a cue for the system to challenge the user and request further identification by other means.

Copyright © 2003, Idea Group Inc. Copying or distributing in print or electronic forms without written permission of Idea Group Inc. is prohibited.

Monitoring of keystrokes has the potential to be done without the awareness or consent of the user. Monitoring could be done by software on the computer being used by the individual, or a wireless device could be embedded within the keyboard and used to transmit keystrokes to a remote monitoring unit.

Context of Use

Most biometric systems separate the processes of enrollment and acquisition/comparison. Enrollment involves the precise identification of an individual, the acquisition of biometric data from that individual and storage of that data in some secure location. Acquisition/comparison involves the identification of an individual, retrieval of the enrolled biometric data and comparison with the biometric data presented.

Some biometric devices store the data locally within the device. The biometric data is not transmitted or stored in any form outwith the device itself. Individuals must enroll and authenticate with the same device. Such systems are often limited in scope of the number of distinct individuals that they can identify. However, they are suitable for high-security applications, particularly where there is a single access point to a controlled resource.

Other biometric systems allow the enrolled biometric data to be stored in a database that can be accessed from multiple locations. For example, consider a system that allowed controlled entry via a biometric scan. There might be many devices distributed over a wide area and many potential users. Allowing the device to retrieve the biometric data from a database and then perform comparisons provides a solution for this distributed context of use.

Most biometric systems do not perform "brute-force" searches of enrolled data in order to perform a match, although this is possible in many systems. Since the comparison time is generally slow and there may be many individuals enrolled, a biometric system may key the biometric data to some form of identifier, for example a username, a badge or ID number, a public encryption key, etc. When the user presents their biometric, they also present the key information. The biometric system retrieves the associated enrolled data and compares it with the acquired sample.

For some types of biometric, such as speech recognition or keystroke patterns, some form of training process may take the place of enrollment. The system "learns" the characteristics of the individual over some period of time and adjusts its recognition algorithms to suit.

Vulnerabilities

Considering a biometric system as a pattern-matching system, (Ratha, Connell & Bolle, 2001) describe eight possible attacks that could be made by a malicious individual attempting to breach the integrity of the system:
1.   Presentation of a fake biometric at the sensor.
2.   Replay of pre-recorded digital biometric data to bypass the sensor.

Copyright © 2003, Idea Group Inc. Copying or distributing in print or electronic forms without written permission of Idea Group Inc. is prohibited.

3.   Overriding the feature extraction portion of the sensor.
4.   Tampering with the template generation.
5.   Overriding the matching algorithm.
6.   Attacking the database of stored templates.
7.   Intercepting templates being communicated between the sensor and the database.
8.   Overriding the final decision to match or reject the biometric data.

For attack Type 1, (Matsumoto, 2002) demonstrated how many contemporary fingerprint scanners could be fooled by presenting a fake finger made of a gelatin mould with the original fingerprint pattern embedded. This method worked even on some scanners that incorporated "biometric sensors" to detect a live finger. Going one stage further, Matsumoto's team developed a technique for recovering a fingerprint from a latent print and etching it onto a printed-circuit board (PCB). Presenting these images to the sensor also managed to fool the devices. While a user might notice if a mould was taken directly from their fingertips, who is able to completely eliminate the latent prints they leave behind? Deflecting a Type 1 attack needs careful design of the protocol for acquisition to eliminate the possibility of presenting a fake biometric (manual check of fingertips before scanning, human intervention to ensure that no playback device is used to fool a voiceprint sensor).

Attack Types 6 and 7 can be addressed by never storing biometric data in raw form, but instead employing strong encryption to protect it. Encryption may also be employed to avoid attacks of Type 8, encrypting the signals used to indicate acceptance or rejection of the biometric data. Deflecting the other attack types depends on maintaining the integrity of the biometric sensor itself, a strong argument for tamper-proof sensors and human supervision in security sensitive applications.

Many biometric systems cannot be directly used for a challenge-response protocol that is generally used as a second security factor. The only information that the sensor has is the biometric data itself and this does not change regardless of how it is challenged.

False Acceptance and False Rejection

Imagine that we have a situation where a number of different individuals are granted access to some resource and some are not. In order to gain access to the resource, biometric data is acquired from an individual, compared with biometric data previously enrolled by that individual and a decision made on whether or not to grant access. If a biometric has been registered for that individual and it matches with the sample presented, then access should be granted — otherwise it should not.

The ideal process would be:
1.   Enroll biometric for individual and store.
2.   Acquire biometric sample from individual.

Copyright © 2003, Idea Group Inc. Copying or distributing in print or electronic forms without written permission of Idea Group Inc. is prohibited.

3.   Compare with enrolled biometric.
4.   If match obtained, grant access, otherwise deny access.

However, the uncertainty associated with the biometric forces us to admit some doubt and to consider the probability that a biometric is not unique or that some flaw in the measurement and comparison process causes either a false rejection or a false acceptance.

A false rejection, or false negative, represents the situation where an individual presents their biometric data and the device does not match it correctly with the enrolled data. This could occur for any one of a number of reasons: a major change in the form of the biometric since enrollment, imprecise measurement by the device or a major difference in the environments of the enrollment and acquisition processes.

A false rejection may be inconvenient for the individual concerned. The outcome is that they will need to repeat the presentation of the biometric — often multiple times — before a correct match is obtained, or in more extreme circumstances, to repeat the enrollment process to have their data re-established in the system. A false rejection does not represent a breach of security of the system; it is merely inconvenient for the individual concerned.

The more serious situation is that of a false positive. In this case, the system authenticates an individual who should not gain access to the resource. This represents a breach of the security of the system and is clearly a case that we want to avoid.

In most devices, there exists the ability to trade-off the false acceptance and false rejection rates. For example, with a fingerprint scanner, the system could be arranged so as to compare a certain number of minutiae (the unique characteristics of fingerprints). Comparing a greater number of minutiae would tend to result in a more accurate match; however the accuracy of the measurement might not be high enough to allow the comparison to be made. Comparing fewer minutiae would result in a less precise match, but one that might be within the capabilities of the device to perform.

Normally, it is of greater importance to reduce the false acceptance rate in order to reduce the potential for breaches of security. However, this is done at the expense of convenience to the individuals using the system, who may have to present biometric data multiple times for authentication or repeatedly enroll biometric data. The level of inconvenience will impact on the usability of the system in terms of user satisfaction.

Many biometric devices do not perform the comparison on the raw biometric data; instead they perform some transformation on the data to reduce it to a template. The template contains sufficient information to allow a comparison to be made, but will often eliminate redundant information in the raw data, or extract the key features needed for comparison. For example, facial scanning will attempt to identify certain

Copyright © 2003, Idea Group Inc. Copying or distributing in print or electronic forms without written permission of Idea Group Inc. is prohibited.

key features from image data; fingerprint scanners may attempt to extract minutiae from a scanned image. Such transformation methods are usually proprietary algorithms.

Where such transformations are performed, we must admit the possibility that different raw biometric samples could reduce to the same template. More seriously, if the template was ever compromised (intercepted or copied in digital form by some malicious attacker), then the biometric data itself must be considered to be compromised. While the reduction to a template is expedient for the comparison process, the resultant template data must be sufficiently protected to avoid it being compromised. Most biometric authorities recommend encryption for this purpose.

This problem is not new. The original Bertillon system developed in France last century, based on the measurements of criminal's features and precise description of their appearance, has the same fundamental flaw. In the case of Will West and William West in Leavenworth, Kansas in 1903, two individuals with the same name and sharing largely similar appearance were mistakenly identified and the system was discredited as a result (UK Home Office, 2001). This potential flaw lurks at the heart of any template-based biometric system.

A study to independently verify the false acceptance and false rejection rates for a broad sample of biometric devices is underway at the University of Otago in New Zealand. This involves the capture of a large number of biometrics, various measurements of similarities between templates and a large number of comparisons to determine actual error rates with real users. This work will provide a protocol for the independent verification of acceptance and rejection rates for biometric devices. This work is being conducted in line with the best practices for testing biometric devices recommended by the UK Biometrics Working Group (BWG).

SOCIETAL ISSUES, SOLUTIONS AND RECOMMENDATIONS

Irrevocability

Perhaps the most important characteristic of biometric data with respect to security systems is their irrevocability. If a password or security code becomes compromised, or if a key is stolen, then an individual has some recourse: they can select a new password, or change the locks. If a biometric is compromised, there is a more serious problem — the individual cannot change the physical characteristic on which the biometric is based. They cannot easily grow new fingers, or change their iris pattern[1].

Once it has been compromised, biometric data cannot be revoked. This is the single most important reason for the use of strong cryptography to protect biometric data during storage. If not, then the common perception that the biometric is a unique identifier enables perhaps the ultimate in social engineering — identity theft via theft of biometric data.

Copyright © 2003, Idea Group Inc. Copying or distributing in print or electronic forms without written permission of Idea Group Inc. is prohibited.

As a first example, consider the case where authorization is granted to individuals based on the comparison of enrolled biometric data with data acquired from an individual at the point of authorization. If a malicious individual attacked the database where enrolled biometric data were stored, they could substitute their own biometric data for that of an authorized individual. They then present their biometric data, the system matches it with the substituted data, and the malicious individual becomes authorized. The original individual is locked out and must repeat the enrollment process, hopefully this time with a more secure database. The biometric data is still unique to the individual; however the compromise of the database security has compromised the integrity of the correspondence with identity.

To consider a second example, imagine that the source biometric data of an individual is captured by a malicious attacker and a facsimile copy is made. This need not be a perfect copy; it needs to be good enough only for the precision of the biometric device used to scan it. The malicious attacker then presents this data to the biometric scanner and gains access by masquerading as an authorized individual. Such vulnerabilities exist for fingerprint and voiceprint recognition systems.

If we do not afford to an individual strong protection of their biometric data, then a high level of user satisfaction or acceptance of the system is unlikely to be achieved. To enable informed consent to be given, the potential user must be made aware of the purpose for collecting the biometric data, the scope of storage in terms of duration and distribution, and they must be assured adequate protection of their biometric data for the term of storage.

In fact, we would go further than this to recommend that strong encryption be used routinely to protect biometric data and that decryption of the data be made possible only at the point of authorization and in the presence of the individual concerned.

Non-Repudiation

Repudiation is the ability of an individual to disavow knowledge of some action that has taken place or responsibility for it. Non-repudiation is an important property of a secure system in that it assures that all individuals do have responsibility for their actions and that, in case of dispute, sufficient evidence can be provided to identify an individual and establish that they performed a certain action.

For non-repudiation to be successful, we must first have a reliable mechanism for confirming the identity of an individual and then a mechanism for linking that identified individual with the action that has been performed.

For example, imagine that a computer in a locked office is used to access some controlled resource. One person has the only key to the office. Can that person deny that they were the one to access the resource? Quite easily, if we admit the possibility that a second key had been cut, or the original key given to or secretly obtained by another person, or even that the electronic record of access had been forged. Non-repudiation depends on an identifying capability somewhere within the system. The

Copyright © 2003, Idea Group Inc. Copying or distributing in print or electronic forms without written permission of Idea Group Inc. is prohibited.

level of non-repudiation depends on the probability of the integrity of the system being compromised. In this example, nowhere is an individual identified and the possibility of compromise is quite high.

Therefore, for proper non-repudiation, we require not only a 1:1 correspondence between some data and the identity of an individual, we require a secure system for establishing and maintaining that correspondence. It is worth investigating how biometrics coupled with cryptographic techniques can contribute to providing a greater level of non-repudiation.

Firstly, we require a direct biometric, one with an identifying capability. Secondly, we require that both the individual and the system can authenticate the biometric data. An effective security system is one in which at least two out of the following three elements are present: something you have, something you know, or something that you are (Schneier, 2000). Biometrics can provide only one of these elements; for non-repudiation we require at least one additional element. Which one we choose is left to system design: it could be a smart card that is the property of an individual, or a private key, or even another individual to act as witness or participate in the authorization process. The requirement for the individual to be able to verify their own data is important because bits — simple digital representations — can be copied and substituted perfectly.

An encrypted biometric will provide two of the three essential elements for security. If encrypted biometric data is decrypted using the private key of an individual and then matches with a biometric sample acquired from that individual at the same time, then we could be reasonably assured that the designated individual is present.

While this arrangement provides a reasonable level of non-repudiation, it does so only for a single transaction. That is, we know that an individual presented biometric data and that the data was authenticated by both the individual and the system. However, while the individual can no longer claim, "It wasn't me," they can still claim, "I wasn't *there*," or, "I wasn't there *at that time*."

For finer detail of non-repudiation, we must add more properties to the authentication stage. By adding a digital timestamp to the transaction information, we can provide a secure time reference against a known time source. By encoding location information regarding the transaction (such as terminal identifier or even GPS coordinates), we can also identify the exact location of the transaction. However, as we add such detail, we start to invade the privacy of the individual further. A person may not want the location and/or time of the transaction to be known; they may want to know the purpose of gathering such information before consenting to this arrangement. Here, a technical aspect of the system (the ability to add more detail regarding the transaction) starts to interfere with the social and ethical aspects.

The above discussion goes some way toward assuring non-repudiation of presence. It does nothing to assure us of the responsibility for the actions that an

Copyright © 2003, Idea Group Inc. Copying or distributing in print or electronic forms without written permission of Idea Group Inc. is prohibited.

individual might take. If we concern ourselves purely with actions that can be mediated by some kind of automatic control, then we find some application of the techniques described above.

At the point in time when an action is about to be performed, authentication in the form of a biometric is requested from a real live person. The acquired biometric must match with that stored for the individual, and that individual must be authorized for the action in order to proceed. The time of the authentication and the action should be logged with a digital timestamp. If the time source is reliable and the timestamps of authentication and action are synchronized, then we have a reasonable indication that the authentic individual was present and carried out the action.

Such an arrangement does not tell us any information about other actions that the individual might have taken, nor if that person was acting under their own free will or was somehow coerced into performing the action under duress. Some biometric systems have attempted to detect if an individual is under duress when presenting biometric data. For example, if a finger is swiped across a sensor, there might be variations in the speed or direction of swiping if the individual is under stress. Certainly, biometric sensors should make some attempt to verify that the sample is collected from a living individual, although many can be fooled.

Encryption

The organization that is involved in the collection, storage and processing of biometric data as part of some system has a duty of care to protect that data as if it were personal data held about an individual. Privacy legislation in many countries (for example, the Privacy Act in New Zealand and the Data Protection Act in the United Kingdom) has been developed to provide this kind of protection. The United States is still deficient in unified legislation for the privacy of personal data.

Encryption has been recommended for the protection of biometric data by all leading industry organizations (ANSI X9.84 group, International Biometrics Industry Association [IBIA] and the BioAPI Consortium). Many biometric devices already employ encryption to protect biometric data. For example, the Sony FIU-500 fingerprint scanner uses 128-bit DES encryption to protect raw images and templates of fingerprint scans during transfer between the biometric device and the host computer. Such application should be widespread, and no biometric data should be stored in an unencrypted form.

Unfortunately, since most biometric devices generate a template, and this template varies with every acquisition, it is impractical to use the biometric data directly as an encryption key. Instead, various cryptographic techniques are employed to ensure the protection of the biometric data.

The Bioscrypt™ technology described by (Tomko, 1998) uses optical technology to combine a biometric scan with a pass-phrase known only to the user in order to provide authentication. This binding of user credentials with the biometric data is useful, since it enables a cooperation between the user and the system to establish

Copyright © 2003, Idea Group Inc. Copying or distributing in print or electronic forms without written permission of Idea Group Inc. is prohibited.

identity. Developments in the range of BioScrypt™ devices embed this information along with the biometric template on a smart card to enable a distributed security system without a single database that stores all biometric information.

Asymmetric cryptography can be employed to provide a similar kind of protection of biometric data during storage, while preserving the useful property of cooperation between the user and the system when decrypting and comparing the data.

In a system without encryption, an individual enrolls biometric data and has it registered with a database of biometrics. When they require authorization by the system, biometric data is acquired and compared with that registered in the database. The system can perform a brute-force match by comparing the biometric data with all registered samples, or it can use some key information provided by the individual to compare only samples for that individual.

The vulnerability with this arrangement is that enrolled biometric data could be intercepted or substituted in the database. The privacy concern for individuals is that a brute-force match could be conducted against all samples in the database. That is, it can be used to *establish*, not just confirm, the identity of an individual. However, if the integrity of the system has been compromised, as is possible, then there cannot be a guaranteed 1:1 correspondence between the biometric data and the identity of the individual.

Therefore, for the protection of the individual and the assurance of system integrity, we advocate the use of encryption. To enable cooperation (i.e., informed consent), we suggest the use of public-key cryptography as follows.

When the biometric data is acquired, either during enrollment or comparison, it is encrypted by the biometric device using the public key of the individual. The encrypted biometric data is stored in the database and is keyed to some identifier associated with the individual (the public key itself could be used as the identifier). When authorization is required, the encrypted biometric is retrieved from the database and decrypted using the private key of the individual before comparison.

With this arrangement, it is no longer possible to perform an authorization without the consent of the individual, since it requires the private key known only to the individual. It is no longer possible to perform a brute-force comparison of all samples in the database, since the encrypted samples require the private key of each individual before comparison is possible. Non-repudiation is stronger because, for authorization to be given, the biometric data must be decrypted using information known only to the individual and it must match with the credentials provided by the individual at the point of comparison.

The strength of this arrangement depends on the difficulty of breaking public-key cryptography, which is time-consuming, but not impossible, or the difficulty of obtaining both the public key and facsimile of the individual's biometrics. It is worth noting that this technique changes the property of the biometric system from one capable of *identifying* an individual to one that can *confirm* the identity of an individual. That is, the individual is in control of the process, from making the claim

Copyright © 2003, Idea Group Inc. Copying or distributing in print or electronic forms without written permission of Idea Group Inc. is prohibited.

of identity; the role of the system is to use the enrolled biometric information to confirm that claim.

Other cryptographic techniques which may be useful with regard to biometric systems are the use of digital timestamps and the application of digital signatures. By applying a digital timestamp to biometric data at the point of acquisition, we can again enhance the strength of non-repudiation. By applying a digital signature to the biometric data, we can detect any changes that may have been made to the data and reject it as an invalid sample before comparison is attempted.

An implementation of this system could potentially use smart-card technology to provide further privacy assurance to the individual. Their public/private key pair could be embedded on a smart card along with the encrypted copy of the biometric template. On enrollment, the key pair is generated and the enrolled biometric template encrypted with the public key. On acquisition, the enrolled biometric is decrypted by the smart card using the private key and is then uploaded to the biometric device and compared.

The vulnerabilities of this system are still the same as before, only now less risky. In order to break the security of the system, a malicious attacker must substitute an encrypted version of the biometric template both within the database and within the smart card. They must also obtain the private key of the individual in order to be able to decrypt the template or break public-key cryptography. For a masquerade attack, a malicious individual would have to steal the smart card and present facsimile biometric data to the scanner. The risks of these attacks (to the individual) are lower because the raw biometric data is never compromised; it is always encrypted. As soon as a breach of security is discovered (such as the loss or theft of the smart card), the encrypted biometrics can be revoked.

In fact, to further improve the system, we could arrange for the public/private key pairs to be disposable. That is, each pair is used for only a single transaction. When a biometric is enrolled, a key pair is generated and the public key used to encrypt the biometric data. When a biometric is acquired, a new key pair is generated and a new encrypted template is created and stored.

Now we have a system with the additional properties of longitudinal stability and attack discovery. Since new biometric data is being stored at each acquisition point, the system is less prone to recognition failure due to the rejection of natural changes in the biometric.

If an attacker carried out a masquerade attack, then as soon as the source of the attack is discovered (loss of smart card), then all public/private key pairs associated with that individual can be immediately revoked. The attacker is now at risk of discovery on the next transaction using that identity.

Privacy, Awareness and Consent Framework

The biometric system described above using public-key encryption and cooperation with the user at the point of acquisition provides an assurance of privacy,

Copyright © 2003, Idea Group Inc. Copying or distributing in print or electronic forms without written permission of Idea Group Inc. is prohibited.

enables informed consent and raises awareness about the system. These three characteristics are critical to the acceptance of the system by the users.

Privacy is the ability for an individual to control the use of their own personal data, wherever it might be recorded. We consider biometric data to be personal data private to an individual and therefore required to be protected from abuse. Privacy of biometric data is assured only if no raw data is ever stored. In the arrangement described above, the encrypted forms of biometric data are protected by a device that is under the control of the individual.

We consider *awareness* of biometric systems to comprise two aspects: awareness that a biometric system is in use **and** awareness of the legitimate purposes for the collection of the data and the implications for the future use of that data. Indirect biometrics, such as iris or facial scanning, are the biometric technologies that can be operated in a concealed fashion most easily. Indirect biometrics represent the greatest risk to privacy in that there is no need for an enrollment process (provided that we do not want to establish identity, merely to track it).

Consent is a non-trivial concept in the context of biometric systems. It presupposes awareness of the biometric device and what constitutes appropriate use of the resulting data. It presupposes that the user has some control over the enrollment and acquisition of the biometric data. It falls on both parties — the administrators of a system and the users — to *agree* on the purpose of the system, not for the system to be imposed as a prerequisite. If there is no alternative to the use of the biometric system, can the users really be said to be consenting to use it? If a passenger *has* to undergo a retinal scan or have their fingerprints taken before getting on an airliner or passing through immigration, does that constitute consent?

Consent is achieved in the arrangement described above because the encrypted forms are only processed with the agreed cooperation of the user (presentation of the smart card and use of the private key to decrypt the biometric data). The individual is aware that biometric data is being collected, but knows also that it can only be used with their cooperation.

Considering biometric systems within this framework is intended to establish a basis for the design of such systems so that there is scope for an individual user to make the assertion:

> *"My IDENTITY is <state personal identifier>. I present the following CREDENTIALS <supply biometric + supporting non-biometric data>. I confirm that I freely enter into this transaction without duress."*

Some types of biometric device can detect "liveness," that is the presence of a living individual. For example, eye scanners may look for pupil dilation; fingerprint scanners may attempt to detect a warm finger with blood flowing. However, many of these devices can be fooled: recorded voiceprints can still bypass some voice devices; fake fingers can still bypass many fingerprint scanners.

Copyright © 2003, Idea Group Inc. Copying or distributing in print or electronic forms without written permission of Idea Group Inc. is prohibited.

One way to confirm that the designated individual is present in person is to use a challenge-response system of authentication. In such an arrangement, instead of the user initiating the authentication by presenting the biometric, the system requests for the biometric to be presented. For example, in a voiceprint recognition system, an automated security system could request the user to answer a question to which they could not have known the answer beforehand. Challenge-response systems for other biometrics could be employed, for example by asking the user to present a certain finger for scanning. However, such approaches are normally used as a second factor in authentication, to use the biometric first to confirm identity and subsequent challenge-response to verify that the individual is present.

Automatic detection of duress may be possible with some biometrics; for example a voiceprint recognition system could detect stress patterns, a fingerprint swipe device could detect variations in the speed and direction of the swipe. Such signs may be difficult to detect in practice and are more likely to lead to a rejection of the biometric due to the limitations of the accuracy of the device. A more appropriate arrangement would be to issue the individual with two methods of authentication with the system: one for normal use and one for when the individual knows they are being coerced. Both methods would authenticate with the system and grant access, but the "duress signal" would cause an alarm to occur. For a biometric, the duress signal could be to use a certain finger for the scan, or to repeat a different phrase to a voiceprint recognizer.

This framework appears to be useful for the consideration of the capabilities and limitations of biometric devices and the implications for large-scale systems in wider society. Its development grew from the need to meet ethical requirements in the study to verify manufacturers' claims for biometric devices. The research group started to ask questions about the devices that they were using and to explore vulnerabilities and found that they had to go to great lengths to protect the biometric data of individuals used in the study.

FUTURE TRENDS

The upsurge in popularity of biometric devices in recent years has prompted many questions regarding their application. While biometric devices can enhance the security of a system, they do not provide a "silver bullet" to guarantee absolute security. This research set out to investigate the state of the art in biometric devices, to identify risks, possible uses and abuses, and user perceptions of the technology. This work was in progress prior to the traumatic events of September 11, 2001, which, most security analysts would agree, changed the nature of global electronic security completely. In the immediate aftermath, the stock price of five major biometric vendors increased between 20% and 100% (Guevin, 2002).

The perceived need for heightened security in the months following that event has major implications for the uptake of biometric security systems. Almost

Copyright © 2003, Idea Group Inc. Copying or distributing in print or electronic forms without written permission of Idea Group Inc. is prohibited.

immediately, facial scanning systems were established at some airports. Proposals were made for the fingerprinting of foreign nationals entering the United States. Various claims were made about the reliability and usefulness of a wide variety of biometric systems.

A biometric device on its own is no guarantee of security. A combination of two or three security factors may be a more effective way to assure better security (Hong, Jain & Pankanti, 1999). Indeed, the industry trend appears to be towards packaged systems that make use of two or more biometrics, for example combining voiceprint and fingerprint recognition. Such systems will become dominant as customers recognize that individual biometrics do not provide total accuracy.

Legislative developments need to keep pace with technological ones. Already there are concerns regarding the ownership and use of biometric identifiers (California Senate Bill Numbers SB1622 and AB2265) and those concerning the constitutional validity of biometrics (Nuger, 2002).

Digital fingerprinting is finding more widespread application in fraud prevention through better identification. Fingerprints taken from welfare recipients stored in distributed databases provide a better means of tracking multiple claimants to reduce fraud. Fingerprints in driver's licenses provide a means of confirming the identity of the driver of a motor vehicle and eliminate the possibility of obtaining multiple drivers' licenses.

Voiceprint recognition may be the technology to find greatest remote application. Most biometric devices are hampered by the need for secure networks between the sensor and the authorization location. For voiceprint recognition all that is required is a high-quality audio communication. Secure voice-based transactions may become more common; particularly since voiceprint technology has the potential for hardening via challenge-response protocols.

Ironically, given the introduction to this chapter, iris scanning may prove to be the most widespread of all biometric technologies. Already, standards are emerging that provide secure authentication end-to-end between a server and a user via iris scanning (Liedy, 1998). Iris scanning is cheap and reliable, and the biometric templates that are generated are compact and easily transmitted across networks. The indirect nature of iris scanners raises a significant privacy concern.

Biometric devices are divisive in a different way. They do not provide an equal opportunity for every individual in society to interact with them. There will always be those who, due to some physical defect, cannot enroll or be validated by a biometric sensor. For biometric devices to become widespread in society, they must be integrated into a system that provides alternatives for *all* individuals.

CONCLUSIONS

While biometrics do have an important part to play in the design of secure systems in which a user has confidence, their use requires careful consideration in

Copyright © 2003, Idea Group Inc. Copying or distributing in print or electronic forms without written permission of Idea Group Inc. is prohibited.

the design of such systems. By developing various scenarios for the use of biometrics and examining user perceptions of such systems, a framework has been established for the design of systems that incorporate biometric data.

The state of the art in biometrics is such that reliable technologies do exist and the deployment of such technologies is becoming widespread. This area of study is at the stage of development where the careful consideration of ethical and societal implications is important. Legislation will be required in the very near future that addresses the trade-off between the need for security within society and the privacy that should be enjoyed by each individual.

The use of strong encryption is recommended for the protection of biometric data as if it were personal data associated with an individual. Individuals would be correct to be suspicious of devices that operate in public areas and have the potential for brute-force matching. Such application of devices could be deemed to infringe on civil liberties, without providing additional security to the society under surveillance.

As a by-product of the use of encryption of biometric data, we can achieve authorization without identification. That is, a database containing biometric data in encrypted form no longer has the capability to perform a brute-force search since it does not have the cooperation of every individual concerned. Such a biometric system provides the ability to confirm the identity of an individual, but not to be able to specifically identify one individual from many, based solely on the biometric data. This is what we mean by "authentication without identification" and view it as an important property of a biometric system deployed widely in public society.

Finally, the framework presented here is intended as a step towards providing more detailed guidelines to designers of systems that incorporate biometric data. It indicates that awareness of the biometric system is necessary for informed consent and that all factors — privacy, awareness and consent — must be present before the system will be entirely accepted by the users. Experience with the evaluation of user interfaces tells us that if user satisfaction with the system is low, the system is unlikely to be successful as users find workarounds to bypass it. Whether this will yet lead us to walk around in public wearing gloves to avoid leaving latent fingerprints and mirror sunglasses to defeat iris scanners remains to be seen.

REFERENCES

Clarke, R. (1998). Cryptography in plain text. *Privacy Law and Policy Reporter, 3*(2), 24-27.

Davies, S. G. (1994). Touching Big Brother: How biometric technology will fuse flesh and machine. Information *Technology and People, 7*(4).

Fleming, S. T., & Vorst, D. (1998). *Putting your finger on it — Patient identification in a multi-name society.* Paper presented at the IRMA International Conference, (May 1999) Hershey, PA.

Copyright © 2003, Idea Group Inc. Copying or distributing in print or electronic forms without written permission of Idea Group Inc. is prohibited.

Guevin, L. (2002). *From Telecom to Biometrics, To Bonanza?* BiometriTech, Inc.

Jain, A. K., Prabhakar, S., & Pankanti, S. (1999). *Can multibiometrics improve performance?* Paper presented at the Proceedings of AutoID '99, NJ.

Kain, A. K., Prabhakar, S., & Pankanti, S. (2002). Twin test: On discriminability of fingerprints. *Pattern Recognition Journal.*

Liedy, M. V. (1998). *Biometric security systems: The next generation of security.* University of Maryland.

Matsumoto, T., Matsumoto, H., Yamada, K. & Hoshino, S. (2002). Impact of artificial "gummy fingers" on fingerprint systems. In *Proceedings SPIE*, 4677, pp. 275-289.

Meeks, B. N. (2001). Electronic frontier: Blanking on rebellion: where the future is Nabster. Communications *of the ACM, 44*(11), 17.

Nuger, K. P. (1998). *Biometric applications : Legal and societal implications .*

Pankanti, S., Prabhakar, S., & Jain, A. K. (2001). *On the individuality of fingerprints.* Paper presented at the Proceedings Computer Vision and Pattern Recognition (CSVPR), Hawaii.

Ratha, N. K., Cornell, J. H., & Bolle, R. M. (2001). A biometrics-based secure authentication system. *IBM System Journal, 40*(3).

Schneier, B. (1999). Biometrics: Uses and abuses. Inside Risks 100. *Communications of the ACM, 42*(8).

Schneier, B. (2000). *Secrets and Lies: Digital security in a networked world.* Wiley.

Tomko, G. (1998). *Biometrics as a privacy-enhancing technology: Friend or foe of privacy.* Paper presented at the Privacy Laws and Business Privacy Commissioner's/Data Protection Authorities Workshop, Santiago de Compostela, Spain.

United Kingdom Home Office. (2001). *Sci-fi future for detection.*

Copyright © 2003, Idea Group Inc. Copying or distributing in print or electronic forms without written permission of Idea Group Inc. is prohibited.

Chapter VII

User Types and Filter Effectiveness: A University Case Study

Geoffrey Sandy
Victoria University, Australia

Paul Darbyshire
Victoria University, Australia

ABSTRACT

As the amount of content on the Web grows almost exponentially, one of the new growth industries is that of filtering products. The effectiveness of Web-filtering software depends on a number of factors including the architecture of the software itself, and the sophistication of the users operating within its application domain. The main use of filtering software is to "block" access to controversial content such as pornography. This paper reports an investigation of the effectiveness of a filter called squidGuard in the real-world environment of an Australian University. The product is used to "block" pornographic material. This investigation simulates three classes of web users in trying to access pornography. While squidGuard did have limited success in blocking such material from novice users, the blocking rate dropped dramatically for the more experienced users using access lists. In all cases, however, access to

Copyright © 2003, Idea Group Inc. Copying or distributing in print or electronic forms without written permission of Idea Group Inc. is prohibited.

supposedly filtered material was gained in seconds.   Under such testing, the effectiveness of squidGuard as a specific-content filter for "pornographic" material can only be seen as superficial approach at best. The use of anonymous proxy servers was found to be an easy means to by-pass the filter.

INTRODUCTION

Filter software is increasingly used by a wide variety of groups in society and in many societies, its use is mandated by law. Filter software is used in the home and school markets. Parents and teachers use a filter to prevent children from accessing content deemed not suitable for them. Sexually explicit and violent material is of most concern to parents and teachers. The regulation of controversial material in respect to children is also an issue for organizations like libraries and universities. Recently the corporate world has embraced filter technology because of concerns expressed about loss of productivity and risks of litigation.

Fundamental to the acceptance and use of a filter are two questions. First, how effective is it in blocking content that is intended to be blocked? Second, how effective is it in not blocking content that is intended not to be blocked? Vendors claim their product is highly effective. Many vendors also claim that the product is highly effective because, before content is blocked, it is evaluated by a person using a rating or classification system. Another question that concerns effectiveness is the ease with which the software can be disabled or by-passed.

This paper reports on testing the effectiveness of a filter product, called *squidGuard*, that is used in a number of Australian universities. The test is conducted in a real-world environment at one of these universities (Victoria University), and simulates different types of consumers of Internet pornography that may be found in this environment. Victoria University mainly uses the filter to block what the vendor's blacklist describes as pornography. The university does add its own sites to the blacklist, and the product offers a number of blacklists additional to pornography.

In the following sections some background material is provided on the main approaches to filtering and the effectiveness of a range of filtering products. A description of the *squidGuard* filter is then provided. A classification scheme — that classifies users that browse the Web for Internet pornography in terms of their sophistication in browsing for specific-content — is described. A first set of trials to test the effectiveness of *squidGuard* in blocking material intended to be blocked for two levels of users is discussed. A second set of trials to test the effectiveness of *squidGuard* in blocking material that is not intended to be blocked is also discussed. The results of both sets of trials are presented. A third set of trials to test the ease with which *squidGuard* may be by-passed is discussed and the results presented.

Copyright © 2003, Idea Group Inc. Copying or distributing in print or electronic forms without written permission of Idea Group Inc. is prohibited.

BACKGROUND

Filter software is designed to block access to controversial Internet content. Such content can be blocked in three places: at the source (that is the provider or creator of the content); in transit either at the application level or at the packet level; at the receiver. Blocking at the receiver end may be done directly by installation of a filter on the receiver's PC, or indirectly at the receiver's Internet Service Provider (ISP) with a subscription to a "white list." The process of blocking requires the content must be rated based on some classification system. Such a system may be a simple one which produces a rating of allowed/disallowed, or a sophisticated one like the Platform for Internet Content Selection (PICS) that employs many categories and values. Opinion is divided over whether PICS or similar labelling systems are a solution to blocking controversial content (see for instance Kohntopp & Kohntopp, 1999; Chen et al., 1999; Hochheiser, 1997).

There are three main approaches to filtering Internet content. These may be referred to as inclusion filtering, exclusion filtering and content filtering. Inclusion filtering allows access to a relatively small number of sites that are known to be "acceptable" and access to the rest of the Internet content is blocked. The sites that carry the acceptable content are known as "white lists." Obviously, tests of "white lists" often result in 100% effectiveness. Exclusion filtering is based on identifying unacceptable content and adding sites carrying this to a "black list" that is blocked. What determines whether the content is unacceptable depends on the rating or classification scheme employed. Content filtering employs "key words" or other characteristics that suggest unacceptable content, and this is blocked. Often the software vendors combine two approaches in an attempt to improve the product's effectiveness.

There is a growing body of research that challenges the effectiveness claims of filter software vendors. A recent report by the Australian Commonwealth Scientific and Industrial Research Organisation (CSIRO, 2001) evaluated the effectiveness of 14 filter products. All are currently on the list of approved filters of the Australian Government. *SquidGuard* is not on the list and was not tested. According to the CSIRO, an effective filter is one that blocks all undesirable Internet content, it passes all other Internet content through untouched, is not easily by-passed or disabled and securely tracks all attempts to access undesirable content. The study found that filters vary considerably in their effectiveness. This is partly explained by the different approaches to filtering adopted for a particular product. As would be expected, products based on inclusion filtering registered very high levels of effectiveness compared to those based on exclusion or content filtering. Nevertheless, the study found the products to be more effective in blocking pornography and in not blocking unintended content (non-pornographic) than found in earlier studies.

Haselton (2000a), using "zone files" from Network Solutions (which lists all .com files), obtained a list of the first 1000 active .com domains for June 14, 2000.

Copyright © 2003, Idea Group Inc. Copying or distributing in print or electronic forms without written permission of Idea Group Inc. is prohibited.

This list was tested using five popular filters to discover how many sites were blocked as "pornography" and, of those sites, how many were actually pornographic. The products tested were "Cyber Patrol" (Haselton 2000b), "SurfWatch" (Haselton 2000c), "Bess" (Haselton 2000d), "AOL Parental Controls" (Haselton 2000d) and "SafeServer" (Haselton 2000e). The error rate found for each product was computed as the number of non-pornographic sites blocked divided by the total number of sites blocked. The average error rates for each filter product were: "Cyber Patrol," 81%; "SurfWatch," 82%; "Bess," 27%; "AOL," 20%; and "SafeServer," 34%. The researcher believes that the claim of human evaluation of material is false and the error rate would be higher if .org sites were tested.

Haselton (2000f) tested the "BAIR" filter with a sample of 50 randomly selected pornographic images and 50 randomly selected non-pornographic images. Haselton (2000g) retested the filter on July 18, 2000, and found that 34 out of the 50 pornographic images of the first experiment were blocked. Of the non-pornographic images, only eight were blocked. A random selection of 50 images of peoples' faces was selected to test if they were blocked. Out of 50 face images, 34 were blocked. It was concluded that "BAIR" has only negligible ability to distinguish between pornographic images and pictures of peoples' faces.

Finklestein (2000) investigated "SmartFilter." The study provides empirical evidence to confirm the mathematical impossibility of a human evaluation of blacklisted content. It lists many sites blocked by the product that were not intended to be blocked. Possible programming-related reasons are put forth as to why these sites are blacklisted.

The Censorware Project (2000) tested the effectiveness of "Bess." Thousands of URL's were tested against "Bess" proxies in real-world use from July 23 to July 26, 2000. The 10 proxies were configured similarly to each other and to the setup that "Bess" recommends for schools. The major finding is that "Bess" is ineffective in blocking many porn sites, and mistakenly blocks a great deal of useful non-pornographic material suitable for school children. A test was also made by the Censorware Project (1999) of "SmartFilter," used by the Utah Education Network, that resulted in similar findings.

An independent review was conducted of the "Clairview Internet Sheriff" in May 1999 (Electronic Frontiers Australia, 1999). Internet access accounts were purchased with Clairview's Brisbane ISP and Cvue Internet. Cvue start-up packages include 20 hours of access, and customers using this service are anonymous to Clairview. The customers (three reviewers) simulated the use of the Internet as a cautious and reasonably Internet familiar parent would to check the effectiveness of the filter for themselves and children. Approximately 20 hours of testing was conducted by three people for a week. Access was sought to sites unambiguously pornographic. Many pages were accessible. On returning to these pages later, some were now blocked. It was found the blocking mechanism was able to be by-passed using free anonymiser-type services available on the World Wide Web; that is,

Copyright © 2003, Idea Group Inc. Copying or distributing in print or electronic forms without written permission of Idea Group Inc. is prohibited.

blocked sites could be accessed while using the Cvue service. It was also found to block vast numbers of non-pornographic pages.

Over a number of years, Peacefire, a Youth Alliance Against Internet Censorship, has published reports on sites and newsgroups that could not be described as pornographic, but have been blocked by filters online. These include "Cyber Patrol," "Net Nanny," "X-Stop" and "CYBERsitter."

The Electronic Privacy Information Centre (EPIC 1997) conducted 100 searches using a traditional search engine and 100 searches using a search engine described as the "world's first family Internet search site." An attempt was made to locate material that might be useful to children. This included schools and charitable, educational, artistic and cultural institutions. Search terms included "Smithsonian Institute," "American Red Cross," and "San Diego Zoo." It was found that the family-friendly search engine prevented access to 90% of materials available on the Net using the relevant search terms. It was also found that the family-friendly service denied access to 95% to 99% of material otherwise available without filters. The study concluded that the filtering mechanism prevented children from accessing appropriate material likely to be useful to them.

FILTER DESCRIPTION

Information technology management of Victoria University state that *squidGuard* was introduced for two main reasons. The first reason was to minimise risks of litigation and the possible infringement of sexual harassment legislation. The second reason was to contain Internet costs. Notwithstanding this, *squidGuard* is universally applied across Victoria University and applies to both staff and students.

SquidGuard blocks sites at the application level by filtering material from the user based on the destination of the URL requests. Sites can be filtered based on the following:
- User ID
- IP addresses
- Entire domains, including sub-domains (my.domain.com)
- Entire hosts (Host.my.domain.com)
- Directory URL's (my.domain.com/directory/one)
- Specific files (my.domain.com/directory/one/file1.html)

The IP addresses, domain URL's, hosts and files to be filtered are compiled into a database and searched every time a URL request is made through the filtering server. If a match is found then the user is directed to a URL specified through the *squidGuard* configuration. Figure 1 shows an abstraction of squidGuard in operation.

Copyright © 2003, Idea Group Inc. Copying or distributing in print or electronic forms without written permission of Idea Group Inc. is prohibited.

Figure 1.   Abstraction of squidGuard

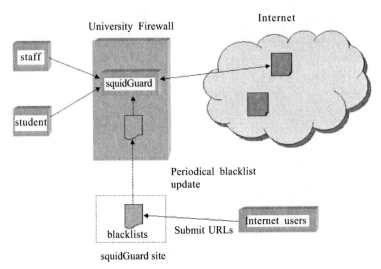

The databases used by *squidGuard* are compiled by periodically initiating a "dumb" Web robot[1] to scan Internet URL's based on keywords and expression lists to find Web pages to block. The robot consumes large amounts of computer resources, so it is recommended that it be used sparingly, or that users of *squidGuard* contribute to common blacklists that can be downloaded from the Internet. Web pages are not checked for content, and in fact *squidGuard* makes the following disclaimer:

> *"The blacklists are entirely products of a dumb robot. We strongly recommend that you review the lists before using them. Don't blame us if there are mistakes, but please report errors with the online tool."*

The size and structure of the blacklists, however, (particularly the one concerned with pornography), are such that a manual check, while not impossible, is certainly not feasible.

USER TYPES

In any organisation containing computer-based technology, there will be varying levels of user sophistication. When filtering software is in place whose purpose is to block entry of users to specific sites, or a class of sites, it will have varying degrees of success depending on the technological sophistication and "software savvy" of the users. In this study, we identify four levels of users with an increasing level of sophistication when browsing for specific content on the Web. These user-levels represent an increasing progression of sophistication from left to right in the diagram.

Copyright © 2003, Idea Group Inc. Copying or distributing in print or electronic forms without written permission of Idea Group Inc. is prohibited.

Figure 2. User sophistication and domain of study

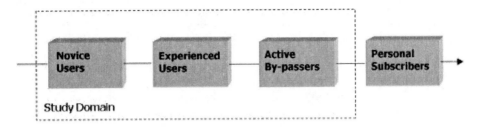

The four classes identified in are:

Novice users: someone who wishes to access filtered material on the Web but has no great experience in doing so. Such a user, in all likelihood, would begin with a standard search engine using obvious keywords from their learned experience.

Experienced users: users who have been successful in previous browsing, and have gained some experience in searching for the specific content. Such a user would be familiar with less obvious keywords to use in standard search engines, or perhaps more likely, follow links on daily-updated specific content lists.

Active by-passers: some users, aware of the filtering technology and techniques they employ, attempt to take active steps to bypass the filtering technology. There are many Web sites devoted to instruction on techniques to use to achieve this goal.

Personal subscribers: this class of user is represented by people who personally subscribe to filtered content by filling out Web forms and subscription lists. The filtered material can then be delivered to their personal mailboxes, sometimes in innocuous format.

The last two classes of users are difficult to dissuade, and quite often the only way to prevent their access is to remove them from the Web altogether. In the remainder of this paper we study the effectiveness of the *squidGuard* filter; the first three classes of users in represent our domain of study. We believe that users belonging to the first two user-types represent people who may be willing to browse the Web for specific content, but may be discouraged depending on the success of the filtering software. Users belonging to the third user-type, (active by-passers), are almost impossible to control using the filter under investigation, as the sections below demonstrate.

FILTER EFFECTIVENESS — NOVICE AND EXPERIENCED USERS

The results used to determine the effectiveness of *squidGuard* as a filter for novice and experienced users centred on a series of trials accessing Internet sites.

Copyright © 2003, Idea Group Inc. Copying or distributing in print or electronic forms without written permission of Idea Group Inc. is prohibited.

These trials attempted to simulate the actions of these types of users while trying to gain access to filtered pornographic material. The following two sections describe the data collection methodology and the results determined from the ensuing trials.

Data Collection Description

In simulating the *Novice User*, two Web search engines were chosen, Google[2], and AltaVista[3]. For both of these search engines, 10 initial trials were conducted. A trial was conducted for each of 10 keywords — that is, 10 Web searches of filtered material. In each of the 10 searches, the first 20 URL's were followed to try and gain access to the filtered material. This represents 200 URL's per search engine. For each search, a tally was kept as to the number of successful accesses (accesses to filtered material) and the number of sites filtered (material was successfully filtered). In some cases, errors may have occurred due to problems with the URL's, and these were also noted. The percentages of the *access rate* and *filtered rate* were than calculated and tallied.

The 10 keywords used for the trials were 10 obvious *porn-keywords*, chosen from an industry-compiled list of unambiguous pornographic terms. The term "*obvious*" is subjective, but the keywords were chosen from the list for two reasons. The keywords were deemed to be socially familiar (if not acceptable) to the wider community, and Web sites indexed using these keywords would contain unambiguous pornography. Unambiguous pornography is material that would be designated as pornographic in any broad-based definition. The keywords and lists used are not presented in this paper, as they may give offence to some readers. Details are available on request from either of the authors.

A second trial was then conducted, similar to the one just described, except a different set of 10 keywords was selected. These keywords were selected, as they were *less-obvious* terms to use when searching. Again, the term "*less-obvious*" is subjective, but they were chosen from the same industry compiled list of unambiguous terms. Such terms represent search criteria used by more experienced users of pornography.

Finally, a trial was conducted to simulate a more *Experienced User* by using comprehensive, daily-updated, specific content lists. These lists are readily accessible via the Internet, and most users browsing for pornographic content will come across them, as the researchers did during the first trials discussed above. Two common lists were chosen and for each list the first 50 URLs were checked for accessibility.

A trial was also undertaken to search the Web using keywords such as "*sexuality,*" "*gay,*" "*lesbian,*" and "*sexual health.*" In each case, the first few links were attempted. If these were blocked, then their content was checked against an un-filtered Internet connection through an external ISP. This test was performed to gauge the extent to which the filter inappropriately blocked access to sites where the content was unambiguously not pornographic in nature.

Copyright © 2003, Idea Group Inc. Copying or distributing in print or electronic forms without written permission of Idea Group Inc. is prohibited.

Table 1.   Trial 1, 10 obvious keywords with Google and AltaVista search engines

Keyword	Google		AltaVista	
	Access Rate%	Filter Rate%	Access Rate%	Filter Rate%
1	58	40	16	84
2	20	80	25	75
3	30	70	35	65
4	40	60	15	85
5	47	53	20	80
6	42	57	10	90
7	32	68	35	65
8	42	58	20	80
9	35	65	5	95
10	55	45	25	75
Average%	40%	60%	21%	79%

Results

In the first trial, checking two common search engines for 10 "obvious" keywords, a table is presented that represents the results from both search engines. Table 1 represents the summarized results of the trial using the Google and AltaVista search engines. In the case of an error (page inaccessible), the page was not counted in the resultant statistics.

The summarized results for the two corresponding trials of the 10 "*less-obvious*" keywords for the Google and AltaVista search engines can be seen in Table 2.

Table 2. Trial 2, 10 less-obvious keywords with Google and AltaVista search engines

Keyword	Google		AltaVista	
	Access Rate%	Filter Rate%	Access Rate%	Filter Rate%
1	15	85	35	65
2	35	65	35	65
3	70	30	40	60
4	20	80	10	90
5	30	70	25	75
6	35	65	25	75
7	25	75	20	80
8	75	25	5	95
9	70	30	20	80
10	45	55	25	75
Average%	42%	58%	24%	76%

Copyright © 2003, Idea Group Inc. Copying or distributing in print or electronic forms without written permission of Idea Group Inc. is prohibited.

Table 3. Trial 3, using pornographic lists

List	Successfully Accessed	Filtered	Errors	Access Rate%	Filter Rate%
List 1	37	13		74	26
List 2	38	12		76	24
		Average %		75%	25%

The results shown in Table 3 represent the simulation of an Experienced User using content specific lists, which are updated on a daily basis.

FILTER EFFECTIVENESS — ACTIVE BY-PASSING

For those users with enough technical expertise and knowledge, there are a number of ways to by-pass the filter technology being employed (CSIRO, 2001; Carey, 2002). These include tunnelling, using re-director services or using little known or uncommon port proxies to bypass the censorship programs on the gateway server (Kennington, 2000; Carey, 2002). The use of tunnelling requires the user to take advantage of Virtual Private Networks, which allow users to create secure private networks that work on top of the public network (CSIRO, 2001). However, the use of tunnelling techniques does require a more sophisticated use of the operating and software to support this. A far easier approach is to use public anonymous proxy server as a re-director service.

Re-director services are extremely simple to use and work by allowing a user to piggy-back a blocked URL on top of a legitimate URL. For instance, if the URL you wanted to reach is:

http://www.thehun.com

This site, which is a list consisting of hundreds of free URL links to porn sites, is currently blocked by *squidGuard* at Victoria University. However, by locating an anonymous public proxy server we can formulate a different URL. One such public proxy server is MagusNet. The URL for MagusNet is:

http://www.magusnet.com/proxy.html

Instructions contained on this site show the user how to reach the desired URL by getting the anonymous proxy server to re-direct the URL you initially enter to the desired destination site. For instance to get to the site above [www.thehun.com] you type in the following URL into your browser:

Copyright © 2003, Idea Group Inc. Copying or distributing in print or electronic forms without written permission of Idea Group Inc. is prohibited.

https://proxy.magusnet.com/-_-http://www.thehun.com

The URL you really wish is piggy-backed onto the end of the URL for the anonymous proxy server. The gateway server, which contains *squidGuard* (or possible another filtering product) generally only sees the first part of the URL (https://proxy.magusnet.com), and if this site is not blocked itself, then the ULR is then passed to the anonymous proxy server. The proxy server, in turn, retrieves the second part of the URL (http://www.thehun.com), then sends this request to the desired destination, and after the page is returned, in turn, sends the retrieved information (Web page) back to the user. The sequence of events is depicted in.

In the case of some filters, which may block on content, pages may still be blocked if the returned material is readable by the filtering software. However, *squidGuard* does not filter on content, and also the MagusNet anonymous proxy returns the page in a secure format, which is not readable, thus thwarting the filters that block on content. The only way to filter material accessed in this way by *squidGuard* is to block the anonymous proxy server site. In fact, in between the time of initial investigation and writing this document, MagusNet have become blocked by *squidGuard*. But it took only a matter of minutes of searching on Google (or any other search engine) to find another, Anonymouse. To read the same page above through the anonymous server, we just send the following URL through our browser software:

http://anonymouse.ws/cgi-bin/anon-www.cgi/http://www.thehun.com

At the time of this writing, the Anonymouse hadn't been blocked by *squidGuard*. By using the URL's obtained in the trials conducted in the previous section, those URL's blocked by *squidGuard* were tested using the Anonymouse anonymous proxy server. It was found that with the *squidGuard* filter, once we had an anonymous proxy server that was not blocked itself, we could access 100% of the sites previously blocked.

We also found other sites, which listed hundreds of anonymous proxy servers (Samaraline, 2001), and even one site (http://leader.ru/secure/), which acted as a portal into a number of such proxy servers. As the anonymous proxy servers are not

Figure 3. Anonymous proxy server operation

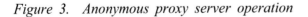
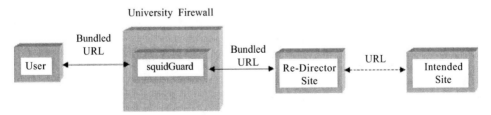

Copyright © 2003, Idea Group Inc. Copying or distributing in print or electronic forms without written permission of Idea Group Inc. is prohibited.

always available, such a portal allowed a user to try a number of such proxies in a matter of seconds.

BLOCKING USEFUL CONTENT

In the trials for testing the filter inappropriately blocking non-pornographic material, 26 sites were identified as containing non-pornographic material and were blocked by *squidGuard*. At this point the researchers stopped, as it seemed clear that many more could be identified if the trial persisted.

Research sites blocked include "The American Board of Sexology," "Male Multiorgasm Response Research," the "Journal of Sexuality and Culture," and "The World Sex Guide (Prostitution Research)." Also blocked was access to the Society for Human Sexuality.

Safe sex practices include teen dating, teen pregnancy, sexually transmitted diseases and information on the use and availability of condoms and latex dams. Links to "personal, relationships, intimacy and sex Eastern spirituality" was blocked on the *Looksmart* site that is dedicated to non-pornographic material. Other sites blocked include "planned parenthood," "spirituality and sexuality," and "sexuality and mental health."

DISCUSSION

The data presented in the "Results" sections indicates a varying degree of success of the filtering mechanism in blocking the intended specific content. The filter rate varied quite widely depending on the keyword used to search, even within the same search engine. Generally speaking, the filtering software was more successful at blocking specific content when the more obvious keywords were used, as opposed to the less obvious ones. The differences between the *obvious* and *less-obvious* keyword results were not significant.

There was a significant difference, however, between the filter rates of the specific content lists and the standard search engine results. The highest average filter rate achieved using the standard search engines was with Alta Vista, at 79%, using the *obvious* keywords. But the lowest filter rate achieved by using the two lists was 58%. The use of daily-updated specific content lists represents a more experienced user, according to our hierarchy of user sophistication. Thus, the more sophisticated users are able to gain access to a greater number of specific content sites. As the lists are updated on a daily basis, it is more probable that many of the new URL entries are actually new to the Web, and hence not already filtered by such products as *squidGuard*. Thus, a lower filter rate could have been anticipated, as proved to be the case.

Copyright © 2003, Idea Group Inc. Copying or distributing in print or electronic forms without written permission of Idea Group Inc. is prohibited.

There are a number of important issues that relate to filter products like *squidGuard*. First is a recognition that they are highly inaccurate, in that they fail to block targeted material, and material is blocked that should not have been. Users are unable to verify the inaccuracy, as access is denied to the material. The reality concerning effectiveness of the product is very different from the claims made by vendors.

The vast size of available material on the Web, its growth rate (in volume), and the frequent changes made to existing sites makes evaluation very difficult. Although vendors claim that sites are evaluated by humans before being blocked, the reality is that vendors largely use computers for evaluation. The vendors of *squidGuard* honestly inform users of the product that its blacklists are entirely the results of a dumb robot. This is inappropriate, as anybody not checking the lists manually could be filtering out invaluable material. Many of the URL's provided in blacklists are the results of personal judgements about the information requirements of Internet users made by anonymous third parties. There is a risk that these third parties adopt a very conservative attitude to material, or worse incorporate their prejudices and biases.

CONCLUSION

In this paper we have investigated the success of filtering software, in particular *squidGuard*, in filtering specific-content from Web browsers. Four levels of Internet users have been identified with increasing sophistication in searching for undesired content. As a user's level of sophistication increases, their chances of gaining access to this material will increase dramatically.

Three trials were conducted to test the effectiveness of *squidGuard* on three levels of user sophistication. This was done by simulating possible access methods by these users. In the first trial, two standard search engines were used to test access success when users searched using obvious keywords. The second trial was similar, except less obvious keywords were used with the search engines. In the third trial, lists containing URL links to the specific-content were used. These lists are readily available on the Web, but it takes some time to find them. Thus, only more sophisticated browsers would use such lists rather than a standard search engine. In the third trial, once we obtained the URL of a non-blocked anonymous proxy server, a user actively by-passing the filter could access 100% of the blocked material.

While the *squidGuard* did have limited success in blocking material from a *Novice User*, the blocking rate dropped dramatically for the more *Experienced User* who used the access lists, and indeed disappeared for active by-passing users. In all cases, however, access to supposedly filtered material was gained in seconds. Under such testing, the effectiveness of *squidGuard* as a specific-content filter for "pornographic" material can only be seen as superficial approach at best.

Copyright © 2003, Idea Group Inc. Copying or distributing in print or electronic forms without written permission of Idea Group Inc. is prohibited.

ENDNOTES

1   http://ftp.ost.eltele.no/pub/www/proxy/squidGuard/contrib/squidGuardRobot/
2   http://www.google.com/
3   http://www.av.com/

REFERENCES

Carey, C. (2002). *Uncommon port proxies: Bypassing censoring firewalls/ proxies*. Retrieved March 2002 from: http://www.ijs.co.nz/proxies3.htm.

The Censorware Project. (2000). *Passing porn, banning the bible*. Retrieved October 1, 2000 from: http://www.censorware.org/reports/bess/.

Chen, D., et al. (1999). Centralized content-based web filtering and blocking: How far can it go? *IEEE*, 115-119.

Commonwealth Scientific and Industrial Research Organisation. (2001). Effectiveness of Internet filtering software products. *Mathematical and Information Sciences*, September.

Electronic Frontiers Australia Inc. (1999). *Report: Clairview Internet Sheriff An Independent Review*. Retrieved October 24, 2000 from: http://www.efa.org.au/ Publish/report_isheriff.html.

Electronic Privacy Information Center. (2000). *Mandated mediocrity: Blocking software gets a failing grade*. Retrieved October 25, 2000 from: http:// www.peacefire.org/censorware/BESS/MM/.

Finklestein, S. (2000). *SmartFilter – I've got a little list: An anticensorware investigation*. Retrieved February 3, 2001 from: http://sethf.com/ anticensorware/smartfilter/gotalist.php.

Haselton, B. (2000a). *Study of average error rates for Censorware Programs*. Retrieved October 25, 2000 from: http://www.peacefire.org/error-rates/.

Haselton, B. (2000b). *Cyber Patrol error rate for 1,000 .com domains*. Retrieved October 25, 2000 from: http://www.peacefire.org/censorwa...atrol/first-1000-com-domains.html.

Haselton, B. (2000c). *SurfWatch error rate for first 1,000 .com domains*. Retrieved October 25, 2000 from: http://www.peacefire.org/censorwa...Watch/ first-1000-com-domains/html.

Haselton, B. (2000d). *Bess error rate for 1,000 .com domains*. Retrieved October 25, 2000 from: http://www.peacefire.org/censorware/BESS/second-1000-com-domains.html.

Haselton, B. (2000e). *SafeServer error rate for first 1,000 .com domains*. Retrieved October 25, 2000 from: http://www.peacefire.org/censorwa...Proof/ first–1000-com-domains.html.

Haselton, B. (2000f). *BAIR "image filtering" has 0% accuracy rate*. Retrieved May 5, 2001 from: http://peacefire.org/censorware/BAIR/first-report.6-6-2000.html.

Copyright © 2003, Idea Group Inc. Copying or distributing in print or electronic forms without written permission of Idea Group Inc. is prohibited.

Haselton, B. (2000g). *BAIR cannot distinguish between pictures of faces and pornographic images.* Retrieved February 3, 2001 from: http://peacefire.org/censorware/BAIR/second-report.7-19-2000.html.

Hochheiser, H. (1997). *Filtering FAQ.* Retrieved December 10, 2000 from: http://www.eff.org/pub/Censorship/Rati...ters_labelling/HTML/filtering_faq.html. Kennington, A. (2000). *Internet censorship.* Retrieved from http://www.topology.org/net/censor.html.

Kohntopp, K. & Kohntopp, M. (1999). *Content rating and selection does not work.* Retrieved June 20, 2000 from: http://www.Koehntopp.de/kris/artikel/rating_does_not_work.html.

Samaraline. (2001). *List of free anonymous proxy servers.* Available Online at: http://www.samair.ru/xwww/proxy.htm.

Sandy, G. (2000). Censorship of the Internet: Theories and Evidence of Pornographic Harm. In J. Barlow & M. Warren (Eds.), *Second Australian Institute of Computer Ethics Conference,* Imation (CD Rom).

Wayne. (2001). *Beating the Net Censor.* Retrieved March 2000 from: http://www.angelfire.com/wy/1waynes/bypassingCensorship.html.

Copyright © 2003, Idea Group Inc. Copying or distributing in print or electronic forms without written permission of Idea Group Inc. is prohibited.

Section II:

Ethics and Social Responsibility in the Information Age

Chapter VIII

What is the Social Responsibility in the Information Age? Maximising Profit?

Bernd Carsten Stahl
University College Dublin, Ireland

ABSTRACT

Social responsibility is a highly popular term, and it seems to be of importance to what is happening in the information age. In this paper, the notion of social responsibility is analysed and its relationship to the information age is discussed. The result is that, while the term social responsibility may make sense, it is imperative to clarify its definition before drawing any further conclusions from it. On this condition, talking about social responsibility can be helpful in expressing some of the normative questions of the information age. If a clear definition is lacking, however, it might be a better idea to forget about the term rather than come to a counterintuitive conclusion as the one hinted at in the title of the paper, namely that it is an expression of social responsibility to maximise profits.

Copyright © 2003, Idea Group Inc. Copying or distributing in print or electronic forms without written permission of Idea Group Inc. is prohibited.

INTRODUCTION

In one of the best-known and most discussed articles about the topic of social responsibility Milton Friedman (1970) argues that it is the social responsibility of businesses to increase their profits. His argument is that a functioning market will lead to optimal allocation of resources and to the maximisation of well-being. So, in effect, what business does is morally responsible anyway, and if we just let people do their job without interfering on the grounds of some misunderstood morality, then everything turns out for the best.

Friedman's article is usually met by ambivalent reactions. On the one hand, the argument does not seem to include any logical flaws and it is hard to see where he is going wrong. On the other hand, the conclusion that it is socially responsible to maximise one's profits seems counterintuitive. Business ethicists have frequently tried to show that Friedman is wrong by pointing to potential weaknesses in the argument and in the assumptions of the argument. In this paper we will not be able to follow these arguments but we will try to clarify one of the concepts used by Friedman, the concept of social responsibility. Friedman's view of the topic is an extreme one and it is certainly not universally recognised. However, up to this day it is frequently discussed. The example is useful because it shows that the term "social responsibility" itself is neither clear nor unequivocal. Different authors think of different things when they talk about social responsibility and it is far from clear whether the term is really meaningful. The purpose of this paper will therefore be to shed some light on the concept of social responsibility and to discuss what impact the information age might have on it. For this purpose, we will begin with a brief discussion of the concept of responsibility and analyse how it changes if the attribute "social" is added. From there we will proceed to see how information technology or computers change this concept, enlarge or decrease the scope and scale of it, and what social responsibility in the information age might mean. In doing this we hope to prove that the term "social responsibility in the information age" is not at all a trivial one. We will demonstrate that responsibility is a concept that by definition aims to lead to concrete results in dealing with normative problems. It can only have this effect if it is clarified and well defined. In this sense, the article tries to impose some responsibility on the debate about social responsibility.

RESPONSIBILITY

In order to find out what the meaning of social responsibility in the information age might be, we will first look at the definition of responsibility and, in a next step, discuss what the specific properties of social responsibility are.

A Definition of Responsibility

In the most general sense, responsibility is a process of ascription.[1] The purpose is to ascribe an object to a subject. The subject is what is named as the answer to

Copyright © 2003, Idea Group Inc. Copying or distributing in print or electronic forms without written permission of Idea Group Inc. is prohibited.

the question: "Who is responsible?"; the object answers the question "What is the subject responsible for?" Thus, if I say, "You are responsible for the accident," then I ascribe the accident (object) to you (subject). This ascription process is usually a social one and it involves more than just a subject and an object. There needs to be some kind of authority or instance to decide about the outcome of the imputation. In the case of legal responsibility, for example, this instance is the judge. The entire process is based on communication and it needs some sort of generally agreed upon normative background. These underlying norms can be social morality, the law, or any other set of rules that the affected parties can agree upon.

Responsibility can be described as a notion with a multitude of different meanings. Parents can be responsible for their children, the storm for the devastation, the criminal for the murder, the councillor for the decision of building a road, or the CEO for the economic success of the enterprise. Just looking at these five random examples shows that the term comprises many facets that sometimes seem not to have too much in common or can even appear contradictory. A closer look at the literature, however, shows that there are several aspects that most, if not all, responsibility ascriptions share. Responsibility transports normative contents but, in difference to many other moral philosophies, it does not insist on a particular material morality. One of the generally shared features is therefore its openness (Etchegoyen 1993; Kreikebaum 1996). Openness in this context means that responsibility ascriptions are always determined by the particular circumstances, by the persons and groups involved, by the relevant norms, etc. This openness is one of the reasons why the concept of responsibility has gained in importance over the last century. It can be argued that the appeal of responsibility is that it is applicable where traditional moral concepts, such as the idea of duty, lost their effectiveness due to their rigidity (Bayertz, 1995, p. 46). This is first of all the area of technical development. The rise of the importance of responsibility as a moral concept is closely linked with industrialisation and with the spread of technology to more and more areas of life. The openness of the term encompasses such characteristics as flexibility and reversibility. This means that responsibility ascription can take human fallibility into account. They apply norms in such a way and to the effect that mistakes can be compensated for.

Apart from openness, another characteristic of responsibility is its affinity to action (Staddon, 1999; Goodpaster & Matthews, 1982). Whenever we speak of responsibility there is an implication that this will lead to some sort of manifest result, to action being taken. When we speak of the parents' responsibility for their children, then the expectation is that the parents will act in such a way as to make sure that their children are safe or that they will reimburse the damage the children produced. When we speak of the politician's responsibility, then we imply that she will resign because of the scandal, or when we speak of the CEO's responsibility for the jump in earnings, then this implies that he will be rewarded for it. Responsibility thus is close to action and this action is inextricably linked to the purpose of the ascription. The purpose is usually to ascribe some sort of sanction, be they positive in the form of a

Copyright © 2003, Idea Group Inc. Copying or distributing in print or electronic forms without written permission of Idea Group Inc. is prohibited.

reward or negative in the form of punishment. In legal, as well as in moral responsibility, the negative side — the punishment — is generally in the centre of attention. The imposition of punishments usually follows some higher purpose, which tends to be the greater good, the facilitation and improvement of social existence.

This leads us to the third overarching characteristic that most sorts of responsibility share, the teleology, the fact that ascriptions are based on factual or expected consequences and less on intentions. This consequentialism often has an Aristotelian undertone, meaning that its ultimate aim is the good life. Whether the judge sentences the accused or public opinion holds a politician responsible, they are motivated by hope that it will make life better in the long run. Responsibility is thus, independent of its specific type, constellation, and realisation, a moral notion but one that implies a certain ethical theory, namely some sort of teleology or consequentialism.

Another point that is important to remember when talking about responsibility is that it is a social construct. There is no such thing as natural or universal responsibility. Every instance of responsibility is a social agreement that includes several parties and is thus subject to potential criticism by everybody involved. Responsibility ascriptions can only claim validity when there is at least a great majority of those affected who agree that it is legitimate. Furthermore, responsibility is never a neutral and purely descriptive category since it always involves some kind of accusation, defence, differing perceptions of realities and rules, and a final decision. The last characteristic of responsibility that seems important to mention is its formal nature. This has become clear in the other points discussed so far, but it is important to emphasise it again. Unlike other concepts that transport normative contents, responsibility is a term that leaves the concrete form of application of the norms open. In this sense it is close to most modern ethical theories from Kantianism to utilitarianism, which also act as formal checks of concrete morality rather than as generators of material norms. This is one of the great strengths of the term, which can be used to transport all different sorts of meanings. At the same time it is also a weakness of responsibility because it no longer allows a prediction of how a concrete ascription will turn out (with the possible exception of highly structured forms of responsibility such as legal responsibility).

If this is a general description of responsibility, then the next question is what defines social responsibility.

Social Responsibility

According to Webster's *New World Dictionary*, "social" means — among other things — "of or having to do with human beings in their living together." Following the description given above, one can see that responsibility is a social process. All responsibility ascriptions are social by definition and therefore the term "social responsibility" is a tautology and redundant. When people speak of social responsibility, however, they presumably want to say something that is not redundant and it is therefore worth asking what the "social" might mean. In order to find an

Copyright © 2003, Idea Group Inc. Copying or distributing in print or electronic forms without written permission of Idea Group Inc. is prohibited.

answer to this question it is helpful to go back to the definition and see which parts of it could be social or might warrant the distinction between individual and social.

All three of the basic dimensions, the subject, the object, and the instance or authority potentially have a social character. The usual subject of responsibility is the individual, the person. A person is someone who fulfils all of the conditions of being ascribed responsibility. She is adult, mentally and physically healthy, aware of her surroundings, acting intentionally, etc. This is the ideal case in which most philosophers admit that an ascription of responsibility makes sense. The problem of the person as the subject of responsibility is that in many of the relevant cases, there are no individuals who can justifiably be said to be the subject and thus responsible for a result. In the modern world governments, societies, companies, and organisations of all forms and sorts are making many, if not most, decisions. There is no single individual who is responsible for technological catastrophes like Chernobyl; there is no one who is individually responsible for global warming and the depletion of the ozone layer; and social developments, such as globalisation or the development of the Internet and e-commerce, cannot be ascribed to one single person either. Therefore, some authors have tried to broaden the concept of responsibility to permit collective subjects. These attempts are centred on medium-sized organisations that have certain characteristics, such as an internal decision structure, a clear organisational boundary, clearly defined objectives, and so forth. Several authors have come to the conclusion that such entities might be considered legitimate subjects of responsibility (cf. French 1972, 1979; Werhane, 1985).[2] In this area, we now find increasing discussions about questions like corporate citizenship and other questions of how collective responsibility in the meso-level of the organisation might lead to results.

Corporate social responsibility can be described as the predominant theory of business ethics in the 1960s and 1970s. It is an area where many different streams of thoughts converged which agreed on the fact that there is more to business than the simple mechanisms described and prescribed by neoclassical economics.

> *"Largely reacting to neoclassical economics, which holds that the sole responsibility of business is to maximize its immediate bottom line subject to only the most minimal constraints of the law, advocates of corporate social responsibility argued that ethical management requires more than merely following the dictates of the law or signals of the market, the two institutions that otherwise guide business behavior. Rather, ethical management is a process of anticipating both the law and the market — and for sound business reasons" (Stark, 1993, p. 39).*

Corporate social responsibility can thus be understood as a direct answer to the question asked in the title of this paper and it would answer it with a "no." The social responsibility in the information age cannot be solely to maximise profits. Proponents

Copyright © 2003, Idea Group Inc. Copying or distributing in print or electronic forms without written permission of Idea Group Inc. is prohibited.

of corporate social responsibility hold that companies, as socio-cultural entities, are many-facetted and therefore have responsibilities in many different areas. However, as became clear from the above quote by Stark, the whole concept is rather equivocal. It is usually agreed that corporate social responsibility takes care of all stakeholders such as employees, neighbouring communities, special interest groups, and many others (Husted & Allen, 2000). The aim is to take these groups' interests into account: first, because it is the good thing to do; and second, because it will be good for the company in the long run (Zadek, 1999). While this sort of reasoning is tempting for managers who see a chance of combining their business activities with their moral aspirations, it has been harshly criticised by business ethicists. If corporate social responsibility will indeed lead to an increase in the business environment by pacifying all of the stakeholders, it can be argued that it is just another management tool. It also means that in the case of a conflict between (long term) profit and (moral) responsibilities the profit will win again.

From the point of view that was developed so far, it is impossible to judge this discussion because the concept of responsibility does not by itself require this interpretation of corporate social responsibility, but it does not contradict it either. Responsibility — understood as the process of ascribing an object to a subject under the condition of openness with the aim of furthering the good life — is in principle open to the idea. The question is, of course, how this can be done when the subject is a collective entity such as a corporation, but we will return to this question later because the technological development may offer some new answers to it that might give a unique sense to the notion of social responsibility in the information age.

Another way of describing a genuine sort of social responsibility is looking at the instance. Depending on the sort of responsibility, it can be quite complicated to figure out who or what is considered as the instance. In the case of legal responsibility the instance is clear; it is the judge or the jury. For moral questions this is much less clear. One can hear suggestions ranging from God to conscience and, pertaining to our question, one possible instance is society. In a way, society is probably the instance in most cases that leads to clear results. When a judge sentences a perpetrator, she does so in the name of the people. When a politician has to accept the responsibility for some occurrence, he does so before the people. Even when we say that our neighbour is responsible for the dirt in our driveway, we refer to social rules and standards that are grounded in socially developed norms. In this sense all responsibility contains a reference to society and again social responsibility is nothing special.

Most people who talk about social responsibility probably associate something concerning the object of responsibility. Social responsibility can then mean that one is either responsible for society or parts of it, or that one is responsible with regard to society. Examples of social responsibility in this sense might be the president who is responsible for his subjects, the teacher who is responsible for the pupils in her class, or the engineer who is responsible for the safety of the bridge, given that members of society will use it. Of course the three dimensions are linked in practice

Copyright © 2003, Idea Group Inc. Copying or distributing in print or electronic forms without written permission of Idea Group Inc. is prohibited.

and the social aspect of all of them interacts. If the engineer is responsible for the safety of the bridge in the face of society, then this means that he may eventually be judged and punished by society if he does not discharge his responsibility according to social expectations.

What we have see so far is that social responsibility can have many meanings and the next question will therefore be what, if anything, is special about it in the information age.

SOCIAL RESPONSIBILITY IN THE INFORMATION AGE

Information technology has several points of impact on responsibility in general, which I will discuss in the first part of this section. In the second part, I will then analyse whether any of these points are relevant in the case of social responsibility and what those consequences might be.

Responsibility and Information Technology

Information technology (IT) brings about changes in the way we perceive and realise responsibility. Some of these changes are clear-cut and obvious. Responsibility is, as was mentioned before, a social process during which an object is ascribed to a subject. This process is based on communication, which offers the first link to IT. The increase of potential scale and scope of communication and information is a precondition for a potential expansion of responsibility. Each user of IT in general, and of the Internet in particular, has the opportunity to communicate about topics that he or she is interested in, to create special interest groups, and to discuss topics of all sorts with fewer time and space restraints than ever before. We are therefore free to realise responsibility ascriptions concerning questions that would have been unavailable before. On the other hand, responsibility may change the nature of communication. It can blend out parts of it and it may distort what we perceive. So far, most of the computer-mediated communication relies heavily on written communication. The increasing use of multimedia technologies may change that in the future, but even then communication via IT is different to classic face-to-face communication.

Let as take a look at one example — e-teaching. Many colleges and universities are planning or implementing new courses or programmes, or changing existing structures, so as to incorporate the use of computers into teaching. While there is a lot to be said for and against this development it seems clear that it is not morally neutral.[3] Being in a seminar and listening to a lecturer or discussing issues with fellow students is categorically different from sitting in front of a computer and listening to recorded messages or even videoconferencing with other participants of a distance learning course. It is not only that the directness of contact changes, it also has to do

Copyright © 2003, Idea Group Inc. Copying or distributing in print or electronic forms without written permission of Idea Group Inc. is prohibited.

with many of the tacit assumptions that are being made. E-teaching applications, as we find them today, often aim at training students in specific subject matters and giving them clearly defined skills. A typical example that can be found in many universities is self-taught tutorials in computer applications where students learn how to work with specific hardware and software by following the instructions on the screen. While this may be helpful for learning these applications, it also sends other, more subtle messages. There are two groups of teaching theories, the constructivist and the objectivist theories, which are both based on metaphysical assumptions. The objectivist theory holds that there is an absolute reality, and truth consists in the correspondence between sentences and the underlying reality. Teaching thus means transmitting the knowledge about reality to learners. The constructivists, on the other hand, believe that reality is socially constructed, and that therefore teaching must incorporate and explain the process of constructing knowledge (Piccoli et al., 2001; Leidner & Jarvenpaa, 1995). While the use of IT in teaching can be aimed at both models (Alavi, Wheeler, & Valacich, 1995), it mostly assumes the objectivist position by positing a given truth that can be taught. This paragraph is not meant to be a critique of e-teaching, but rather it should demonstrate that the use of IT has implication on levels that we frequently do not consider. IT is not a value-neutral tool whose use is the only determinant of its moral value. The mere use already has further consequences that need to be considered.

With regards to responsibility this line of thought can be extended to the implications that IT use has on moral rules and ethical reflections. It is not possible to develop these considerations in full here, but one area where moral consequences of IT use become quite clear is the change of the moral quality in human interaction due to the mediation of computers.[4] Responsibility is a normative construct based on communication. Whenever the quality and quantity of communication changes, this will have direct repercussions on responsibility ascriptions. Some of the same thoughts that were developed with regards to e-teaching also apply to responsibility relationships. The use of computers favours a certain sort of communication, namely written communication, which can blend out some aspects that are relevant for responsibility. Non-verbal communication is sometimes said to carry the bulk of the information in face-to-face interaction. All these subtle cues are lost in computer-mediated communication (CMC). More dangerous yet is the fact that the nature of communication changes partly because of technical media. Following a communication theory like Habermas' (1981) one can state that the purpose of communication is successful social interaction. This includes much more than just factual information. Part of it is the constitution of a shared life-world, the determination of what shared objective truths are, what acceptable norms are, and whether speakers are authentic. The bartering about these different aspects of our world can be severely limited by CMC.

Another philosophical difficulty of CMC is that it suppresses the other from our considerations. The other — as the other human being, the abstract countenance of

Copyright © 2003, Idea Group Inc. Copying or distributing in print or electronic forms without written permission of Idea Group Inc. is prohibited.

humanity, the completely other such as death — is a cornerstone of several moral philosophies, predominantly of French origins (Ricoeur, 1990; Levinas, 1983). The idea that these approaches share is that the other, usually recognisable as someone like me but yet different, induces moral responsibility. Anecdotal evidence for the relevance of these ideas was given during the burst of the dot.com bubble, when allegedly many of the e-commerce *nouveaux riches* fired their former employees by email. In our context, this sort of behaviour could be interpreted as avoiding responsibility by avoiding having to face the other.

Finally, with regards to the interaction of computers and humans, there is the problem of the blurring of the boundaries between the two. The technology of any given age has always been used as a metaphor for the description of human beings. For the ancient Greek Atomists, human beings consisted of nothing but atoms. During the early enlightenment, with the success of newly discovered mechanics, humans became mechanical automatons. Accordingly, in the information age, human beings are increasingly seen as information processors. While this is not a bad thing per se, as long as the metaphor remains recognisable as such, there is a danger that people may start mixing up humans and information processors. Weizenbaum (1976) warned very early in the development of computers of the dangers of assigning tasks and attributes to them that originally belong to humans. His argument was that we lose our identity and dignity if we confer tasks to machines that define human beings, such as decision-making. Worse yet, and related to the problem of the disappearing other, is the fact that, in a world where humans mutate to information processors, there is no more need for morality. Computers that stop functioning can be replaced and the same can happen to humans if they are seen in this light. The fundamental ethical questions that constitute the basis of responsibility such as freedom, dignity, life and death, bodily existence, etc., lose their importance in the light of a changing portrait of humanity. In the worst case, responsibility will simply vanish because it is no longer needed.

Another possible impact that the information age can have on the subject of responsibility is that, increasingly, the question will be asked whether computers might be considered subjects or instances of responsibility. As subjects, they would be held responsible (a difficult idea that I cannot discuss here) (see Stahl, 2001). As instances, they would decide about who is wrong or right (another philosophically contentious thought which I do not have the space to discuss).

The most widely discussed aspect of IT and responsibility, however, is the results IT produces, thus IT as an object of responsibility. IT changes the way we work and live, the way we communicate and perceive reality and ourselves. These changes deeply affect our communities, our norms and morals, and they are thus objects of responsibility ascriptions. The entire field of computer ethics revolves around these questions and offers detailed discussions of questions like power and IT, problems of privacy, accuracy of data, intellectual property, problems of access, hacking, computer fraud, etc. IT as an object of responsibility can be divided into

Copyright © 2003, Idea Group Inc. Copying or distributing in print or electronic forms without written permission of Idea Group Inc. is prohibited.

responsibility because of IT and responsibility for IT. In the first case, responsibility ascriptions become necessary because of a development caused or intensified by IT. Most of the list just enumerated can play a role here. Privacy, for example, is a moral (and legal) problem that is not originally caused by IT, but its social importance has been increased by the fact that IT facilitates infringements. Similar statements can be made for intellectual property, fraud etc. In these cases, the idea of responsibility because of IT is to find a subject to whom the object can be ascribed. With regards to privacy, this could, for example, be a data commissioner, whom we find in many European countries. With regards to intellectual property, a similar role could be held by institutions such as patent offices. The ascription could also aim at individuals, such as the hacker, who could be held responsible for hacking, or the inventor, who might be ascribed responsibility for the protection of her intellectual property. In economic situations this sort of responsibility will often fall on management. All of these examples show the shared characteristics of responsibility developed earlier on. They aim at an open process that will lead to consequences with the aim of improving the social life.

Responsibility for information technology is related to these other forms but it differs in its temporal dimension. While responsibility because of IT aims at rectifying problems and wrongs already incurred in the past, responsibility for IT points towards the future, towards avoiding problems that are to be expected. The different temporal aspect causes different modes of ascription and different sorts of responsibility. The retrospective kind of responsibility tends to aim at third parties and attributes blame or punishment. Its typical representative is legal responsibility, which only comes into effect *ex post* and whose effect tends to be negative sanctions. Prospective responsibility for IT, on the other side, tends to be rather positive, the sanctions often take the form of rewards and the ascriptions will generally be reflective rather than transitive. That means that responsibility is more likely to be assumed voluntarily and, due to its characteristic of being in the future, it is much more uncertain.

These two aspects of IT as an object of responsibility are, of course, related and refer to one another. In many cases retrospective responsibility ascriptions, in the sense of punishments, only make sense under the condition that a prospective responsibility existed beforehand. On the other hand, one of the main reasons for assigning or assuming prospective responsibility will often be the knowledge that there is a likelihood of retrospective responsibility ascriptions resulting from the consequences of an action. To make the difference clearer: Prospective responsibility might be assumed by a person of management rang, say the CIO. The CIO can assume responsibility for the development of the information infrastructure of an organisation and make sure that it corresponds to the long-term business strategy. In our terms this would be responsibility for IT. This responsibility is in a feedback relation with the responsibility that is to be expected ex post. If the CIO fails to deliver, then she may be sanctioned for that. At the same time, the discovery of responsibility problems that have to be dealt with ex post may lead to new ascriptions ex ante. If

Copyright © 2003, Idea Group Inc. Copying or distributing in print or electronic forms without written permission of Idea Group Inc. is prohibited.

management during the implementation process notices, for example, that a certain element, say ergonomics, has been neglected so far, then this can lead to the explicit ascription of responsibility for that element in the future.

Now that we have seen what social responsibility can mean, and we also know some of the effects that information technology can have on responsibility ascriptions in all of the major dimensions, the last aspect to be discussed is what the specificities of social responsibility in the information age are.

What is the Social Aspect of Responsibility in the Information Age?

Since we are not the first ones to think about this question, it may be helpful to look at the pertinent literature and, indeed, one can find that there is an organisation calling itself "Computer Professionals for Social Responsibility" (CPSR). This organisation, however, seems to have a narrow idea of what social responsibility in relation to information technology might be about. When the director of CPSR says during a speech before the American Congress that his organisation emphasises "individual accountability as the cornerstone of computer ethics" (Rotenberg 1995, p. 136), then this indicates a somewhat limited idea of the problems in question. It implies the theory of corporate social responsibility discussed earlier and makes the questionable assumption that individual human beings are best equipped to deal with it. Given what we know about responsibility so far, it seems sensible to look for a more satisfying answer to what social responsibility in the information age might mean.

In order to come closer to that goal, we will combine what was said so far about social responsibility, on the one hand, and responsibility and IT on the other hand. The purpose of this is to see which meanings the term "social responsibility in the information age" might have. The most promising approach to go about this is to work along the lines of the major dimension and see how they are affected.

Let us start with the subject. Social responsibility — understood as collective responsibility as described in the first part of this paper — is clearly related to modern organisational forms and these are in turn often based on technologies, especially IT. Computers and IT allow for new ways of interacting and communicating, and therefore they can facilitate the emergence of collectives as subjects. The obvious example for this is the corporation. IT helps the construction of this entity called the corporation, and therefore it helps make it a subject of responsibility. However, the use of IT brings about a change in organisations that are constituted faster than ever before. One can find discussions of this phenomenon under the heading of "virtual organisation." If one admits the corporation as a subject of quasi-moral responsibility, as we have suggested elsewhere (Stahl, 2000), then the question is: do we also admit virtual communities, corporations, or organisations?

Another problem with regard to the subject of responsibility is whether there is something like a collective subject consisting of the users of IT. Are, for example, all of the "netizens" responsible for the changes that happen in their name and

Copyright © 2003, Idea Group Inc. Copying or distributing in print or electronic forms without written permission of Idea Group Inc. is prohibited.

allegedly in their interest? It can be argued that the Internet changes not only the way we communicate, but also the way we do business, the way we educate ourselves, and much more (Schiller, 1999). These developments are of high moral relevance, and we have to ask whether this might be a case of social responsibility as collective responsibility. In a way, this seems a sensible idea because the users of IT are one of the driving forces behind it; and it can be argued that they should be held responsible for the developments that they cause. On the other hand, such a form of large group responsibility runs into several problems. The large and heterogeneous group of IT users, or IT developers or programmers, or any comparable group, lacks many of the characteristics traditionally associated with responsibility subjects. They do not act according to any collective plan, they have no collective aim, and they cannot even be punished or rewarded collectively.

The next example of where one might talk of social responsibility is where a social entity is the object of responsibility. As mentioned before, one can be responsible for one's children, for the pupils in one's class, for one's colleagues, for the members of a given society or for humanity. These are mostly examples of role responsibility, since the parent is responsible for her children, the teacher for the pupils, the president for his people, and nobody (apparently) for humanity. Of course one can also feel responsibility for social beings outside of one's roles. How does this change in the information age? Again the most important impact is that many of us have more information than ever before and thus more ways of being aware of possible responsibilities. We may also find new ways of discharging our responsibilities in the information society. The American President's response to the terrorist attacks in New York and Washington was first the use of mass media to communicate with the American people. This was certainly a typical, if drastic example, of social responsibility in the information age.

Another interesting aspect is whether the adjective "social" changes anything about responsibility because of, or for, information technology. In fact, the idea of social responsibility seems to open new aspects of potential responsibilities in this respect. While traditionally IT as an object of responsibility is a quite limited term because of the subject's limits of knowledge and power, the scope of responsibility might be widened by conceiving it as a social task. What this means is the following. An individual human being has only a very limited capacity of being responsible, because she cannot possibly predict all of the results of her actions, she often lacks the power to change the course of history, and she may not even be aware of what she might be considered responsible for. Similar restrictions apply to collective entities such as corporations. Even large companies such as Microsoft or IBM only have a very limited grasp of the results that their actions cause, of potential moral problems, and of the way their products change the social fabric. Many of the problems caused by the use of IT and the advent of the information society are therefore outside of the reach of the classical subjects of responsibility. However, it seems quite clear that there are a lot of developments on the societal level that

Copyright © 2003, Idea Group Inc. Copying or distributing in print or electronic forms without written permission of Idea Group Inc. is prohibited.

responsibility should or could be ascribed for. The question now is whether there is such a thing as society's responsibility for, or because of, information technology. A tentative answer to this might be that, at least insofar as developments are predictable and can be influenced by societies or governments, one can stipulate the existence of such responsibility. This would probably constitute "social responsibility in the information age" in its purest form. What this social responsibility would look like is out of the scope of this paper. However, one thing seems quite probable, which is that it will encompass aspects of a responsibility of a second order, meaning responsibilities for the facilitation of responsibility. The idea is that social responsibility should not be seen as an excuse for the individual but quite the opposite, as enabling the individual or corporation to assume responsibility.

Finally, the social entity may act as the instance or authority of responsibility. We can be responsible in the face of a social group. This social group can be the basis of the moral norms that underlie the responsibility ascription and it can determine the sanctions that are the result of responsibility. This is what I believe to be the most commonly found example of social responsibility discussed in the literature. When an author speaks of social responsibility he or she often implies that the responsibility ascription in question is social because it happens in public. What happens to this in the information age? Obviously we again have to take into account the multiplicity of information channels. Due to information technology, a huge number of acts and their results are perceived in the public realm and can thus be called social.

The three dimensions and their impacts on social responsibility are, of course, not neatly divided, but they can be combined at will. One can, for example, imagine a case where, say, the computer programmers are held responsible for the Internet users in the face of society that can follow their acts on TV. This would be a case where responsibility has several links to social beings and to the information age at the same time. But where does all of this lead us?

CONCLUSION

The purpose of this paper was to analyse what social responsibility might mean and how it changes in the context of the information age. The result of this analysis is that social responsibility is at best a contentious topic. Responsibility viewed alone is already sufficiently complex and the addition of the attribute social does not make it easier to handle. Using the typical distinction of dimensions of responsibility, we demonstrated that social responsibility can have several meanings. These meanings are partly dependent on circumstances, and thus change in the information age. It can therefore make sense, and this is my first conclusion, to speak of social responsibility in the information age.

The second conclusion is that the acceptance of the idea of social responsibility does not suffice as a basis of discussion. Social responsibility in the information age can have different meanings and these have to be clearly defined if they are to be

Copyright © 2003, Idea Group Inc. Copying or distributing in print or electronic forms without written permission of Idea Group Inc. is prohibited.

useful. If we do not define the term clearly then the maximisation of profits can also be seen as an expression of social responsibility, a result that would probably be perceived as counterintuitive by most of us. This would then open the door to arguments, such as that cutting of jobs, reduction of benefits, etc., are all expressions of social responsibility. Thus, if the necessary clarity of the concept is lacking, it is probably more beneficial to simply forget about social responsibility than to talk about it.

However, all is not lost. A thorough analysis of the concept of responsibility allows us to draw several non-trivial conclusions with regards to social responsibility in the information age. First, the nature and character of responsibility has to be taken into consideration. That means that it must be clear that responsibility is a social construct used for ascribing an object to a subject. Responsibility ascriptions are not expressions of a material morality but a formal means for applying ethical theories to concrete problems. Second, the three characteristics of responsibility — openness, affinity to action, and consequentialism — should be kept in mind. They will apply to social responsibility in the information age, as well as to all other forms of responsibility. That means that the formal construct of responsibility should be checked with regards to its openness and consequences. If a given ascription lives up to these, then there is a good chance that it can live up to its implicit promise of delivering an improvement of our lives. The formal, open, and goal-oriented structure of responsibility makes it a good concept for dealing with problems of information technology, which shares the same characteristics. It is therefore a promising concept for dealing with moral issues in IT. However, it can only live up to this promise if the notion is made clear and the ascriptions are made in accordance.

In this sense, this paper can be viewed as an attempt to start a discussion about the content of social responsibility with the purpose of rendering the notion useful.

ENDNOTES

[1]   For a more detailed discussion of responsibility see the following texts: Bayertz (1995), Fischer (1999), French (1992), Lenk (1998), May/Hoffman (1991), Neuberg (1997), Paul et al. (1999), and Sänger (1991).

[2]   Most of theses thoughts refer to moral responsibility. In the case of legal responsibility the idea of a company as the subject is not new and organisations have been recognised as legal persons for a while.

[3]   For a discussion of the moral challenges arising from e-teaching see Stahl (2002a).

[4]   We have discussed these problems of the relationship of anthropology, responsibility, and IT in more detail in Stahl (2002b).

Copyright © 2003, Idea Group Inc. Copying or distributing in print or electronic forms without written permission of Idea Group Inc. is prohibited.

REFERENCES

Alavi, M., Wheeler, B. C. & Valacich, J. S. (1995). Using IT to reengineer business education: An exploratory investigation of collaborative telelearning. *MIS Quarterly, 19*(3), 293-312.

Bayertz, K. (ed.). (1995). *Verantwortung: Prinzip oder problem?* Darmstadt: Wissenschaftliche Buchgesellschaft.

Bechtel, W. (1985). Attributing responsibility to computer systems. *Metaphilosophy, 16*(4), 296-305.

Etchegoyen, A. (1993). *Le temps des responsables.* Paris: Editions Julliard.

Fischer, J. M. (1999). Recent work on moral responsibility. *Ethics, 110*(1), 93–139.

French, P. A. (1992). *Responsibility matters.* Lawrence, KA: University Press of Kansas.

French, P. A. (1979, July). The corporation as a moral person. *American Philosophical Quarterly*, 16(3), 207-215.

French, P. A. (Ed.). (1972). *Individual and collective responsibility - Massacre at My Lai.* Cambridge, MA: Schenkman Publishing Company.

Friedman, M. (1970, September 13). The social responsibility of business is to increase its profits. *The New York Times Magazine.*

Goodpaster, K. E. & Matthews, J. B., Jr. (1982, January/February). Can a corporation have a moral conscience? *Harvard Business Review*, 132-141

Habermas, J. (1981). Theorie des kommunikativen Handelns. Frankfurt, Germany: Suhrkamp Verlag.

Husted, B. W. & Allen, D. B. (2000). Is it ethical to use ethics as a strategy? *Journal of Business Ethics*, 27, 21-31.

Kreikebaum, H. (1996). *Grundlagen der Unternehmensethik.* Stuttgart: Schaeffer-Poeschel.

Leidner, D. E. & Jarvenapaa, S. L. (1995). The use of information technology to enhance management school education: A theoretical view. *MIS Quarterly, 19*(3), 265–291.

Lenk, H. (1998). Konkrete humanität: Vorlesungen über verantwortung und Menschlichkeit. Frankfurt, Germany: Suhrkamp Verlag.

Levinas, E. (1983). *Le temps et l'autre.* Paris: Quadrige/Presses Universitaires de France.

May, L. & Hoffman, S. (eds.) (1991). *Collective responsibility: Five decades of debate in theoretical and applied ethics.* Savage, MD: Rowman & Littlefield Publishers.

Neuberg, M. (ed.) (1997). *La responsabilité - questions philosophiques.* Paris: Presses Universitaires de France.

Paul, E. F., Miller, F. D., & Paul, J. (Eds.). (1999). *Responsibility.* Cambridge, MA: Cambridge University Press.

Copyright © 2003, Idea Group Inc. Copying or distributing in print or electronic forms without written permission of Idea Group Inc. is prohibited.

Piccoli, G., Ahmad, R., & Ives, B. (2001). Web-Based virtual learning environments: A research framework and a preliminary assessment of effectiveness in basic IT skills training. *MIS Quarterly, 25*(4), 401– 426.

Picht, G. (1991). Georg Picht: Die dimension der verantwortung. In M. Sänger (Ed.), *Arbeitstexte für den Unterricht: Verantwortung* (pp. 28-32)   Stuttgart: Philipp Reclam.

Ricoeur, P. (1990). *Soi-même comme un autre.* Paris: Edition du Seuil.

Rotenberg, M. (1995). Computer virus legislation. In D. G. Johnson & H. Nissenbaum (Eds.), *Computers, Ethics and Social Values* (pp. 135-147). Upper Saddle River, NJ: Prentice Hall.

Sänger, M. (ed.) (1991). *Arbeitstexte für den Unterricht: Verantwortung.* Stuttgart: Philipp Reclam.

Schiller, D. (1999). Digital capitalism — Networking the global market system. Cambridge, MA: MIT Press.

Staddon, J. (1999). On responsibility in science and law. In E. F. Paul, F. D. Miller, & J. Paul (Eds.), *Responsibility,* (pp. 146-174) Cambridge, MA: Cambridge University Press.

Stahl, B. C. (2000). Das kollektive Subjekt der Verantwortung. *Zeitschrift für Wirtschafts- und Unternehmensethik 1*(2), 225-236

Stahl, B. C. (2001, October 30-31). Constructing a brave new IT-World: Will the computer finally become a subject of responsibility? In *Proceedings of Constructing IS-Futures*, 11th BIT Conference, Manchester.

Stahl, B. C. (2002a, March 25-27). Ethical issues in e-teaching — A theoretical framework. In G. King et al. (Eds.), *Proceedings of INSPIRE VII, Quality in Learning and Delivery Techniques,* (pp. 135-148) Limerick, Ireland: The British Computer Society.

Stahl, B. C. (2002b, January 7-10). Information technology, responsibility, and anthropology. In *Proceedings of the 35th Hawaiian Conference on Systems Sciences.* Hawaii.

Stark, A. (1993). What is the matter with business ethics? *Harvard Business Review, 71*(3), 38-48.

Stewart, I. (1997). Mathematische Unterhaltungen. *Spektrum der Wissenschaft, 07.*

Weizenbaum, J. (1976). *Computer power and human reason.* San Francisco, CA: W. H. Freeman and Company.

Werhane, P. (1985). *Persons, rights, and corporations.* Englewood Cliffs, NJ: Prentice-Hall.

Zadek, S. (1999, June 3-4). Can corporations be civil? Presentation given at *Dezentralisierung und weltweite Kooperation.* (3). Ethikforum Regio Bodensee, Konstanz, Germany.

Copyright © 2003, Idea Group Inc. Copying or distributing in print or electronic forms without written permission of Idea Group Inc. is prohibited.

Chapter IX

The Social Contract Revised: Obligation and Responsibility in the Information Society

Robert Joseph Skovira
Robert Morris University, USA

ABSTRACT

This chapter introduces the social contract as a basis for personal and corporate responsibility and obligation. I briefly discuss three perspectives on the nature of the social contract: the Hobbesean, the Lockean, and the Rousseauean. I discuss the idea that information technology and the information society are in the process of revising the social contract. It sees the Internet as a key transformer of the sense of the social contract. It ends with a discussion of three revisionary frames: virtual communitarianism, radical individualism, and social capitalism.

INTRODUCTION

This paper began as a discussion of obligation and responsibility within the frames of the social contract and the information society. The paper has evolved into a discussion of information technology as a cultural paradigm and the social contract.

Copyright © 2003, Idea Group Inc. Copying or distributing in print or electronic forms without written permission of Idea Group Inc. is prohibited.

The essay is about delineating versions of the social contract. The discussion sees the World Wide Web (in all its many evolving forms) as an artifact of the information technology paradigm and a phenomenon of the information society (others may call this the information age, or the digital age). I prefer information society; ages do not have any pretense to fostering or enhancing a social contract.

One final note here is that I find the constellation of social contract, ethics, law, information technology, and information society to be like a black hole. The notes I attempt here are written on the slippery slope of these ideas. Taking responsibility for behavior is based, in part, on a sense of obligation that shapes responsibility. A sense of obligation rests within the sense of a social contract. Being responsible, in the other part, is personal justification of behavior. Some may refer to this as a conscience. This also answers expectations derived from the social contract. For individuals and corporations in the information society, and conducting e-commerce activities, obligation and responsibility rest upon the sense of the social contract within the information society.

This essay raises the issue of a moral sense of taking responsibility for one's behavior and what this means to individuals or corporations living in the information society. In the literature of business ethics, there is a long tradition of discussion of the responsibility of corporations and individuals to the society of which they are a part.

Corporate and individual obligations are derived from a sense of social contract. The ethos of the Internet, the World Wide Web, and the information society contribute to and determine this sense of social contract. We must (we are obligated to) analyze and understand the conceptions of the social contract in the information society. We unfold the meaning of social contract. What are the notions of the information society and the social contract and how do we need to analyze and understand them? What does the idea of a social contract mean within the frame of information society?

Social responsibility and business practices are linked in corporate behavior. Corporate and personal behaviors are expressive of the conjunction of responsibility and obligation and business practices. Business practices are habitual ways and means of doing business, buying and selling. The business world expects actions that are accountable and that carry out agreed upon tasks. Usually these accountable and obligated behaviors are explicitly stated in legal contracts. But even the legalized versions that enforce responsible and expected actions are dependent upon expectations of a moral worldview of the social contract. The practices of e-commerce and eBusiness should satisfy the behavioral expectations of the same moral worldview. However, in the brave new world of e-commerce, the view is much more stark. In this digital world of business practices, the prevailing perception is Darwinian, where corporate and personal survival may be a matter of innovative practices adapting the firm or the person to the digital business circumstances. Digital Darwinism is a phenomenon of doing business on the World Wide Web. This discussion of

Copyright © 2003, Idea Group Inc. Copying or distributing in print or electronic forms without written permission of Idea Group Inc. is prohibited.

responsibility and obligation delves into the contextual foundation of behaviors and expectations of behavior among World Wide Web sojourners.

A SENSE OF OBLIGATION AND RESPONSIBILITY

So even as these notes have moved away from discussing obligations and responsibilities, we find that we should say something about them. Obligations and responsibilities are a major influence on our everyday give-and-take with others. They might be explanatory constructs for judgments about behavior. While some obligations and responsibilities are shaped into legal contracts, many that govern the daily situations in which we find ourselves never see the light-of-day.

In our locales, we make sense of our transactions by casting our behavioral reasons as obligations and responsibilities. This state-of-affairs is more than likely a cultural thing. Moral behavior is a cultural artifact. So also are responsibility and a sense of duty. So too is the notion of social contract. The cultural context is, in a general way, the national culture of the United States of America, but that is too general and nebulous. Responsible behavior is always local behavior and always personal.

Information technology, in the guise of the World Wide Web, and its companion paradigm, information society, confounds this view of the immediacy of responsibility and obligation. Local sensibilities become global (universal). In becoming universal, they become anonymous and impersonal. These explanatory moral and social constructs drift and blur as they move into cyberspace. They are no longer anchored in the rocky harbor of everyday existence. Responsible behavior — as is the sense of obligation — are logical constructs in cyberspace, a matter of language. And while language use is a form of action in the world, in cyberspace it is the only way to act.

The lens of information technology, which we use to see the constructs of responsibility and obligation, is complex. Actually, as we will discuss later, there are several different lenses. They refract things differently. If information technology is a morally neutral state-of-affairs or if it is its own ideological paradigm, or a combination of these, then any behavior based on a social contract changes purpose. In either case, the issue of the social contract must be taken up. Obligations and responsibilities may be localized social and moral constructs arising from a communal sense and from the sensibility of persons in the flow of everydayness. Information technology in its many forms stretches the localized sensibilities to global proportions. There is an incipient universalism in information technology and its offspring, the information society.

Social circumstances and personal relationships are infused with obligations and responsibilities; they are the fabric of lived experience. Obligations are norms that structure human interaction and locate human relationships within a moral universe

Copyright © 2003, Idea Group Inc. Copying or distributing in print or electronic forms without written permission of Idea Group Inc. is prohibited.

of discourse. Obligations are normative structures of personal transaction within everyday situations. Obligations situate human relationships within a moral universe of discourse. Because information technology is a way of human interaction in corporate environments and personal contexts, the use and growth of information technology change collective obligations. Information technology is a mode of corporate and personal transaction across the Internet. Information technology affects the fulfillment of obligations and responsibilities. Information technology is a cultural force, a shaper of obligations and responsibilities. Information technology manipulates the social fabric, the social contract.

Social responsibility is related to a constellation of supporting values. Accountability within a social group functions effectively when private and confidential arenas of behavior are recognized. Being responsible carries an expectation of also being left alone. Other expectations that form the ground of responsibility and obligation are access to information and freedom to voice one's opinion. Ownership, physical and intellectual, also sets the stage for responsibility (Dhillon, 2002, p. 1).

Obligations and responsibilities are social expectations founded in the social contract. The social contract has a communal side and an individual side. Just as obligations and responsibilities are transactions based on expectations, so too is the social contract

PRIOR PERSPECTIVES ON THE SOCIAL CONTRACT

A social view of obligations and responsibilities is dependent upon a social contract. A social contract is an assumption that is needed to get things started. A social contract is usually implicit for any society and culture. The social contract is never written. Formal documents establishing a civil government are created after the societal establishment. A common understanding of how to act is assumed after the association of persons into a community. A social network, a society, is the basis for a developing culture or a society's pool of ways and means of living in the world. A social network is the occasion for a social contract; a social contract entails association. There are three conceptions of the social contract that western civilization usually discusses: the Hobbesean, the Lockean, and the Rousseauean. They are perspectives about the nature of society and human nature.

Hobbes

According to Thomas Hobbes (1988), persons who incorporate as a community constitute the establishment of a social contract. The social contract is a tacit affair formulating a communal association. The social contract is a tacit affair and constitutes the foundations of communal association.

Copyright © 2003, Idea Group Inc. Copying or distributing in print or electronic forms without written permission of Idea Group Inc. is prohibited.

Community is a natural restraint on humanity's natural perversity and propensity to selfishness and conflict. A community, and its social contract, is a result of self-interested preservation. The social contract that results from the incorporation means individuals must give up their natural rights. The social contract is the basis of societal authority, or the power of a society to sanction behavior. For Hobbes, the social contract, which is a substrate of any society, is an unnatural state of affairs. Individuals are intuitively selfish and prone to violence to achieve their selfish ends.

The social contract is a restraint on humanity's Darwinian-like tendency to reduce all interactions to power relationships and to coercion (Hobbes, 1988). The social contract is a consequence of alignments into social groups to overcome the natural predatory nature of human relationships outside the conventions of a social group. Hobbes argues that even within the social group, a higher authority is needed to enforce the rules, to sanction behavior, and to judge non-cooperative members of the society to be excomunicatio, or outlaws, beyond the pale of the group. Communal behavior replaces individualistic or egocentric behavior (Hobbes, 1988, pp. 87-89).

Social responsibility comes only with the agreement to the implicit and even explicit rules of a Hobbesean community: the social contract. Living an incorporated life means accepting the sanctions by the normative and legal systems of the society. Individuals, not for mutual safety but for personal safety, accept the dictates of a duly constituted governmental body (and if they do not accept these, the duly constituted governmental organization has the power, given in the social contract, to impose norms and laws). The social contract redefines the individual in accordance with the agreed upon and accepted norms and laws. The social contract confers the rights of citizenship and the duties — being responsive (responsible) to the now common or mutual interests (Hobbes, 1988, pp. 87-90; Solomon, 1992, pp. 174-175, p. 191; Solomon, 1993, p. 182; Halverson, 1972, pp. 60-61).

Locke

Persons begin, for Locke, with freedoms to act, to do what they will with their property, and to live as they see fit. All persons are equal to one another. This natural state of freedom and equality rests on the bed of natural law. When individuals agree to join in a community, a society, it is because certain affairs can be better managed and pursued. The convention that is a mutual agreement to become a community and political body. Government is a result of the social contract (Locke, 1960, pp. 393-396; Kendall, 1959, p. 64).

The social contract from a Lockean perspective on the surface appears similar to the Hobbesean notion. Persons freely agree to associate within a community. The community serves as a protective situation (Locke, p. 397). The social contract forms a basis for society and for society's civil government. Society exists as an organized free association of individuals. Government exists in, through, and for the community (Barker, p. vi, pp. xii-xiii, p. xxx). For Locke, government is the result of the social contract. But individuals do not give up natural rights, i.e., rights that people have

Copyright © 2003, Idea Group Inc. Copying or distributing in print or electronic forms without written permission of Idea Group Inc. is prohibited.

because of their humanity. The social contract for Locke is founded not on wild, savage existence, but on natural law, which posits certain rights for persons (Barker, p. xi). The notion of the social contract, according to Locke, is expressive of the values of freedom and fairness; power and coercion are not reasons for the social contract (Barker, p. vi).

Rousseau

For Rousseau, each person naturally tends to self-preservation and to maintenance of personal concerns. But no individual has any natural power or right to such over any other person. So socially agreed upon norms are the basis of any authority within a group. The social contract, the conventions of association, is a solution to the problematic situation created when persons band together to defend self and property (Rousseau, 1998, pp. 6-14).

For Rousseau, persons are naturally self-centered and aggressive. Society is established by agreement of individuals who are expected to give up any natural rights for rights founded in the collective. Individuals depend upon the community; the common will encompasses the individual will (Crocker, p. 35, pp. 45-46, pp. 55-57).

The social contract is the solution to the social problem of persons associating together to defend property and selves of all those agreeing to join the community. Membership in such a community means giving up natural tendencies, which Rousseau considered selfish. The act of joining others communally constructs the society and forms the ground of moral behavior. The community designates behavior as moral. Moral behavior is lawful behavior. Persons submit their personal will to the common will (Rousseau, 1998, pp. 9-15).

The Hobbesean and Rousseauean notions of social contract are collectivist while the Lockean idea of social contract is individualist.

INFORMATION TECHNOLOGY AS BASIC PARADIGM

Information technology is a metaphor, a slogan, and a descriptor of hardware and software applications to informational situations and flows, i.e., information systems, corporate or personal. From the home, to educational institutions, to medical institutions, to governmental venues, to legal circumstances, to business organizations, information technology shows up everywhere, in ubiquitous informational appliances. Information technology shows up in our use of cell phones. Information technology shows up in all manner of software applications: personal and business-oriented. Information technology shows up and transforms people into information workers or knowledge workers (even as information technology deskills). Information technology shows up in email and Internet connectivity, changing how we

Copyright © 2003, Idea Group Inc. Copying or distributing in print or electronic forms without written permission of Idea Group Inc. is prohibited.

communicate, with whom we communicate, and the frequency of communication. And we never just write or talk; we communicate.

Technology is an ideological stance that argues that all problems that are soluble are defined within technological space (Postrel, 1998, p. 16; Barbour, 1993, p. 3, p. 15). Technology or technologism is the application of a particular methodological approach and body of knowledge to problematic situations in order to resolve the situation to a desired end. This approach has a significant position in today's society as the only means to solving societal problems (in many individuals' opinion). Technology is not value free because technology is an intentional activity. Technologies are unique in terms of the adaptation of certain knowledge, processes, procedures, and materials to specific ends-in-view, and consequently embody the worldview or paradigm of their creators (Monsma, 1986, p. 25, pp. 31-34; Barbour, 1993, p. 14). Responsible living in today's world requires understanding technology (Monsma, 1986, p. 10, p. 14).

Information technology enhances accountability or responsibility in business affairs. Behavior is easily monitored and tracked, underscoring the habits of honesty and fairness (Galvin, 2000, pp. 97-99). Information technologists must be accountable for clarifying the costs and benefits of information technology for society (Stoll, 1999, p. xii).

Information technology is key to access to information. Information access is an important state-of-affairs. Information technology opens up societal structures and allows global access to the marketplace. Information technology provides for the inclusion of the disadvantaged in the global marketplace (Burn & Loch, 2001, pp. 5-6, p. 11).

There are several different views of information technology. They define our sensibilities of the use of information technology within our lives. One approach sees information technology as a mere tool, a subsystem within its socio-cultural environment. Societal members use information technology, but its use is framed by the cultural sensibilities of the users. Individuals and society are not constructs of information technology. A second approach is that information technology is the culture that orients the person and the society. Information technology, and technology in general, is the world in which we live, and by which we live, and through which we live. Our mode of being in the world is technological; everything is technique. A third approach, a hybrid of sorts, is that information technology, and technology in general, contributes in a major way to how we understand and live in the world, but it is only a facet of our experiences in the world. In different ways, and to varying degrees, these perspectives frame how we are. Each view is a different approach to understanding the mix of individual and community. Each approach frames, in a unique manner, a notion of the social contract. The use and consequences of information technology determine a view of the social contract and, hence, of the virtues of responsibility and obligation.

Because information technology insinuates itself into our social existence, there is some affect on the nature of the social contract. Information technology appears

Copyright © 2003, Idea Group Inc. Copying or distributing in print or electronic forms without written permission of Idea Group Inc. is prohibited.

in the guise of local and global interconnectivity (Friedman, 2000). We have become increasingly reliant upon information technology's presence. In many areas of corporate and personal living, information technology is the weave of everydayness; we exist as we do because of the information technology in place; we are information technology junkies.

One view of how information technology intrudes into life, work, and play defines information technology as a tool, or a set of tools, to handle the informational flows and situations of our daily lives, personal and institutional. This view considers information technology to be value-neutral. This frame of reference is a sub-frame of more inclusive frames of reference, forming a continuum from the personal through the institutional to the social; i.e., the cultural environment. Information technology is merely part of the cultural landscape, as is a car, or horse and wagon, or bicycle. As an instrumental part of the socio-cultural context, information technology is expressive of many of the core scientific values maintained by its socio-cultural matrix. Information technology is a cultural surrogate, representing the values of the society that has spawned it. The culture provides the framework for what is considered to be appropriate and inappropriate information technology use and information technology's consequences.

A second possible frame sees information technology as a socio-cultural force in information technology's own right. Information technology is an ideology. As a major socio-cultural frame, information technology embodies a set of values that is a catalyst in the transformation of the culture. This view sees information technology as providing a new context for living; information technology embodies a set of assumptions and constraints that shape the circumstances differently. An important assumption is that information technology, if deployed appropriately, solves social problems. Another assumption is that problems are technologically fixable. A basic constraint is that information technology defines the problem spaces.

These technological values represent major shifts in how human problems and issues are resolved. Information technology is a sub-frame of the societal, and is part of the socio-cultural dialectic. The dialectic changes to a monologue. This is an overwhelming perspective that, like an avalanche, carries everything away, utterly changing the cultural landscape forever. As a result, just as information technology is changing our personal views of reality, information technology is a transforming agent of our social lives.

This frame changes the notion of the social contract. Information technology also changes the nature of the social, spanning virtual communities, transforming businesses, recreating personal identities, etc. A cornerstone of this framework is the ability to digitalize anything and everything, and to collect, store, and retrieve anything as wanted. This information technology paradigm is the foundation of the information society.

A possible third frame of reference is a hybrid. This is a compromise. Information technology is a socio-cultural force, a sign of progress, but one that is and

Copyright © 2003, Idea Group Inc. Copying or distributing in print or electronic forms without written permission of Idea Group Inc. is prohibited.

can be managed and controlled. Information technology is embedded in information technology's cultural context or circumstances, but is also a change agent of information technology's context, especially in the business world. Information technology is also a change agent in the world of the Internet and the World Wide Web.

THE INTERNET AS eLEBENSWELT

To consider the ethics of the Internet, with all of the anonymity the network provides a user, the very issue of anonymity and the result of operating in a culture where there is no accountability needs to be addressed. Does this non-accountability skew the action of the participant, perhaps making them change their ethics? Isolation is the characteristic of Internet existence. Virtual experience is isolating experience (Stoll, 1995, pp. 57-58, p. 101).

The World Wide Web is a society that is intentionally created by its users. The technologists are accountable to raising and discussing any moral questions within their environment. Users of the World Wide Web must be self-regulators, according to accepted standards and rules (Berners-Lee, 1999, pp. 123-124, p. 137). The Internet is an electronic (digital) informational network of associated individuals whose ecology consists of social, technological, and political spheres of behavior (Chapman & Dhillon, 2002, p. 76).

The Internet, a.k.a., the information highway or the digital highway, as the interconnections of people and groups, is an ethos or cultural environment, as our interactions and our conversations demonstrate, even if they are electronic. Viewing the Internet and the World Wide Web as a cultural environment is especially the case if we are proponents of the second perspective on information technology. The Internet and the World Wide Web are manifestations of information technology as a cultural paradigm. Where there is a culture, there is a morality. Where there is a moral sense, there are obligations, duties, and responsibilities.

The World Wide Web has shrunk space in terms of access to informational sources. Users of the Web ignore where the information is stored. Further, our sense of time has changed. Immediacy is in. Informational access also means instantaneous access. Information technology has reformed our ethos, the place where we live. We now live and speak (and write) in cyberspace. Anyone can have a presence in cyberspace by having a web site. Having a web site means having the possibility of joining or being joined in conversations. This raises a basic issue about the new world we exist in: trust. Trust is based on a sense of authenticity of the voices in the discursive space of cyberspace. Joining a cyber-conversation, an e-conversation, broaches the problem of self-authentication. To believe the conversation, one must believe the conversationalist. One must trust and consider discourse in light of its perspective and ideology (Mitra, 2002, pp. 27-28; Palen, 2002, p. 79).

Copyright © 2003, Idea Group Inc. Copying or distributing in print or electronic forms without written permission of Idea Group Inc. is prohibited.

The Internet is viewed as a society of multiple local communities. These local communities embody the social and ethical values. Social relationships express the values. The values bind the relationships. The Internet is an expression of, or embodies a normative architecture. It is a structure for responsible self-governance. The architecture is made up of free choice, free speech, honesty, and openness or disclosure (Dyson, 1997, pp. 2-3). The many discussion lists, news groups, and all of the various web sites are expressive of this; they are subcultures of a subculture (the Internet).

Cyberspace is a different mode of being social. Cyberspace is a structure that is socially constructed by linguistic relationships and transactions. The Internet is as much a social construction of personal relationships as it is a matter of networks and computers. As an individual creates or recreates a social identity via the Internet, the social character of the Internet is formed. As individuals maintain their membership in social gatherings via the Internet, the ethical character of the Internet is formed. The Internet generates and maintains a sense of communal values.

The sense of anarchy, of lawlessness, or immorality arises from the instability of authentic self-identities. Persons may not be who they say they are. We have to accept what they say they are. That is why security has become a major issue on the Internet. Security concerns means a lack of trust. Self-identification is a movable feast, actually the consequence of gamers influencing the development of the Internet. Dissenting views are easily voiced. The outward manifestation of identity and even markers of social position are not there. We have to take a person's word for it, a person we do not know, and this is not something we do (Poster, 1995, pp. 135-136).

According to Stoll (1995, p. 9, pp. 21-28, pp. 30-33), the World Wide Web is hyped as the ultimate form of democratic life, but shows up more as a socially (and perhaps politically) anarchistic state-of-affairs. Much of this extreme individualism is adolescent attitude rendered as virtual identity and personality (Stoll, 1995, pp. 56-57; Turkel, 1995). On the Internet and the World Wide Web, a rugged individualism prevails with anarchistic tendencies. Gates (1995, pp. 7-8) once referred to this mentality as frontier-like. The Internet is a subversive social network, an electronic ideology that is revolutionary for civil governments, as they are currently constituted (Negroponte, 1995, p. 7). The Internet, as a world-wide social state-of-affairs, that follows anarchist and libertarian ideologies in a nebulous and incoherent way, appears as the ultimate experience of democratic living (Kinney, 1995, p. 94; Stoll, 1995, p. 31).

The information highway, the Internet and World Wide Web, reflect a new social contract. This new social contract is evolving in terms of the so-called netiquette. As the World Wide Web becomes the new town meeting, a new social contract is being created (Gates, 1995, p. 161). The new social contract is digital and, while its major focii are about decentralization and world-wide in scope, the social contract is also about harmony and empowerment (Negroponte, 1995, pp. 228-229). Cyberspace creates a different social contract (Poster, 1995, p. 136).

Copyright © 2003, Idea Group Inc. Copying or distributing in print or electronic forms without written permission of Idea Group Inc. is prohibited.

The Internet and World Wide Web provide a different view of the public sphere of behavior. Persons creating Web sites for personal use, especially, and business use, to a smaller degree, place their ideas, as text and pictures, into a public arena. The Internet and World Wide Web are public places for the display of subjectivity. The act of display recreates the subjective meanings in an objective, albeit electronic space. Whatever may be considered private does not show up on the Web. Privacy is an offline consideration (Rothstein, 1996, p. C21).

The Web is still in the process of shaping new understandings of everyday objects such as documents, images, and books. Being an author on the Web is also being reconsidered, as is also what it means to be a teacher or publisher. The Internet necessarily has forced a wider sense of these roles. The focus is now on the act of teaching or the act of publishing. Consequently, because the views of these behaviors have changed, the conceptions of intellectual property are in the process of changing. If everything placed on the Web, or written in emails, is public in some fashion, ownership is an illusion. The notion of copyright, as currently conceived in terms or paper and electronic formats, appears to be outmoded and is being reformulated by actual practices on the Web (Gates, 1995, p. 178; Negroponte, 1995, p. 58).

This communal sensibility forms the digital society (commonly called the information society). This social network of like-minded Websters is a dynamic and growing force. It is a decentralized social grouping and world-wide in reach. The digital society, the Internet, is a global, social and economic source of power (Negroponte, 1995, pp. 228-229). The globalization of social discourse and the subsequent natural unfolding of electronic local communities will be an alternative perspective on government. The Internet's character reflects a cooperative sensibility that can arise out of a decentralized and chaotic social network, where no one is in charge.

The Internet as a world-wide social network, based on commonly held views, supported by a sense of trustworthiness of personal transactions, provides a moral mode of being in cyberspace. As a world-wide community whose members are from differing cultures and backgrounds, the Internet provides an interesting experiment in universal morality, even if there may not always be perfect harmony of some electronic ethical stances. The Internet, as a social network of persons who seem to share common values, is a source of moral agency and a social contract of sorts.

The interpersonal discourse among individuals on the Internet transform the digital network into a social network. At the base of these Internet transactions is a growing sense of trust. Trust is an essential virtue of online discourse and building of community. Trust is also an ingredient that supports persons sharing all manner of information about themselves. A networked community of similar thinking people develops via the Internet (Rheinghold, 1993, p. 49, p. 166; Negroponte, 1996, p. 286).

Even while a seemingly new view of the social contract is represented by social behavior in cyberspace, there is an egocentric sensibility that prevails in this new social space and time. Discourse is always about information. Information access

Copyright © 2003, Idea Group Inc. Copying or distributing in print or electronic forms without written permission of Idea Group Inc. is prohibited.

and use are individualized. Social networks consist of individuals. Individuals will want to control and manage the information flows and their interactions with these information flows (Coleman, 1998, p. 90).

The person exists as a digital being, egocentric and seeking personal satisfaction within the webs of social discourse on the Internet (Negroponte, 1995, pp. 164-165). Despite the interconnectivity and communal behavior, cyberspace is a place of a heightened sense of privacy. At least so it seems. Isolation may be a more appropriate term to use. Perhaps the openness of the interconnectivities fosters this desire for privacy. An expectation of individual privacy holds as long as the individual can trust the social group or the organization. There is an implicit arrangement between the individual and the organization; trust is another name for this arrangement (Dhillon & Moores, 2002, p. 68).

The Internet is the cyber-social structure of the new digital community. Any network's value resides in the communal sense created through the informational flows themselves. The World Wide Web is about the constitution of a global society; information access is only a part of the world-wide communal development. The World Wide Web fosters discourse among its users; discourse is always social. Electronic communities develop over time in the conversations and the interactions across the Internet. Networked personal relationships grow into communal sensibilities in cyberspace (Negroponte, 1995, p. 183; Rheinghold, 1993, p. 5). The World Wide Web use signals a rise of digital democracy. This idea is problematic and based on information access. It is questionable whether the Internet can be democratic and preserve individual privacy (Papazafeiropoulou & Pouloudi, 2002, pp. 145-146).

INFORMATION SOCIETY AS FRAME OF REFERENCE

The Information Society is an important aspect of the discussion about social responsibility. According to Vannear Bush, this era began at the end of WWII. However, it is important to attempt to determine how the information society shows up in people's lives. One way it shows up is the ever-growing technological presence and use of computer information systems and computer networks. This is probably unremarkable. But, the infusion of technology into every aspect of existence gives rise to the notion of technological determinism. This is simply that technology changes and determines not only the socio-cultural environment, but also human thinking (Webster 1995, pp. 7-10).

The information society is a globalized world (Friedman, 2000, p. 9). The information society is a way of describing the global connectivity of commercial interests, governmental venues, as well as individual and personal ways of being linked around the world (Friedman, 2000, p. 50). The information society exists globally in the digitalization of all societal and personal affairs, whether it is the economic world, or the educational world (Friedman, 2000, pp. 48-49).

Copyright © 2003, Idea Group Inc. Copying or distributing in print or electronic forms without written permission of Idea Group Inc. is prohibited.

The information society [although some argue that the type of society we live in is knowledge-based (Drucker, 1994)], is the perspective that reality is information based; it is digital. Information is in the details. All details are equal. Informative details require an interpretative framework. Digitized information, such as email, managerial reports, and the content of Web sites, is not always contextualized. Furthermore, information can be easily abstracted from its context. We are mesmerized by the details, not understanding their significance because we are immersed in them; we have become informationalized (Heim, 1993, p. 10).

Reality, the world, is informational flows. Or, more accurately, the information society is an information field or space (Liu, 2000, p. 7). The information society is a global information system, embodied in the Internet and the World Wide Web. There are several ways of defining information society.

The information society is signified by the individual — the personal — within communities of use or practice whose mode of existence is informational. They are information systems or situations. The individual or the person is an informational entity; a person is informationally in the world. The world is an informational universe, a.k.a., World Wide Web. A community of practice is a social network self-organized in the informational way of being in the world. The social group is founded on the information and the knowledge that are needed to pursue a specific goal (Harney, 2002, pp. 52-53).

The information society shows up in the ever-growing technological presence and use of computer information systems and computer networks. This configuration of information technology changes and determines not only the socio-cultural environment, but also human thinking (Webster, 1995, pp. 7-10). Information technology reduces the social aspects of human interaction to nothing more than individuals and information flows (Borgmann, 1999, pp. 204-208). Society is nothing but information and people (Brown, 2000, p. 22). Ultimately, even people exist as information entities. Information is the focus of everything; it is everything (Brown, 2000, p. 31). The information society is not a mass society. Because informational flows are the basis, society is not centralized; there is a diffusion of information (Brown, 2000, p. 22). Information access is a significant issue for the existence of the information society (Burn & Loch, 2002, p. 14).

The information society is about the ability and willingness to collect, in digital format, everything. The information society is the presence of digital economic and financial markets worldwide. The rise and commercialization of the Internet is the most significant event in the construction of the information society. The Internet signals the democratization of information flows globally. Information technology is available worldwide. Worldwide connectivity is the information society.

Because it is now possible to not only collect but store large amounts of information about anything, this information suddenly becomes valuable. It can be sold or exchanged. Information is a commodity. Further, information is a commodity

Copyright © 2003, Idea Group Inc. Copying or distributing in print or electronic forms without written permission of Idea Group Inc. is prohibited.

because information workers produce it. Making information is an economic activity (Webster, 1995, pp. 10-13; Friedman, 2000, pp. 77-79). Information technology is a mode of acting in the information society. In the past, wealth was based on property or labor, but now information is the foundation of wealth. The information society, with its electronic marketplace, is a creator of new wealth (Boar, 2000, February 9, p. 14, p. 16).

The information society is also defined by the governmental occupational classifications of workers in today's rationalistic society. The job category of information worker suggests the existence of the information society (Webster, 1995, pp. 13-17). The presence of computers and the Internet in the workplace has turned employees into users and producers of information. Capturing, recording, and retrieving information are daily tasks. The digitization of information creates information workers.

The presence of the Internet, electronic mail, and the World Wide Web create new spatial and temporal dimensions of human reality. The information society is cyberspace and virtual reality. Open access to information changes how we interact with others and view the world (Friedman, 2000, p. 61). The information society signals a new lebenswelt (Webster, 1995, pp. 18-20).

For example, prior to the information society in the form of the Internet and the use of email to connect locales, individuals may have corresponded with friends in other countries using letters sent via air-mail. This was laborious and time consuming. Letters would take months to arrive. The interconnectivity was very loose. The advent of email (as a result of Internet connectivity) fostered a growth in correspondence between individuals. Now it is possible to carry on conversations via email between the U.S. and Slovakia (as an example) in the time of a few seconds. When the virtual social relationship is bolstered by actual visits between friends, the sense of community (as an aspect of the information society) is enhanced. The world has changed. In the information society, a friend is only an email, and a second, away.

The information society actually consists of local informational spaces that become the lived world (lebenswelt) of many people (Brown, 2000, p. 39). Cyberspace and virtual reality are both informational spaces. In this world, cyberspace or virtual world, culture is technology and informational flows (Borsook, 2000, p. 117). Culture is informational space. The traditional boundaries between the political sphere, culture, national security, business and financial markets disappear in the information society (Friedman, 2000, p. 20).

The basic cultural metaphor for the information society is digital. The neighborhoods are digital; physical place is irrelevant (Negroponte, 1995, pp. 228-229; Stoll, 1995, p. 3, p. 50). Individuals in the information society are not restrained by national or natural borders; they are crossed with virtual impunity. Individuals are not confined to one physical place when they can ride the informational waves to other places in the world (Borsook, 2000, p. 155).

In the information society, social identities and roles are redefined both locally and globally (Dyson, 1999, p. 2). Information is personalized; there is an audience of

Copyright © 2003, Idea Group Inc. Copying or distributing in print or electronic forms without written permission of Idea Group Inc. is prohibited.

one (Negroponte, 1995, p. 164). Personal identity is a matter of information. A person can be, digitally, anyone he or she wants to be. This identity formation is solipsistic (Stoll, 1995, pp. 57-58). The social sensibilities and human bonding that normally help form human personality are not present, except informationally. There is no physical social presence or group. Presence is linguistic. Presence is virtual (translated: unreal presence) (Brown, 2000, p. 77). Human identity is information dependent; identity is the personal information on file in governmental and corporate databases (Rheingold, 1993, p. 169; Turkel, 1995). A person also exists on the informational level. Personal information is acquired and stored in corporate and governmental databases. This information is the person in the information society. In cyberspace, existence is in the informative details that presume to capture how a person is in the world. Confidentiality of personal information is a major moral problem and is a common expectation of the citizens of the information society (Henderson, Snyder, & Byrd, 2002, p. 91).

The information society exists in the rise of new media (mostly visual and supposedly interactive). Consciousness is on the screen; we project our image of self into the screen's display. We watch soccer, hockey, and baseball (in the U.S.) instead of actually playing it. We experience the wilds of Africa, its sights and sounds (but no smell) through the World Wide Web and multimedia shows. Cultural significance (culture itself) is created and maintained on a CD (Webster, 1995, pp. 21-27).

No matter what set of markers constitute the attributes of information society, the pervasive and invasive effects of information technology have dramatically changed our lives and our worldviews (Webster, 1995, p. 182).

The information society's worldview is the information technology paradigm or ideology that technology is culture. Contemporary life for citizens in the information society is digital behavior. Cultural behavior in the information society is the semantic behavior associated with digital existence (Borsook, 2000, pp. 117-119).

THE eSOCIAL CONTRACT

The eSocial contract is digital. But this is merely metaphoric. The digital social contract resides in the expectations, assumptions, and constraints of online behavior, namely conversations carried on in emails, chat rooms, and instant messaging services. It resides in guest books and other forms of relationship building on the Web. The forms of behavior on the Internet still rely on the tacit conventions of right or appropriate behavior, at the right times, in the right places, to the right people. Moreover, being responsible in the digital world is being genuine and trustworthy. The revised eSocial contract supports in cyberspace being authentic in an environment where being inauthentic is easy. There is an unexpressed connection between anonymity and inauthenticity. This revision of the social contract in cyberspace has

Copyright © 2003, Idea Group Inc. Copying or distributing in print or electronic forms without written permission of Idea Group Inc. is prohibited.

at least three different faces to show the world. They are virtual communitarianism, radical individualism, and social capitalism.

Virtual Communitarianism and Social Contract

Davenport (2002, pp. 33-35) argues that, contrary to the commonly accepted value of anonymity of the ethos of virtual communities, anonymity does not lead to responsible behavior. A social network, community or society must have some hierarchical set-up to guide and manage affairs so that transactions are fair and just. Responsibility maintains claims of rights and freedoms. The consequences of anonymity are inappropriate behaviors that take advantage of the situation.

Responsible behavior is trustworthy because it is public or visible behavior. Public behavior is framed by the purpose of public space (or the virtual community, or cyberspace), and what the public space has been created for, i.e., an expectation that behavior is not anonymous or private in the midst of social networks (Erickson et al., 2002, p. 44).

Virtual communities are communities of practice, which are constituted by a set of expectations. These expectations are the netiquette values of reciprocity and trust; people helping people (Blanchard & Horan, 2000, pp. 11-12, p. 14; Stoll, 1995, pp. 112-113).

Each virtual community generates its own set of sanctioned online behaviors and underlying policies. A virtual community has jurisdiction only over individuals who freely elect to join the group. A community has no right of authority over outsiders. Such normative prescriptions freely entered into have more moral force than civil governments (Dyson, 1997, p. 9). Communal norms or rules are tacit and implicit in the relationships that create the group and remain so until individuals abuse them or raise issues that make the normative structures visible. Resolution of alienating conflict is arrived at by consensus. Dyson proposes a few rules for virtual communal living. First, each member, although free to join and free to leave, belongs because of recognizable benefits and costs. Virtual communities are intentional communities. Second, the communal boundaries are obvious and straight-forward. Community identity markers are apparent. A boundaryless community makes no sense. A poet could have written that, besides making good neighbors, good fences make good members. Third, leaving a community would be difficult because of the cost of belonging. By imposing a cost of investiture on new members, the social group imposes a cost if a member wishes to terminate membership. Fourth, communal behavior ought to be rule-governed, and sanctions of inappropriate behavior are available to punish offenders (Dyson, 1997, pp. 37-38).

Members of virtual communities decide about the honesty of e-conversations of their fellow Netizens. The rhetoric force of the conversations is grounded in the conversational space, the virtual community. Engaging in virtual discourse of a virtual community means to trust the various conversational actors on the basis of the semantics (Mitra, 2002, pp. 28-29).

Copyright © 2003, Idea Group Inc. Copying or distributing in print or electronic forms without written permission of Idea Group Inc. is prohibited.

Radical Individualism and Social Contract

The Internet constructs a social contract for the empowering of individuals. It is also a basis for autonomy. This social contract is an agreement in support of anarchy (Kinney, 1995, pp. 94-95).

Digital Darwinism is an approach that argues that the economic, biological, and the Internet environments influence one another. These spheres of influence are evolutionary. Evolutionary change is a consequence of technological change. Technological adaptation to its environment means pushing adaptation in societal and economic spheres (Stewart & Williams, 2000, p. 50). The World Wide Web encapsulates the economic and the biological. The Internet is basically an environment where a survivor mentality ensures, for the day, the existence of the individual and perhaps the group. This view pertains to the World Wide Web as a business domain and a global marketplace (Schwartz, 1999, pp. 3-4). To counter extinction of Web-based commerce, constant innovation or adaptation to the environment is in order. Innovation aims at the individual and the specialized, to unbridled desires and greed (Schwartz, 1999, p. 8, pp. 17-18; Borsook, 2000, pp. 42, 46).

Radical individualism, or political libertarianism, is political egoism. Persons of such ilk ideologically follow or admit to communal beliefs in the information society or any of the many virtual communities. Those who espouse technolibertarian ideals view existence on the Web (and what else is there) in technoeconomic terms. Innovation is analogous to biological and genetic adaptation and modification. Thus the person self-selects membership in, or out of, the information society. Thus the inability to maintain an Internet presence, to be competitive, is a form of natural selection. Only the innovative and competitive survive (Borsook, 2000, p. 10, p. 32).

The worldview of the individualist or egoist (the technolibertarian) holds human nature to be a model of rational economic behavior always guided by enlightened self-interest (or a self-interest framed by greed). The individual is responsible or accountable for holding his or her way within the virtual marketplaces in cyberspace. Digital existence is a matter of being able to compete, i.e., to innovate and adapt to the situation. This worldview does not believe in an implicit social contract about expected appropriate behavior in social groups, electronic or otherwise [unless you count enlightened self-interest (Borsook, 2000, p. 110)].

The technolibertarians are asocial and do not want (as their ideology) to balance individualism, even in its extremes, against any virtual communal membership. Self-reliance and independent action is the individualist approach to Internet behavior (Borsook, 2000, pp. 216-217, p. 237; Kinney, 1995, p. 92).

The political form of technolibertarianism is an ideology that fosters self-regulation and the free market. Any form of government is viewed as repressive and ought to be done away with. The view is that government presents unnecessary obstruction to individuals (Borsook, 2000, p. 10). The philosophical approach to technolibertarianism is an ethos (Borsook, 2000, p. 15) that argues for individualism,

Copyright © 2003, Idea Group Inc. Copying or distributing in print or electronic forms without written permission of Idea Group Inc. is prohibited.

asocial behavior (Borsook, 2000, p. 90), self-selection, and self-organization (Borsook, 2000, p. 212). This ideology embraces digital Darwinism and sociobiology (Borsook, 2000, p. 42, p. 46)

Social Capitalism and Social Contract

Social contract is the substance of social capital. Social capital is the stuff of communal relationships. Community implies trust as an important element of social association. Societal endeavors are grounded in shared beliefs, mores, and free collaborative activities. Coming together in a social group to accomplish some shared purpose rests on a foundation of trust among the individuals. Such trust shows up in a common semantical universe and worldview (Cohen & Prusak, 2001, pp. 3-4, p. 9). The social contract is a tacit set of reciprocal expectations and commitments among individuals. The unspoken and unwritten obligations of social living show up in common trust and loyalty (Cohen & Prusak, 2001, pp. 13-14, p. 29). Trust also depends upon human character; social capital is a consequence of like-minded individuals living and working together in communities of practice or use (virtual communities).

Social relationships are personal and are important to the development of social capital, and hence reflective of the strength or force of the implicit social contract (Cohen & Prusak, 2001, pp. 30-37, p. 79). Collaboration and social dependency are aspects of social capital. Such behaviors rely on the implicit, but acted upon, promises, expectations, and benefits of the social contract joining persons into a social entity. The social contract is the tacit compact or set of conventions consisting of acceptable behaviors, commonly held beliefs, and the expectations of reciprocal benefits accruing between individuals and community (Cohen & Prusak, 2001, p. 81, pp. 143-145).

Social capital refers to implicit willingness of individuals to work together. An important element that shows up is trust. Social capital maintains communal behavior. Commonality of purpose is the stuff of social capital. Social networks are cooperative relationships (Preece, 2002, pp. 3-9).

CONCLUSION

This discussion has looked at the foundational contexts of behavioral expectations of travelers of the World Wide Web. Our own journey in this essay started with a discussion of responsibility and obligation. These notions were framed by the ideas of the social contract and the information society. The essay expanded into explorations of some previous views of the social contract and the fit of responsibility and obligation. A portion of the way involved a discussion of information technology as a cultural frame of reference. The essay envisaged the World Wide Web as an electronic lebenswelt. The Internet showed up as a major archeological find in our

Copyright © 2003, Idea Group Inc. Copying or distributing in print or electronic forms without written permission of Idea Group Inc. is prohibited.

digging through the information technology paradigm and the information society. The combinatorial constellation of social contract, ethics, information technology, the Internet, and the information society, when joined to the star of e-commerce, is still a black hole whose gravitational pull threatens to collapse all this to nothingness.

Responsible action and business practices are united in corporate behavior. Actions are accountable in their intent and their consequences. Such behaviors, both corporate and personal, assume the putative existence of a tacit but binding set of conventions: the social contract. Corporations and individuals conducting electronic forms of business rely upon this sensibility of right actions and trustworthiness to continue to do business in the information society. A sense of responsible business practices and obligations exists within the borders of the information society.

The only caveat to this is wondering about the bias of the social contract. The bias shows up in the global reach of the information society. One wonders about a Confucian version, or a Hindu version, or an Islamic version of the social contract (to name a few), and how these worldviews change the circumstances of the revised social contract of the information society. The moral sensibility about responsible behavior and fulfillment of obligations within the information society still remains an interesting issue.

REFERENCES

Barbour, J. (1993). *Ethics in an age of technology* (Vol. 2). New York: HarperCollins.

Berners-Lee, T. (1999). *Weaving the Web.* New York: HarperSanFransico/ HarperCollins.

Blanchard, A. & Horn, T. (2000). Virtual communities and social capital. In G. D. Garson (Ed.), *Social Dimensions of Information Technology,* (pp. 6-21) Hershey, PA: Idea Group Publishing.

Boar, B. (2000, February 9). The dawn of IT fighting. *Intelligent Enterprise, 3*(3), 14, 16, 18.

Borgmann, A. (1999). *Holding on to reality: The nature of information at the turn of the millennium.* Chicago, IL: University of Chicago Press.

Borsook, P. (2000). *Cyberselfish: A critical romp through the terribly libertarian culture of high tech.* New York: PublicAffairs.

Brown, J. S. & Dugwid, P. (2000). *The social life of information.* Boston, MA: Harvard Business School Press.

Burn, J. M. & Loch, K. D. (2001, October-December). The societal impact of the World Wide Web – Key changes for the 21ˢᵗ Century. *Information Resources Management Journal, 14*(4), 4-14.

Burn, J. M. & Loch, K.D. (2002). The societal impact of the world wide web—Key challenges for the 21ˢᵗ century. In G. S. Dhillon (Ed.), *Social Responsibility*

Copyright © 2003, Idea Group Inc. Copying or distributing in print or electronic forms without written permission of Idea Group Inc. is prohibited.

in the Information Age: Issues and Controversies (pp. 12-29) Hershey, PA: Idea Group Publishing.

Chapman, S. & Dhillon, G. S. (2002). Privacy and the internet: The case of DoubleClick, Inc. In G. S. Dhillon (Ed.), *Social Responsibility in the Information Age: Issues and Controversies* (pp. 75-88) Hershey, PA: Idea Group Publishing.

Coleman, A. D. (1998). *The digital evolution: Visual communication in the electronic age.* Tucson, AZ: Nazraeli Press.

Crocker, L. G. (1968). *Rousseau's social contract: An interpretative essay.* Cleveland, OH: The Press of Case Western Reserve University.

Davenport, D. (2002, April). Anonymity on the Internet: Why the price may be too high. *Communications of the ACM,* 45(4), 33-35.

Dhillon, G. S. (2002). Understanding social responsibility issues in the information age. In G. S. Dhillon (Ed.), *Social Responsibility in the Information Age: Issues and Controversies* (p. 1-11) Hershey, PA: Idea Group Publishing.

Dhillon, G. S. & Moores, T.T. (2002). Internet privacy: Interpreting key issues. In G. S. Dhillon (Ed.), *Social Responsibility in the Information Age: Issues and Controversies* (pp. 66-74) Hershey, PA: Idea Group Publishing.

Dhillon, G. S. & Moores, T.T. (2001, October-December). Internet privacy: Interpreting key issues. *Information Resources Management Journal, 14*(4), 33-37.

Drucker, P. F. (1994). *Post-capitalist society.* New York: HarperBusiness/HarperCollins.

Dyson, E. (1997). *Release 2.0: A design for living in the digital society.* New York: Broadway Books.

Erickson, T., Halverson, C., Kellog, W. A., Laff, M. & Wolf, T. (2002, April). Social translucence: Designing social infrastructures that make collective activity visible. *Communications of the ACM, 45* (4), 40-44.

Friedman, T. L. (2000). *The lexus and the olive tree.* New York: Anchor Books/Random House.

Galvin, J. (2000, June). The new business ethics. *Smart Business for the New Economy, 13* (6), 86-90, 92, 94, 97, 98-99.

Gates, B. (1995). *The road ahead.* New York: Penguin.

Halverson, W. H. (1972). *A concise introduction to philosophy.* New York: Random House.

Heim, M. (1993). *The metaphysics of virtual reality.* Oxford, UK: Oxford University Press.

Henderson, S. C., Snyder, C. A. & Byrd, T. A. (2002). Electronic commerce and data privacy: The impact of privacy concerns on electronic commerce use and regulatory preferences. In G. S. Dhillon (Ed.), *Social Responsibility in the Information Age: Issues and Controversies* (pp. 89-113) Hershey, PA: Idea Group Publishing.

Hobbes, T. (1988). *The Leviathan.* Amherst, NY: Prometheus Books.

Copyright © 2003, Idea Group Inc. Copying or distributing in print or electronic forms without written permission of Idea Group Inc. is prohibited.

Liu, K. (2000). *Semiotics in information systems engineering.* Cambridge, MA: Cambridge University Press.

Locke, J. (1960). Two treatises of government. In W. Ebenstein (Ed.), *Great Political Thinkers: Plato to the Present* (pp. 393-413) New York: Holt, Rinehart and Winston.

Kendall, W. (1959). *John Locke and the doctrine of majority-rule.* Urbana, IL: University of Illinois Press.

Kinney, J. (1995, September). Anarcho-emergentist-republicans. *Wired*, 3.09, pp. 90, 92, 94-95.

Mitra, A. (2002, March). Trust, authenticity, and discursive power in cyberspace. *Communications of the ACM, 45*(3), 27-29.

Monsma, S. V. et al. (1986). *Responsible technology: A christian perspective.* Grand Rapids, MI: William B. Eerdmans.

Negroponte, N. (1996, November). Being local. *Wired*, 4(11), 286.

Negroponte, N. (1995). *Being digital.* New York: Alfred A. Knopf.

Palen, L. (2002, March). Mobile telephony in a connected life. *Communications of the ACM, 45* (3), 78-82.

Papazafeiropoulou, A. & Pouloudi, A. (2001, October-December). Social issues in electronic commerce: Implications for policy makers. *Information Resources Management Journal, 14*(4), 24-32.

Papazafeiropoulou, A. & Pouloudi, A. (2002). Social issues in electronic commerce: Implications for policy makers. In G. S. Dhillon (Ed.), *Social Responsibility in the Information Age: Issues and Controversies* (pp. 144-159) Hershey, PA: Idea Group Publishing.

Poster, M. (1995, November). The net as a public sphere? *Wired*, 3(11), 135-136, 138.

Postrel, V. (1998). *The future and its enemies: The growing conflict over creativity, enterprise, and progress.* New York: The Free Press.

Preece, J. (2002, April). Supporting community and building social capital. *Communications of the ACM, 45*(4), 37-39.

Rheingold, H. (1993). *The virtual community.* New York: HarperCollins.

Rothstein, E. (1996, April 29). Technology: Connections: Tuning into Timothy Leary's last trip, live from his death bed. *The New York Times*, p. C21.

Rousseau, J-J. (1998). *The social contract or principles of political right.* (H. J. Tozer, Trans.). Hertfordshire, UK: Wordsworth Editions Ltd.

Schwartz, E. I. (1999). *Digital darwinism.* New York: Broad Way Books/Random House.

Social contract: Essays by Locke, Hume, and Rousseau (With an introduction by Sir E. Barker). (1970). London: Oxford University Press.

Solomon, R. C. (1993). *Ethics and excellence.* Oxford/New York: Oxford University Press.

Solomon, R. C. (1992). *Morality and the good life.* New York: McGraw-Hill.

Stewart, J. & Williams, R. (2000). The co-evolution of society and multimedia

Copyright © 2003, Idea Group Inc. Copying or distributing in print or electronic forms without written permission of Idea Group Inc. is prohibited.

technology: Issues in predicting the future innovation and use of ubiquitous technology. In G. D. Garson (Ed.), *Social Dimensions of Information Technology* (pp. 46-62) Hershey, PA: Idea Group Publishing.

Stoll, C. (1999). *High-tech heretic*. New York: Doubleday.

Stoll, C. (1995). *Silicon snake oil: Second thoughts on the information highway*. New York: Doubleday.

Turkle, S. (1995). *Life on the screen: Identity in the society of the internet*. New York: Simon & Schuster.

Webster, F. (1995). *Theories of the information society*. London/New York: Routledge.

Copyright © 2003, Idea Group Inc. Copying or distributing in print or electronic forms without written permission of Idea Group Inc. is prohibited.

Chapter X

The Influence of Socioeconomic Factors on Technological Change: The Case of High-Tech States in the U.S.

Rasool Azari
University of Redlands, USA

James Pick
University of Redlands, USA

ABSTRACT

This paper examines the technological level of 74 counties in technologically advanced states in the United States at the end of the 1990s. The conceptual framework is that selected socioeconomic dimensions influence the level of technological development for advanced communities; i.e., technology does not develop by itself but in concert with pre-disposing characteristics of the environment. The influence of socioeconomic factors was studied through correlation and regression analysis. The findings reveal that, on a national basis, factors that are important across several technology sectors are college education, ethnicity, income, and federal grant funds.   There are distinctive

Copyright © 2003, Idea Group Inc. Copying or distributing in print or electronic forms without written permission of Idea Group Inc. is prohibited.

influences for high-tech counties in the "rust belt" versus the "sunbelt." Taken together, the results highlight the association of socioeconomic factors with the per capita magnitude of the technology sectors. The findings are discussed relative to research literature and data collected, and policy and ethical implications are presented.

INTRODUCTION

Over the past century, technological development has been reshaping the material basis of U.S. society and economy at an ever-increasing pace. Especially the rapid development and diffusion of the new information technologies have altered the process of production, raised productivity, and improved living standards. This transformation is taking place on a global basis. Yet, there is evidence that this revolution is still in its beginning stages and its effects are not yet well understood and predictable. But there is general consensus that the advances in the information technology are global, irreversible, and will continue to transform the way we live and work.

As the complexity of technological change accelerates, the need to maximize its benefits and minimize its risk increases. In recent years, the subject of technological change and information technology has received a great deal of attention from economists, sociologists, and psychologists (Stein, 1995, p. 38). One issue, which frequently surfaces, is the question of how these sweeping changes will affect the fabric of our lives. Will the revolutionary advances of the information and communication technology (ICT) widen the "digital divide" and increase the gap of inequality, which already is prevalent throughout societies, or will we be able to direct these forces to work more equitably for the benefit of everyone? This is the daunting challenge the global economy and U.S. economy now face (ILO, 2001).

The aims of this paper are to better understand the relationships between socioeconomic factors and technological change within U.S. high-tech states, to raise some relevant questions that may help policy makers and experts to identify and address potential and already developing social and economic problems based on the recent changes, and to increase the social dialogue and partnership amongst employers, workers, government, and civil society.

In the next section, we briefly review some of the existing theories about technology and its impact on wage inequality, the "digital divide," business ethics and corporate social responsibility, and present our research questions. In the following section, we turn to the methodology used in this paper. The chapter then looks at the empirical evidence and explains the findings. This is followed by a discussion on the research results and a discussion of the review policy implications and ramifications for future research. The final section presents the conclusion of this study.

Copyright © 2003, Idea Group Inc. Copying or distributing in print or electronic forms without written permission of Idea Group Inc. is prohibited.

BACKGROUND

Technological change has been central to U.S. economic growth and is the major force in raising the factor productivity at an accelerated rate. In order to sustain economic growth and prosperity, companies must adjust to a faster pace of change (Landau, 1988, p. 47). New information technology (IT) is reshaping organizations and business enterprises, and is redefining work processes and employment structures. "Indeed, the potential of the ICT revolution to transform the global economy has been at the centre stage in international fora and discussions…" (2, p. v).

The rapid development of new technologies in the information age is a source of problems for the old socioeconomic structures "…until society and social institutions are able to match perfectly with them" (OECD, 1998, p. 126). "If there is technological advance without social advance, there is, almost automatically, an increase in human misery" (Harrington, 1987, p. 960). The recent technological innovations and their impact on economic performance, especially in industrial countries, seem not only to affect the way we live and work, but they also seem to determine the course of action in our society. Nevertheless, technology alone does not determine society, and neither can society script the activities of technological innovation; technological change and innovation depend on many complex patterns of interaction, including individual inventiveness and entrepreneurship (Castells, 1996, p. 5). Fortunately, the advances in technology and the risks associated with its applications can be shaped by social and political choices. Society, through state intervention and policy changes, can stall or accelerate the process of technological change.

In this paper we discuss both the business use of technology and the consumer use of technology. We believe that literacy in technology is good for both industry and consumers. Our review of literature addresses the increasing inequality of wages between technologically skilled and unskilled workers and the term digital divide, "to refer to unequal access to information technology" (Light, 2001, p. 709) by consumers. This also raises the questions of ethics of the emerging technologies and how the future of corporate social responsibility evolves in this increasingly ever-changing environment. Wage inequality, digital divide, and ethics will be more explored in the following three subsections.

Wage Inequality

One phenomenon related to technological change that received the attention of many labor and trade economists (Autor, 1998; Baldwin, 2000; Burtless, 1995; Davis, 1998; Feenstra, 1997; Haskel, 2001; Johnson, 1997; Krugman, 1995) was the emergence of wage divergence in the late 1970s and early 1980s. It is widely believed that the development of the new technology increased the demand for skilled workers, thereby increasing the wage differential between skilled and unskilled

Copyright © 2003, Idea Group Inc. Copying or distributing in print or electronic forms without written permission of Idea Group Inc. is prohibited.

workers (Breshnan, 1999, p. 1). Haskel and Slaughter (2001) examined international trade and technical change by measuring trade as changes in product prices and measuring technical change as the total factor productivity (TFP), which revealed macroeconomic gains from productive innovations. They concluded that changes in prices are behind the rises of the wage inequality. Baldwin and Cain (2000) indicated that none of the economic forces alone can account for the observed wage inequality. They emphasized that education-biased technical progress played important roles in bringing about the increase in wage inequality during the 1980s and 1990s. Autor et al. (1998) agree that education is playing a crucial role in skill-based technological change, such as computerization.

Some refer to trade as the reason for the wage inequality, while others argue that technological change is the primary explanation for the widening gap in inequality of wages — the so-called skilled biased technical change. Even though empirical evidence from the literature on wage inequality is inconclusive and fragmented (Deardorff, 1998, p. 371), there is, however, increasing consensus that technological change and innovation is the primary factor for the increasing gap in wages.

Digital Divide

The rapidly widening disparity in the utilization of technology is apparent worldwide. There are also income and wealth inequalities within the United States that limit the advances of technologies into some sectors, regions, and parts of society. This is commonly referred to as the "digital divide," i.e., that society has major divisions in intensity of IT utilization and application. The U.S. government has recognized this, but not acted substantially on it. For instance, a major report from the National Telecommunications and Information Administration (NTIA, 1999) utilized U.S. Census national sample data to examine household distribution of access to technology, including computers, phones, and the Internet. It defined "digital divide" as the divide between those with access to new technologies and those without. It concluded that the digital divide is substantial and growing over time. The poor side of the digital divide consists of households with low education, low income, minority status, single parents with children, and rural residence.

The "patchiness" of IT benefits across the U.S. was also emphasized by analysts. Baker (2001) suggests that the inequity in the diffusion of the technologies is not a simple socioeconomic concern, but it is "a policy problem related to the use and deployment of ICTs with multiple geographic, social, economic and organizational components." Just correcting disparities in accessibility is not enough. Furthermore, he suggests a public dialogue about adopting the market-driven practices of the private sector, in order to understand the fundamental dimensions of the digital divide, and to develop policy initiatives that target more efficiently and effectively the limited resources of government.

Crandall (2001) likewise identified a sharp digital divide between the middle class, white segments of the population and deprived minorities in the U.S. The

Copyright © 2003, Idea Group Inc. Copying or distributing in print or electronic forms without written permission of Idea Group Inc. is prohibited.

important factors contributing to the increase of the divide are income, occupation, rural residence, large household size, and female head of household. When these factors are statistically controlled for, the Hispanic divide disappears, but the divide for blacks remains.

Some states have recognized this problem and tried to change it. In the well-known case of Digital Georgia (GCATT, 2001), the governor's office established policy guidelines that sought to increase participation of citizens of the state of Georgia in the digital society. The report points out that the hardware itself is not enough, but awareness and relevant, timely applications are critically important. It also underscores the need to learn more about the causes of technology non-adoption, and the need to focus on and foster technology education. Georgia is now categorized as a high-tech state (AEA, 2001), and is included in our study sample.

There are studies, besides those recent ones, on the digital divide that have examined socioeconomic influences on IT use, intensity, and impacts. These have had a variety of geographic locales, units of analysis, methodological designs, and research questions. In a survey study of end use of microcomputers in Finland (Igbaria, 1999), the extent of influence of demographic variables (age, gender, education, organizational tenure), computer experience, and job training on micro-computer utilization at the level of the individual were examined. Utilization consisted of frequency of use, time of use, type of business task, and category software application. Some socioeconomic factors were important correlates of utilization, especially gender and age. By contrast, in a similar study of North America, the overall level of use was higher and gender was not a factor (Igbaria, 1989). Continuing education and specialized training were recommended. An earlier study of attitudes of elderly people towards computers (Brown, 1990-91) confirmed that the age factor can reduce use, although age was difficult to sort out from other age-related variables affecting attitudes, such as education and occupational level.

In a comparative study of utilization and impacts of IT applications on end users in the U.S. and Mexico, Torkzadeh (1999) found strong similarities between the countries on how the technology is utilized, but many differences in levels of use. The study surveyed individuals and measured uses based on problem solving, decision rationalization, horizontal integration, vertical integration, and customer service. IT impacts overall were about 20 percent higher in Mexico. The policy implications of the study were that firms can benefit by evaluating portfolios of applications, regarding users differently and individually, and assessing training needs. At the national level, Dasgupta et al. (2001) examined urban, economic, and telecommunication policy predictors of Internet intensity and cell phone diffusion for a sample of 44 countries in developing nations. Both Internet intensity and cell phone subscriptions were influenced by urban population, favorable national telecomm policy, and location in particular world regions.

These and other studies of socioeconomic influences on IT impacts and uses underscore the importance of the socioeconomic factors. They also suggest that the

Copyright © 2003, Idea Group Inc. Copying or distributing in print or electronic forms without written permission of Idea Group Inc. is prohibited.

factors vary in complex ways depending on the unit of analysis, region, and dependent variable, such as IS utilization, impact, application area, or IT investment. This study differs from these nationwide "divide" studies by emphasizing socioeconomic differences in IT intensity within high-technology states. It seeks to determine what factors are significant in distinguishing technology use within states generally better off in IT. Is there a "graininess" in socioeconomic factors that makes the digital divide persist, even in high-tech states?

The geographic side of this area of research is important. The characteristics of nations, states, and counties have numerous features that influence studies such as this one. At the state level in the U.S., a wealth of high-tech data appeared in *Cyberstates 2001* (AEA). This volume presents data, rather than analyzing it. It is useful as a data source, including in the present paper. A geographical-based study of how technology influences intra-metropolitan and inter-metropolitan change (Atkinson, 1998) focused on the present and future impacts of technological advancement on cities and metropolitan areas. This study analyzes an opposite pathway from our study, i.e., how technology influences cities and their characteristics, versus how characteristics influence technology levels in counties.

Since technology is used in businesses, homes, criminal justice systems, educational institutions, medicine, science, and government, in short "in a social context rich with moral, cultural, and political ideas," (Johnson, 2001, p. 11) and is inextricable from society, it is crucial to understand its impact and to exert our social responsibility in steering its course. This is the topic of the following section.

Business Ethics and Social Responsibility

The Oxford Dictionary describes ethics as "a set of moral principles," a definition which embraces a huge subject area beyond the scope of this paper. We are, however, concerned here primarily with ethics as it applies to business issues that corporate decision-makers are facing in developing policies regarding various interest groups. Since corporations, in order to run their business, bring together different groups, which sometimes have conflicting interests, the question arises of whose interests should be served and at what costs to others. These questions came more to the forefront, especially in the last three decades, because regulation by itself did not resolve the problems of unethical behavior, and because corporations increased their influence on society by taking over activities of businesses that normally are part of the government's responsibility. "Is the corporation the private property of stockholders who choose to do business in the corporate form, or is a corporation a public institution sanctioned by the state for some social good?" (Boatright, 2000, p. 348).

Grappling with the difficulties of answering this and similar questions and the discussion on corporate social responsibility (CSR) is not new to communities involved with business. The debate around this topic has also been the concern of

Copyright © 2003, Idea Group Inc. Copying or distributing in print or electronic forms without written permission of Idea Group Inc. is prohibited.

academia, the government and legislators, and society in general, and it has consistently gained momentum over the last half century.

The aim here is not to verify the need for corporations to adhere to the existing economic and legal rules. This is usually accepted as the most important element of performance society demands of any business. This section focuses on the ethical and social responsibility in business, meaning guidelines and standards of conduct and doing what is right, which go beyond what society sets forth as its strictly legal requirements. Although we do not presume to resolve the questions surrounding business ethics and social responsibility, our goal is to acknowledge its legitimate existence and to point out some of the issues and controversies evolving around it.

Even though it is often used interchangeably, we distinguish business ethics from social responsibility. The former specifies principles and standards in terms of individual and group decisions, while the latter refers to the responsibility of an organization towards its stakeholders. By stakeholders we mean customers, owners, employers, community, suppliers, and the government (Ferrell, 2002, p. 73).

The idea of social responsibility for corporations is by no means a clearly defined concept and generally accepted idea. The conservative economist Milton Friedman states: "Few trends could so thoroughly undermine the foundations of our free society as the acceptance by corporate officials of a social responsibility other than making as much money for the stockholders as possible... It is the responsibility of the rest of us to establish a framework of law such that an individual pursuing his own interest is, to quote Adam Smith..., 'led by an invisible hand to promote an end which was no part of his intention'" (Friedman, 1962, p. 133).

It probably is true that organizations that focus their business solely on making profits and increasing the shareholders assets avoid a host of unresolved questions. What does it mean to be socially responsible? What are the rights of stakeholders and how should we protect them? Who determines corporate actions? Is it sufficient to respond to ongoing issues or should causes be anticipated? Since causes may exert opposing reactions, which opinion the company should heed? How much of committed resources constitutes sufficient social responsibility and who decides on these and other questions? It may also be that the gain of one group is the loss of another, that contributing to a cleaner environment may bring hardship to whole professions, and so on. The fact that commitment very often carries with it a certain trade-off increases the complexity of the situations. Furthermore, it may be that the internal structures and strategies along which corporations and businesses are formed and operate are such that genuine social responsible involvement becomes futile.

The questions abound and there are no clear guidelines on how to proceed. But despite the difficulties to reach some consensus, these questions are not disappearing, rather they are more and more moved to the forefront by a public that demands to be involved and heard. After all, it is substantial sections of the public that suffer the consequences; for instance, when a corporation like the energy giant ENRON

Copyright © 2003, Idea Group Inc. Copying or distributing in print or electronic forms without written permission of Idea Group Inc. is prohibited.

collapses, when the California Department of Consumer Affairs (DCA) seeks to shut down the 72 Sears Auto Centers in that state, and when the tragedy at the Union Carbide plant in Bhopal, India kills more than 3,500 and injures at least 200,000.

The magnitude of these and other disastrous events leave their mark. Corporations and their conglomerates have grown to a size and level of influence so that their decisions regularly reach and possibly alter thousands of lives. Their activities affect us all, often positive, sometimes negative, and so their conduct of business is, and should be, a matter of concern to everyone.

Undoubtedly, a major reason for the transformation of many of our business organizations and social institutions has been the steady and progressively rapid innovations in technology and we can, with certainty, argue that especially the "information technology is a critical enabler of the re-creation (redefinition) of the organization" (Kling, 1996, p. 158). The information technology has had (and will continue to have) the greatest impact on businesses and other organizations by revolutionizing the processes of operations, global competition, and many other business activities. For example, in the past, business organizations tended to focus inward and their main relations were with their immediate suppliers. Recently, corporations have broadened their focus to include the entire supply chain. This and e-business is continuing to change the way in which business organizations deal with each other. The increasing interrelatedness created by these technologies proceed to open up possibilities to interact, expand and evolve on a worldwide scale, and global competition and markets are having growing impact on organizational strategies and structures around the globe.

These revolutionary changes in business organizations, as a result of technological innovation, also bring about changes in the way we live and work. How and to what extent society embraces and adjusts to them is the topic of many debates. But their impact is already transforming the character and quality of our lives. Therefore it is important to analyze and understand what is driving this transformation and how it might be influenced and directed. In the proceeding sections, we looked at the connection between technological change and the digital divide and the widening gap in wages. These are two negative consequences of the technological transformation with which society has to grapple. "Unequal access poses a serious threat to democracy. Indeed, a good deal of concern has been expressed in recent years about computer and information technology and the Internet widening the gap between haves and have-nots within the United States and among countries of the world" (Johnson, 2001, p. 218). We believe that these problems can and should be dealt with. Corporations have the resources and means to impact and shape these negative outcomes of technology.

This varied literature is informative on many dimensions to the present paper. Some literature on the impacts of technological change neglects the link to socioeconomic factors. Our paper has the objective to examine this issue and shed more light on the phenomenon of technological differences, and to discuss the findings in terms of some ethical dimensions as well.

Copyright © 2003, Idea Group Inc. Copying or distributing in print or electronic forms without written permission of Idea Group Inc. is prohibited.

Research Questions

This paper has the following research questions:

1. What are the socio-economic factors that influence the per capita economic size of the information systems-data processing sector for counties in high-tech states in the United States?
2. What are the socio-economic factors that influence the per capita economic size of the broadcasting-telecommunications sector for counties in high-tech states in the United States?
3. What are the socio-economic factors that influence the per capita economic size of the motion picture/sound recording sector for counties in high-tech states in the United States?
4. Are there differences between high-tech counties in northern "traditional" states in the center and northeast of the U.S. and "sunbelt" states in the south and west in the socioeconomic factors that influence the per capita economic sizes of the three technology sectors?

DATA AND METHODS

This paper investigates the association of technological development with socioeconomic factors for 74 counties from the 12 highest tech states in the United States. These states were selected as the most high-tech ones based on criteria in a recent study of the American Electronics Association (2001), which examined national and state trends in employment, wages, exports, venture capita investments, research and development (R&D) expenditures, and computer and internet use at home. We identified the 12 states ranked as the "leading cyberstates": in particular, California, Texas, New York, Massachusetts, Washington, Virginia, Illinois, New Jersey, Colorado, Florida, Pennsylvania, and Georgia. These states accounted for 84 percent of U.S. high-tech payroll and 62 percent of high-tech establishments in 1999 (AEA). As seen in Figure 1, the average high-tech payroll is eight times higher in the 12 high-tech states, versus 40 other "low-tech" states plus District of Colombia and Puerto Rico. On a per capita basis, the average high-tech payroll is twice as large in the "leading cyberstates." The counties in our study sample consist of all those in these 12 states that had complete county data sets available on three technology sectors discussed later in this section. The paper focuses on the high-tech states because they currently not only dominate the U.S. but also the world in technology. We are interested in examining the particular socioeconomic influences within these states due to their importance for technology worldwide. Due to scope limitations, the paper does not intend to compare their patterns to low-tech states.

For this research project, the basic assumption is that socioeconomic factors, such as education, income, service sector composition, ethnicity, and population growth, are associated with the size of technology investment and development. It is evident that socioeconomic factors and technology are frequently intertwined and

Copyright © 2003, Idea Group Inc. Copying or distributing in print or electronic forms without written permission of Idea Group Inc. is prohibited.

Figure 1. Technology payroll, high tech versus low tech state in U.S., 1999

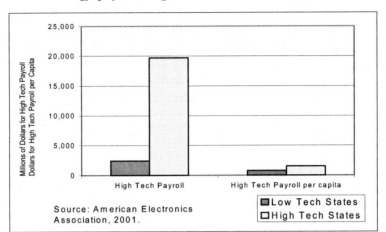

interrelated. For instance, in a county the presence of a wealthy population, a highly educated labor force, and high R&D expenditures may increase technology level by attracting capital investment. At the same time, a county with high-technology level may attract highly educated people; may create prosperity and wealth in its citizenry; and may foster R&D. However, in this paper, we are concerned with the directionality of effects from socioeconomic factors towards technology level, not the converse (see Figure 2). A study of bi-directional effects would require more sophisticated data collection and intermediate variables than we undertook for this study. Future expanded research is discussed later in the chapter.

Data for this study came from a special series on the information sector of the 1997 Economic Census (1997) and from the U.S. Census of Population and Housing of 2000. Although the socioeconomic data were collected three years following the information sector data, they are considered sufficiently stable, at the level of counties, over the three-year period to be suitable for the purposes of our study.

The independent variables that we examined are the following:
- Per Capita Federal Grants and Funds
- Per Capita Number of Employees in Services
- Per Capita Annual Payroll in Services

Figure 2. An unidirectional framework of changes in technology

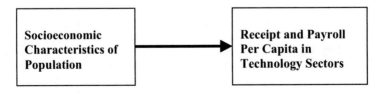

Copyright © 2003, Idea Group Inc. Copying or distributing in print or electronic forms without written permission of Idea Group Inc. is prohibited.

- Median Household Income
- Per Capita Number of Employees in Educational Services
- Per Capita Annual Payroll in Educational Services
- Per Capita College Graduates
- Percentage of Black Population in the County
- Percentage of Asian Population in the County
- Percentage of Latino Population in the County
- Percentage of White Population in the County
- Percentage of Female Population in the County
- Percentage Change in Population, 1990-2000

These 13 socioeconomic dimensions for counties were selected as being relevant to the technology level through prior research studies.

We reason that technology will have higher levels in counties that receive higher levels overall of federal funding. The federal grants overall can stimulate greater technology use, technology education, and research and development. Practical examples are the Boston and Los Angeles regions, which have very high rates of federal funding that, in turn, stimulates technology use in business and the economy through emphasis on higher tech products and services, and associated employment.

We examine whether counties with higher service components will also have higher levels of technology. We justify this variable by the substantial proportion of high-tech employees who work in services versus other sectors, and the growth in this proportion over time. For instance, in 2000, 63 percent of high-tech workers were in services, a proportion 11 percent higher than in 1994. Hence, we reason that more service-oriented counties will have higher levels of technology workers, and the technology sectors will be more ample.

U.S. Department of Commerce studies (NTIA, 1999) have emphasized the differences in technology utilization based on demographic attributes. For instance, in 1998 the difference in Internet utilization between very low-income households (under $20,000) and high income ones (over $75,000) varied between 8 percent and 60 percent (NTIA, 1999). At the level of developing nations, per capita income was one of the most important influences on Internet and cell phone use (Dasgupat, 2001). Likewise, 47 percent of white households had a computer, versus 23 and 25 percent, respectively, for Blacks and Hispanics. In a recent study, Lentz (2000) emphasizes that race and ethnicity should not be excluded from studies of high-tech jobs. Slowinski (2000) points to large differences between the ethnic groups as a cause of differences in high-tech workforce. Crandall (2001) identifies ethnicity and income as important variables for access to computers and technology.

The survey study of workers by Igbaria and Iivari (1999) confirmed that education and training were key predictors of microcomputer utilization. That study also substantiated the importance of gender for microcomputer utilization. The U.S.

Copyright © 2003, Idea Group Inc. Copying or distributing in print or electronic forms without written permission of Idea Group Inc. is prohibited.

Department of Commerce identified a gender gap, with about 3 percent more utilization of the Internet by surveyed males versus females (NTIA, 1999).

We included percent change in county population based on our own reasoning that growing counties draw in workforce and capital investment, and tend to have growing educational institutions that encourage technology use. This attribute has not been included in prior studies in this field that we are aware of.

Even though the units of analysis, i.e., individuals, firms, and nations, have varied in prior research, the importance of these demographic variables justifies including them. We re-iterate that although the directionality of effect may be in two directions, we emphasize in this study how socioeconomic attributes affect technology level.

We further submitted these variables to preliminary correlation analysis to analyze for possible adverse effects from multi-colinearity (Neter, 1996). We eliminated six of them through their high inter-correlations, which are known to bias regression analysis results. Seven were found to be less inter-correlated and were selected for regression analysis of the full sample. They are: percentage change in population, 1990-2000, per capita college graduates, Black percentage of the population, Latino percentage of the population, household income, per capita number of service employees, and per capita federal grant funds. Among other things, based on multi-colinearity considerations, we did not include the percent white population, percent Asian population, percent female, and variables on educational services and employment. The latter two were highly correlated with percent college graduates. However, we added percent Asian and percent female as eligible variables for the stepwise regressions for regional sub-samples. The few variables entered in stepwise procedures did not exhibit multi-colinearity.

The three dependent variables measure per capita technology levels for the ICT sector in the 1997 Economic Census. These three variables constitute the main components of the information sector of the 1997 U.S. Economic Census (AEA, 2001). They are defined as receipts and payrolls for the following three sub-sectors: Information Systems/Data Processing (IS/DP), Broadcasting/Telecommunications (B/T), and Motion Picture/Sound Recording (MP/SR) industries. The Census classified MP/SR as a technology industry. We think this is justified because of the growing role of technology in MP/SR. The dependent variables represent the per capita economic importance of different technology sectors in a county.

Linear regression analysis was conducted to examine the influences of all seven independent variables on each of the dependent variables. Statistical processing was done utilizing standard statistical software (SPSS, 2001). For the full sample of 74 counties, fixed regression was applied with forced entry of all seven variables. For comparison of "sunbelt" high-tech counties with "rust belt" high-tech counties, both sample sizes are 37. The stepwise algorithms prevented more than three variables to enter. Stepwise approach with this stopping rule is appropriate given the small sizes of these two samples.

Copyright © 2003, Idea Group Inc. Copying or distributing in print or electronic forms without written permission of Idea Group Inc. is prohibited.

FINDINGS

The mean values of variables in the full sample variables are given in Table 1. These indicate that the high-tech counties were not so different, on the average, than the typical U.S. profile. However, the median household income is higher; educational level is higher; and the percent Latino is somewhat higher. The average amounts of technology receipts and payroll per capita are also significantly higher than the national average.

Correlation analysis (see Table 2) reveals that within each dependent variable category, receipts and payroll of employees are significantly correlated. Also, receipts and payroll are significantly inter-correlated between IS/DP and B/T. This makes sense, since today the technologies of information systems and telecommunications are intertwined in systems and services. Payroll for motion picture/sound recording is correlated with the other categories. On the other hand, receipts for the motion pictures/sound recording industry are not correlated with the other dependent variables. This reflects that differences in county geographic patterns still persist between motion pictures/sound recording and information systems and telecommunications. These differences may diminish in the future, as the three types of technologies become more inter-mixed.

For the full sample, all six regressions are significant in estimating technology sectors (see Table 3). This confirms that the socioeconomic attributes are associated

Table 1.   Mean values of selected variables for 74 sample counties

Independent Variables	
Population	976,071
Percent change in population 1990-2000	14.7
College graduates per capita	0.1552
Percent White	73.9
Percent Black	10.5
Percent Asian	5.4
Percent Latino	13.5
Percent Female	51.0
Service Employees per capita	0.1160
Educational Services Employees per capita	0.0243
Median Household Income (in dollars)	45,000
Federal Grants and Funds (in 1000's of dollars)	4,980,565
Dependent Variables	
IS-Data Processing Receipts (in 1000's of dollars)	241,196
IS-Data Processing Payroll (in 1000's of dollars)	75,456
Motion Picture-Sound Receipts (in 1000's of dollars)	615,355
Motion Picture-Sound Payroll (in 1000's of dollars)	102,481
Broadcasting-Telecomm Receipts (in 1000's of dollars)	1,877,634
Broadcasting-Telecomm Payroll (in 1000's of dollars)	349,500

Data Sources: U.S. Census, 1997, 2000

Copyright © 2003, Idea Group Inc. Copying or distributing in print or electronic forms without written permission of Idea Group Inc. is prohibited.

Table 2.   Correlation matrix of dependent variables

	Receipts for IS-DP/capita	Payroll for IS-DP/capita	Receipts for Broadcasting-Telecomm/cap.	Payroll for Broadcasting-Telecomm/cap.	Receipts for Motion Picture-Sound/cap.	Payroll for Motion Picture-Sound/cap.
Receipts for IS-DP/capita	1.000					
Payroll for IS-DP/capita	0.974 0.000***	1.000				
Receipts for Broadcasting-Telecomm/cap.	0.569 0.000***	0.604 0.000***	1.000			
Payroll for Broadcasting-Telecomm/cap.	0.565 0.000	0.606 0.000***	0.950 0.000***	1.000		
Receipts for Motion Picture-Sound/cap.	0.073 0.538	0.089 0.452	0.201 0.086	0.165 0.159	1.000	
Payroll for Motion Picture-Sound/cap.	0.208 0.076	0.258 0.026*	0.617 0.000***	0.526 0.000***	0.757*** 0.000	1.000

* correlation significant at 0.05 level
** correlation significant at 0.01 level
*** correlation significant at 0.001 level

Note: The top of each cell gives the Pearson correlation and the bottom gives the two-tailed significance level. Sample size N = 74.

Table 3. Standardized regression results for seven socioeconomic independent variables

	Receipts for IS-DP/capita Beta Value	signif.	Payroll for IS-DP/capita Beta Value	signif.	Receipts for Broadcast.-Telecomm/cap. Beta Value	signif	Payroll for Broadcast.-Telecomm/cap. Beta Value	signif.	Receipts for Motion Picture-Sound/cap. Beta Value	signif	Payroll for Motion Picture-Sound/cap. Beta Value	signif
Percent Change in Population, 1990-2000	0.039	0.717	0.067	0.534	0.262	0.015*	0.246	0.035*	-0.032	0.821	0.182	0.136
College Graduates per capita	0.426	0.001***	0.522	0.000***	0.861	0.000***	0.779	0.000***	0.336	0.048*	0.850	0.000***
Percent Black	0.205	0.027*	0.113	0.214	0.310	0.001***	0.276	0.006**	0.012	0.920	0.061	0.549
Percent Latino	0.140	0.124	0.108	0.235	0.135	0.132	0.133	0.171	0.308	0.012*	0.285	0.006**
Median Household Income	0.235	0.075	0.154	0.242	-0.381	0.004**	0.115	0.248	-0.150	0.386	-0.500	0.001***
Service Employees per capita	0.124	0.203	0.148	0.128	-0.018	0.846	0.014	0.895	0.127	0.321	-0.162	0.139
Federal Grant Funds per capita	0.438	0.000***	0.374	0.000***	0.110	0.234	-0.287	0.042*	-0.091	0.464	-0.118	0.264
Regression Adjusted R Square	0.433		0.498		0.516		0.433		0.125		0.368	
Significance Level		0.000***		0.000***		0.000***		0.000***		0.025*		0.000***

N = 74
* signif. at 0.05
** signif. at 0.01
*** signif at 0.001

with receipts and payrolls for technology sectors. There are distinctive influences for each of the three technology sectors. In particular, receipts and payroll for the IS/DP industry sector are associated strongly with college graduates, per capita federal grant funds, and with percent African American (for receipts only).

Receipts and payroll for the telecommunication/broadcasting industry are associated with college graduates and population growth in the 1990s. Median household income is inversely associated with B/T receipts, and federal grant funds per capita are related oppositely to payroll of B/T. For the motion picture/sound recording industries, receipts and payroll are associated with college graduates and percent Latino. In addition, household income is inversely related to MP/SR payroll.

Copyright © 2003, Idea Group Inc. Copying or distributing in print or electronic forms without written permission of Idea Group Inc. is prohibited.

Table 4. Standardized stepwise regression results for all independent variables, North, "traditional" high-tech region

	Receipts for IS-DP/capita Beta Value	signif.	Payroll for IS-DP/capita Beta Value	signif.	Receipts for Broadcast.-Telecomm/cap. Beta Value	signif	Payroll for Broadcast.-Telecomm/cap Beta Value.	signif.	Receipts for Motion Picture-Sound/cap. Beta Value	signif	Payroll for Motion Picture-Sound/cap. Beta Value	signif
Percent Change in Population, 1990-2000												
College Graduates per capita	0.318	0.027*	0.396	0.007**	0.840	0.000***	0.671	0.000***	0.709	0.000***	0.727	0.000***
Percent Black												
Percent Latino					0.251	0.030*	0.314	0.009**	0.351	0.007**	0.325	0.011*
Percent Asian	0.408	0.006**	0.366	0.012*								
Percent Female							0.239	0.042*				
Median Household Income					-0.376	0.008**			-0.336	0.026*	-0.458	0.003**
Service Employees per capita												
Federal Grant Funds per capita	0.440	0.000***	0.387	0.001***								
Regression Adjusted R Square		0.623		0.619		0.571		0.544		0.485		0.496
Significance Level		0.000***		0.000***		0.000***		0.000***		0.000***		0.000***

N = 37
* signif. at 0.05
** signif. at 0.01
*** signif. at 0.001

Table 5. Standardized stepwise regression results for all independent variables, South, "sunbelt" high-tech region

	Receipts for IS-DP/capita Beta Value	signif.	Payroll for IS-DP/capita Beta Value	signif.	Receipts for Broadcast.-Telecomm/cap. Beta Value	signif	Payroll for Broadcast.-Telecomm/cap Beta Value.	signif.	Receipts for Motion Picture-Sound/cap. Beta Value	signif	Payroll for Motion Picture-Sound/cap. Beta Value	signif
Percent Change in Population, 1990-2000												
College Graduates per capita									0.321	0.049*	0.405	0.013*
Percent Black					0.278	0.011*						
Percent Latino									0.302	0.063		
Percent Asian												
Percent Female												
Median Household Income	0.266	0.028*	0.358	0.005**								
Service Employees per capita	0.700	0.000***	0.644	0.000***	0.679	0.000***	0.690	0.000***				
Federal Grant Funds per capita												
Regression Adjusted R Square		0.514		0.489		0.691		0.461		0.123		0.164
Significance Level		0.000***		0.000***		0.000***		0.000***		0.041*		0.013*

N = 37
* signif. at 0.05
** signif. at 0.01
*** signif. at 0.001

Note: "South" refers to high-tech states in the south, southwest, and west of the U.S.

Copyright © 2003, Idea Group Inc. Copying or distributing in print or electronic forms without written permission of Idea Group Inc. is prohibited.

For the full sample, there are not significant associations with service employees per capita.

To test the socioeconomic influences between the northern "rustbelt" high-tech region and south/southwestern/western "sunbelt" high-tech region, we divided the sample into two sub-samples. The North sub-sample consists of counties in the high-tech states of Illinois, Massachusetts, New York, New Jersey, Pennsylvania, and Virginia. The south sub-sample includes counties in the south, southwestern, and western high-tech states of California, Washington, Colorado, Texas, Georgia, and Florida. Stepwise regression yields the findings shown in Tables 4 and 5. All the regressions in these tables significantly estimate the technology sectors. For the northern states, college graduates has a consistently strong influence on all dependent variables. Ethnic categories are likewise influential for all dependent variables. The percentage of Latinos is significant for B/T and MP/SR sectors, while the percentage of Asians is significant for the IS/DP sector. Household income has inverse effects on MP/SR and on receipts for B/T. Federal grant funds per capita are associated with IS/DP. Finally, the percentage of females is associated with payroll for B/T.

The South sample is entirely different. The most important influence for IS/DP and B/T is the number of service employees per capita.   Although service employment was insignificant in the full sample, it becomes the largest effect for the South sample. We expect that its importance was "hidden" in the national sample. Median household income is statistically significant for the IS/DP sector, while education only impacts the MP/SR sector. Ethnic influences in the South are much reduced versus the North.   Only the percentage of the Black population is significantly related to the B/T sector in the South.

In summary, the major differences between the high-tech counties in the North and South are:
- College graduates is influential across all technology sectors in the North, but has lesser impacts — only on MP/SR — in the South.
- Ethnic groups (Latino and Asian) have strong effects on all technology sectors in the North, but minor effects in the South.
- Service workforce per capita strongly affects both IS/DP and B/T sectors in the South.
- Household income impacts all technology sectors, but is different in the North versus the South.
- Federal grant funds per capita is strongly associated with IS/DP in the North.

DISCUSSION OF RESULTS

The results of this research on high-technology U.S. counties raise several important issues. First, education is a crucial factor for technology sectoral size. This factor has been pointed to as an important factor in other studies (NTIA, 1999:

Copyright © 2003, Idea Group Inc. Copying or distributing in print or electronic forms without written permission of Idea Group Inc. is prohibited.

Crandall, 2001; GCATT, 2001; Igbaria, 1999), including at the national level (NTIA, 1999; Crandall, 2001), state level (GCATT, 2001), and individual level (Igbaria, 1999). The technology educational gaps were notable enough that the above studies all recommended additional training and education. The importance of education may be highlighted by extreme examples, such as the Silicon Valley, which was nourished by the education offered by Stanford and Berkeley. In ordinary high-tech counties over many years, expanded college educated population can create environments of talent, R&D, adoption, and creativity that assist in growing of technology sectors.

Second, for the IS/DP sector, federal grant funds per capita are influential. Federal grants are helpful in stimulating need for governmental services in IS/DP. They sometimes include training and education components that encompass IS/DP. The grants can also stimulate private sector firms to expand into new areas of IS/DP products and services. For unknown reasons, there is a weak inverse association of federal grants with payroll for B/T. The lack of influence of federal grants on MP/SR may be because that sector depends much less on the government, but rather is driven by the private sector.

Third, the statistically significant correlation between B/T and county population growth suggests that population growth may intensify technology. Much of B/T industry serves the immediate county, so increasing population expands local markets. Although not the focus of the present research, an interpretation with opposite causality is that telecommunications-intensive counties may attract more population through an economic multiplier effect — that is, telecommunications infrastructure and services to a greater extent foster broader employment growth across economic sectors. The positive effect of services on IS/DP and B/T technology levels reflects greater availability of service workforce and service entities to support these sub-sectors.

Fourth, there is an inverse association of average household income for receipts in B/T and payroll in MP/SR. Later, this is shown to be more characteristic of the North. It may be that lower income is a proxy variable for something else, since it does not make sense to us as a reducing factor. Further, a number of studies have identified income as a positive correlate (NTIA, 1999; AEA, 2001). We interpret this finding as reflecting the influence of older, northern high-tech cities. In some of these cities, substantial wage inequalities are known to have occurred. The average city wage may be lower in these cases, even with significant presence of technology workforce. This explanation requires further research, which could try to gather similar data for geographic regions within these cities that represent extremes of wage inequalities.

Fifth, there are significant positive effects from ethnic composition. Percent African American is associated with the B/T sector. This finding is contrary to other studies that have identified inverse relationships between the African American component and various facets of technology (NTIA, 1999; Crandall 2001; Slowinski, 2000). Our regional results hint at an explanation. This effect appears in the South

Copyright © 2003, Idea Group Inc. Copying or distributing in print or electronic forms without written permission of Idea Group Inc. is prohibited.

sub-sample, but not in the North. In the South sub-sample, African American population is more characteristic of larger cities and urban areas. These are also regions that have higher B/T. Hence, ethnic composition may act as a proxy for metropolitan/urban character, especially in the South. The positive association between Latino population and motion picture/sound recording technology is contrary to prior studies (NTIA, 1999; Crandall 2001; Slowinski, 2000). However, it is less surprising, considering recent demographic shifts in the U.S. The southwestern states, especially southern California, and several northeastern metropolitan areas, in particular the New York city region, which have high levels of Latino population, also have high motion picture/sound recording technology prevalence. We regard this as a demographic settlement effect, i.e., it reflects the coincidence that Latinos are concentrated in regions that have more entertainment industry. This needs to be considered for the future, since high intensity of MP/SR industry may be associated more strongly with Latino people and culture as a result of their presence in the regions.

Finally, there is a diversity of socioeconomic influences by technology sectors. In other words, the influences on the three sectors are distinctive. Except for college graduates, which goes across all sectors, influences for the national sample are distinctive. This means that generalizations about influences on technology must be taken cautiously. What is the "technology" that a particular study or argument refers to? Grouping all "technology" too closely together may hide finer sectoral distinctions of impacts of socioeconomic factors.

However, all three industrial sectors in this study are information and knowledge-based. The goods they produce are, unlike traditional goods and services, intangible. The transfer of these goods from the supplier to the consumer does not involve or require direct contact, because their value lies in the information they are delivering — which may be educational, cultural, political, or for entertainment purpose. This information may be delivered by the motion picture and sound recording industry in the form of movies and videos, by the broadcasting and telecommunication industry in the form of radio and TV, etc. How does the size of the technology sectors affect different income levels in a county? What are the advantages and disadvantages of a large or small technology sector? There are no easy answers to these and similar questions.

Nevertheless, as discussed before, the higher the level of education in a county, the higher the industrial sector's payroll and receipts. Besides this possibly being the result of increased investment in educating the workforce, this may also be due to the fact that ample investment in information technology may attract a more educated workforce to a county. On the other hand, investing more in IT does not necessarily translate into higher efficiency, customer satisfaction, and increased profit. This may be due to the intangible aspects of IT, which are difficult to quantify and measure (Papp, 1999). This phenomenon is dealt with in the literature under the term "IT productivity paradox."

Copyright © 2003, Idea Group Inc. Copying or distributing in print or electronic forms without written permission of Idea Group Inc. is prohibited.

Even though there are no clear answers to the question of why this paradox occurs, since the new technology evidently brings with it obvious advantages for the people who are able to use it, investing in it seems to make sense in the long-run. Making these technologies accessible to the greatest number of people possible seems vital, not only because an ever-greater educated workforce will be needed by the industry, but also because the benefits associated with them should not be the privilege of a specialized, overworked, qualified minority. If we want to be a democratic and humane society, it is our ethical responsibility to find the ways and means to make these benefits available to all.

In addition, the North-South differences in socioeconomic impacts on technology levels are substantial and have not been identified before. Of course, we have identified these differences only for high-tech U.S. counties. They may not apply to other frameworks, for example, comparing states between these regions, or comparing individual survey responses in North and South. The importance of service employees per capita in the South, in contrast to its absence in the North, may be due to the differences in the types of services and products being provided. One explanation is that technology products and services are geared to be distributed and utilized in local service firms and service workforce more in the South. In the North, those products and services are more widely distributed, i.e. outside of the county, or are not geared to service-industry users. This explanation requires further investigation to distinguish finer grade differences in the technology sectors and markets between North and South.

The presence of much stronger ethnic influences (Latino and Asian) in the North, versus their near absence in the South, may relate to workforce demands in technology industries. Certainly the importance of Asian workforce has been documented in the trade publications. Latino workforce may serve mostly lower skilled, yet vital, workforce in these industries. It may be that in the North, the ethnic composition between counties is more sharply different, which would accentuate the impact. An explanation for the greater importance of federal grant funds in the North versus South is that technology sectors may be more based on the public sector in the North, including government, education, R&D, and public works, whereas in the South it is more influenced by private markets for products and services. More studies are called for to determine just what the impacts of government grants are in the North versus South.

The regional differences for high-tech counties are sharp and point to a new dimension in understanding socioeconomic contrasts. Digital divides and wage inequalities may be present across the nation, but are influenced by different factors in the "sunbelt" versus the "rust belt."

Our study is different from some prior studies in that we included several socioeconomic variables in order to see the broader aspect of correlation among variables and policy implementations. The emphasis here is more on broad influences on technological change and level of investment in high-tech industries rather than

Copyright © 2003, Idea Group Inc. Copying or distributing in print or electronic forms without written permission of Idea Group Inc. is prohibited.

on trade and wage inequalities. Nevertheless, wages are important for IS/DP industry. In particular, higher income stands out as the most important positive influence on technology level. Here, higher income level, and associated higher level of skills, supports greater technology. The absence of income level as a factor for B/T and MP/SR implies that high per capita income and associated high skills are not as important for them.

The present research may be summarized in terms of the research questions.

1. *What are the socio-economic factors that influence the per capita economic size of the information systems/data processing sector for counties in high-tech states in the United States?* The most important factors for IS/DP are college educated workforce and the per capita amount of federal grant funds.

2. *What are the socio-economic factors that influence the per capita economic size of the broadcasting/telecommunications sector for counties in high-tech states in the United States?* The key factors affecting B/T are college-educated workforce, percent African American, and population change in the 1990s.

3. *What are the socio-economic factors that influence the per capita economic size of the motion picture/sound recording sector for counties in high-tech states in the United States?* The most important factors are college-educated workforce, percent Latino, and household income (which has an inverse relationship).

4. *Are there differences between high-tech counties in northern "traditional" states in the center and northeast of the U.S. and "sunbelt" states in the south and west in the socioeconomic factors that influence the per capita economic sizes of the three technology sectors?* College graduates is dominant in the North, but minor in the South. Ethnic effects are important in the North, but minor in the South. Service workforce is strong in the South. Household income influences sectors in both North and South, but different sectors. In the North, IS/DP is associated with federal grant funds.

POLICY IMPLICATIONS AND FUTURE RESEARCH

Technological change will increase the demand for more skilled workers. Current trends indicate that the rate of skill upgrading in computer and ICT intensive industries has been greater than in other industries, although the need for considerably more upgrading remains. This trend will exclude many talented individuals from participating and benefiting in the growth of the economy. "Whole communities and countries may be excluded on account of historical, cultural and economic forces, the gulf between technology-rich and technology-poor countries and continents may be

Copyright © 2003, Idea Group Inc. Copying or distributing in print or electronic forms without written permission of Idea Group Inc. is prohibited.

as stark as that between local communities and individuals. To some extent, the digital divide is simply a deepening of existing forms of exclusion" (OECD, 2000, p. 11).

This research emphasizes the advantages for technology the development of college-educated workforce.   A county that focuses on retraining for service industries and upgrading the educational level of employees will reduce the problem of accessibility and will have a positive impact on the technological level, which in turn will influence economic growth in general.

The association between the amount of income and the level of receipts in the information and broadcasting/telecommunication industries points to a version of the digital divide, even within high-tech states. That gap will deepen if the information revolution is not transformed into jobs and benefits for those counties having lower median household money incomes. Wise policies and the participation of civil society will be crucial at county, state and federal levels in order to maximize the economic benefits obtained from the information technology. "To fully understand today's digital inequities, educators must look beyond the machines" (The Editors, 2001, p. 5).

The association between the number of service employees with the level of receipts in the information and broadcasting/telecommunications industries implies the importance of these positions in the service industry in fostering technology levels in these high-tech counties. This impact may be limited to technologically skilled employees, and hence the potential gains associated with this transformation are likely to be limited. This dynamic needs to be adjusted by appropriate institutions and policy choices. Markets alone cannot dictate the course of this transformation. The extent of the success of technological change depends very much on the socioeconomic context: "technological development, in its final innovative outcomes, is both supply-pushed (by scientific knowledge) and demand pulled (by social and economic needs)" (OECD, 1998, p. 123).

As has been shown in this study, counties possessing certain socioeconomic factors have higher technology-based business receipts and payrolls. Thus, if socioeconomic factors significantly affect technology payroll and receipts and encourage a widening divide even within high-tech states, then policy intervention must be targeted towards reducing the gap in social and economic factors. This is easier said than done. Also, the challenge is greater in low-tech states, which are not the focus of this paper. A major problem with technology arises from its inadequate distribution to society, and consequently, its unequal access to some members of society.

However, the proposal of more equitable access to all available forms of technologies is not sufficient to address the problem of the digital divide. "While the advantages of accessing these services is well accepted, the benefits of the use of these technologies has been observed to occur in a distressingly uneven or patchy manner…more accurately there is a policy problem related to the use and deployments of ICTs with multiple geographic, social economic and organizational components" (Baker, 2001, p. 1). He further emphasizes that studies conducted by the U.S.

Copyright © 2003, Idea Group Inc. Copying or distributing in print or electronic forms without written permission of Idea Group Inc. is prohibited.

Figure 3. Future research: A bi-directional framework of technological change

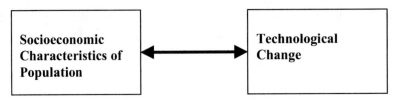

Department of Commerce (17) have indicated that the digital divide is affected by education, geography, race, and income. Other studies (Hoffman, 19998; Benton Foundation, 1998) support these findings and add more dimensions. The Benton Foundation reports about the technology gap in the U.S. and arrives at "the conviction that the design of the communication system through which we will talk to one another, learn from one another, and participate in political and economic life together is too important to be left to the free market alone" (Lentz, 2000, p. 361).

The increasing pressure by society for demanding greater social responsibility of corporations challenges the business community to face the many questions associated with technological change. But unless the involvement with these social demands are incorporated into their strategic planning, corporations will not be able to meet the changing market forces driven by growing public expectations. The present research has indicated that certain socioeconomic characteristics of counties such as education, federal grant funds, certain ethnic composition, and others can influence the sizes of three technology sectors. We raise a further ethical discussion point about these findings. It consists of the ethical questions of the benefits versus costs, good versus bad, of having larger technology sectors. We are not debating that generally larger county technology sectors are good thing — good for the companies constituting it, for their employees, and for the surrounding communities in the county. However, the ethical literature referred to earlier in this paper introduces some cases where a bigger technology sector in a county or region was a bad influence on the companies and people in the region. Consider Enron, which had very high levels of information technology and telecommunications for its sometime vast trading networks. Houston and surrounding counties did not benefit in the end by the larger technology sectors created.

Therefore, studies of differences in technological level and of the digital divide must exert the caution, after gaining quantitative knowledge of the processes and correlates, in interpreting the findings and offering policy recommendations. It is that those processes, although generally beneficial, may sometimes lead to large sectors causing harm, losses and high social costs. Policy recommendations therefore should include concern about social responsibility.

Suggested practical policies for decreasing the digital divide within high-tech counties are the following:

Copyright © 2003, Idea Group Inc. Copying or distributing in print or electronic forms without written permission of Idea Group Inc. is prohibited.

- Invest in education, training, and lifelong learning.
- Allocate resources more efficiently.
- Shift the focus of unemployment protection to skills upgrading and retraining.
- Encourage and facilitate corporate and governmental social responsibility.
- Increase the possibility that business organizations are truly accountable to stakeholders and the larger society.
- Increase accessibility to computers, the Internet and technology in communities and schools, especially among minorities and disadvantaged groups.
- Increase awareness of the possible negative and exclusionary effects that the digital divide may have on individuals and society in general, and its possible unpleasant results — unemployment, accounting failures, privacy invasion, social unrest, and others.
- Establish a comprehensive dialogue between different stakeholders in communities — government, businesses, educational, institutions, citizens — to foster a unified approach to economic development and its benefit to all.

The current research project can be expanded in a number of ways. One is to increase the sample to include all the counties in the U.S. This would allow the observation of trends and comparisons for medium- and low-technology states as well. Additional research might also consist of a survey of individuals in selected counties in the U.S. That survey might collect interview responses shedding light on the bi-directionality of effects, i.e., not only socioeconomic influences on technology level but also the opposite causality (see Figure 3). This could help to measure the benefits and economic contribution of IT across regions. In that way, methods could be applied that take into account feedback loops and bi-directional flows.

Furthermore, a multi-nation study of socioeconomic factors and technology levels could be conducted, with counties or states as units of analysis, in order to determine if there are cultural and international differences. This could be supported by utilizing variables, such as age, gender, ethnicity, education, high-tech employment trends, venture capital investments, international trade, high-tech average wage, R&D per capita, and technology transfer. The ethical dimensions raised in the discussion of findings could be examined in more detail by gathering data on possible untoward impacts of technology in counties.

CONCLUSION

This paper has focused on the association between socioeconomic factors and changes in technology measured by the level of receipts and payrolls in counties of the highest technology states in the U.S. Because of the complexity of the subject matter, no single study can provide all the appropriate answers. Only in conjunction with other studies may it be possible to come to a greater confidence of the underlying

Copyright © 2003, Idea Group Inc. Copying or distributing in print or electronic forms without written permission of Idea Group Inc. is prohibited.

social and economic causes of technological change and the digital divide. This is " a steerable revolution whose impact will be shaped by wise and or foolish policies and societal choices" (Mathews, 2000, p. 11). For appropriate policy formulation, insight into the dynamics that affect the digital divide is of paramount concern. Some studies on information technology and its utilization, including the present one, emphasize that future research needs to address the links between technological change and socioeconomic factors, available resources, multicultural content, behavior of population, corporate social responsibility, the building of communities, and ethnic group compositions.

Technology is embedded in social relationships and institutions. Policy decisions addressing the technological issue and its economic effects cross several levels of government and interest groups and hundreds of programs, and are complex. To complicate the matter even more, policies must survive political tests, regardless of scientific evidence. Even though technological changes and innovations seem miraculous, the heart of the business is still the people, their activities and social interactions, and products built to serve them. Therefore, focusing on the social and economic context of technological change will be beneficial to all stakeholders — businesses, citizens, educational institutions, and government. Good corporations acquire values and principles that become a part of their business strategy, culture, and day-to-day operations. As Atkins (2000, p. i) points out: "…information technology can have an appropriate and positive impact only if we design technology and social systems holistically." In setting policies to encourage more technology in counties, it is important also for policy leaders to emphasize social responsibility alongside technological growth.

REFERENCES

American Electronics Association. (2001). *Cyberstates (2001): A state-by-state overview of the high-technology industry.* Santa Clara, CA: American Electronics Association.

Atkins, D.E. (2000). In J.S. Brown & P. Duguid (Eds.), *The social life of information.* Boston, MA: Harvard Business School Press.

Atkinson, R.D. (1998). Technological change and cities. *Cityscope: A Journal of Policy Development and Research, 3*(3), 129-170.

Autor, D. L., Katz, L.F. & Krueger, A.B. (1998, November). Computing inequality: Have computers changed the labor market? *Quarterly Journal of Economics,* 1169-1213.

Baker, P. M. A. (2001). Policy bridges for the digital divide: Assessing the landscape and gauging the dimensions. *First Monday, 6*(5). Retrieved from http://www.firstmonday.org.

Baldwin R.E. & Cain, G.G. (2000, November). Shifts in relative U.S. wages: The

Copyright © 2003, Idea Group Inc. Copying or distributing in print or electronic forms without written permission of Idea Group Inc. is prohibited.

role of trade, technology, and factor endowments. *The Review of Economics and Statistics*, 82(4), 580-595.

Benton Foundation. (1998). Losing ground bit by bit: Low-Income communities in the Information Age. Washington, DC: Benton Foundation.

Boatright, J.R. (2000). *Ethics and the conduct of the business* (3rd ed.), NJ: Prentice Hall.

Boatright, J.R. (2001). The future of corporate social responsibility. *Business & Professional Ethics Journal, 20*(3 & 4), 39-48.

Breshnan, T. (1999). Information technology, workplace organization and the demand for skilled labor: Firm level evidence. *NBER Working Paper*, No.7136.

Brown, T. S., Brown, J.T., & Baack, S.A. (1990-1991, Winter). Attitudes of the Elderly Toward Computers. *The Journal of Computer Information Systems*, 31 (2).

Burtless, G. (1995, June). International trade and the rise in earnings inequality. *Journal of Economic Literature,* 33, 800-816.

Castells, M. (1996). *The rise of the network society.* Oxford, UK: Blackwell Publishers.

Crandall, R. W. (2001). The digital divide: Bridging the divide naturally. *Brookings Review*, 19(1), 38-41.

Dasgupta, S., Lall, S. & Wheeler, D. (2001). Policy reform, economic growth, and the digital divide: An econometric analysis. *Research Paper, World Bank.* Washington D.C: Development Research Group.

Davis, D.R. (1998). Technology, unemployment and relative wages in a global economy. *European Economic Review,* 42(9), 1613-1633.

Deardorff, A.V. (1998). Technology, trade, and increasing inequality: Does the cause matter for the cure? *Journal of International Economic Law*, 353-376.

The Editors. (2001, May 10). The new divides. *Education Week on the Web*, 1-5. Retrieved from http://www.edweek.org.

Feenstra, R. C. & Hanson, G. H. (1997, June). Productivity measurement, outsourcing, and its impact on wages: Estimates for the U.S., 1972-1990. *NBER Working Paper*, No. 6052.

Ferrell, D. C., Fraedrich, J., & Ferrell, L. (2002). *Business ethics: Ethical decision making and cases* (5th ed.). Boston, MA: Houghton Mifflin Co.

Friedman, M. (1962). *Capitalism and freedom.* Chicago, IL: University of Chicago Press.

Georgia Center for Advanced Telecommunications Technology (GCATT). (2001). Digital Georgia.

Harrington, M. (1987). In T. Rohda (Ed.), *The International Thesaurus of Quotations.* Tripp, Harper and Row.

Haskel, J. & Slaughter, M.J. (2001, January). Trade, technology and U.K. wage inequality. *The Economic Journal*, 111, 163-187.

Copyright © 2003, Idea Group Inc. Copying or distributing in print or electronic forms without written permission of Idea Group Inc. is prohibited.

Hoffman, D., Novak, T. & Venkatesh. (1998). Diversity on the Internet: The relationship of race to access in usage. In A. Garmer (Ed.), *Investing in Diversity: Advancing Opportunities for Minorities and the Media* (p. 130) Washington, D.C.: The Aspin Institute.

Igbaria, M. & Huff, S. (1989). Microcomputer Application: An Empirical Look at Usage. *Information and Management, 16*(4), 187-196.

Igbaria, M. & Iivari, J. (1999). Microcomputer utilization patterns among managers and professionals: The case of Finland. *Journal of Computer Information Systems, 33*(3), 28-43.

International Labor Office. (2001). *World Employment Report: Life at Work in the Information Economy.* Geneva: International Labor Office.

Johnson, D. (2001). *Computer Ethics* (3rd ed.) NJ: Prentice Hall.

Johnson, G.E. (1997). Changes in Earning Inequality. *The Journal of Economics Perspectives, 11*(2), 41-54.

Kling, R. (1996). *Computerization and controversy: Value conflict and social choices* (2nd ed.). San Diego, CA: Academic Press.

Krugman, P.R. (1995). Technology, trade, and factor prices. *NBER Working Paper, No. 5395.* Cambridge, MA: National Bureau of Economic Research.

Landau, R. (1988). U.S. economic growth. *Scientific American, 258*(6), 44-56.

Lentz, R.G. (2000). The E-volution of the digital divide in the U.S.: A mayhem of competing metrics. *Info, 2*(4), 355-377.

Light, J. (2001). Rethinking the digital divide. *Harvard Educational Review, 71*(4), 709-733.

Mathews, J. (2000, Summer). The information revolution. *Foreign Policy.*

National Telecommunication Information Administration (NTIA). (1999). *Falling Through the Net: Defining the Digital Divide.* Washington, D.C.: U.S. Department of Commerce.

Neter, J., Kutner, M.H., Nachtsheim, C. J., & Wasserman, W. (1996). *Applied linear statistical models.* Boston, MA: WCB/McGraw-Hill.

OECD. (2000). *Learning to Bridge the Digital Divide.* Organisation for Economic Cooperation and Development.

Organisation for Economic Cooperation and Development (OECD). (1998). *21st Century technologies: Promises and perils of a dynamic future.* Organisation for Economic Cooperation and Development.

Papp, R. (1999). Business-IT alignment: Productivity paradox payoff? *Industrial Management Data Systems, 99*(8), 367-373.

Slowinski, J. (2000). Workforce literacy in an Information Age: Policy recommendations for developing an equitable high-tech skills workforce. *First Monday, 5*(7). Retrieved from http://firstmonday.org.

SPSS. (2001). *SPSS for Windows. Release 10.1.* Chicago, IL: SPSS Inc.

Stein, J.R. (1995). Towards a socioeconomic framework on technological change. *International Journal of Social Economics, 22*(6), 38-52.

Copyright © 2003, Idea Group Inc. Copying or distributing in print or electronic forms without written permission of Idea Group Inc. is prohibited.

Torkzadeh, R. & Gemoets, L.A. (1998-1999). Utilization and impacts of information technology application on end-users in U.S. and Mexico. *Journal of Computer Information Systems*, *39*(2), 6-14.

U.S. Census Bureau. (1997). 1997 Economic census: Information. *Geographic Area Series* (EC97551A). Washington, D.C.: U.S. Census Bureau.

U.S. Census Bureau. (2000). *2000 Census of population and housing*. Washington, D.C.: U.S. Census Bureau.

Wilson, I. (2000, May-June). The new rules: Ethics, social responsibility, and strategy. *Strategy and Leadership*, 12-16.

Copyright © 2003, Idea Group Inc. Copying or distributing in print or electronic forms without written permission of Idea Group Inc. is prohibited.

Chapter XI

Social Responsibility and the Transition Toward a Knowledge-Based Society in Latin America

Heberto J. Ochoa-Morales
University of New Mexico, USA

ABSTRACT

In Latin America, the proliferation of regional and multilateral agreements with integration as a purpose has generated a high flow of goods, services, and investments among these countries. From the economic perspective, the outcome is trade and, therefore, stimulus to economic growth. Information technology is a relevant parameter in this endeavor. The "digital gap" between developed countries (DC) and less developed countries (LDC) is greater than the gap in the "standard of living" between them. The uneven distribution of wealth among and within countries, and the lack of communication infrastructure and computer-based power, situate them at a transitional stage within the "knowledge-based society," which emanates social changes, and therefore new roles to be achieved by private and public institutions within the framework of social responsibility.

Copyright © 2003, Idea Group Inc. Copying or distributing in print or electronic forms without written permission of Idea Group Inc. is prohibited.

INTRODUCTION

In Latin America, regional as well as multilateral integration schemes have a predominant role within integration agreements. Good representations of the above include MERCOSUR: Brazil, Argentina, Uruguay and Paraguay. The Andean Community (AC) is composed of Bolivia, Ecuador, Colombia, Peru, and Venezuela, and the Group of Three (G3): Colombia, Mexico, and Venezuela. These organizations have the intent to establish, among other components, free trade areas, customs unions, common markets, and economic unions — all covenants that, in the future, may evolve into a political union (S.C.A. et al., 1998).

Under the scheme of regional integration, a high flow of goods, services, and investments between countries will be originated primarily under the format of foreign direct investments (FDIs). From the economic perspective, the outcome is trade and, therefore, stimulus to economic growth. By the year 2000, Latin America's regional agreements AC and MERCOSUR, without considering other regional pacts with Chile, had a potential market of 310 million consumers (UN-CEPAL, 1999a). Chile's contribution alone is 15.2 million potential customers. It should be emphasized that the AC countries will have, by the period 2000-2005, an average increase in population rate of 17.98 per thousand, while MERCOSUR will have 13.96, and Chile 11.8 per thousand increases, respectively (UN-CEPAL, 1999b).

The research literature concurs in the importance of technology as a main factor imbedded in the productivity equation. The "digital gap" between developed countries (DC) and the less developed ones (LDC) is greater than the gap built by economic indicators, such as productivity, and socio-economic ones, like "standard of living." In March 2000, the number of users on the Internet was approximately 304 million. The United States of America and Canada have 45%, Europe 27%, the Asia-Pacific region 23%, and Africa and the Middle East 1.5%. Latin America and the Caribbean hold 8% of the world population, but only 3.5% of Internet users and less than 1% of the global e-commerce. Although, in the year 1999, a noticeable increase in Internet host computers was extant. The growth rate has been the highest in the world, and the number of users is 14-fold within the 1995 to 1999 period (UIT, 2000).

The literature emphasized the growth of e-commerce in the decade of the 1990s that has occurred by improvement of computer-based power and the convergence taking place with telecommunications. Nevertheless, there are other factors associated with the developments, which include, but are not limited to, the role and social responsibilities of the public and private sectors in driving and sustaining infrastructure development. Currently, businesses that transact on the Internet have had relevant cost reduction, and an increase in revenues. A high correlation does exist between the growth of benefit and the increase of businesses performing such transactions within the network (U.S.D.C., 1998). E-commerce has shown a rapid development in Latin America. Brazil reached 4 million users in 1999. This

Copyright © 2003, Idea Group Inc. Copying or distributing in print or electronic forms without written permission of Idea Group Inc. is prohibited.

represents 50% of the interconnected population — Mexico with 18%, Argentina 12%, and Chile 4%. It is necessary to emphasize the fact that 80% of electronic commerce is realized within six realms: supermarkets, books, hardware and software, electronic equipment, music, and financial services (UN-CEPAL, 2000b).

Another "gap" present in Latin America that has great repercussions on the digital economy is the one that could be defined by its components: socio-economics and technology. Further, there is an uneven distribution of wealth between countries, and within them. A large price differential regarding telecommunications cost and coverture exists. There is fundamental lack of human resources, and managerial level staff with the expertise needed, for an inevitable digital economy. The latter generates a negative impact on the development of such economy (Applegate et al., 1999).

The governments of the region have accomplished basic strides so that the mass population will have access to the Internet. Peru has created the Peruvian Scientific Network, known by its Spanish abbreviation, RCP. The network is composed of 1,000 public centers that provide service to 40% of the network. In Argentina, the program argentina@internet.todos has approximately 1,000 tele-centers located in low income and remote areas. Brazilian commercial banks are offering free access to the Internet, and Costa Rica is one of the first countries in the world that provides free email to its citizens through estate agencies (UIT, 2000).

The position of the Latin American countries within the framework of a "knowledge-based society" could be described as a transitional one. To acquire the objective of a knowledge-based society, state intervention through laws and regulations and, furthermore, private and public actions, will be essential in view of the peculiar contrasts in the region. It will be wearisome to expect the market forces alone to furnish the needed mechanisms. Also, the implementation of an adequate legal framework which determines the rules and regulations, not only for the suppliers of services, but to compensate for power concentration generated by the technology in the hands of the industrialized countries and multinational enterprise (MNE), are imperative (Katz & Ventura-Dias, 2000).

The literature coincides that computer information systems is a function of various parameters. Among them, the ones that could be identified, related to communication and diffusion, are: cost of telephone service and the structure and behavior of the markets that compose the Internet services. There are at least five relevant parameters in the market of information transmission that will be identifiable, which contribute to shaping the Internet: (1) the carriers; (2) the access providers; (3) the service providers; (4) the content providers; and (5) the end users. These schemes generate conflict and competition. International firms cover the first two levels, meanwhile the rest are national enterprises within country members of regional or multilateral agreements (UN-CEPAL, 2000b).

Carr and Snyder (1997) stated that one occurrence causing great effect in the realm of computing information system is the convergence that is taking place with

Copyright © 2003, Idea Group Inc. Copying or distributing in print or electronic forms without written permission of Idea Group Inc. is prohibited.

computing and telecommunications, because organizations perceive the means of combining the preeminence of computer-based information and telecommunications networks. The rapid evolution of the Internet and Intranet extant play a preponderant role in this new array.

BACKGROUND

In the last decade, the telecommunication sector in Latin America has grown enormously. Privatization and the development of new technologies have performed a critical role in this process. During the decade of the 1990s, two-thirds of the countries of the region totally or partially privatized the telecommunication domain. Uruguay and Costa Rica are examples of the fact that privatization is not *sine qua non* to modernize or acquire new technology — competition is. At the same time, the arrival of new technologies, such as cellular telephones and cable television, has generated substantial changes in the sector. During 1990, 100,000 cellular telephones were in use; 3.5 million during 1995; increasing to 38 million in 1999. The case of Venezuela and Paraguay deserves special attention due to the fact that there are more cell phones than conventional ones (UIT, 2000).

In Latin America, only one-third of all homes have telephone service. The growth and coverture of the telecommunication sector are functions of the regulatory framework in which they are developed, as well as the influence of the responsible regulatory agency. In many cases, monopolies have been created. During the 1980s, 100 people were served by seven telephone lines in the region — Argentina (12), Chile (10), and Mexico (50) each (per 100). Installation of services took an average of five years, and repairs took 15 days. In the last decade, Argentina and Chile users' ratio was increased to 22%. Other good indicators of improvement in the sector are the digitalization of the telephone systems, an increase in the number of public telephones, and the improvement of repair time (UIT, 2000).

Social factors have to be taken into consideration regarding the infrastructure of telecommunications; 25% of the region's population lives on an income of $1 a day. The access to the Internet services in absolute terms is less than the U.S., although it is prohibitive to the great majority of the population, due to poverty. Government involvement could provide a solution to the problem, subsidizing services and the necessary hardware and software (UN-CEPAL, 2000b). A notion does exist that the Internet revolution would narrow the gap between the world's rich and poor. The evidence shows that the opposite could happen, and many developing countries are located on the wrong side of a widening knowledge gap if they do not act almost immediately. The DC's use different approaches to deal with the digital divide. The U.S. approach comes out of the "trade vector," because U.S. firms have large investments in the New Economy. They aggressively seek market expansions. The "state vector," represented by European firms, emphasizes the state responsibility and sustainable development. The northern hemisphere countries, "donor states,"

Copyright © 2003, Idea Group Inc. Copying or distributing in print or electronic forms without written permission of Idea Group Inc. is prohibited.

approach is to find the best way to penetrate foreign markets and use their investments in the most cost-effective mode. The southern hemisphere countries, "host states," are concerned with how to attract investments that could generate growth and, therefore, jobs and wealth that will assist in the struggle to reduce social inequities (Conhaim, 2001).

Across the literature, authors agree in a definition of social responsibility as moral obligation of business organizations to seek goals that will provide common good for the communities that are beyond those required by business itself. According to Adams (2000), the business' main responsibility is the shareholders' concerns, therefore society should not expect large investment or involvement within the communities where they function. Also, the author stated that business organizations look toward the government to provide and maintain the necessary infrastructure for them to operate. Epstein (1998) confirmed that corporations are institutions that exist to fulfill societal purpose, and that the common good of the community is the underlying principle for their continued existence. The author defined corporate social policy process (CSPP) as a concept to provide the tools and operational framework to assist business managers in the consideration of social policies in the decision making process. The foundation of CSPP is the internalization, within business organizations' key elements, of business ethics, corporate social responsibility and corporate social responsiveness (Epstein, 1998). The latter eliminates a vacuum in the decision-making process that could have, as a result, the instance that the literature recognized as "bounded rationality," which is the "good enough solution" for a particular problem. Brazil, member of MERCOSUR, has the privilege to count within its information technology assets the Committee for Democracy in Information Technology (CDI). This not-for-profit organization has as its goal to reduce the "digital gap" affecting individuals of low-income communities, not only in the country, but throughout the world. In addition to bringing information technology (IT) to the less privileged, CDI promotes notions of human rights, literacy, ecology, health, and non-violence (among other important social teachings), that will help to cover the social responsibility vacuum created by the lack of involvement of domestics, MNEs, and public and private institutions. Currently, Brazil has 19 regional CDI centers with 311 schools of information technology and citizenship. Internationally, CDI operates 25 centers located in Chile, Colombia, Japan, Mexico and Uruguay, for a grand total of 336 schools. The Japan Center, located in Tokyo, is mainly used to collect hardware that later is sent to LDC. CDI was created in 1993, by a young professor of information technology, Rodrigo Baggio, with an initial slogan "Computers for Everyone" (htpp://cdi.org.br).

The United Nations' Economic and Social Council, based on the decision 1999/281, resolved that the high level segment of the agenda for the year 2000 would be dedicated to "The Development and International Cooperation in the XXI Century: The Function of Information Technology in the Context of a World Economy Based in Knowledge." Therefore, representatives of Latin American and Caribbean

Copyright © 2003, Idea Group Inc. Copying or distributing in print or electronic forms without written permission of Idea Group Inc. is prohibited.

Countries met in the town of Florianopolis, Santa Catarina, Brazil, from June 20 to 21, 2000, to issue the guidelines to design and implement the necessary mechanisms to move these countries into the "knowledgeable society" (UN-CEPAL, 2000a).

The mechanism of social responsibility will need to be based on an agenda that will contain several public policies to increase the efficiency and equity during the transition to a knowledge-based society. These include, but are not limited to: cost of telecommunication services, access to the digital network, and cost and accessibility to the computational structure. Education of the users at any level is necessary, and access must be provided to the mass population with scarce financial resources for the information society. To reach the latter, the establishment of terminals in public places and community centers is necessary. All the above have to be performed within a legal framework that provides the essential elements to guarantee electronic transactions and, therefore, the ability to generate a large volume of trade using this media.

CONCLUSION

A "Framework for the Virtual Society," Figure 1, depicts the parameters in which the virtual society evolved (Igbaria, 1999). The regional trading block already in place in Latin America will generate an expansion of business into global markets, creating a global economy in which new standards for trade will be present, which include, but are not limited to, electronic payments like e-cash, and electronic data interchange (EDI) among businesses located elsewhere. Due to economic and social factors in Latin America, the role of regional governments to provide oversight for this new arrangement is not only preponderant, but could be controversial. Elements, such as the amount of control to be adopted by the government, regulations, and privatization, will be relevant to the development of the knowledge-based society within the legal framework — same as the education and exposure of the population to the new virtual society (Ochoa-Morales, 2001). The Peruvian case portrays the importance of privatization versus a state monopoly in the telecommunication industry. It shows that privatization not only increased the amount of investments and the growth of many parameters within the telecommunication area, but also allows the mass population to have access to the technology (Ochoa-Morales, 2002). Any new policies should contain essential provisions addressing the importance of social responsibility and accountability. This will aid in reaching the goals of helping in the realm of social inequalities. Pertaining to the technology sector, a component that will exert large influence is the volatility of the communication segment, due to the availability of new technology and changes thereof. The workplace arrangements, such as tele-work, computer-supported cooperative work (CSCW), among others described in the model (Figure 1), are elements that will change the way business is done conventionally and will cause a great impact in social and cultural values within the context of society.

Copyright © 2003, Idea Group Inc. Copying or distributing in print or electronic forms without written permission of Idea Group Inc. is prohibited.

Figure 1. A framework for the virtual society (M. Igbaria)

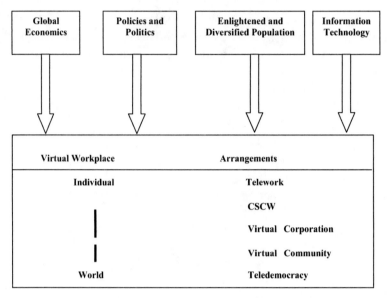

© 1999 ACM, Inc. Reprinted by permission

The synergism generated by countries, as members of regional and/or multilateral agreements, allows them to obtain the necessary endowment to develop the infrastructure required for a virtual society. This synergism also contributes to dissipate the concentration of power originated by the technology in the hands of the DC and multinational enterprises, and provides the necessary significance to establish policies that eliminate the vacuum created by the lack of involvement of business organizations regarding the social implications cause by the virtual society.

In summary, the above gives rise to the following questions that have direct relevance to the solution of how to close the existing digital gap and establish the relevance of social responsibility within the framework of the knowledge-based society:

1. What kind of agenda should be implemented to avoid the uneven distribution of wealth among countries, and within them, that allows the creation of the necessary information technology infrastructure?

2. How will the countries implement an agenda to address and prioritize the issues of social responsibility, with regard to the implications inherent in the cultural diversity and the existence of economic and social inequality pervasive within the countries and among them?

REFERENCES

Adams, J. D. (2000). Dominant institutions and their responsibility. *The Futurist*, 34(2), 65.

Copyright © 2003, Idea Group Inc. Copying or distributing in print or electronic forms without written permission of Idea Group Inc. is prohibited.

Applegate, L. M., McFarlan, F. W., & McKenney, J. L. (1999). *Corporate information systems management: Text and cases* (5th ed.). New York: Irwin McGraw-Hill, pp. 404-417.

Carr, H. H. & Snyder, C. A. (1997). *The management of telecommunications: Business solutions to business problems.* New York: Irwin McGraw Hill, pp. 680-682.

Committee for Democracy in Information Technology (CDI). *Institutional Profile.* Retrieved from: http://www.cdi.org.br.

Conhaim, W. (2001). The global digital divide. *Information Today, 18*(7).

Epstein, E. M. (1998). Business ethics and corporate social policy. *Business and Society, 37*(1).

Igbaria, M. (1999). The driving forces in the virtual society. *Communications of the ACM, 42*(12), 64-70.

Katz, J. & Ventura-Dias, V. (2000). America Latina y el Caribe en la Transicion Hacia Una Sociedad del Conocimiento. Una Agenda de Politicas Publicas. Informe, LC/L.1383/E, Junio 1.

Ochoa-Morales, H. J. (2001). The digital gap between the industrialized countries and the less developed ones (LDC): The transition toward a knowledgeable society in Latin America. *Issues in Information Systems, 2,* 337-342.

Ochoa-Morales, H. J. (2002). The impact of reforms in the telecommunication sector and its effects on Latin America. *Journal of Issues in Information Systems, 3,* 483-489.

Secretaria de la Comunidad Andina (S.C.A.), Cooperacion Francesa y CEPAL. (1998). Multilaterismo y Regionalismo. Seminario efectuado en Santa Fe de Bogota, 26 de Mayo, 1-2.

UN-CEPAL (Comision Economica Para America Latina y El Caribe). (1999a). America Latina: Poblacion Total, Urbana y Rural y Porcentaje Urbano por Paises. Cuadro 11. *Boletin Demografico, 63,* 1-6. Retrieved from http://www.eclac.cl/publicaciones/Poblacion/2/LCG2052/BD63.11html.

UN-CEPAL (Comision Economica Para America Latina y El Caribe). (1999b). America Latina: Tasa de Crecimiento de la Poblacion Total, Urbana y Rural por Paises. Cuadro 12. *Boletin Demografico, 63,* 1-3. Retrieved from http://www.eclac.cl/publicaciones/Poblacion/2/LCG2052/BD63.12html.

UN-CEPAL (2000a). *Declaracion de Florianapolis. Reunion Regional en Tecnologia de Informacion para el Desarrollo,* Brasil, 1-9.

UN-CEPAL (2000b). *Latin America and the Caribbean in the Transition to a Knowledge-Based Society: An Agenda for Public Policy,* LC/L.1383, 5-25.

Union International de Telecomunicaciones: UIT. (2000). Indicadores de Telecomunicaciones de Las Americas 2000. *Resumen Ejecutivo,* 1-22.

U.S. Department of Commerce. (1998). The Emerging Digital Economy. Retrieved from http://www.ecommerce.gov. 2, 4, 21, 23, 35.

Copyright © 2003, Idea Group Inc. Copying or distributing in print or electronic forms without written permission of Idea Group Inc. is prohibited.

Chapter XII

Information Systems Ethics in the USA and in the Arab World

Husain Al-Lawatia
Utah State University, USA

Thomas Hilton
Utah State University, USA

ABSTRACT

This chapter explores similarities and differences between two cultures, the USA and the Arab World, in BIS ethics, through a survey of American and Arab students on personal use of organizational computers, use of organizational IS resources for non-organization gain, and monitoring of organizational IS resource use. While interesting statistical differences were found in the average strength of several responses, there was no disagreement as to the ethicality or non-ethicality of any survey item. The authors view this consistency as encouraging evidence of a common foundation for IS-related commerce between the two cultures. The findings of this study can be a basis for future cooperation, as legislators, educators, and employers in the Arab World and the USA develop acceptable BIS practices.

Copyright © 2003, Idea Group Inc. Copying or distributing in print or electronic forms without written permission of Idea Group Inc. is prohibited.

INTRODUCTION

The past two decades have shown a rapid, though unequal, spread of computers throughout businesses worldwide. Despite this spread, the information systems (IS) field is still considered relatively young (Pierce & Henry, 2000). One result of this youth is a general dearth of IS-related laws and clear-cut codes of conduct to regulate this challenging, fast expanding sphere (Udas, Fuerst, & Paradice, 1996). Thus, ethical issues in the IS field are highly influenced by less obvious factors, such as a nation's general legal system, and other disciplines, such as business law, internal organizational policies, culture, social, etc. (Pierce & Henry).

Research suggests that cultural values and traditions have a substantial influence on many IS ethics issues (Whitman, Townsend, & Hendrickson, 1999). As a consequence, what is considered 'right' IS use by one culture may be considered 'wrong' by another culture. This cultural factor may often supersede internal policies and codes that multinational corporations have issued to guide their personnel in using information systems consistently, ethically, and legally. Certainly such internal policies are necessary, but they are often perceived as ineffective (Loch, Conger, & Oz, 1998).

In our opinion, unauthorized copying of software has received a lot of research attention due to its huge negative effect on developers. Other IS ethical issues, however, have not received a similar level of attention.

This study aims to explore similarities and differences in IS ethics between two different cultures: the USA and the Arab World. The authors hope to begin identifying specifics of how these two cultures vary in deciding what is 'right' and what is 'wrong' in IS ethics issues.

LITERATURE REVIEW

In building a framework for investigating differences and similarities in information systems ethics among computer users in the Arab world and those in the USA, the following areas of literature are reviewed:

- Ethics defined
- Ethics in the USA
- Ethics in the Arab world
- Law and ethical behavior
- Personal code of ethics as a function of culture

Ethics Defined

Ethics is defined in different and sometimes conflicting ways depending on one's philosophical background (Regan, 1984, as cited by Udas et al., 1996). Therefore, Udas et al. suggest, that a definition of ethics that could be meaningfully applied in the business arena must be flexible. As this study aims to explore

Copyright © 2003, Idea Group Inc. Copying or distributing in print or electronic forms without written permission of Idea Group Inc. is prohibited.

similarities and differences in IS ethics between two different cultures, the USA and Arabian, it is important to understand the basis from which the people of these two cultures view and define ethics, particularly as it applies to business computing.

Ethics in the USA

Historically, religion has had a considerable cultural influence on business ethics throughout the world (Wienen, 1999), and the USA is no exception. However, in the United States today, like other western countries that are considered highly secular (Kruckeberg, 1996), religion has declined in its influence on defining the ethics that could be generally accepted by the various socio-economic sectors of society.

Secular Ethics

The definition of ethics in the USA is now based on secular philosophic views centered in different philosophical schools of thought such as the utilitarian (most popular), teleological, deontological, etc. According to Kimberly and Jonathon (1999), those schools of thought are the foundation of ethical decision-making, and thus they shape personal values and beliefs in the U.S., on which ethics are rooted. As a result, it is difficult to find in the ethics literature a generally accepted definition of ethics from the western perspective. However, several definitions of ethics from general and business perspectives offered by scholars from different academic and business domains are considered representative. Hiller (1986) views ethics as an instrument that "attempts to find good reasons for holding certain values or adopting certain principles or duties as a guide to decision making" (p. 6). Price (as quoted in Kimberly & Jonathon, 1999) defines ethics as "an explanation of what ought to be done and why, the study of why we have the particular belief system that we have, and the analysis of how moral codes relate to what we value." Finally, Cook (1997) espouses "situational ethics," the belief that rules of ethics may change because in certain cases ordinarily acceptable ethical principles may not apply.

Business Ethics

According to Newton and Ford (1994), "'business ethics' is sometimes considered to be an oxymoron.... Business and ethics have often been treated as mutually exclusive. But ethics is an issue of growing concern and importance to businesses..." (p. xii). Fort (1998) presents ethical business behavior in a formula form introduced by William Frederick (1995). Fort states, "in this 'Philosopher's Formula,' ethical business behavior (B_E) is a function of Kantian rights (R_K), Rawlsian justice (J_R), and Jamesian utilitarianism (U_J)."

U.S. business ethics is also asserted as globally applicable. According to Buller, Kohls and Anderson (2000), "global business ethics is the application of moral values and principles to complex cross-cultural situations." This recent definition of business ethics seems to be general enough to be accepted by most cultures, including those of the Arab world.

Copyright © 2003, Idea Group Inc. Copying or distributing in print or electronic forms without written permission of Idea Group Inc. is prohibited.

Ethics in the Arab World

Kruckeberg (1996) states that "Islam is the state-sanctioned religion in many Middle East countries" (p. 187). Similarly, Wienen (1999) observes that "Islam is a driving force behind the cultural development in the Muslim World" (p. 18). This implies that Arab ethics are influenced significantly by Islam. As a result, the definition of ethics — or "Akhlaq," the comparable term used by Muslims — cannot be defined in isolation from Islam. Knowing this is important both in defining Arab ethics and in distinguishing it from ethics in the USA. According to Siddiqui (1997),

"The comparable word for ethics in Islam is Akhlaq, and this is construed as morality. The problem rises when we study akhlaq vis-à-vis ethics. In western vocabulary the terms 'ethics' and 'morality' have different origins; one derived from the Greek ethos, 'ethics,' and the other derived from the Latin mores or 'morals.' Both mean habits or customs, but the distinction in European (and U.S.) thought and language has been maintained. One is what is 'commonly felt and done' (morals) as opposed to what is 'appropriate and rational' (ethics). In Islamic thought, the predominant feature is knowledge of morality (ilm-ul-Akhlaq), i.e., what we could call the 'science of ethics'" (p. 2).

In a similar vein, Beekun (1997) attempts to define ethics from an Islamic perspective, how Allah views ethical individuals and what should be the role of ethics in the Muslim's life. He states, "Without specifying any situational context," Allah describes, "people who attain success as those who are "inviting to all that is good (Khayr), enjoining what is right (ma'ruf) and forbidding what is wrong (munkar). In Islam, ethics governs all aspects of life" (pp. 1-2).

Relating this perspective to business ethics, Abeng (1997) states, "Besides its general appreciation for the vocation of business, the Qu'ran often speaks about honesty and justice in trade (see Qur'an 6:152; 17:35; 55:9). The Qur'an also presents Allah as the prototype of good conduct. The Muslims, therefore, are supposed to emulate Him throughout their lives including, of course, their conduct in business" (p. 50). This means that ethics is viewed similarly in all circumstances from the Islamic point of view, that ethics in business is not essentially different from ethics in other contexts.

Consequently, it is important to understand that the term "ethics" in the Arab world has a significantly different meaning than it does in the USA. Keeping this in mind, the factors that affect human ethical behaviors, including IS-related acts, are discussed in the next two sections.

Law and Ethical Behavior

Laws are a strong deterrent of behaviors legislatively defined to be illegal. Generally, unlawful acts are also viewed as unethical (Hilton, 1989). According to

Copyright © 2003, Idea Group Inc. Copying or distributing in print or electronic forms without written permission of Idea Group Inc. is prohibited.

the general theory of deterrence, laws' effect on illegal behavior depends on the certainty and severity of the punishment (Harrington, 1996). The outcome of law enforcement influences both behavior and decision-making and is usually due more to fear and creation of habits of compliance than to the integrity of the individual (Pierce & Henry, 1996). Law could, therefore, play a superior role in deterring people from conducting acts that are considered illegal (or unethical) in the IS discipline. However, IS laws throughout the world are not consistent, and so the certainty and severity of punishment varies between cultures. For example, unauthorized copying of software, or so-called "software pirating," is considered illegal in many countries (including the United States) yet legal in others (such as China); this is the case with many IS issues. The authors thus believe that laws cannot be looked to presently for a definition of IS ethics. Every single IS matter has not been — nor could it ever be — legislated. Moreover, the authors see no imminent prospects for reconciling IS legislation in all (or even most) of the legal systems of the world to produce a globally accepted body of IS law. Thus we agree with Whitman et al. (1999), who found that cultural traits can generate illegal acts despite legislation and must not be ignored.

Personal Code of Ethics as a Function of Culture

Guthrie (1997) writes that a personal code of ethics is a framework inside a person for making "ethical decisions and discuss[ing] their values as they relate to society as a whole"; such personal codes are a function of a variety of philosophies, social and cultural norms, and surrounding laws and other codes (p. 1). Personal codes of ethics can be viewed as influenced by business policies as well as by the broader culture.

Business Policies and Personal Codes of Ethics

Pierce and Henry (2000) write that employees are influenced by their personal norms, co-worker norms, and organizational norms as a whole when making an ethics decision. However, although individual ethics decisions are influenced by formal ethics codes (Pierce & Henry, 1996), Lewellyn (1996) found that a person's personal ethics, shaped over time, have more impact on such decisions than any other factor. Therefore, being ethical is not like a switch to be turned off and on; it is an inseparable trait that shapes all aspects of a person's life (Plenert, 1995). In short, then, formal organizational codes of ethics appear to help in guiding behavior, but the personal ethics code is what allows or prevents a behavior (Pierce & Henry).

Pierce and Henry (1996) point out that it is, therefore, important to be sure formal codes do not conflict with the more influential personal codes of IS users. As an example, they describe the ideological conflict between western-based concepts of copyright protection and Chinese traditions of intellectual property. In the west, intellectual property can be owned by a single person or organization, whereas, in China, intellectual property is presumed to be owned collectively by the people.

Copyright © 2003, Idea Group Inc. Copying or distributing in print or electronic forms without written permission of Idea Group Inc. is prohibited.

Therefore, they characterize the so-called problem of Asian software copyright infringement less as unethical behavior than as basic cultural difference (Whitman, Townsend & Hendrickson, 1999).

Whitman et al. (1999) describe another IS controversy that shows the importance of cultural differences: they report that in Singapore and Hong Kong the personal use of company equipment and time is viewed as unethical whether the company prohibits it or not, whereas in some other countries it is not unethical to use company equipment and time for personal matters unless such use is specifically forbidden by the company.

Personal Code and Culture

According to Randlesome and Myers (1995), "many definitions of culture have appeared in the literature" (p. 42). Two interesting and matching views about culture seem acceptable for the purpose of this study. The first one views culture as "a whole way of life of a people, i.e., their interpersonal relations and their behaviours as well as their attitudes" (Randlesome & Myers). The other perspective is more comprehensive, and views culture as "a generic term...made up of a host of interrelated elements. These include family, language and communication, religion, government and politics, education, technology, society, and economic structures and activities" (Baligh, 1994, as cited by Dunning & Bansal, 1997). Based on these definitions, many cultural factors influence individuals' behaviors and attitudes. (However, the authors observe that some factors may be much more influential in one culture than in another; for example, religion plays a different role in U.S. ethics than in Arabian akhlaq.)

Undoubtedly, this effect of culture would extend to business activity. According to Hiller (1986), cultural issues are the source of several ethical dilemmas in management. For example, "Managed care competition has resulted in a healthcare system in which provider choice is restricted" (Kimberly & Jonathan, 1999, Sec. 2). This shows the strong influence of culture on individual morality in business/IS settings.

Conclusion of Literature Review

Questions of right and wrong in Information Systems use, then, are hardly isolated from outside influences. As Kimberly and Jonathan (1999) write, "Ethics is humanistic, personal, and dependent on one's conscience" (p. 9). Therefore, laws or organizationally defined policy codes are not enough by themselves to maintain ethical behavior; such relatively public statements must be supported by personal values derived from morals based on experience interpreted through the lens of culture. And it must be understood that religion, although ostensibly minimized in U.S. ethics, plays a major, even preeminent, role in Arabian akhlaq. Wienen (1999) reinforced this point with his finding that the influence of religion is obvious as a cultural influence on management in the Muslim world.

Copyright © 2003, Idea Group Inc. Copying or distributing in print or electronic forms without written permission of Idea Group Inc. is prohibited.

However, having said that, the literature also shows that cultural factors other than religion contribute to the development of personal ethics. Moreover, individual differences play a major role: personal codes of ethics develop variously according to individual experience with law, employment, profession, etc.

In conclusion, literature supports the view that culture has a substantial influence on personal ethical decisions and contributes significantly to the ethical framework through which any act is judged right or wrong, ethical or unethical. Based on this review, the authors hypothesize significant divergence in ethics opinions between U.S. and Arab computer users.

RESEARCH QUESTION

This pilot study investigates and explores similarities and differences in ethics between the American culture and the Arabian culture as they manifest in the BIS field. The specific research question is:

How does the American culture differ from the Arabian culture in their views regarding IS ethical issues?

METHODOLOGY

Instrument

After considerable review of the instruments in the area of IS, the researchers decided to develop an instrument deemed appropriate and suitable for the purpose of the study. Thus, the instrument is based on a series of vignettes illustrating various computer uses. Three types of IS ethical issues that are likely to face computer users in any business setting were adopted as the backbone of the survey. These areas are employee's use of company IS resources and time for personal use and entertainment; employee's use of company IS resources (hardware, software, and/or information) for personal, friend's, and or relatives' gain; and finally, the company's use of non-trust systems — either manual or computerized — to monitor its employees. The questions in all three parts of the survey are derived from the studies of Lewellyn (1996), Loch et al. (1998), and Whitman et al. (1999).

The respondents were asked to judge each ethical issue in the survey on a five-point Likert-type scale (Pierce & Henry, 2000) from usually ethical to usually unethical. Instructions were provided to respondents stating that their answer should reflect their personal opinion. Also, they were asked to respond to all issues even if they were unsure of their opinion. Every effort was made to obtain unbiased responses. To assure anonymity to subjects, the surveys were not coded or numbered. Also, the subjects were informed before giving answers that the data would only be reported in an aggregate form.

Copyright © 2003, Idea Group Inc. Copying or distributing in print or electronic forms without written permission of Idea Group Inc. is prohibited.

Data Collection Procedure and Sample

Unlike other ethics research that used mail surveys in obtaining data (Pierce & Henry, 2000), the unique situation of this study forced the researchers to approach the subjects personally. The reason for using this approach was because the number of Arab students in the two universities that were selected for conducting this study was small. Therefore, Arab students were approached outside the classroom setting. On the other hand, all U.S. undergraduate and some graduate students were approached in the classroom. Other U.S graduate students were approached personally. Additionally, the number of U.S. undergraduate respondents was higher than the number of Arab respondents. In order to avoid problems that might arise concerning equal variance and make the t-tests more robust, surveys of 33 U.S undergraduate students were randomly dropped from the study making the number of respondents of both groups equal.

All computer users across both cultures, not only IS or computer science (CS) professionals, were deemed appropriate for this study. A convenience sample of students from two U.S. universities was used. The demographic characteristics of the entire sample are shown in Table 1.

RESULTS

To check the survey's reliability, Chronbach's alpha was calculated for each part of the survey. Results generated from this test were, Part 1 (.86), Part 2 (.84), and Part 3 (.77). These results suggest that the instrument appears to be acceptably reliable.

As mentioned earlier, the sampling scheme in this study was not drawn to be statistically representative of any particular population. Thus, generalizing the results presented here must be left to the reader. However, on the assumption that at least some readers will be tempted to generalize, we include here a power analysis of the study's statistics. Surprisingly, despite a medium effect size (.25), the power statistic

Table 1. Respondent demographics (n = 136)

		Arabs		American	
		Frequency	Percent	Frequency	Percent
Gender	Male	66	97	52	76
	Female	2	3	16	24
	Total	68	100	68	100
Academic Level	Undergraduate	40	59	42	62
	Graduate	28	41	26	38
	Total	68	100	68	100
Age	Under 21	22	32	8	12
	21 to 30	31	46	46	68
	31 to 40	15	22	11	16
	Over 40	0	0	3	4
	Total	68	100	68	100

Copyright © 2003, Idea Group Inc. Copying or distributing in print or electronic forms without written permission of Idea Group Inc. is prohibited.

turned out to be high (98.5). This is due primarily to the relatively large sample size (n = 136) and should not be misinterpreted as compensating for the non-representative sampling scheme.

Setting the rejection criterion of significance at 0.05, the following tests were conducted to obtain results from the data collected. First, a t-test was used to analyze the difference in survey responses of the two cultures. Results obtained were t (df = 134) = 1.423, p = .157, which indicates no significant differences between cultures.

Second, t-tests were used to analyze the mean difference between the two groups for each question. Results in Table 2 revealed that eight out of the total 24 questions were found to have significant differences between the two groups.

Third, a t-test was carried out to assess the mean difference between the two groups for each of the three parts of the survey. Results in Table 3 show that only the first part of the survey, concerning employee's use of company computers for personal use and entertainment, was found to be significantly different (t (df = 134) = 2.189, p = .030). However, the other two parts, employee use of company IS resources for personal, relatives, and or friends gain (p = .801); and the company use of non-trust systems to monitor employees (p = .138), were not found significantly different.

DISCUSSION AND CONCLUSIONS

Despite the fact that research indicated that culture has a significant influence on personal ethical decisions, including some aspects of IS, the results of this study indicate that there is no overall significant difference between subjects from the Arab World and those from the United States in their views regarding IS ethical issues.

Personal Use of Organization Computers

However, when each of the three parts of the survey was independently examined, the first part, which is about the use of company computers for personal matters and entertainment, revealed statistically significant differences (p = .030): while both groups viewed the practice as unethical, Arab respondents viewed this practice as more unethical than did the non-Arab Americans. As discussed in the literature, these results are consistent with the findings of Whitman et al. (1999) (Singapore and Hong Kong, both eastern cultures, were found to be less tolerant of the use of company resources and time for personal matters than most of western cultures, including that of the United States).

This finding is clarified by another interesting result in Part 1 that was revealed when survey questions were examined independently. Questions 2, 4, and 6 evaluate the morality of using company computers for personal use and entertainment *after* working hours, and questions 1, 3, and 5 ask about using company computers *during* working hours. There was no significant difference between the two groups regarding use of company computers for personal matters during working hours; the

Copyright © 2003, Idea Group Inc. Copying or distributing in print or electronic forms without written permission of Idea Group Inc. is prohibited.

Table 2.   Mean responses by question and culture

PART 1: EMPLOYEE USES EMPLOYER COMPUTERS FOR...	Culture	Mean*	S.D	t	p 2-tailed	Diff.
Q1: games during work	Arab	4.03	1.20	1.07	0.29	0.24
	U.S.	3.79	1.37			
Q2: games after work	*Arab*	*2.87*	*1.27*	*4.02*	*0.00*	*0.84*
	U.S.	*2.03*	*1.16*			
Q3: personal matters during work	Arab	3.68	1.38	0.25	0.80	0.06
	U.S.	3.62	1.34			
Q4: personal matters after work	*Arab*	*2.60*	*1.31*	*3.11*	*0.00*	*0.63*
	U.S.	*1.97*	*1.05*			
Q5: personal web browsing during work	Arab	3.40	1.44	-0.31	0.76	-0.07
	U.S.	3.47	1.37			
Q6: personal web browsing after work	*Arab*	*2.34*	*1.30*	*2.45*	*0.02*	*0.50*
	U.S.	*1.84*	*1.07*			
PART 2: EMPLOYEE...	Culture	Mean*	S.D.	t	p 2-tailed	Diff.
Q7: uses employer data for personal gain	Arab	4.35	1.13	-1.09	0.28	-0.19
	U.S.	4.54	0.90			
Q8: uses employer data for the gain of family or friends	Arab	4.41	0.95	0.60	0.55	0.10
	U.S.	4.31	1.04			
Q9: installs employer-licensed software on employee's own PC	*Arab*	*3.78*	*1.22*	*-2.42*	*0.02*	*-0.44*
	U.S.	*4.22*	*0.88*			
Q10: installs employer-licensed software on the PC of a friend or relative	*Arab*	*4.16*	*1.20*	*-2.67*	*0.01*	*-0.46*
	U.S.	*4.62*	*0.73*			
Q11: uses employer e-mail system for personal e-mail	Arab	2.66	1.40	0.27	0.79	0.06
	U.S.	2.60	1.12			
Q12: uses but does not install employer licensed software on employee's own personal PC	*Arab*	*3.00*	*1.25*	*-2.31*	*0.02*	*-0.49*
	U.S.	*3.49*	*1.20*			
Q13: prints personal documents on employer's printer and uses employer's paper	Arab	3.50	1.31	0.48	0.63	0.10
	U.S.	3.40	1.20			
Q14: prints personal documents on employer's printer but uses employee's own paper	Arab	2.81	1.43	0.58	0.56	0.13
	U.S.	2.68	1.23			
Q15: stores personal documents on employer's computer	Arab	2.68	1.38	0.56	0.57	0.12
	U.S.	2.56	1.03			
Q16: logs into and uses employer's computer using a different employee's password	Arab	4.38	1.20	0.63	0.53	0.12
	U.S.	4.26	0.96			
Q17: discloses sensitive customer information to an authorized third party without customer permission	*Arab*	*4.59*	*0.97*	*3.64*	*0.00*	*0.71*
	U.S.	*3.88*	*1.28*			
Q18: discloses sensitive customer information to an unauthorized third party without customer permission	Arab	4.78	0.73	-1.12	0.26	-0.12
	U.S.	4.90	0.46			
PART 3: EMPLOYER...	Culture	Mean*	S.D.	t	p 2-tailed	Diff.
Q19: monitors employee e-mail without informing employees	*Arab*	*3.96*	*1.29*	*2.61*	*0.01*	*0.59*
	U.S.	*3.37*	*1.34*			
Q20: monitors employee e-mail after informing employees	Arab	2.26	1.32	1.52	0.13	0.32
	U.S.	1.94	1.16			
Q21: makes surprise checks for personal documents on employer PCs without informing employees of the possibility	Arab	3.68	1.31	0.94	0.35	0.21
	U.S.	3.47	1.25			
Q22: makes surprise checks for personal documents on employer PCs after informing employees of the possibility	Arab	2.29	1.36	1.40	0.16	0.29
	U.S.	2.00	1.08			
Q23: makes surprise checks for non-employer software on employer PCs without informing employees of the possibility	Arab	2.71	1.35	0.25	0.80	0.06
	U.S.	2.65	1.37			
Q24: makes surprise checks for non-employer software on employer PCs after informing employees of the possibility	Arab	1.74	1.20	-0.72	0.47	-0.15
	U.S.	1.88	1.18			

n = 136
*Mean = Average responses on five-point Likert-type scale from 1 (usually ethical) to 5 (usually unethical).
Statistically significant questions are in bold italics.

Copyright © 2003, Idea Group Inc. Copying or distributing in print or electronic forms without written permission of Idea Group Inc. is prohibited.

Table 3.   Mean response by part and culture

	Culture	Mean*	S.D.	t	p 2-tailed	Diff.
Part 1: Q1 to Q6 *Personal Use of Employer Computers*	*Arab*	*18.91*	*5.74*	*2.189*	*.030*	*2.19*
	U.S.	*16.72*	*5.93*			
Part 2: Q7 to Q18 Use of Employer Computers for Family or Friends	Arab	45.10	9.10	(.252)	.801	(.35)
	U.S.	45.46	7.10			
Part 3: Q19 to Q24 Monitoring Employee Use of Employer Computers	Arab	16.63	5.27	1.492	.138	1.32
	U.S.	15.31	5.08			

N = 136

*Mean = Average responses on five-point Likert-type scale from 1 (usually ethical) to 5 (usually unethical) after being multiplied by the number of questions in each part.
Statistically significant parts are in bold italics.

difference became statistically significant only when considering computer use after working hours.

Use of Organization Resources for Non-Company Gain

Comparison of the overall mean responses to the questions in Part 2 revealed no significant difference between Americans and Arabs. However, analysis of individual questions did reveal significant differences.

Questions 9, 10, and 12 appraise the morality of installing or using company-licensed software off-premises by the employee, by friends of the employee, or by relatives of the employee for non-company purposes. The outcome of these questions showed Americans to be more conservative than Arabs. While both cultures agree the above acts are unethical, American subjects viewed these acts as significantly more unethical than their Arab counterparts. Again, this outcome is consistent with the results of Whitman et al. (1999), who found that Americans are significantly less tolerant of copyright infringement than all other countries.

Question 17 assesses the morality of disclosing potentially damaging personal information to an authorized third person. Responses to this question indicate that Arab respondents consider this more unethical than do American respondents. However, the authors find these results counterintuitive (since authorized persons would presumably be justified in receiving information), and therefore did some informal checking with respondents. These informal checks reveal a possible wording problem in the question that, if verified, would invalidate this result.

Monitoring Employee Computer Use

Analysis of Part 3 of the survey as a whole, which asked about monitoring employee use of employer computers, revealed no significant difference between Arab and American respondents. However, question-by-question analysis did reveal one significant difference. Question 19 assesses the morality of monitoring employee email by the company without informing employees of the monitoring. While both groups considered the practice unethical, the Arab respondents considered it to be worse than did American respondents.

Copyright © 2003, Idea Group Inc. Copying or distributing in print or electronic forms without written permission of Idea Group Inc. is prohibited.

Conclusions

In conclusion, there appear to be two main points identified in this study. First, there is a remarkable consistency between Arabs and non-Arab Americans in their answers to questions: in no case did one group consider ethical an act that the other group considered unethical. Second, there were statistically significant differences between the groups on eight individual questions, suggesting a different level of concern for some issues between the two groups as discussed above; again, even these differences were always on the same side of the response scale. Thus, although culture presumably remains a primary determinant of ethics, there seems to be no more than a modest differentiating effect of these two particular cultures on IS-related ethics opinions of their members. This is generally in conformity with the literature.

LIMITATIONS AND RECOMMENDATIONS FOR FUTURE RESEARCH

Several traits of this study necessarily moderate the confidence that can be placed in its results. The use of students in a study about ethical issues in relation to the business environment raises generalization questions. Students, particularly undergraduates, are likely to have limited experiences in practical business settings. What's more, using students in this study forced the researchers to ignore internal IS codes that large corporations and careful entrepreneurs usually view as an important influence on professional activities. Hence, future studies in this area should target respondents from a real business environment. It is possible that results of such a future study could vary significantly from those reported here.

The use of convenience samples in this study raises several concerns about its validity. It is possible that the samples used in this study are not representative of Arabs or Americans. Moreover, the entire Arab sample was living in the United States. These subjects are possibly affected by the U.S. culture to some extent, thus possibly making them less representative of their population. This weakness should be addressed in future studies. The samples should be selected from the respective cultures.

Lastly, the Arab sample was comprised of people from a variety of countries that presumably have greatly differing access to information systems. Although religion and language were common to all Arab respondents, the authors have no way of determining the effect of nationality on the responses. As is clear in the literature, culture is comprised of several other factors beside religion and language factors. Depending on the magnitude of each factor in shaping cultural values in each country, IS-related ethical decisions could be different among different countries throughout that part of the world. Therefore, it is recommended that future studies should either control for the effect of nationality or sample one country.

Copyright © 2003, Idea Group Inc. Copying or distributing in print or electronic forms without written permission of Idea Group Inc. is prohibited.

REFERENCES

Abeng T. (1997). Business ethics in Islamic context: Perspectives of a Muslim business leader. *Business Ethics Quarterly, 7* (3), 47-54.

Beekun, R. I. (1997). *Islamic business ethics*. Herndon, VA: International Institute of Islamic Thought.

Buller, P. F., Kohls, J. J., & Anderson, K. S. (2000). Managing conflicts across cultures [electronic version]. *Organizational Dynamics, 28* (4), 52-66.

Cook, F. W. (1997). Guidelines for developing a code. *Compensation & Benefits Review, 29* (2), 24-28.

Dunning, J. H & Bansel, S. (1997). The cultural sensitivity of the eclectic paradigm [electronic version]. *Multinational Business Review, 5* (1), 1-16.

Fort, T. L. (1998). Goldilocks and business ethics: A paradigm [electronic version]. *Journal of Corporation Law, 23* (2), 245-276.

Guthrie, R. (1997). The ethics of telework. *Information Systems Management, 14* (4), 29-32. Retrieved on January 16, 2003, from Business Source Premier Databases.

Harrington, S. J. (1996). The effect of codes of ethics and personal denial of responsibility on computer abuse judgments [electronic version]. *MIS Quarterly, 20* (3), 257-278.

Hiller, M. D. (1986). *Ethics and health administration: Ethical decision making in health management*. Arlington, VA: Association of University Programs in Health Administration.

Hilton, T. (1989, Summer). A framework for teaching computer ethics. *Instructional Strategies: An Applied Research Series: A Refereed Publication of Delta Pi Epsilon*, 1-4.

Kimberly, S. & Jonathon, S. (1999). Ethical decision making in health care management [electronic version]. *Hospital Topics, 77* (4), 7-13.

Kruckeberg, D. (1996). A global perspective on public relations ethics. *The Middle East Public Relations Review, 22* (2), 181-189.

Lewellyn, P. A. (1996). Academic perceptions: Ethics in the information systems discipline. *Journal of Business Ethics, 15,* 559-569.

Loch, K. D., Conger, S., & Oz, E. (1998). Ownership, privacy and monitoring in the workplace: A debate on technology and ethics. *Journal of Business Ethics, 17,* 653-663.

Newton, L. H. & Ford, M. M. (1994). Taking Sides: Clashing Views on Controversial Issues in Business Ethics and Society (Ed.), *The Study of Business Ethics: Ethics, Economics, Law and The Corporation* (pp. xii-xiii). Guilford, CT: The Dushkin Publishing Group, Inc.

Pierce, M. A. & Henry, J.W. (1996). Computer ethics: The role of personal, informal, and formal codes. *Journal of Business Ethics, 15,* 425-437.

Copyright © 2003, Idea Group Inc. Copying or distributing in print or electronic forms without written permission of Idea Group Inc. is prohibited.

Pierce, M. A. & Henry, J.W. (2000). Judgments about computer ethics: Do individual, co-worker, and company judgments differ? Do company codes make a difference? *Journal of Business Ethics, 28,* 307-322.

Plenert, G. (1995). Of course I'm ethical [electronic version]. *Journal of Systems Management, 46,* 58-63.

Randlesome, C. & Myers, A. (1995). Cultural fluency: The results of a UK survey [electronic version]. *Journal of Management Development, 14* (8/9), 42-56.

Siddiqui, A. (1997). Ethics in Islam: Key concepts and contemporary challenges. *Journal of Moral Education, 26* (4), 423-431. Retrieved on October 4, 2001, from Academic Search Elite Database.

Udas, K., Fuerst, W. L., & Paradice, D. B. (1996). An investigation of ethical perceptions of public sector MIS professionals. *Journal of Business Ethics, 15,* 721-734.

Whitman, M. E., Townsend, A. M., & Hendrickson, A. R. (1999). Cross-national differences in computer-use ethics: A nine-country study [electronic version]. *Journal of International Business Studies, 30* (4), 673-687.

Wienen I. (1999). Impact of religion on business ethics in Europe and the Muslim world. Frankfurt, Germany: Frankfurt Peter Lang Gmbh.

Copyright © 2003, Idea Group Inc. Copying or distributing in print or electronic forms without written permission of Idea Group Inc. is prohibited.

Chapter XIII

Lemon Problems in the Internet Transactions and Relative Strategies

Li Qi
Xi'an Jiaotong University, China

Zhang Xianfeng
Xi'an Jiaotong University, China

ABSTRACT

Based on some new traits of the Internet environment, this chapter discusses lemon problems in the Internet transactions. It points out that the information asymmetry does not disappear, but develops to be even worse under the new Internet environment. By virtue of mathematical tools, the authors analyze products and services' lemon problems in the new environment. It is found that many new traits of digital products and services lead to new appearances of "lemon" problems. In the end, relative strategies are provided in order to lessen these problems. The authors further hope that through the discussion, some implications can be made to e-sellers and online service providers.

Copyright © 2003, Idea Group Inc. Copying or distributing in print or electronic forms without written permission of Idea Group Inc. is prohibited.

INTRODUCTION

Lemon problems were initially proposed by Akerlof in the 1970s (Akerlof, 1984). He discussed the existence of the information asymmetry in American second-hand car markets and relative results caused by the problem. Based on his discussion, many scholars have conducted related research during these years. In the Internet environment, market conditions involve some new changes when comparing with that of the old economy. Consequently, lemon problems will also vary somewhat. In this chapter, the lemon problems in the Internet transactions are to be discussed. The chapter also takes related results of Akerlof as the research ground, through insight in the unique traits of the Internet transactions and by virtue of relative mathematical tools, new forms of lemon problems are discussed.

Akerlof suggests that it was the information asymmetry in the market to push the superior goods out of the market and leave only the inferior ones. On the other hand, the advent of the Internet seems to bring an era of fast information communication, more selection opportunities and much better matching. However, things do not go as it appears. Information asymmetry not only exists in the Internet environment, but also increases because of some unique traits.

In this chapter, some strategies for avoiding or lessoning lemon problems in the Internet transactions are provided. These suggestions are especially useful to e-sellers and online service providers.

BACKGROUND

There is no denying that information is very important in our daily life. One presupposition of the perfect market's existence in microeconomics is the full information between buyers and sellers (Edwin & David, 1988). Coase (1990), on the other hand, divided companies' costs into manufacturing costs and transacting ones in his company-origin research. He further points out that the transacting costs of one individual company are used mainly to solve the information communication problems and to end up with successful businesses. Information economics (Meheroo & Helene, 1984) explores this field even further. One paramount concern of the information economics is the information asymmetry. Due to the existence of the asymmetric information in each transaction, dealing partners have to input more extra efforts in searching information, assessing materials, negotiating and setting restrictions during the whole process. All those steps will undoubtedly lead to the inefficiency of the market.

The advent and widespread use of the Internet have changed not only the commercial activities companies are conducting, but also the outside environment people are living in. This has turned out to be an incontestable fact all over the world. The Internet develops in an unusually rapid speed. In only four years, Internet users have reached 50 million; whereas the spread of computers to the same level took

Copyright © 2003, Idea Group Inc. Copying or distributing in print or electronic forms without written permission of Idea Group Inc. is prohibited.

about 16 years, and that of TV also needed 13 years (Marilyn & Todd, 2000). Since the application of the Internet into every sphere has been widespread, the relative research about its traits has also been done. Now it is known that in the Internet economy, consumers' marginal utilities are not decreasing as similar as that of the traditional ones, but increasing instead. Therefore, the more consumers join in the Internet environment; the more utilities the existing consumers will obtain. Consequently, the spread of the Internet is actually accelerating in every sphere, and electronic commerce is accordingly popularizing. Commodities and services dealing through the Internet turn to be very common in the reality, so-called Internet transactions are herein realized.

The Internet transactions involve a large scope. It not only means the traditional transactions conducted through the Internet, but also includes the new digital ones. Broadly speaking, the Internet transactions can be defined as all the transacting activities dealing through the Internet, in which there is comprised setting up relationship, enquiring, quoting, signing contracts and relative delivering. In this paper, we are mainly concerned with the static relationships between buyers and sellers and their trading objects. It will include both online selling and online service providing.

As we know, the Internet connects all independently working computers, all over the world, through TCP/IP protocol, and realizes the sharing of information. Undoubtedly, the Internet also eliminates the space restrictions and time limit, making information communication much faster, and transacting costs even lower. Hence, some people (Yin & Wang, 2000) point out that the information asymmetry in the Internet environment differs from that of the traditional one, and the information asymmetry has been greatly weakened now. They further say that many models in the information economics have lost their use in the new environment. However, this kind of statement lacks thorough analysis. According to the information economics, the asymmetric information is caused by peoples' opportunism. Therefore, the problems are not merely a matter of technology, but an economic issue. As they are caused by people's opportunistic inclinations, as long as these inclinations exist, people will hide private information to pursue certain interests. Accordingly, the information asymmetry problems still exist in the Internet transactions.

Based on this condition, the following chapter will try to seek the degree of information asymmetry in the Internet transactions and, accordingly, discuss the dissimilar appearance of lemon problems and relative results towards the market.

MAIN THRUST OF THE CHAPTER
Information Asymmetry in Products' or Services' Qualities Worsen in the Internet Transactions

It is true that communication problems have been greatly relieved in the Internet environment, however, the alleviation of space restriction and time limit simulta-

Copyright © 2003, Idea Group Inc. Copying or distributing in print or electronic forms without written permission of Idea Group Inc. is prohibited.

neously indicates the uncertainty of counterparts' identities, not to speak of other information. Apparently, since the emergence of the Internet, the relative development of electronic commerce has promoted many commercial opportunities. According to Albert Angehrn (Marilyn & Todd, 2000), electronic commerce application in companies can be divided into four layers, which are: the information layer, communication layer, transaction layer and distribution layer. He points out that among those layers the most basic and also the easiest one for companies to achieve is the virtual information layer. Therefore many traditional companies set up their own Websites, while renascent network companies are also growing. In this newly growing trend, the scope of entities involved in the Internet transactions are enlarging, and dealing objects also become abundant. In this way, parties dealing now not only refer to the traditional ones, but also the Internet companies and many consumers, while the objects include physical products, services and digital ones. Physical products' and services' quantity problems have been analyzed in the traditional economies and consequently multiple strategies have been adopted. However, in the Internet transactions, the Internet is usually deemed as the information medium that causes the separation of physical products and services' goods flow and logistics. Though this medium executes rapid and 24-hour information transformation, the separation of physical products and Website, the non-simultaneity of goods ordering and practical delivering make it difficult to transfer the quantity of information. This always results in wrongly-delivered goods or products of inferior quality. On the other hand, freed from many restrictions of space or time, all dealers in the Internet transactions are equal, this will inevitably engender the deterioration of products and services' quantities trading through the Internet.

Coincidently, the digital products and services dealing through the Internet possess many new traits that, altogether, may worsen the quality information asymmetry in the Internet transactions. As Andrew B. Winston (2000) defined, the digital products and services refer to all the products or services that have been digitalized or can be digitalized soon. Due to those many traits, trading processes and both partners also come to show many new features.

Digital Products or Services are Usually Experiential Products

That is to say, people can only know the qualities after practical use because of the intangible feature. Meanwhile, digital products cannot be destroyed easily, so most of the time they are likely durable products and bought for only once. This feature makes the quality information transformation even more difficult. Generally, non-experiential product sellers can easily convey their quality information through on-site demonstration, and buyers can also obtain certain information just through observation. Things like chairs or desks belong to such category. Sometimes sellers can achieve effective information transmission by advertising or giving free samples, helping buyers know the products' qualities. As to non-experiential products, such as the Internet music supplying or personalized news broadcasting, it is difficult for sellers to show their high-quality simply through demonstrations. When the products

Copyright © 2003, Idea Group Inc. Copying or distributing in print or electronic forms without written permission of Idea Group Inc. is prohibited.

or services are purchased for once, giving free samples also turns out to be impractical. With no doubt, all these factors worsen the qualities' information asymmetry problems in the Internet transactions.

Many Digital Products or Services Largely Rely on Time

To supply each city's weather forecast through the Internet is one such service. As for this kind of service, apart from verbal promises, suppliers cannot find a much better way to demonstrate their high qualities. Suppose one supplier consents to give each potential buyer a free chance searching for one city's weather, so as to see how effective the system can be. However, there may exist an underlying threat that the buyer initially just wants one item of service. Thus the seller's potential customers disappear co-instantaneously. Therefore, this trait also worsens the existence of the qualities' information asymmetry between buyers and sellers.

That the Digital Products can be Copied Numerous Times Results in the Overflow of Duplicates in the Market

In the Internet economy, the variable costs and marginal costs of the digital products remain small (someone says it's zero). Usually fixed costs for digital products are high during the development period. Once the products are manufactured, the companies can realize scale manufacturing simply through copy process. Therefore, in the market there exist many fake digital products that possess the similar functions and almost same appearance. On the other hand, those fake products' prices are much lower than the real ones' prices, hence the real digital products have the threat to be squeezed out the market.

Digital Products and Services Supply Highly Personalized Service

Personalized service is the demand of the market, and the application of the Internet makes the level of personalization even more flexible. Unlike with standardized physical products, this feature inevitably brings out problems created by the variety of products and services the producers may offer. Hence the power of verbal recommendation has been greatly weakened in this new market, making it difficult for the loyalty built in one consumer to diffuse to others. The information asymmetry problems therefore are potentially increased.

Suppliers of Digital Products and Services Have Difficulty in Showing Information Signals

Information signal (Wang & He, 1999) is one way to solve the asymmetric information problems in the information economics. In the traditional economics, sellers generally own their physical stores. Therefore they can send out signals through splendid decoration, showing that they are selling high-quality products. In addition, they also adopt methods like satisfactory after-sale services or promising refunds. Yet in the Internet environment, companies can set up their Websites

Copyright © 2003, Idea Group Inc. Copying or distributing in print or electronic forms without written permission of Idea Group Inc. is prohibited.

regardless of the actual size of their business. The signals accordingly may be misleading. Lack of abundant and exact information signals makes it more difficult for consumers to identify appropriate sellers, furthermore worsening the information asymmetry problems.

Through the above analyses, it turns to be true that the qualities' information asymmetry of physical products and services still exist owning to external factors like the separation of goods flow and logistics. And this trend has the tendency to be growing. As for digital products and services, many internal traits decide the existence, and further worsen, their information asymmetry problems.

Findings of Lemon Problems in the Internet Transactions

As the above parts have discussed, the existence of the information asymmetry in products' or services' qualities of the Internet transactions and their tendency to be deteriorated. Therefore, the lemon problems still exist and have the inclination to be worsened. Owning to many new traits of the digital products and services, the lemon problems are also different.

Here we mainly discuss the lemon problems in the Internet transactions. Suppose there are two products or services suppliers, as Figure 1 shows. We assume that customers' demand for high-quality products are D_1 and the demand for low-quality products are D_2. There exists in the market both high-quality and low-quality products or services. Also, the information about the qualities is asymmetric between trading parties. Therefore, the supply curve of the market is that of the high-quality products or services S.

If the information transmission is complete in this market and the consumers can distinguish high-quality products or services from low-quality ones, the market price of high quality and low-quality ones will respectively be P_1, P_2. But, in reality, sellers may hide certain information about their products or services so as to earn large profits. This action will undoubtedly lead to the information asymmetry in the market.

Figure 1.

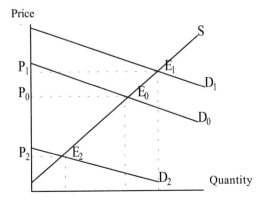

Copyright © 2003, Idea Group Inc. Copying or distributing in print or electronic forms without written permission of Idea Group Inc. is prohibited.

In this way, the consumers can estimate the possibility of buying each kind of product or service and, accordingly, decide the demand for those products or services.

Suppose the estimated possibility of buying high-quality products and low-quality products are: e, $1\text{-}e$ and the real demand curve is D_0.

In this case the actual price in the market will be:

$$P_0 = e\,P_1 + (1\text{-}e)P_2.$$

Assume the products or services industries' normal profit rate is r, the costs of high-quality products or services and low-quality ones are respectively C_1, C_2.

As discussed before, the dealing objects are greatly enlarged in the Internet transactions. As usual, different kinds of objects may cause different influences.

As for physical products and services, they are still subject to the traditional economic theories. Whatever the producers are processing the high-quality ones or the low-quality ones, there remains a relationship:

$$C_1 > C_2.$$

On the contrary, it is the fixed variable costs/marginal costs of the new economy (Shapiro & Varian, 2000) that contributes to the Internet transactions. This trait, in detail, means large fixed costs and small and unalterable variable costs. American scholar Soon-Yong Choi (2000) points out: owning to the fact that the fixed costs are far greater than the variable costs, there exists a high barrier to low-quality digital producers. Once they decide to enter into this field, the large sunk costs compel them to take other things into consideration. If the products cannot sell well, the large input cost will not pay-off. Therefore, in the production of digital products, there exist many duplicate producers instead of low-quality product producers. For all the manufacturing costs of copied products equal the variable costs of the high-quality ones. Hence, here copied digital products represent the low-quality digital products we are concerned with. That is to say:

$$C_1 \gg C_2.$$

As to the Internet services, inputs are also large. For example, in order to service well and set up their own reputation, an Internet personalized news supplier has to input large amounts of money for the service system. That is to say, he should find the appropriate news according to the demand of customers and send them to customers through certain processes. However the inferior services producers basically input very little. They just randomly select some news and offer it to customers. Hence for the Internet services, there also exists the relationship like $C_1 \gg C_2$.

Suppose the normal profit rate of two kinds of producers remain r, thus in the market which sellers and buyers can enter freely (something like a perfect competitive market), there lies the relationship:

Copyright © 2003, Idea Group Inc. Copying or distributing in print or electronic forms without written permission of Idea Group Inc. is prohibited.

$$P_1 = C_1 (1+r) \qquad P_2 = C_2 (1+r).$$

Consequently the actual market price is:
$$P_0 = [e\, C_1 + (1-e)\, C_2](1+e).$$

Therefore when the actual price is P_0, the profit rate of the high-quality products suppliers can be shown:

$$r_1 = \frac{p_0 - c_1}{c_1} = r - (1+r)(1-e)(\frac{c_1 - c_2}{c_1})$$

and the profit rate of the low-quality ones is:

$$r_2 = \frac{p_0 - c_2}{c_2} = r + (1+r)e(\frac{c_1 - c_2}{c_2})$$

Because the costs of the two kinds of physical products and services retain a relationship like $C_1 > C_2$, thus the profit rate of the superior products and services (r_1) are lower than the normal profit rate (r), while the profit rate of the inferior products and services (r_2) are higher than r. That is to say:
$$r_1 < r, r_2 > r.$$

As for the digital products and services, there remains $C_1 \gg C_2$. The profit rate of the superior ones (r_1) are far lower than the normal profit rate (r), and that of the inferior ones (r_2) are far higher than r. That is to say:
$$r_1 \ll r, r_2 \gg r.$$

In this case, for the physical products or services, the final market price P_0 will greatly benefit the producers of inferior products instead of the producers of superior ones. Accordingly, the profits of the superior products or service producers cannot offset their relative costs, those producers have to retreat from the market. This withdrawal reduces the possibility e that customers choose superior products and services, and creates a new market price that is much lower. Finally, when the possibility is reduced to 0, the market leaves only inferior products or service producers. When this happens, the fact that whatever the consumers buy are inferior products and services may promote the Internet customers' suspicion and resistance upon Internet purchasing. With lack of confidence in purchasing, the Internet shopping demands are reduced, as is the relative development of other industries related with online shopping. This vicious cycle grows and further greatly restricts Internet transactions.

Copyright © 2003, Idea Group Inc. Copying or distributing in print or electronic forms without written permission of Idea Group Inc. is prohibited.

As for the digital products and services, the negative effects of the final market price P_0 to the producers of superior products or services are doubled, so is the positive influence to the producers of inferior ones. At last, the superior products and services producers have to retreat from the market. With the disappearance of these products, the number of copied products is also decreasing. These kind of digital products will eventually disappear from the market. Similar to the physical products or services market, the digital services market will also finally vanish.

In Figure 2, the relative results of the lemon problems have been showed clearly. Therefore, it turns out to be obvious that the lemon problems appear different with dissimilar dealing objects. Whatever they are, it is very true that the lemon problems in the Internet transactions may cause the market failure and lead to large social losses.

Recommendations to Resolve the Lemon Problems in the Internet Transactions

The lemon problems lead to the inefficiency of the whole market, while the inefficiency, on the other hand, will deteriorate transactions in the market. In the Internet transactions, many new traits of the digital products and services make it difficult for lemon problems to be solved. Therefore, we should actively search for information transmission channels, helping the successful conveyance of information signals; for appropriate markets, ensuring the accuracy of the information spread. In addition, high restriction systems are also necessary, for they can guarantee that each

Figure 2. The results of lemon problems in the Internet transactions

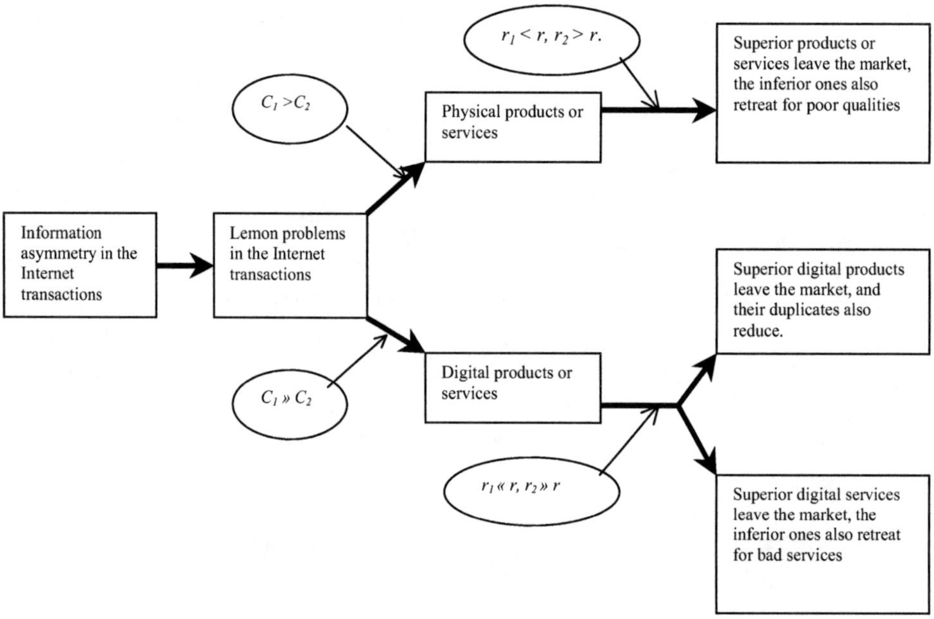

Copyright © 2003, Idea Group Inc. Copying or distributing in print or electronic forms without written permission of Idea Group Inc. is prohibited.

dealer to issue accurate information, and further protect private information or moral risks from engendering.

Suppliers Should Find Channels to Convey their Products' Information

Modes like advertisement, mass-media and Websites are surely the optional choice for suppliers to spread their products' information: Though these are the traditional methods to resolve the information asymmetry problems, they are still suitable in the Internet transactions. It is unavoidable that the inferior products' sellers may spread false information, but if the superior products' suppliers do not promote, how can millions of potential consumers know their products? As we know, consumers usually choose the ones they are familiar with or know about when they are buying, hence the relative promotions are to capture this consumption philosophy. In the Internet transactions, it is simple for sellers to set up their own Website and spread basic information about the products, this will furnish 24-hour continuous service. In addition, good customer feedback systems should be designed, since they are helpful in improving relative functions according to customers' requirements.

Suppliers also can adopt promotion methods like free-samples offering, tryout products distributing: If customers can only know the real value of the products after use, it may be a good communication way to permit consumers to use it before purchase. Digital products or services in the Internet transactions fit this category. Commonly-seen free software and tryout software in the market are supplied by developers in order to get large profits. For another example, many commercial software suppliers furnish the products, which have been deprived of key parts, to consumers. Obviously, those actions can divide the existent market so as to gain maximum margin. Suppose there sells a fine software. The high price accepters are willing to pay a price which is much higher than the cost of the software, whereas the low price accepters are only willing to pay lower price (much lower than the cost). If the suppliers take no steps, the software will be sold at the lower price. Though this can get all the consumers, the profits are surely not the maximum. However, if the suppliers allow consumers to try certain parts for a period of time, the potential market may be divided substantially and the products can be sold to high price takers in a higher price. Usually, when the costs of the products are higher than the price low-price accepters can take, the companies can only take the high-price accepters into consideration. On the other hand, if the costs of the products are lower than the price low-price accepters can pay, to focus at both kinds can help.

Sellers and Buyers can Turn to the Authorized Information Evaluation Agents for Help

In the traditional economies, there exist quality evaluation and identification agencies. Ordinarily, this work is undertaken by state authorized organizations. Since

Copyright © 2003, Idea Group Inc. Copying or distributing in print or electronic forms without written permission of Idea Group Inc. is prohibited.

246   Qi & Xianfeng

those parties hold a certain reputation, and assessment results are relatively more equitable, they are usually deemed as the last resort of other dealing parties. Besides, this quality evaluation agency always stand on the consumers' side and sets up certain systems to estimate the suppliers' credit. Thus, they may be effective communication channel for consumers to get information about the sellers. From this point of view, these evaluation agencies can be deemed as a motivation and a threat to sellers, encouraging them to enhance their quality, and threatening with the loss of customers in ease of poor quality. Now, with the development of the Internet transactions, authorized evaluation agencies can also be established in the Internet environment, exploiting their information communication channels and facilitating the queries of both buyers and sellers.

Information Brokers or Private Information Agents can Effectively Restrain the Behavior of Sellers

When certain information becomes one kind of product and can be sold everywhere, the information brokers step in. They are just information third parties, for example the house agency, governess center, and so on. Here the information agencies are self-operating companies with the aim of the largest profit. Their main business is to evaluate the information about products' and services' qualities, then they sell them to customers just like products.

The participation of third parties in solving the lemon problems actually raises the transaction costs, because the agent may need certain technological knowledge in order to accurately estimate the quality concerned. For other experiential products, the agents may need to use the products to get the information about the products or services concerned. All those things need large investment. Despite of the increased transaction costs for individual buyers, the market efficiency may be enhanced too, for the markets are not closed any more.

Those agencies should present a bulletin board, to provide a place for customers to exchange information about the products' or services' qualities they have used, and a blacklist to put the names of deceiving sellers. If the agency is for individual products, it may collide with the product suppliers, share profits and neglect complaints from consumers. However, if the agent is for multi-products, once they collude with certain product's sellers and continue to spread fake information, consumers will immediately stop to buy information from the agencies. This "fame overflow" mechanism will prevent the agencies and sellers from colluding, and fairly evaluate the quality information.

Dealers can Come to an Incomplete Contract, and Restrict Sellers from Selling Inferior Products or Services

Hatte (1998) defined incomplete contracts like this: "the contract is incomplete, that is to say, there exist gaps and omissions. Specifically speaking, the contract may mention responsibilities of each party in one respect, while in other situations, the

Copyright © 2003, Idea Group Inc. Copying or distributing in print or electronic forms without written permission of Idea Group Inc. is prohibited.

responsibilities are only ambiguously or cursorily stipulated." Owning to the speculative philosophy, sellers may reduce the qualities of products and services with the continuance of the trading. In order to restrict this kind of behavior, buyers cannot regulate each specific detail of the dealings, and also cannot examine the qualities of products or services each time. Therefore, the incomplete contracts are utilized. In this kind of contract, buyers and sellers need not point out specific requests for products or services, but to make it clear that the return for high-quality products and services is at the heart of the transactions. Once low-quality products are found, the contracts will be terminated at once. No doubt, this mechanism will restrict out of the line behavior and compel seller to perform according to their duties.

FUTURE TRENDS

Lemon problems in Internet transaction are initially based on the Internet environment. That is to say, with further development of the Internet and its wider applications in different spheres, lemon problems will emerge and disturb natural transactions as long as no or few solutions are used.

According to this viewpoint, the basic precondition to solving lemon problems in the Internet transactions is better Internet environment and larger applying scope. Without well-equipped Internet basic infrastructures, the customers' due demands for EC and online transactions can only stay in the lower level. EC is not simply an integration of well-established IT platform, high-edged IT technologies and excellent IT intellectuals. It involves more than them. Only under the Internet environment can the unique lemon problem exist, and also only with the help of relative strategies, can lemon problems be reduced.

Generally speaking, the overall Internet environment is turning better and more people are using online means. Due to the world-leading resource for internet trends and strategies (http://www.nua.ie), comparing 1997 and July 2001, Internet users in America increased to 23 times that of Korea is 32 times, of Japan six times, of Hong Kong is eight times, and that of China is 133 times. Until July 2001, Internet users make up 59.4% of the total population in America. In Korea, the number is 46.4%, in Hong Kong, 54.5%, and 37.2% in Japan. As to China alone, from 1997 to 2001, China's Internet users have increased from 620,000 to 3.37 million, with a growth of 53 times. The WWW Websites growth from 1,500 to 277,100 clearly states that more and more enterprises and communities are using the Internet to issue information. The total bandwidth of 2001 is 299 times the former level (www.cnnic.com.cn). Based on this trend, more and more people will turn to e-sellers and online service providers. With the customers' growing demands, companies and relative entities will consequently devote themselves to seeking efficient solutions to alleviate lemon problems, so that online transactions can flourish. Accordingly, when the outside circumstances turn to be better, even larger groups of customers will eventually buy online.

Copyright © 2003, Idea Group Inc. Copying or distributing in print or electronic forms without written permission of Idea Group Inc. is prohibited.

CONCLUSION

Generally speaking, lemon problems are the results of the radical analyses of inferior products or services. In traditional economies, the quality of the products is one important aspect people are concerned with. Accordingly, people find ways to constrain the overflow of the inferior markets. In Internet transactions, the dealing objects are not only confined to physical products and services, but also to many digital ones. All of those new features cause the increase of the lemon problems. Therefore, online products and services suppliers should actively search for solutions.

REFERENCES

Akerlof, G. (1984). The market for lemons: Quality, uncertainty, and the market mechanism. *Quarterly Journal of Economics*, 488-500

Choi, S.Y., Stahl D.O., & Whinston A. B. (2000). Electronic commerce economics. Beijing: Electronic Industry Publishing House.

Coase, R. H. (1990). The tirm, the market and the law. Shanghai: Shanghai Sanlian Press.

Edwin G. D. & David, E. L. (1988). Microeconomics. Chicago: Dryden Press.

Hatte. (1998). Companies, contracts and financial structures. Shanghai: Shanghai People's Publishing House

Marilyn, G. & Todd, M.F. (2000). Electronic commerce: Security, risk management and control. Beijing: Mechanical Industry Publishing House.

Meheroo, J. & Helene, E. (1984). Communication and information economics: New perspectives. New York: Elsevier Science.

Shapiro C. & Varian, H. (2000). Information rules: A strategic guide to the network economy. Beijing: People's University Publishing House.

Wang, Z.K. & He, J. (1999) Information economics overview. Beijing: Chinese Economic Publishing House.

Yin, B.C. & Wang, L.W. (2000). New economy and traditional theories. *Economies Dynamics*, 11, 63-65.

ADDITIONAL REFERENCES

http://www.cnnic.com.cn.
http://www.nua.ie.

Copyright © 2003, Idea Group Inc. Copying or distributing in print or electronic forms without written permission of Idea Group Inc. is prohibited.

Chapter XIV

Reputation, Reputation System and Reputation Distribution — An Exploratory Study in Online Consumer-to-Consumer Auctions

Zhangxi Lin
Texas Tech University, USA

Dahui Li
University of Minnesota Duluth, USA

Wayne Huang
Ohio University, USA

ABSTRACT

Reputation is an important organization asset, particularly in the era of e-commerce. In an online consumer-to-consumer (C2C) auction market, a trader's reputation sends an important signal to his/her trading partners in their decision-making on C2C transactions, due to the nature of the anonymous transaction process. While prior research has shown that reputation systems,

Copyright © 2003, Idea Group Inc. Copying or distributing in print or electronic forms without written permission of Idea Group Inc. is prohibited.

such as eBay's Feedback Forum, facilitated buyer-seller transactions, several fundamental issues with the transaction mechanism remained unclear. Based on the empirical reputation data directly collected from eBay.com, we find that the distribution of reputation scores can be approximated in a geometric function. We analyze the formation of the distribution with a stochastic process model. The computer simulation using the Monte Carlo approach further validates the findings of the empirical study.

INTRODUCTION

The advent of e-commerce has brought about a new era, in which our daily life has undergone profound revolutions in social and economical aspects. However, Internet fraud in online marketplaces, rooted in the effect of information asymmetry (Akerlof, 1970), has been wearing away consumer benefits from the e-commerce. By the end of year 2000, about 31% of online American users participated in online auctions, and 41% of them encountered fraud-related problems. According to fraud.org (http://www.fraud.org), the total loss in 2001 from Internet fraud almost doubled that of 2000. The average loss per person increased about one third in the same period. In the last three years, online auction has remained the leader of 10 top scams. In particular, the fraud in "Nigerian money offers" increased nine times in 2001 (see AARP.org, 2002). As online auction traders have been faced with vital risks from frauds in online transactions, the vulnerable consumer trust could be easily hurt. This could be the main reason why 69% of American Internetters still keep a distance from online auctions (Selis, Ramasastry & Wright, 2001).

Because online trading allows anonymous transactions, an invisible, guileful trader may easily defraud his trading partners to exploit more benefits, and then may change his identity because of the cost in reputation damage. To promote safer online trades, some online market providers, such as eBay, have offered online reputation reporting services for its traders. A reputation reporting service system can provide up-to-date reputation status of a trader, normally in the numerical scores. According to Friedman and Resnick (2001), the higher a reputation score, the higher the cheating cost to the trader, and the lower the probability the trader will cheat. Therefore, a trader's reputation score sends a critical signal to his trading partner in estimating the risk of trading. The reputation reporting service is apparently one of the important factors leading to the fast growth of C2C online businesses. In this chapter, we present the outcomes of an empirical research on online reputation and its distribution, using the data directly collected from eBay.com. The research is intended to examine the nature of reputation, such as its distribution and formation, in order to provide the empirical evidence and basis for further exploring the effect of reputation on perceived risk and trust.

The chapter is organized as follows. First, we present a brief literature review on reputation research; second, we summarize recent research progresses in online

Copyright © 2003, Idea Group Inc. Copying or distributing in print or electronic forms without written permission of Idea Group Inc. is prohibited.

reputation systems — a key effort in promoting online markets; third, we report the findings from data analyses; finally, a stochastic process model explaining the formation of reputation score distribution is derived with the supportive outcomes from the computer simulation using the Monte Carlo method.

Reputation

Reputation is generally regarded as the impression and assessment of a social entity's esteem or desirability (e.g., Kollock, 1999; Standifird, 2001; Weiss et al., 1999). Although a social entity has many different ways to signal and build its reputation, e.g., through advertising or promotion, reputation is ultimately judged by some external entities rather than the entity itself (e.g., Fombrun & Shanley, 1990; Fombrun, 1996). Reputation signals the consistency of an entity's behavior over a certain period of time. It is a record of the history of an entity's interactions with others. Reputation also manifests whether an entity is willing and able to perform an activity in an expected fashion. This notion is supported by various studies on reputation building and continuous prisoner's dilemma game.

Reputation building is based on the sum of all the past behaviors of the entity, rather than a one-time effort. Reputation can be either positive or negative. A positive reputation manifests all the favorable assessment of an entity, while a negative reputation shows the unfavorable aspects. The potential sacrifice associated with a negative or bad reputation is so high that an entity with a positive reputation is predicted to behave consistently in a favorable manner in the future.

Reputation is a universal topic across many academic fields. A comprehensive summary of the roles of reputation can be found in several studies (e.g., Yoon et al., 1993; Mohamed et al., 2001). In business and marketing strategy studies, a firm's reputation resides in its brand name that carries the image of the firm. A brand name is relied on more heavily than other indicators (e.g., price, physical appearance, retailer's reputation) in judging the quality of a product (Dawar & Parker, 1994). A manufacturer with a more favorable reputation has a higher level of intention to use its own sales force and a lower level of intention to switch sale representatives (Weiss et al., 1999). On the other hand, the lower perception of a representative's reputation motivates a firm to switch to a new representative. A good reputation prevents a firm from being attacked when the potential attacker considers the firm as a minor competitor (Clark & Montgomery, 1998).

In relationship marketing literature, a positive reputation will affect future short-term and long-term marketing success. Reputation has been found to be important, theoretically and empirically, in all business-to-business (B2B), business-to-consumer (B2C), and consumer-to-consumer (C2C) transactions. Regarding the buyer-seller relationship, the seller's reputation has a positive effect on buyer's trust in the seller and buyer's long-term orientation with the seller (Ganesan, 1994). Reputation is positively associated with credible transactions between firms (Herbig et al., 1994). During the ongoing process of interactions, previous favorable

Copyright © 2003, Idea Group Inc. Copying or distributing in print or electronic forms without written permission of Idea Group Inc. is prohibited.

transactions strengthen the perception of the firm's reputation in the next round of transactions.

Unlike a firm's reputation, the reputation of an individual person is based on the person's traits and past behaviors, which are usually studied as impression management. Researchers have found that impression is influenced more by the person's negative attributes than his positive attributes (Fiske, 1980). For example, unfavorable information was found to be more influential than favorable information in judging an individual's morality. The term of "negative bias" is used to reflect the effect of negative information on impression ratings (Yaniv & Kleingerger, 2000). According to Yaniv and Kleingerger, unfavorable information indicates conflict between general perception of social norms and a particular person's deviation behavior. The phenomenon of "negative bias" is consistent with "trust asymmetry" (Slovic, 1993), which means that negative events decrease trust far more than positive events serve to increase trust. Yaniv and Kleingerger (2000) suggest that it is easier to lose a good reputation than to gain it.

While people devote much to monitoring their own and others' reputation, they also act to manage their own reputations (Bromely, 1993). Both positive and negative reputations are managed in daily life. Reputation management need not occur in response to any problem related to unfavorable reputation. Social entities with good reputations also manage to maintain and enhance their standings. On the other hand, entities with bad reputations aim to change their present reputations or establish new reputations under new identities.

Researchers are drawn to reputation issues of electronic markets in recent years. In business-to-consumer electronic markets, Internet buyers are found to favor Websites that sell familiar products manufactured by familiar merchants (Quelch & Klein, 1996). The reputation of an online store is positively associated with an online consumer's trust in the store, which further influences the consumer's intention to buy (Javenppa et al., 2000). Unlike conventional reputation of a person or a firm, online reputation is difficult to be evaluated. Because the Internet allows anonymous transactions, traders cannot track the real identities of their transaction partners.

Internet technology is superior to traditional transmission media in several ways to promote the effectiveness and efficiency of business transactions. However, it cannot resolve the problem of information asymmetry. In online auction markets, a buyer does not always have the full knowledge of a business transaction, i.e., the product, the seller, or both. Similarly, a seller does not know the background of a buyer or his credit history. Thus, before a transaction is closed, a buyer does not know whether the products will be the same as described and be shipped with appropriate packaging (Resnick et al., 2000). Meanwhile, a seller does not know whether he can get correct payment from a buyer without errors. Whether a transaction can be successfully conducted depends on whether both parties have good reputation and whether they trust each other.

Copyright © 2003, Idea Group Inc. Copying or distributing in print or electronic forms without written permission of Idea Group Inc. is prohibited.

In the above scenarios, the online reputation associated with a pseudonym created by a trader will critically affect his trading partners' perceived risk in the transaction and their trust toward the trader. The effect will result in the change of premium price and degree of willingness-to-buy (Kollock, 1999; Ba & Pavlou, 2001). Due to world-wide exposures, a trader's reputation becomes an important asset that is sensitive to the trader's online performance (Tadelis, 1999). An effective reputation system that can record and report traders' reputation scores in the online auction market is becoming a critical fraud-depressing mechanism in promoting and securing online trading.

ONLINE REPUTATION SYSTEMS

Reputation Systems

In a traditional context, the experience of interacting with an entity is the basis for judging the entity's reputation. If this experience is shared with other people who will interact with the entity, those people can be benefited. Likewise, if one trader's online transaction experience with another trader is shared it will benefit future traders. Promoting the share of transaction experience can be done through a reputation reporting system, or, in brief, a reputation system.

A reputation system "collects, distributes, and aggregates feedbacks about participants' past behavior" (Resnick et al., 2000). It is built on the assumption that people in future transactions will look back at their partner's transaction history. The reputation system provides incentive for both parties to trust each other and encourages trustworthy behavior online. Because a future trader may lack personal interaction experience with a particular trader, he may rely on public archives of the particular trader to make decisions on transactions. A good reputation assures that a trader will continue to act in a favorable manner and minimize opportunistic behavior. The damaging effect of a bad reputation is so huge that both parties may not risk themselves by cheating the other party. Thus, both parties of a transaction may feel more secure even though the transaction requires a separation of delivery and payment.

Reputation systems can be classified as non-computational and computational (Zacharia et al., 2000). Better Business Bureau Online is an example of non-computational reputation systems, whose main functions are to handle disputes and track complaints. Computational systems range from rating of Web page to rating of peoples. The application domains of these computational systems range from auction sites, expert sites, to product review sites. Further, most retailer Websites provide functions for consumers to rate the products they have purchased. Based on how a reputation is represented, a reputation system can be either positive or negative (Whitmeyer, 2000). A positive reputation system records only a trader's positive reputation, which signals desirable or favorable comments. All the successful transactions are recorded under that trader's name. In a positive system, traders do

Copyright © 2003, Idea Group Inc. Copying or distributing in print or electronic forms without written permission of Idea Group Inc. is prohibited.

not want to change their identities because the accumulated reputations cannot be carried onto a new name (Kollock, 1999). A negative reputation system distributes information of untrustworthy parties and unsuccessful transactions. In such a system, people tend to change their identity as soon as they have negative or bad reputations and are marked as untrustworthy people. This also occurs in positive systems, in which people will change their identities whenever they get bad reputations or their reputations are damaged. Because people of a negative system often change their identities, it is seldom seen a long negative record under a name, and there is a lot of trash information in the system. Currently, most online reputation systems are positive.

eBay's Feedback Forum

One of the most popular and successful reputation systems is eBay's Feedback Forum. Founded in 1995, eBay.com is the world's largest online C2C auction market. There are more than 10 million registered members and over four million items transacted a day. Unlike several other online auction Websites, eBay does not provide warranty or guarantee services for its traders. All the traders assume the inherent risks in the auction process. eBay just works as a central listing catalog of various items and products.

Contrary to common sense that there is a high risk in eBay's system, the fraud and deceit rate of transactions at eBay's site is very low. This could be partly attributed to the proper function of its Feedback Forum. With eBay's Feedback Forum, both buyers and sellers have the chance to rate each other after transactions are completed. The rating is generally related to a specific auction and is designated as a number. A positive comment from a unique trading partner adds one point to the accumulated score, a negative comment reduces one point from the accumulated score, and a neutral comment does not affect the overall score. Every buyer or seller has the overall score attached to his registered user name. Hence, a score of 100 might mean 100 positive comments and no negative comments, or 110 positive comments and 10 negative comments. At different threshold levels, a name is awarded a color star, which marks the number of net positive comments. For example, a yellow star means a rating of 10-99, and a red star means a rating of 1000-9000. To enforce the efficiency of the feedback system, eBay will not allow the existence of a trader with a net negative score of negative four or lower. In addition to the rating, traders can post some specific comments about a transaction, such as "good transaction" or "highly recommended." Future traders can see both feedback scores and written comments of a particular trader they want to transact with. A trader's overall reputation score and the statistics of different types of feedbacks in last six-month, one-month and one-week can be easily accessed from eBay.com (see Figure 1).

In general, a high feedback rating shows that a trader is experienced and has a track record. A low rating indicates either a new trader or an experienced trader who has changed his identity and registered again under a new name. Regarding a

Copyright © 2003, Idea Group Inc. Copying or distributing in print or electronic forms without written permission of Idea Group Inc. is prohibited.

Figure 1.   A seller's reputation profile (the overall reputation score 61 is rated in a yellow star)

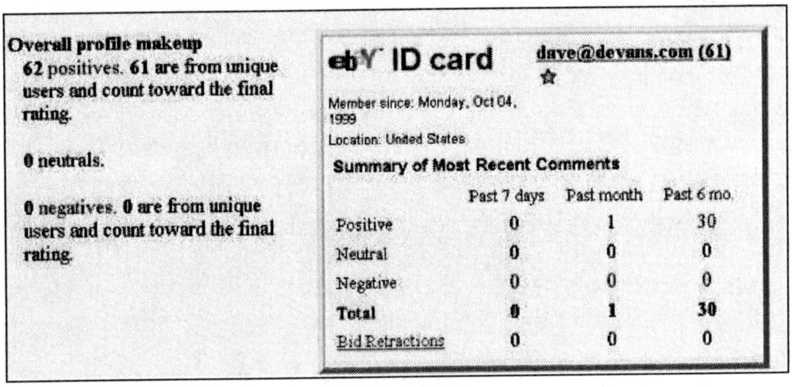

single score, a positive feedback score indicates a successful and satisfactory transaction. A neutral feedback score may suggest that one party hesitates to rate the other party because of various reasons. A neutral score may be related to slight problems, such as delays and poor communication (Resnick & Zeckhauser, 2001). A negative feedback score is used for very problematic transactions, such as products never shipped, broken products, or counterfeit. However, a negative score does not always indicate that the trader has a bad reputation. It may indicate an unresolved dispute or a fight-back occurred during the transaction process. Hence, a trader's reputation cannot be judged only based on a single negative feedback score. Instead, the ratio of overall negatives vs. overall positives, the situation under which the negative score occurs, or whether the feedback is related to the quality of the item, should be examined. The accumulation process of reputation scores is also interesting, which can be described by an attenuation model (Whitmeyer, 2000). In an attenuation model, each additional single point contributing to the overall rating score is less than the previous single point. The model suggests that the more positive ratings a trader has, the more trustworthy the trader is. However, the effect of each additional rating declines as the total reputation score increases.

Resnick and Zeckhauser (2001) report several interesting findings about general characteristics of traders in eBay.com. First, the study has shown that sellers have higher feedback scores than buyers. Because sellers have more transactions than buyers, they seem to be more experienced traders than buyers. They may have stayed in the auction site longer than buyers do. They may also be professional traders, who make livings by conducting auction transactions. For buyers, the percentage of low feedback scores is much higher than that of high feedback scores. This may indicate that there are not many professional buyers. Further, experienced traders less frequently received negative feedbacks. Less experienced traders are likely to get negative feedbacks. This may imply that experienced traders are more careful with their reputation, because they have already built their reputation over a period of time.

Copyright © 2003, Idea Group Inc. Copying or distributing in print or electronic forms without written permission of Idea Group Inc. is prohibited.

Second, regarding the transactional relationship between buyers and sellers, only 17.9% of all sales involved a buyer and a seller who have done business with each other before. Most seller-buyer pairs have conducted just one transaction during the investigated time period. This may suggest that there is no long-term relationship formed between buyers and sellers, unlike conventional buyer-seller relationships. Buyers are also found to have less problematic feedbacks than sellers. This may be because buyers do not have much ambiguous information communicated with the seller. Sellers, on the other hand, must present information about their items, and may cause misunderstandings with buyers.

Third, over 99% of the feedbacks provided by buyers are positive. Regarding neutral and negative ratings, if an item does not match the description, or if the shipment is slow, neutral, rather than negative, feedback is given. If the item is not shipped after payment, negative rather than neutral feedback is given. Sellers are found to care about their reputation very much. They often write more detailed messages in resolving the dispute with buyers after buyers have issued their negative feedbacks.

Fourth, although some eBay traders do both selling and buying, most are primarily a seller or a buyer. Organizational sellers and buyers are also found in eBay's system. In this way, eBay.com is not only a consumer-to-consumer marketplace but also a business-to-consumer or business-to-business marketplace.

Effects of Reputation Systems

In general, reputation systems help manage risks and promote cooperation (Kollock, 1999; Resnick et al., 2000). Whitmeyer (2000) reports that when the proportion of cooperators in a population is low, reputation obtained under a tough system will convey the most information for future traders to discriminate cooperator and non-cooperator. On the other hand, if the proportion of cooperators in the population is high, reputation earned in a lenient system will convey the most information. The proportion of honest and dishonest traders in a population must be also examined.

Further, reputation systems also impact transactional price and the formation of trust perception of one party toward the other. Both positive reputation and negative reputation scores have effects on sellers' abilities to command premium prices. Theoretically, the easier to get a reputation, the less the reputation is worth, and the more the price of a transaction is discounted (Whitmeyer, 2000). However, the effect of negative reputation seems to be more salient than that of positive reputation. Sellers with higher positive reputation scores are not found to be able to sell their products at higher prices than will sellers with lower positive reputation scores (Standifird, 2001). This is in consistency with the finding from the study by Resnick and Zeckhauser (2001), which found that it is easier for sellers with better reputations to sell their products but there is no significant boost in price for the two types of products examined in the study.

Copyright © 2003, Idea Group Inc. Copying or distributing in print or electronic forms without written permission of Idea Group Inc. is prohibited.

A strong positive reputation reduces buyers' risk perception and enhances their trust perception only when there is no negative feedback (Ba & Pavlou, 2002). With the introduction of negative feedback, the story is different. The effect of "negative bias" studied in conventional contexts is very significant in online transactions. People with negative feedback scores are at disadvantaged positions in electronic markets. Empirical studies shows that higher negative scores are significantly related to lower bidding auction price in the Internet auction (Lee et al., 2000), and that a negative reputation has a greater impact on the ability of sellers to sell their products at higher prices than a positive reputation (Standifird, 2001). Sellers with higher negative reputation scores are forced to sell their products at lower prices than will sellers with lower negative reputation scores (Standifird, 2001). Potential buyers are more sensitive to negative feedbacks than positive feedbacks when they plan to buy used or refurbished products (Lee et al., 2000). Negative ratings are found to have greater opposing effects than positive ratings in the formation of a buyer's trust perception toward a seller (Ba & Pavlou, 2002).

The reputation also affects traders' decisions to adopt online risk relief service. A risk relief service is provided by a trusted third party, via the Internet, to protect online transactions from fraud, such as online escrows and credit card protection programs (Selis, Ramasastry & Wright, 2001). A risk relief service does not increase trader's trustworthiness, but reduces or eliminates the risk in online trading (Sweeney, Soutar & Johnson, 1999). Hu et al. (2001) investigated the interactions between a seller and a buyer in a C2C online auction, and how an honest trader makes the decision to adopt online escrow service. They propose that reputation scores are significantly associated with perceived risk (Hawes & Lumpkin, 1986). Antony, Lin and Xu (2001) further test the model in a controlled laboratory experiment. In a computer-simulated C2C auction market, subjects conducted many rounds of transactions. With their trading partners' reputation scores constantly shown on the Website, subjects could refer to these scores to decide whether they needed to adopt online escrow service. The analysis shows that the higher the reputation score, the less the perceived risk in the dynamic process.

Although it has been well accepted that the reputation system plays an important role in electronic markets, the nature of reputation score distribution and how the distribution affects online traders' risk decisions have not been fully explored. Based on prior studies, the next section reports some preliminary research findings on these important issues.

AN EMPIRICAL STUDY OF ONLINE REPUTATION SCORES

We randomly collected three sets of traders' reputation profile data from eBay.com. Two sets were for sellers and one set for buyers, all containing overall reputation credits of each account in a whole life cycle, and positive and negative

Copyright © 2003, Idea Group Inc. Copying or distributing in print or electronic forms without written permission of Idea Group Inc. is prohibited.

feedback scores respectively in a six-month window. There were 200 trader records in each set. A trader was classified as a seller (or buyer) when he was selling (or buying) an item in a trade, although he could be a buyer (seller) in another trade. Samples were randomly chosen from several different item categories, such as consumer electronics, clothes, antiques, toys, etc. Seller samples were collected from a few ongoing transactions in each category, and buyer samples were chosen from the ones currently leading the bid in each selected auctioned item. Seller data and buyer data were collected separately in different days without seeking for any connection between the data sets.

The current empirical study is focused more on reputation score distribution and the relationship between different types of feedbacks. Three main findings are reported below.

Finding 1: The reputation score can be approximated in a geometric distribution.

The trend curve of the histogram from reputation scores can be approximated in an exponential function $y = Ae^{-Bx}$. $B = -0.0016$ ($R^2 = 0.8611$) when the sample is classified in a 100-score increment (see Figure 2). This can be converted into a geometric function, $y' = Ar^{x'}$, a discrete form, where $0 < r < 1, x' = 0, 1, 2, ...$ The statistics from the three sets of data demonstrate the same distribution pattern.

Overall, about one third of traders have reputation scores less than 100; about two thirds of them less than 500; and about 90% of them under 2000 (see Table 1). The overall reputation scores of 534 traders, 89% of 600, range from 0 to 2000.

Finding 2: The positive feedbacks can be approximated in a geometric distribution

Figure 3 shows the histograms of positive reputation scores in last six-months for selected buyers and sellers who had less than 1000 positive scores. The trend

Figure 2. A histogram of reputation scores from a pool of 600 traders

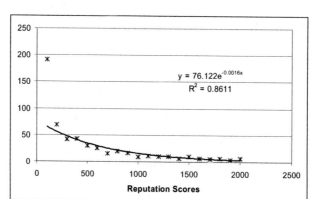

Copyright © 2003, Idea Group Inc. Copying or distributing in print or electronic forms without written permission of Idea Group Inc. is prohibited.

Table 1: The statistics of overall reputation scores

Data Set	<100	<500	<1000	<1500	<2000	<2500
Buyers	28.50%	61.00%	77.00%	86.50%	93.50%	95.00%
Sellers 1	28.50%	59.00%	75.50%	83.00%	86.50%	88.50%
Sellers 2	38.50%	67.50%	77.50%	84.00%	87.00%	89.00%
Average	31.83%	62.50%	76.67%	84.50%	89.00%	90.83%

curve of the histograms matches an exponential function with $B = -0.0034$ ($R^2 = 0.8386$) for buyers and $B = -0.0031$ ($R^2 = 0.8219$) for sellers. This outcome implies that the distribution of positive feedbacks also fits a geometric function as discussed in Finding 1.

The statistics shows, based on current data sets, about a half of the traders have received positive feedbacks less than 150. About 90% sellers' positive feedbacks fall in the interval from 0 to 1050 and 90% buyers' positive feedbacks range from 0 to 900. The positive reputation scores of 95% traders (sellers and buyers together) are less than 1850.

Finding 3: The ratio of negative and positive feedbacks can be approximated in a geometric distribution.

How are trader's negative scores distributed? Data analysis shows that the trend curve of the histogram from negative reputation rate, i.e. the ratio of negative feedbacks and positive feedbacks, can be approximated in an exponential function

Figure 3. A histogram of trader's positive feedbacks in a six-month period

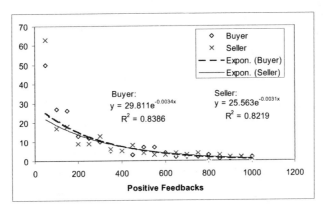

Copyright © 2003, Idea Group Inc. Copying or distributing in print or electronic forms without written permission of Idea Group Inc. is prohibited.

Figure 4. The histograms of negative/positive feedback ratios

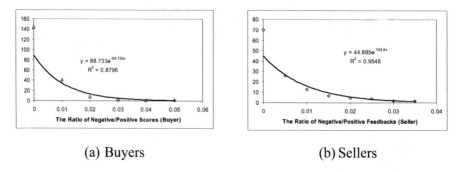

(a) Buyers   (b) Sellers

(see Figure 4). This lines up with Findings 1 and 2 that the discrete form for the distribution of negative/positive feedback ratios is a geometric function.

A STOCHASTIC PROCESS MODEL OF REPUTATION SCORING

In this section we propose a stochastic process model to further explain why the distribution of reputation scores is exponentially shaped, as found in the above empirical study. The model has been further tested in computer simulations using the Monte Carlo approach.

Moral Traders Versus Opportunistic Traders

We assume that the there are two types of traders in electronic markets, the *moral type* and the *opportunistic type*. These traders are distinctive with regard to their self-interest attitudes. This categorization of trader follows a similar scheme in economics literature (Kreps, 1990); traders are classified as the types with guile and without guile. In this study, we assume that a moral trader will never cheat under any circumstances, and an opportunistic trader will cheat when there is an opportunity that increases his benefits.

A trader's type, inherent as an ethical nature, can only be reflected through his trading strategy. The type is not identifiable without finalizing a transaction, because a potential opportunistic trader's trading strategy is subject to change in a specific transaction. Therefore, a trader's honesty is subject to change from trade to trade and can only be justified after a transaction is done.

A trader in a specific transaction can be an honest trader or a cheater according to their ethical behavior. In any transaction, a moral trader will always act honestly. An opportunity trader can choose between an honest trader and a cheater in different transactions, depending on which action benefits him the best. Here, the opportunistic trader has taken into account the opportunity cost being caught and punished. Fearing

Copyright © 2003, Idea Group Inc. Copying or distributing in print or electronic forms without written permission of Idea Group Inc. is prohibited.

of the loss from the punishment, an opportunistic trader may have to behave honestly. In this way, a group of honest traders is composed of moral traders who are naturally honest, and opportunistic traders who decide to be honest because this will bring them better benefits.

We also assume that a reputation score has a value to its bearer. Opportunistic traders are fully aware of the consequences if they make a fraud. One of the costs to them is the damage of the reputation, because a good reputation score could bring them better benefits in future trades. Therefore, how to value their reputations becomes one of the key factors in opportunistic traders' decision-making. Once the reputation of an online identity has been damaged, a rational trader will naturally consider discarding the pseudonym and starting a new one. This causes the loss of previously accumulated reputation credits, but he may be compensated by the illegal income from the fraud.

In general, we define *irresolvable dispute* for the scenario that a severe negative feedback or even a lawsuit will substantially ruin a trader's reputation. This includes two cases: the trader defrauded his trading partner, or more broadly, any violations to the online contracts, such as breaking the contract by stopping payment or shipment without the consent from the trading partner; the trader did not commit any fraud, but his trading partner threw him in an adverse status that would damage his reputation totally. In either of these two cases, the trader will consider restarting a new account because his current reputation no longer brings him as good benefits as a new one.

Stochastic Process Model for the Reputation Scoring System

Based on the above discussion, we propose a reputation-scoring model to explore the formation of the reputation score distribution. Consider a simplified reputation scoring system with only a positive score for a trader:

- When a trader initially participates in an online auction market, his score is 0;
- The trader's score increments one point after he has transacted honestly in a trade;
- The trader's score is reset to 0 if either he naturally quits from the market or he has cheated; and
- Assume that all traders have the same probability to abort their accounts at every level of reputation score.

This reputation scoring system can be modeled as a discrete-time Markov chain (Ross, 1997).

Define a stochastic process $\{X_n, n = 0, 1, 2, ...\}$ that takes on a countable number of possible values. Denote $\{0, 1, 2, 3, ...\}$ the score state set, $\{p_0, p_1, p_2, ...\}$ the distribution of the score, and $q_i = P\{X_n = i | X_{n-1} = i - 1\}$ the probability of the reputation score increments one, where $i > 0$ and $0 < q_i < 1$. Then:

Copyright © 2003, Idea Group Inc. Copying or distributing in print or electronic forms without written permission of Idea Group Inc. is prohibited.

$$p_0 = \cfrac{1}{1+\sum_{i=1}^{\infty}(\prod_{j=1}^{i}q_j)} \text{ and } p_i = p_0 \prod_{j=1}^{i}q_j, \quad i = 1, 2, \dots$$

If $q_i = q \ \forall \ i$, i.e., the probability that a trader abort his current account is irrelevant to the reputation score, when $n \to \infty$:

$$p_0 = 1 - q \text{ and } p_i = q^i(1 - q), \ i = 1, 2, \dots$$

It clearly shows that $X = lim_{n \to \infty} X_n$ has a geometric distribution, the discrete form of exponential distribution.

When we assume that a trader's reputations score is naturally reset to 0 if he did not trade in last six months, this model can explain the distribution of reputation scores in a six-month window.

A Monte Carlo Simulation of Reputation Scoring

We tested the above reputation model in a simulated C2C auction system, in which virtual traders were set up to use online escrow service (OES) to protect their transactions. In Figure 5, PRR is an abbreviation for *perceived risk rate* (Hu et al., 2001), a subjective probability evaluating the risk that a fraud may happen in a trade.

The system starts from a given number of traders. At the very beginning, every trader's reputation score is initialized as a zero. The following parameters are randomized in each trade:

Figure 5. A flow chart for the C2C auction simulation

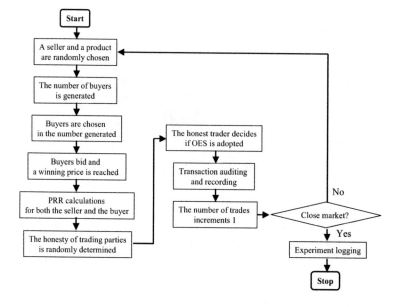

Copyright © 2003, Idea Group Inc. Copying or distributing in print or electronic forms without written permission of Idea Group Inc. is prohibited.

Figure 6.   Histogram of reputation scores after 200,000 transactions (trader samples: 320 virtual traders including buyers and sellers)

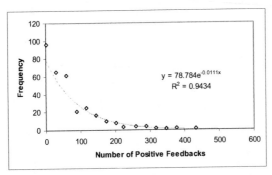

- The item to be sold, which is a specific merchandise chosen from a set of products;
- The seller chosen from a trader pool;
- The number of buyers bidding for the item;
- The perceived value of the underlying product for the buyer and the seller;
- The winning price; and
- The type of traders, either the moral type or the opportunistic type.

Honest traders make decision on how they trade and whether they need a trusted third party's protection for online frauds, which are randomly generated. A trader is scored regarding whether he behaves honestly or not. If a trader cheats, his score will be reset to zero, meaning he will escape and restart with a new appearance. If he trades honestly, his score will be increased by one. There is no negative reputation scoring in this simplified simulation system, because negative scores are considered as resolvable disputes not as frauds.

Figure 6 is a histogram of reputation scores from 320 traders after 200,000 trades were run in the simulation system. The trend curve in Figure 6 is consistent with the one as shown in Figure 2. An adjusted logarithm of reputation scores, $y = ln(x + 1)$, has a linear-like decreasing curve and further supports the distribution. Although $A = 78.784$, $B = 0.0111$ in Figure 6, they can be calibrated by changing a few parameters. Therefore, the reputation scores can be approximated in a geometric distribution.

CONCLUSIVE REMARKS

This chapter is based on our previous research work (Lin, Li & Huang, 2002). The findings in the reputation score distribution support the study in the game-theoretic model between moral traders and opportunistic traders as conducted by Hu et al. (2001). With the approximated distribution of reputation scores, further

Copyright © 2003, Idea Group Inc. Copying or distributing in print or electronic forms without written permission of Idea Group Inc. is prohibited.

computer experiments will have a solid background to calibrate other important parameters, such as those for the calculation of perceived risk.

While reputation systems provide significant benefits to the development of online transaction markets, there are various inherent problems regarding the reliability of these systems (Dellarocas, 2001; Zacharia et al., 2000). Resnick et al. (2000) summarize several problems in reputation expression, distribution, and aggregation. Online traders may not have the incentive and intention to spend extra time providing feedbacks. They may also have the apprehension of being evaluated and evaluating others, so they do not post any negative feedback. Traders may also intentionally provide unfairly high or low ratings (Dellarocas, 2001) toward a specific person. The sellers may also perform "discriminatory behavior," providing favorable services for one group of buyers and unfavorable services for another to get inflated ratings from the favorable group of buyers (Dellarocas, 2001). Additional insights are expected to explain the important issues of the reputation distribution with the imperfections of current reputation systems.

Further research can emphasize on the validation of the research findings from consumer behavior perspectives, with the aim to study the theoretical implications of the reputation distribution with mathematic modeling techniques. Specifically, the properties of negative feedback scores are not well studied. Negative feedbacks are actually not negative enough in eBay.com. In fact, if we look into the comments and the final settledown associated to each negative feedback we can find that most of negative feedbacks are finally resolved and many were caused by third parties, such as a shipping company which did not deliver the item on time. Since the experience and risk attitude vary from trader to trader, the real effect of negative feedbacks may also change. Furthermore the correlation of negative feedbacks with other factors, such as overall reputation credits, is to be studied for better understanding of the nature of negative feedbacks.

ACKNOWLEDGMENT

The authors would like to thank Vasuki M. Basavanahalli for his work in data collection.

REFERENCES

AARP.org. (2002). Nigerian money offer scams. Retrieved from the World Wide Web: http://www.aarp.org/confacts/money/nigerianscams.html.

Akerlof, G. (1970). The market for "lemons": Quality under uncertainty and the market mechanism. *Quarterly Journal of Economics, 84*, 488-500.

Antony, S., Lin, Z., & Xu, B. (2001). Determinants of online escrow service adoption: An experimental study. In the *Proceedings of the 11th Workshop on Information Technology and Systems.*

Copyright © 2003, Idea Group Inc. Copying or distributing in print or electronic forms without written permission of Idea Group Inc. is prohibited.

Ba, S. & Pavlou, P. A. (2002). Evidence of the effect of trust building technology in electronic markets: Price premiums and buyer behavior. Forthcoming in *MIS Quarterly*.

Bromley, D.B. (1993). *Reputation, image, and impression management*. West Sussex, UK: John Wiley & Sons.

Clark, B. H. & Montgomery, D. B. (1998). Deterrence, reputation, and competitive cognition. *Management Science, 44*(1), 62-82.

Dawar, N. & Parker, P. (1994). Marketing universals: Consumers' use of brand name, price, physical appearance, and retailer reputation as signals of product quality. *Journal of Marketing, 58*(2), 81-95.

Dellarocas, C. (2001). Analyzing the economic efficiency of eBay-like online reputation reporting mechanisms. In *Proceedings of the 3rd ACM Conference on Electronic Commerce*.

Fiske, S.T. (1980). Attention and weight in person perception: The impact of negative and extreme behavior. *Journal of Personality and Social Psychology, 38*, 889-906.

Fombrun, C. (1996). *Reputation: Realizing value from the corporate image*. Boston, MA: Harvard Business School Press.

Fombrun, C. & Shanley, M. (1990). What's in a name? Reputation building and corporate strategy. *Academy of Management Journal, 33*(2), 233-258.

Friedman, E. & Resnick, P. (2001). The social cost of cheap pseudonyms. *Journal of Economics and Management Strategy, 10*(2), 173-199.

Ganesan, S. (1994). Determinants of long-term orientation in buyer-seller relationships. *Journal of Marketing, 58*(2), 1-19.

Hawes, J. M. & Lumpkin, J. R. (1986). Perceived risk and the selection of a retail patronage mode. *Journal of Academy of Marketing Science, 14*(4), 37-42.

Herbig, P., Milewicz, J., & Golden, J. (1994). A model of reputation building and destruction. *Journal of Business Research, 31*(1), 23-31.

Hu, X., Lin, Z., Whinston, A. B., & Zhang, H. (2001). Perceived risk and escrow adoption: An economic analysis in online consumer-to-consumer auction markets. In *Proceedings of the 22nd International Conference on Information Systems*. Retrieved from http://zlin.ba.ttu.edu/s/published/ICIS01-full.pdf.

Jarvenpaa, S. L., Tractinsky, N., & Vitale, M. (2000). Consumer trust in an internet store. *Information Technology and Management, 1*(1-2), 45-71.

Kollock, P. (1999). The production of trust in online markets. In E.J. Lawler et al. (Eds.), *Advances in Group Processes*. Greenwich, CT: JAI Press.

Kreps, D. M. (1990). Corporate Culture and Economic Theory. In E. A James. & K. A. Shepsle (Eds.), *Perspectives on Positive Political Economy* (pp. 90-143). New York: Cambridge University Press.

Lee, Z., Im, I., & Lee, S. J. (2000). The effect of negative buyer feedback on prices in internet auction markets. In W. Orlikowski et al. (Eds.), *The Proceedings*

Copyright © 2003, Idea Group Inc. Copying or distributing in print or electronic forms without written permission of Idea Group Inc. is prohibited.

of the 21st International Conference on Information Systems (pp. 286-287).

Lin, Z., Li, D., & Huang, W. (2002). Modeling trader reputation distribution in an online consumer-to-consumer auction market. In *The Proceedings of IRMA 2002* (pp. 19-22).

Mohamed, A. A., Orife, J. N., Slack, & Frederick, J. (2001). Organizational reputation: A literature review and a model. *International Journal of Management, 18*(2), 260-268.

Quelch, J. A. & Klein, L. R. (1996). The Internet and international marketing. *Sloan Management Review, 37*(3), 60-75.

Resnick, P. & Zeckhauser, R. (2001). Trust among strangers in Internet transactions: Empirical analysis of eBay's reputation system. University of Michigan.

Resnick, P., Zeckhauser, R., Friedman, E., & Kuwabara, K. (2000). Reputation systems. *Communications of the ACM, 43*(12), 45-48.

Ross, S. M. (1997). *Introduction to probability models* (6th ed.). Academic Press.

Selis, P., Ramasastry, A. & Wright, C. S. (2001). BIDDER BEWARE: Toward a fraud-free marketplace – Best practices for the online auction industry. *2001 Annual LCT Conference*, April, http://www.law.washington.edu/lct/publications.html#Online.

Slovic, P. (1993). Perceived risk, trust, and democracy: A systems perspective. *Risk Analysis, 13*, 675-682.

Standifird, S. S. (2001). Reputation and e-commerce: eBay auctions and the asymmetrical impact of positive and negative ratings. *Journal of Management, 27*(3), 279-295.

Sweeney, J. C., Soutar, G. N., & Johnson, L. W. (1999). The role of perceived risk in the quality-value relationship: A study in a retail environment. *Journal of Retailing, 75*(1), 77-105.

Tadelis, S. (1999). What's in a name? Reputation as a tradeable asset. *American Economic Review, 89*(3), 48-563.

Weiss, A. M., Erin, A., & MacInnis, D. J. (1999). Reputation management as a motivation for sales structure decisions. *Journal of Marketing, 63*(4), 74-89.

Whitmeyer, J. M. (2000). Effects of positive reputation systems. *Social Science Research, 29*(2), 188-207.

Yaniv, I. & Kleinberger, E. (2000). Advice taking in decision making: Egocentric discounting and reputation formation. *Organizational Behavior & Human Decision Processes, 83*(2), 260-281.

Yoon, E., Guffey, H. J., & Kijewski, V. (1993). The effects of information and company reputation on intentions to buy a business service. *Journal of Business Research, 27*(3), 215-228.

Zacharia, G., Moukas, A., & Maes, P. (2000). Collaborative reputation mechanisms for electronic marketplaces. *Decision Support Systems, 29*(4), 371-388.

Copyright © 2003, Idea Group Inc. Copying or distributing in print or electronic forms without written permission of Idea Group Inc. is prohibited.

Chapter XV

Privacy Perspective from Utilitarianism and Metaphysical Theories

Hasan A. Abbas
Kuwait University, Kuwait

Salah M. Al-Fadhly
Kuwait University, Kuwait

ABSTRACT

The Internet is a hot issue nowadays because of its important role at different levels. The topic of privacy is a debatable issue: we read in the research field scholars for and against applying this concept in real life and how to deal with it. Most researchers mainly focus on this subject from a social studies perspective. This chapter takes a new approach and discusses this issue from a philosophical perspective where we use two ethical theories (Mill & Kant) to raise the important relevant points regarding this subject.

INTRODUCTION

The Internet, which is the revolution of information technology, has initially been used for research and advancements in scientific fields through connecting scholars around the continent. However, the open environment of such use, and the enormous

Copyright © 2003, Idea Group Inc. Copying or distributing in print or electronic forms without written permission of Idea Group Inc. is prohibited.

advantage that provides for the scientific sector, made the need for such use highly urgent from the private high management levels. Therefore, difficulties are introduced as a result of the flexible environment this technology provides, such as eavesdropping, password sniffing, data modification, and spoofing (Bhimani, 1996).

Still, the scholars in the field have not agreed upon definition of the privacy concept (Alter, 1998; Laudon & Laudon, 1994; Reiter & Rubin 1999; Wang, Lee, & Wang, 1998). Laudon and Laudon (1994) define privacy as the lonely condition that people ask for to be away from other individuals, institutions, or governmental surveillance. Moreover, Wang, Lee, and Wang (1998) identify four characteristics of privacy:

1.   Solitude
2.   Intimacy
3.   Anonymity
4.   Reserve

On the other hand, Milberg et al. (1995) focus on the legal aspect of the privacy issue. Their study identifies the relationship between privacy and the given society's heritage of knowledge. This means that societies differ according to their understanding of privacy. In addition, other researchers (Sipior & Ward, 1995; Weisbank & Reining, 1995) give more attention to the legal issue of privacy. Specifically, they study the legal perspective of email, the most important tool facilitated by the Internet. Their argument is that email is a sensitive tool for both sides (i.e., employee and employer). The employer provides this tool to facilitate its employees' job related tasks. However, employees consider it part of their legal rights and a private tool that should not be intervened with by outsiders, including their employers. Other studies concentrated on the technical aspect of privacy and how technology can be formulated to maintain people's privacy (Bernassi, 1999; Clarke, 1999; Gabber et al., 1999; Goldshlag et al., 1999; Reagle & Cranor, 1999; Reiter & Rubin, 1999).

In this chapter, we concentrate on the convergence point which plays the important part of the communication technology revolution and on the ethical standards that the users are asked to respect and obey. Precisely, this chapter gives more attention to the limits of the legitimacy of violating the privacy of other parties. The paper is divided into four sections. First, the chapter concentrates on the concept of privacy in general and information privacy in particular. Then, it presents John Stuart Mill's *Utilitarianism* and examines how it offers a solution to the ethical problems. Next, the chapter introduces Immanuel Kant's theory of ethics. The chapter then deals with the ethical issues of privacy from the two theories' points of view and whether these theories are capable addressing all Internet and technology privacy-related cases. Finally, the last section contains recommendations and a conclusion.

Copyright © 2003, Idea Group Inc. Copying or distributing in print or electronic forms without written permission of Idea Group Inc. is prohibited.

PRIVACY CONCEPT

Almost everyone believes in the necessity of privacy. In spite of this, what do we mean by privacy in the first place? The literature does not uniformly define and describe the meaning of privacy. In this regard, we will first make some effort to unify the different meanings of privacy before we continue our discussion of how we deal ethically with the concept and with cases where there is a violation of privacy .

The concept of privacy can be shown on a scale with two extreme points. On one extreme side, privacy means that the individual is completely immune from any interference and that no personal information is known by others, which is called *complete privacy.* On the other extreme, the individual is under surveillance of others at all times. These two extremes do not exist in reality and cannot be practically developed. This is what made Horney (1945, p. 76) claim that asking for higher degrees of privacy is a symptom for a neural disease.

The concept of privacy called *individualist privacy* is where the individual wants to keep himself physically away from others' observation, such as being in his own bedroom. The second concept of privacy, *informatic privacy,* is related to the individual's personal information such as their nationality, ethnic group, health situation, social level, address and phone number. Individuals give away these pieces of information relative to their social status in the society. This means that for a person higher on the familiarity scale, i.e., a public figure, the more personal information is being held in the hands of others. On the contrary, ordinary individuals live in higher degrees of privacy.

After agreeing upon the fact that each individual has the right to stop others from interfering in his/her own personal life, we should raise another question: whether privacy is categorized as a human right or as a constitutional right?

Giving more attention to the concept of privacy leads us to the conclusion that it is a natural component of a human's spiritual life. On the other hand, the more we know about the private life of the individual, the more we can use this knowledge to abuse them. Consequently, this human, whose privacy is continually violated, loses more and more of his dignity because the invaders may know more pieces of information than he is reluctant to publicize.

It is important to note that privacy differs from all other human right. For example, the right to freedom and the right to life are absolute and can only be relinquished by legal acts. Privacy, on the other hand, is scalable and the owner may control its limits.

The human manipulates his own related information in the same way he manipulates other properties. Thus, the same way he uses his own home (renting, selling, etc.), for instance, in a manner that produces the best gain, he can comparatively deal with his own information. As a result, not all information regarding any individual means a privacy violation occurred, unless we are sure that the individual considers such information as part of his privacy. The range of privacy

Copyright © 2003, Idea Group Inc. Copying or distributing in print or electronic forms without written permission of Idea Group Inc. is prohibited.

for one person does not mean the same for another. As an example, the first individual may not consider knowing the specifications of his marriage life a privacy violation, whereas the other may and will refuse to relinquish such pieces of information. This may lead us to define privacy as the set of information that the individual refuses to reveal to others.

There is an important debatable issue in this subject and that is whether there are other areas where privacy can play an important role in the evaluation. James Rachels (1995, p. 351) considers privacy to sometimes be important to keep a competitor in a positive position in any competition (social, scientific, professional, etc.). Imagine how badly the situation of an applicant who is asking for a new job will be when his past criminal history is revealed.

Other researchers relate privacy to spiritual and psychological stability. Sidney Jouard (1966) claims that individuals are victims of spiritual and psychological diseases as a result of the violation of their privacy.

Keeping or revealing information about oneself is subject to different standards such as social customs, traditions, religion and many others. Note, though, that society also has the right to keep its population protected, even if this leads to violating an individual's privacy.

THE UTILITARIAN THEORY

The privacy concept is related to the philosophy of ethics and specifies the criteria that should be followed to measure the correctness of our actions.

The pursuit of happiness is an innate component of humanity and it is the ultimate motive for his deeds. This is why most of the researchers consider happiness as the most sublime of our actions, which is called by Aristotle the *ultimate goal.*

Although there is a collective agreement about happiness, philosophers disagree upon how to reach this end. One school of thinking looks at happiness as having life without difficulties and acquiring the maximum pleasure with lowest possible pain. On the other side, the second school of thinking looks at happiness as having a restriction following the ethical standards, regardless of the direct gain, or through strict obedience to mental rules.

Aside from the two previous schools of thinking, there is another type of thinking that neither relates happiness to sensory pleasure, as does the first school, nor to mental foundation, as does the rationalist school. Instead, it relates happiness to the magnitude of pleasure of the greatest number of people who have been affected by an action, which Mill considers as ethical criteria for human deeds.

For Mill, happiness means the presence of intended pleasure and the absence of pain; and this is the only thing that is pursued. Everything else is pursued as a tool that leads us to this goal, which is called the *greatest pleasure principle.*

Copyright © 2003, Idea Group Inc. Copying or distributing in print or electronic forms without written permission of Idea Group Inc. is prohibited.

Some people raise claims against Mill's view that any act is based upon the virtue incentive. This might be true, answers Mill, but a virtual act gives the feeling and a way to reach happiness, and lacking such feeling brings pain and suffering.

There are some types of pleasure that are more desirable than other types (Mill, 1993). Many people feel pleasure at a sensual level, but there are others who are equipped with higher spiritual and mental capabilities that are highly impressed and feel in-depth and lengthy pleasure. There is a positive relationship between the level of pleasure and one's own internal capabilities. The scientist, for example, who is hardly inventing a new creation may not feel satisfied and happy until a lengthy time of research and experimental efforts are exhausted.

The *utilitarianism* theory specifies how much an act is ethical based upon the maximum satisfaction to the maximum number of individuals. This does not mean that the persons are not asked to follow their own utility. It means, however, that every one should follow their own interests, as well as the community's.

There is one important issue left unsolved: how to keep the balance between the conflicting interests and pleasures of individuals and of the community. Mill's answer is to maximize the society's pleasure, because the final gains are more than the individual's happiness. If there is no conflict, the individuals should be left undisturbed to satisfy their own interests.

THE METAPHYSICAL THEORY

The metaphysics of morals theory is one of three well-established theories in the field of ethics (Aristotle's *Nichomachean Ethics*, Kant's *The Fundamental Principles of the Metaphysic of Morals*, and Mill's *Utilitarianism*). Kant's main argument in his theory, and the core difference between his and others, is that any action should not be performed in accordance with duty. However, one must act mainly for duty's sake.

The theory mainly intensifies the point that a good will is good, not because of its effects, but simply because of the virtue of the volition, and because of the good in itself. One other important proposition in the theory is that duty is the necessity of acting from respect for the law (Kant, 1999, p. 26). This means an action should have no inclination or motive at all. Instead, the law itself and only the law can determine will, and it is the maxim that the individual should follow it, even if it thwarts all of the individual's inclinations.

At this point Kant reaches his main principle, which he calls the *categorical imperative*. The categorical imperative argues that a person must never perform an act unless he or she consistently believes that the maxim or principle that motivates the action could become a universal law.

Copyright © 2003, Idea Group Inc. Copying or distributing in print or electronic forms without written permission of Idea Group Inc. is prohibited.

PRIVACY DISCUSSION THROUGH UTILITARIANISM

As we discussed previously (see The Utilitarianism Theory section) that utilitarianism classifies an act as ethical if its return of pleasure is sublime and to the maximum number of people.

Privacy is an acquired right of humanity, and cannot be given to or eliminated from anyone by the positive legal system of the community. Moreover, this right belongs to its owner, who can minimize or maximize the definition of personal privacy.

What is the utilitarian view of the concept of privacy? It is clear that information technology and the communications revolution played an important role in the previous century. However, this revolution has a negative side effect, as a result of the many incidents of hacking and intruding into unauthorized sections of personal information. The fundamental question to ask at this point is how ethical is it to intrude and interfere with the information of individuals and organizations? According to Mill's theory, we cannot judge if an act is ethical unless we measure the consequences. If the results are positively oriented the theory endorses it, otherwise it is rejected.

Mill's theory gives greater weight to the pleasure of many over an individual's happiness, as we discussed previously. The essential component, therefore, is the competition between interests. We categorize the different interests of privacy violations as follows:

- Violating the individual's privacy by another individual
- Violating the individual's privacy by a community
- Violating the community's privacy by an individual
- Violating the community's privacy by another community

Violating the Individual's Privacy by Another

Regardless of how much scientists and software organizations spend on efforts to free users from hacking and interference, technology can be used to intervene and be used harmfully. Individuals are continuously suffering from such acts. Let's concentrate on the following two cases:

Case 1: A chatting program user is interested in chatting with others, and in hacking and intruding upon their machines.

It is obvious from this case that there are conflicts of interest. The one side feels satisfaction and success as a result of having the power to look into other's private information; whereas the second party feels degraded as a result of being under the extortion of the hacker.

Copyright © 2003, Idea Group Inc. Copying or distributing in print or electronic forms without written permission of Idea Group Inc. is prohibited.

This case has both positive and negative effects. The first party feels positive, because of the feelings of satisfaction, and the second party feels negative, because of being abused. We need, at this point, to measure which of the results is greater: the pleasure of the first or the pain of the second? The theory in this case directs us to experience the history and the experts. It is obvious, from the pragmatic and experimental history, that the suffering of the second party is greater than the acquired pleasure of the first and the conclusion is that such an act is unethical.

Case 2: A divorced man is trying hard to interfere with his ex-wife's system to download important files that may be used in court for his advantage in their conflict for custody of the children.

This is a crucial case for both parents. We need to find how ethical this act is, according to theory. It is understandable that the custody of the kids is very sensitive for the parents. In this case we need to identify which interest is greater for the children. If the returned value of utility for the kids under the custody of the mother is more, then the theory's decision is to condemn the father's act, otherwise it is justifiable. The utility that we mean in this regard is the type of guidance the kids will receive in order to make them useful citizens of their community. Hence, the violation of privacy in this case is subject to whoever can serve better and produce a healthier generation.

Violating the Individual's Privacy by the Community

We mean by community here either the private or general society. The general society is the one in which the individual is one of its units, who has different relationships with it, such as economical, social, and political. The private society is the one that has a specific relationship with this specific person, and not the others, such as a professional or medical community where this individual belongs. Kenneth Laudon (1995) classifies the different ethical theories under different titles. According to Laudon, utilitarianism is classified under the title *collective consequentialist*. This specific set of theories gives the priority to the group over the individual. This means that the group act is ethical under Mill's theory. The utility that results from an intrusion to the individual's privacy exceeds the pain resulted from such act. Lets consider the following example:

Case 3: Eugene Wang used to work at the giant software company Borland International. While he was there, he used his electronic mail facility to send secret data to the new company he is planning to join. The administration at Borland discovered the matter and held the electronic mails to use against Mr. Wang in the court of law.

Copyright © 2003, Idea Group Inc. Copying or distributing in print or electronic forms without written permission of Idea Group Inc. is prohibited.

It is notable in this case how Eugene misused the facilities that he was equipped with by the company, and threatened Borland's interests by revealing its secrets. The utilitarianism directly concludes that the community's (Borland) act is ethical, because the losses that will face the professional community are enormously higher than the advantages gained by Eugene. In other words, the value of return for such an act is of a higher degree than the suffering of Eugene because of the legal case against him.

Violating the Community's Privacy by the Individual

As previously declared, according to Mill's theory, the well being of the community is preferable over the well being of the individual. Hence, it is always unethical for the individual to violate the community's privacy.

Violating the Community's Privacy by Another

Discussing this type of violation can follow the same direction as we did in the first type of violation. There are different cases and examples, such as spying acts, that are committed between rival governments or organizations.

It is hard to reach a final decision in such situations. The invader justifies its act that the control over the other communities in any field (political, economical, etc.) has a higher advantage over any other interests, which is the same argument that can be raised by the defender.

PRIVACY DISCUSSION THROUGH THE METAPHYSICAL THEORY

In the previous section we discussed issues of privacy using Mill's theory. In this part of the chapter we need to understand how Kant's ethical theory deals with the issue.

The theory is simple in the point that it does not need to build upon previous history, or to collect enough information in order to evaluate the different options the individual may have (which is the case that faces the individual according to the utilitarianism). Instead, the agent has to act based upon on the maxim or principle that the way he or she thinks can be used universally.

Privacy, as we stated above, is a right given to individuals as a result of being human. Hence, it is not a constitutional right that may be supported by the institution he or she lives in. Therefore, Kant's argument is that the persons' privacy can be violated. The reason is simply stated that the individual or institution should determine the will behind any action, regardless of the effect that is expected from it. The important fact here is that universal conformity of actions to the law in general should be maintained all times. Hence, the agents (i.e., individuals or institutions) should never act unless this action follows a universal law.

Copyright © 2003, Idea Group Inc. Copying or distributing in print or electronic forms without written permission of Idea Group Inc. is prohibited.

If we take this point into consideration, and try to evaluate the violation of one's privacy, it is true that at some moments the violation may be necessary in order to check if the individual has any illegal transactions or movements. However, this act, according to the theory, cannot be used as a universal law. The exception destroys the justification of such actions and would be rejected by the theory.

Kant has another argument that makes such a violation a prohibited act. The second formulation states that one must act so as to treat people as ends in themselves and not, and never, merely as means. Let's then focus on the violation of privacy as an action. This violation means using the unawareness of the individual to gain an advantage. Again, we don't argue what type of gains the violator may have as a result of such an act. The theory only discusses if such an act uses the other as means, which is the case in the privacy violation act.

FINAL DISCUSSIONS, FUTURE TRENDS, AND CONCLUSIONS

In the previous section, we covered different practical cases and how ethical the acts are in each according to utilitarian theory. Additionally, we noticed that the theory mainly decides upon the amount of utility that can be returned from each act. However, this theory has different problems that make its decisions regarding real life acts unfair.

Imagine a society where discrimination against its employees is acceptable. This negative ideology in the society justifies the violation of privacy of minorities without any logical justification other than discrimination. Moreover, Mill uses the personal experience for the individuals to judge the new cases. This means it uses the history as help the future cases. What if the new cases are totally different and no experience can be used to reach a decision? Third, utilitarianism does not give the mind its chance to decide. It seems that the theory always has the solution, even if this output conflicts with rational thinking. Fourth, there are cases which are unique and have no similarities to past or present cases. Utilitarianism cannot give a decisive answer in such occurrences. To clarify the issue, imagine two democratic societies with equal capabilities in a semi-war situation with the same ambitions and history. The theory will not be able to answer these difficulties.

Kenneth Laudon (1995) argues that ethics is the ability of the intelligent entity to conceptualize and process incidents based upon deep understanding and reasoning. It is not a static tool where the decision can be reached initially. Henceforth, the theory is definitely incapable of reasoning all ethical acts that are related to information technology and, specifically, if we know that it is in continuous improvement and change, makes the theory even more deficient.

The act cannot be ethically judged from the interested perspective solely. It is important, in this regard, to understand which one is the prime component: individual or the society? The society and the individual are both important and cannot be

Copyright © 2003, Idea Group Inc. Copying or distributing in print or electronic forms without written permission of Idea Group Inc. is prohibited.

separated in any study. They both should be considered, and the interest of the community has the precedence over the individual if there is a conflict between the two. Furthermore, we also should not forget that any ethical action is based upon the importance of our minds and its logical deductions. It is not uncommon to reach a judgment using pure logical thinking of the justifications without measuring the consequences. This is true when fear increases at places where a bad society is available, because Mill's theory will be used for societies' advantage, and the minorities will be oppressed with supposedly ethical justification.

Kant's metaphysical theory has a totally different view of the problem. A core understanding of Kant's theory is to know that Kant does not say it is false to use others as a means. He does say, though, that one cannot use another as a mere means. For example, checking into a country through the border necessarily needs to use the border man as mean, without whom I cannot get in. The border man, in turn, uses me as a means to earn his or her living. One way of using others as mere means is through deception, if, for instance, someone gives a misleading account or information or gives a false promise. Another way of using others as mere means is through coercion. This occurs when the force that is in the hand of influential and powerful individuals is used unjustly against the helpless.

The theory has a clear limitation in the differentiation between intentions and results (O'Neill, 1999). Since it assesses actions by looking to the principles of agents, it can only assess intentional acts. Therefore, all individuals or agencies that have intentions may be assessed by the theory through looking at their maxims. This means the theory can do nothing regarding acts of groups lacking decision-making procedures (O'Neill, 1999).

The great difficulty of the theory comes from the fact that it focuses on the intentions, and neglects the results. The theory fails to consider acts that may not result into the expected end. In other words, what does the theory say about acts where the intentions are bad, but have good results; or acts that have good intentions, but with bad results?

REFERENCES

Alter, S. (1999). *Information Systems: A Management Perspective* (3rd ed.). Reading, MA: Addison-Wesley.

Benassi, P. (1999). TRUSTe: An online privacy seal program. *Communications of the ACM, 42*(2), 56-59.

Bhimani, A. (1996, June). Securing the Commercial Internet. *Communications of the ACM, 39*(6), 29-35.

Chlapowski, F. S. (1991, January). The constitutional protection of informational privacy. *Boston University Law Review*, 71.

Clarke, R. (1999, February). Internet privacy concerns confirm the case for intervention. *Communications of the ACM, 42*(2), 60-67.

Copyright © 2003, Idea Group Inc. Copying or distributing in print or electronic forms without written permission of Idea Group Inc. is prohibited.

Cranor, L. F. (1999). Internet Privacy. *Communications of the ACM, 42*(2), 29-31.

Gabber, E., Gibbons, P. B., Kristol, D. M., Matias, Y., & Mayer, A. (1999). Consistent, yet anonymous, web access with LPWA. *Communications of the ACM, 42*(2), 42-47.

Goldschlag, D., Reed, M., & Syverson, P. (1999). Onion routing for anonymous and private Internet connections. *Communications of the ACM, 42*(2), 39-41.

Horney, K. (1945). *Our inner conflicts: A constructive theory of neurosis.* New York: W.W. Norton and Co.

Iaccarino, G. (1996). A look at Internet Privacy and security issues and their relationship to the electronic job search: Implications for librarians and career services professionals. *The Reference Librarian, 55,* 107-113.

Johnson, G. D. & Nissenbaum, H. (1995). *Computers ethics and social values.* Upper Saddle River, NJ: Prentice Hall.

Jouard, S. (1966). Some philosophical aspects of privacy. *Law & Contemporary Problems, 31,* 307-318.

Kant, I. (1999). The fundamental principles of the metaphysic of morals. In J. Arthur (Ed.), *Morality and Moral Controversies (5ᵗʰ Ed.)* (pp. 24-33) .

Laudon, K.C. (1995). Ethical concepts and information technology. *Communications of the ACM, 38*(12), 33-39.

Laudon, K.C. (1996, September). Markets and privacy. *Communications of the ACM, 39.*

Laudon, K.C. & Laudon, J. P. (1994). Management information systems: Organization and technology (3rd ed.). New York: Macmillan.

Mason, R.O. (1995). Applying Ethics to Information Technology Issues. *Communications of the ACM, 38*(12), 55-57.

Milberg, S. J., Burke, S. J., Smith, H. J., & Kallman, E. A. (1995). Values, personal information privacy, and regulatory approaches. *Communications of the ACM, 38*(12), 65-75.

Mill, J. S. (1993). *On Liberty and Utilitarianism (A Bantam Classic).*

O'Neill, O. (1999). Kant and utilitarianism contrasted. In J. Arthur (Ed.), *Morality and Moral Controversies (5ᵗʰ ed)* (pp. 47-52).

Rachels, J. (1995). Why privacy is important. In D. G. Johnson & H. Nissenbaum (Eds.), *Computers, Ethics & Social Values* (pp. 351-357). NJ: Prentice-Hall.

Reagle, J. & Cranor, L. F. (1999). The platform for privacy preferences. *Communications of the ACM, 42*(2), 48-55.

Reiter, M. K. & Rubin, A. D. (1999). Anonymous web transactions with crowds. *Communications of the ACM, 42*(2), 32-38.

Sapsford, J. (1999). *Wall Street Journal.*

Sauter, V. L. (1997). *Decision support systems: An applied managerial approach.* New York: John Wiley & Sons.

Sipior, J. C., & Ward, B. T. (1995). The ethical and legal quandary of email privacy. *Communications of the ACM, 38*(12), 48-54.

Copyright © 2003, Idea Group Inc. Copying or distributing in print or electronic forms without written permission of Idea Group Inc. is prohibited.

Teich, A. H. (2000). *Technology and the future.* New York: Bedford/St. Martin's.

Turban, E. (1995). Decision support and expert systems: Management support systems (4th ed.). Englewood Cliffs, NJ: Prentice Hall.

Wang, H., Lee, M. K. O., & Wang, C. (1998). Consumer privacy concerns about Internet marketing. *Communications of the ACM, 41*(3), 63-70.

Weisband, S. P. & Reinig, B. A. (1995). Managing user perceptions of email privacy. *Communications of the ACM, 38*(12).

Copyright © 2003, Idea Group Inc. Copying or distributing in print or electronic forms without written permission of Idea Group Inc. is prohibited.

About the Authors

Rasool Azari is currently Assistant Professor of Operations Management in the School of Business at the University of Redlands, USA, and the previous associate chair of the Department of Management and Business. He holds a Doctor of Science in Engineering Management and an MBA in International Business from George Washington University, a master's Degree in Electrical Engineering from UCLA and a BS in Electrical Engineering from California State University Sacramento. He also was a graduate student of Political Economy and International Affairs at the Freie Universität, Berlin, Germany. His work experience includes years as Project and Design Engineer in interdisciplinary multi-national corporations in the United States and Europe. Since 1995 he has been a Consultant to the United States Department of Commerce/National Institute of Standards and Technology. He has published more than 15 papers in journals and in national and international conference proceedings, and served as track-chair, chair, and discussant for the Western Economic Association (WEA), Western Decision Sciences (WDS), Information Resources Management Association International (IRMA), and the American Society of Business and Behavioral Sciences (ASBBS). He has served as a member of the program committee for IRMA and was a manuscript reviewer for the *Journal of Management Education* and the Mountain Plains Management Conference. He is a member of the Academy of Management, Decision Sciences Institute (DSI), Institute for Operations Research and the Management Science (INFORMS), Information Resources Management Association International (IRMA), Western Decision Sciences Institute (WDSI), Western Economics Association (WEA), Association of Integrative Studies (AIS), and World Future Society. His research interests include: the impact of technology on society; technological change and

Copyright © 2003, Idea Group Inc. Copying or distributing in print or electronic forms without written permission of Idea Group Inc. is prohibited.

globalization and their impact on organizations, economies, and society in general; science and technology policies; and management of technology and innovation.

*   *   *

Hasan A. Abbas is a Member of the faculty at Kuwait University, Department of QM and IS. He holds a 1998 PhD in Computer Science from Illinois Institute of Technology, a 1995 MS in Computer Science from Illinois Institute of Technology, and a 1990 BS in Economics from Kuwait University. His interest research areas include: artificial intelligence, expert system, natural language, knowledge base, decision support systems, database, artificial neural networks, intelligent tutoring systems, systems analysis and design, ethics, and cognitive sciences.

Salah M. Al-Fadhly is a Member of the faculty at Kuwait University, in the Department of QM and IS. He holds a 1998 MS in Philosophy from Kuwait University and 1990 BS in Computer Science from Bradley University. His interest research areas include: artificial intelligence, expert system, natural language, knowledge base, decision support systems, database, artificial neural networks, intelligent tutoring systems, systems analysis and design, ethics, and cognitive sciences.

Husain Al-Lawatia is a Doctoral Student in the Department of Business Information Systems at Utah State University, USA. Prior to coming to USU, Mr. Al-Lawatia worked for the Central Bank of Oman (CBO) in the Banking Supervision Department. He started as a New Bank Examiner and rose to the rank of Senior Assistant Manager, the second highest position in his department. His current position of Manager-on-Leave entitles him to head a department at CBO when he completes his degree. Mr. Al-Lawatia has participated in several international and regional meetings, conferences, and seminars held in different countries around the world in the areas of banking, auditing, and information systems. His research emphasis is information ethics in banking and financial information systems. Mr. Al-Lawatia holds a BS in Accounting from Beirut Arab University and an MBA from Utah State University.

Peik Åström is a BSc (Eng) Student in Electrical Engineering and Information Technology Student at Arcada Polytechnic, Espoo, Finland. He has, since May 2002, been working for Arcada Polytechnic as a research assistant in Network Security research.

Vlasti Broucek has been working in the computer industry since 1985 in various positions. Currently, he is a Researcher at the School of Information Systems, University of Tasmania and a Network Administrator at the School of Psychology,

Copyright © 2003, Idea Group Inc. Copying or distributing in print or electronic forms without written permission of Idea Group Inc. is prohibited.

University of Tasmania, Australia. His current research interest is in computer security and forensic computing. He has an extensive knowledge of systems administration on a range of systems (Novell Netware, Unix flavours); computer security, mathematics and artificial intelligence. He has an MSc degree from the Czech Technical University in Prague, where he worked on applications of expert systems, and currently is pursuing a PhD at the University of Tasmania working on technical and legal issues of forensic computing.

Paul Darbyshire is a lecturer in the School of Information systems at Victoria University, Melbourne, Australia. He holds a Bachelor of Science, Graduate Diploma in Computing and a Masters of Engineering. Paul is undertaking doctoral studies in the field of Intelligent Agents. He has worked for many private and public organisations including many years in the University sector. Paul is a member of the ACM and IEEE. He has published widely on the Internet.

Stewart T. Fleming received the Bachelor of Engineering Degree in Information Engineering from the University of Strathclyde, Glasgow, in 1990. He studied under the supervision of Professor Alistair Kilgour at the Department of Computing and Electrical Engineering, Heriot-Watt University, Edinburgh, graduating with a PhD in 1996. Between 1993 and 1996, he worked in industry, developing systems for digital mapping and sales and marketing consultancies. From 1996 to 1998, he was Head of Information Systems in the Department of Business Studies at the Papua New Guinea University of Technology. He is currently a Lecturer within the Department of Computer Science at the University of Otago, on the South island of New Zealand. His current research interests include software engineering, computer security and the information needs of developing countries.

Maria Grazia Fugini is a Professor of Computer Engineering at Politecnico di Milano, Italy. She received her PhD in Computer Engineering in 1987 and was a visiting professor at the University of Maryland, Technical University of Vienna and Technical University of Stuttgart. She teaches Fundamentals of Computer Science and Information Systems. Her research interests are in information system security and development, software reuse, information retrieval, information systems development and re-engineering. She participated in the TODOS, ITHACA, F3, WIDE and DEAFIN UE Projects, working on information system development and re-engineering, software reuse, data security, information retrieval tools, and workflow and web application design. She participates in, and coordinates, UE and national Projects on security, web based information systems for public administrations, in particular on web services to citizens and enterprises. She is co-author of the books, *Database Security* (Addison-Wesley, 1995) and *Sicurezza dei Sistemi Informatici* (in Italian, Apogeo, 2001). She cooperates with Public Administrations in the design of the Portal of the Workfare for services to Employment.

Copyright © 2003, Idea Group Inc. Copying or distributing in print or electronic forms without written permission of Idea Group Inc. is prohibited.

Kaj J. Grahn, PhD Tech, is presently Senior Lecturer in Telecommunications at the Department of IT and Electronics of Arcada Polytechnic, Espoo, Finland. He is also Program Manager of the Electrical Engineering Programme.

Thomas Hilton is a Professor and the Director of graduate programs in the Business Information Systems Department, Utah State University, USA. Dr. Hilton has been in business computing for 24 years. Presently he teaches user interface design, data communications, and research methods. Before joining USU, Dr. Hilton designed systems for what is now Accenture Management & Technology Services. There he worked on systems for the U.S. Navy, IBM, and other clients. He also helped define the METHOD-1® systems development methodology. Dr. Hilton also worked as a Flight Simulation Designer for Singer Aerospace and Marine Systems, Inc. There he designed flight simulators for the U.S. Air Force. Dr. Hilton holds a PhD in system design and a BA in English, both from Brigham Young University. He has published and presented on various topics in information systems. His primary research emphasis is the ethics of information use.

Wayne Huang is an Associate Professor at the MIS Department, College of Business, Ohio University, USA. He has worked as a faculty member in universities in Australia, Singapore, and Hong Kong. His main research interests include group support systems (GSS), electronic commerce, eLearning, knowledge management systems, and software engineering. He has published 50 academic research papers, including published papers in leading IS journals such as the *Journal of Management Information Systems (JMIS)*, the *IEEE Transactions on Systems, Man, and Cybernetics*, *Information & Management*, *IEEE Transactions on Professional Communication*, *Decision Support Systems (DSS)*, and the *European Journal of Information Systems*.

Alexander D. Korzyk, Sr. received a BS in Systems Engineering from the United States Military Academy, West Point and numerous military awards during his military career, culminating with the United States Presidential Award for Reinventing the Government in 1993. He also served overseas in Germany twice during the height of the Cold War. During most of his military assignments, he was in charge of information systems security and software development. After retiring from the military, Korzyk consulted extensively in industry and government during which time, he wrote three computer security books, and developed and certified seven major information systems. He received an MBA from Florida Tech and an MS in Information Systems from the United States Naval Postgraduate School, Monterey, CA and his doctorate from Virginia Commonwealth University, Richmond, VA. He is currently an assistant professor in the College of Business and Economics at the University of Idaho, USA, and Center for Secure and Dependable Software. He has over 20 publications on information systems security.

Copyright © 2003, Idea Group Inc. Copying or distributing in print or electronic forms without written permission of Idea Group Inc. is prohibited.

Dahui Li is an Assistant Professor of Management Information Systems in the School of Business and Economics at the University of Minnesota Duluth, USA. He received his PhD in Management Information Systems from Texas Tech University, USA. His research focuses on Internet buyer behavior, business-to-consumer relationship, and diffusion of information technology innovation. He has co-authored several scientific papers and presented his findings at national conferences.

Zhangxi Lin is currently an Assistant Professor of Information Systems in the College of Business Administration at Texas Tech University, USA. He obtained an MEng degree in computer science from Tsinghua University in 1982, an MS degree in Economics in 1996 and a PhD in Information Systems in 1999 from the University of Texas at Austin. His research interests include network traffic pricing, software engineering, economic experimental system design and experimental testing, and knowledge-based systems. He has published more than 30 academic research papers in referred journals and conferences. He worked in computer application development and held a number of senior positions since 1982.

Heberto J. Ochoa-Morales is an Assistant Professor at the University of New Mexico, USA, in the Business Management and Technology Department. He holds a Bachelor in Civil Engineering, a Master of Science in Engineering Management, a Master in Management, and a Master of Business Administration (MBA), with a major in MIS. His doctoral degree in Business Administration with a major in International Management is anticipated in the Fall of 2003. He has published and presented more than a dozen papers in international conferences and journals on the subject of information technology, and international management related to Latin America, especially the Andean Community of Nations (CAN). His academic career has spanned the past 10 years. He has also held positions as CEO and Executive Director of international companies in the US, Latin America and abroad.

James Pick is Professor in School of Business at University of Redlands, USA, and former department Chair of management and business. He holds a BA from Northwestern University and PhD from the University of California, Irvine. He is the author of seven books and 100 scientific papers and book chapters in the research areas of management information systems, geographic information systems, environmental systems, population, and urban studies. He has received several university research and teaching awards, and in 2001 was senior Fulbright scholar in Mexico.

Pierluigi Plebani is a PhD Student at Politecnico di Milano, Italy. His research interests are in information system security, development of cooperative information systems, e-service technologies, and data quality on cooperative information system. He participates in national and international projects on modelling and development of multi-channel information systems.

Copyright © 2003, Idea Group Inc. Copying or distributing in print or electronic forms without written permission of Idea Group Inc. is prohibited.

Göran Pulkkis, PhD Tech., is presently Senior Lecturer in Computer Science and Engineering at the Department of IT and Electronics at Arcada Polytechnic, Espoo, Finland.

Li Qi holds a PhD in Economics, is Professor of Electronic Commerce Discipline, and, in 1997, published *China Electronic Commerce,* which is the first EC book in China. Until now, he has published more than 50 papers and more than 10 books, accomplished 20 projects, and certified one patent. There are 13 doctoral students and 22 postgraduates under his instruction. He is also the Director or Dean of the following organizations: Electronic Commerce Department, Xi'an Jiaotong University; EC Research Institute of Xi'an Jiaotong Uni, (the first EC research center in China); EC Commission of Chinese Information & Economics Association; The Coordination Group for the Establishment and Development of Electronic Business Specialty of China's Higher Education Institutes.

Geoffrey Sandy is Head, School of Information Systems of the Faculty of Business and Law, Victoria University, Melbourne, Australia. He holds a Doctor of Philosophy from RMIT University and a bachelor's and master's degree in Economics from Melbourne University. Geoff is a member of the Australian Computer Society, the Australian Institute of Computer Ethics, and Electronic Frontiers Australia. He has over 26 years experience in university teaching, research and consultancy, and six years of private sector experience where he worked for International Harvester and the ANZ Bank. His major research interests are Internet censorship, filter software, computer use policies and adding value via the Internet. He has published widely in these and other areas.

Robert Joseph Skovira is a Professor of Computer Information Systems in the Computer and Information Systems Department of the School of Communications and Information Systems at Robert Morris University, USA. He has taught courses in business ethics and legal and ethical dimensions of technology. A focal area of research is moral and societal issues and information systems. Currently, his teaching and research focus on Web design and development, theories of information and information architecture, knowledge management, object-oriented programming, and ethnography of information systems. He teaches undergraduates and masters students. He is a member of the doctoral faculty at Robert Morris University.

Vernon Stagg is currently completing his Doctorate at Deakin University, Australia. His research is focusing on information warfare and he is developing a framework for application in the private/civilian sector. As part of this research he has developed a model of the National Information Infrastructure that incorporates non-critical elements. More details about his work and general information security issues are available at http://www.infowar.com.au.

Copyright © 2003, Idea Group Inc. Copying or distributing in print or electronic forms without written permission of Idea Group Inc. is prohibited.

Bernd Carsten Stahl, Dipl-Wi-Ing, MA, DEA, studied Mechanical Engineering, Commerce, and Philosophy in Hamburg, Hagen, Bordeaux, and Witten. From 1987-1997, he was an officer of the German Armed Forces. Since 2000, he has been working a *DAAD Fachlektor f/r Wirtschaftswissenschaften* (lecturer) at the Department of Management Information Systems and the German Department in University College Dublin, Ireland. His area of research includes questions concerning the relationship of business, information technology, and ethics with a particular emphasis on the notion of responsibility. His second field of research includes normative problems caused by the use of computers and IT in education.

Paul Turner is Senior Research Fellow of the School of Information Systems, University of Tasmania, Australia. He previously was a Research Fellow at CRID (Computer, Telecommunications and Law Research Institute) in Belgium where he worked on a variety of European Commission contracts in the field of electronic commerce, telecommunications and intellectual property rights. Dr. Turner has also worked as an Independent Information and Telecommunications Consultant in a number of countries in Europe and was for three years editor of the London-based monthly publication *Telecommunications Regulation Review*. Dr. Turner's strong research focus in the field of electronic commerce continues both in his work as senior research fellow at the University of Tasmania and in his concurrent position as Research Manager for the Tasmanian Electronic Commerce Centre (TECC). In Paul's work for the TECC he is responsible for coordinating research at basic, applied and strategic levels across a range of industry sectors with a focus on small to medium sized enterprises electronic business practices.

Matthew Warren is an Associate Professor in the School of Information Technology at Deakin University, Australia. He has a PhD in Computer Security Risk Analysis Methods from Plymouth University, UK. He is a member of the Australian Standards Committee IT/12/4 Security Techniques, the Chair of IFIP TC 11 Working Group 11.1 - Security Management, Co-Director of the Australasian Institute Of Network And Information Warfare (AiNiW) and the Director of the Australian Institute of Computer Ethics.

Zhang Xianfeng is a PhD Student in the Economic and Financial School of Xi'an Jiaotong University, China, and a Member of EC Research Institute of Xi'an Jiaotong Uni. Research interests include electronic commerce theory, online banking, information asymmetry and business EC strategies. Over 10 papers have been issued in journals and international conferences.

Copyright © 2003, Idea Group Inc. Copying or distributing in print or electronic forms without written permission of Idea Group Inc. is prohibited.

Index

Copyright © 2003, Idea Group Inc. Copying or distributing in print or electronic forms without written permission of Idea Group Inc. is prohibited.

Copyright © 2003, Idea Group Inc. Copying or distributing in print or electronic forms without written permission of Idea Group Inc. is prohibited.

Copyright © 2003, Idea Group Inc. Copying or distributing in print or electronic forms without written permission of Idea Group Inc. is prohibited.

Copyright © 2003, Idea Group Inc. Copying or distributing in print or electronic forms without written permission of Idea Group Inc. is prohibited.

InfoSci-Online Database

30-Day free trial!

www.infosci-online.com

Provide instant access to the latest offerings of Idea Group Inc. publications in the fields of INFORMATION SCIENCE, TECHNOLOGY and MANAGEMENT

During the past decade, with the advent of telecommunications and the availability of distance learning opportunities, more college and university libraries can now provide access to comprehensive collections of research literature through access to online databases.

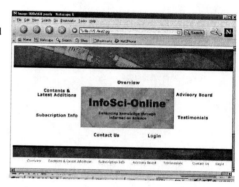

The InfoSci-Online database is the most comprehensive collection of *full-text* literature regarding research, trends, technologies, and challenges in the fields of information science, technology and management. This online database consists of over 3000 book chapters, 200+ journal articles, 200+ case studies and over 1,000+ conference proceedings papers from IGI's three imprints (Idea Group Publishing, Information Science Publishing and IRM Press) that can be accessed by users of this database through identifying areas of research interest and keywords.

Contents & Latest Additions:
Unlike the delay that readers face when waiting for the release of print publications, users will find this online database updated as soon as the material becomes available for distribution, providing instant access to the latest literature and research findings published by Idea Group Inc. in the field of information science and technology, in which emerging technologies and innovations are constantly taking place, and where time is of the essence.

The content within this database will be updated by IGI with 1300 new book chapters, 250+ journal articles and case studies and 250+ conference proceedings papers per year, all related to aspects of information, science, technology and management, published by Idea Group Inc. The updates will occur as soon as the material becomes available, even before the publications are sent to print.

InfoSci-Online pricing flexibility allows this database to be an excellent addition to your library, regardless of the size of your institution.

Contact: Ms. Carrie Skovrinskie, InfoSci-Online Project Coordinator, 717-533-8845 (Ext. 14), cskovrinskie@idea-group.com for a 30-day trial subscription to InfoSci-Online.

A product of:

INFORMATION SCIENCE PUBLISHING*
Enhancing Knowledge Through Information Science
http://www.info-sci-pub.com

*an imprint of Idea Group Inc.

Journal of Electronic Commerce in Organizations (JECO)

The International Journal of Electronic Commerce in Modern Organizations

ISSN: 1539-2937
eISSN: 1539-2929
Subscription: Annual fee per volume (4 issues):
Individual US $85
Institutional US $185

Editor: Mehdi Khosrow-Pour, D.B.A.
Information Resources
Management Association, USA

Mission

The *Journal of Electronic Commerce in Organizations* is designed to provide comprehensive coverage and understanding of the social, cultural, organizational, and cognitive impacts of e-commerce technologies and advances on organizations around the world. These impacts can be viewed from the impacts of electronic commerce on consumer behavior, as well as the impact of e-commerce on organizational behavior, development, and management in organizations. The secondary objective of this publication is to expand the overall body of knowledge regarding the human aspects of electronic commerce technologies and utilization in modern organizations, assisting researchers and practitioners to devise more effective systems for managing the human side of e-commerce.

Coverage

This publication includes topics related to electronic commerce as it relates to: Strategic Management, Management and Leadership, Organizational Behavior, Organizational Developement, Organizational Learning, Technologies and the Workplace, Employee Ethical Issues, Stress and Strain Impacts, Human Resources Management, Cultural Issues, Customer Behavior, Customer Relationships, National Work Force, Political Issues, and all other related issues that impact the overall utilization and management of electronic commerce technologies in modern organizations.

For subscription information, contact:

Idea Group Publishing
701 E Chocolate Ave., Ste 200
Hershey PA 17033-1240, USA
cust@idea-group.com
URL: www-idea-group.com

For paper submission information:

Dr. Mehdi Khosrow-Pour
Information Resources Management
Association
jeco@idea-group.com

Information Resources Management Journal (IRMJ)

An Official Publication of the Information Resources Management Association since 1988

Editor:

Mehdi Khosrow-Pour, D.B.A.
Information Resources Management
Association, USA

ISSN: 1040-1628; eISSN: 1533-7979
Subscription: Annual fee per volume (four issues): Individual
US $85; Institutional US $265

Mission

The *Information Resources Management Journal* (IRMJ) is a refereed, international publication featuring the latest research findings dealing with all aspects of information resources management, managerial and organizational applications, as well as implications of information technology organizations. It aims to be instrumental in the improvement and development of the theory and practice of information resources management, appealing to both practicing managers and academics. In addition, it educates organizations on how they can benefit from their information resources and all the tools needed to gather, process, disseminate and manage this valuable resource.

Coverage

IRMJ covers topics with a major emphasis on the managerial and organizational aspects of information resource and technology management. Some of the topics covered include: Executive information systems; Information technology security and ethics; Global information technology Management; Electronic commerce technologies and issues; Emerging technologies management; IT management in public organizations; Strategic IT management; Telecommunications and networking technologies; Database management technologies and issues; End user computing issues; Decision support & group decision support; Systems development and CASE; IT management research and practice; Multimedia computing technologies and issues; Object-oriented technologies and issues; Human and societal issues in IT management; IT education and training issues; Distance learning technologies and issues; Artificial intelligence & expert technologies; Information technology innovation & diffusion; and other issues relevant to IT management.

It's Easy to Order! Order online at www.idea-group.com or call our toll-free hotline at 1-800-345-4332!
Mon-Fri 8:30 am-5:00 pm (est) or fax 24 hours a day 717/533-8661

Idea Group Publishing

Hershey • London • Melbourne • Singapore • Beijing

An excellent addition to your library